Charles Rogers

The Book of Robert Burns

Vol. 3

Charles Rogers

The Book of Robert Burns
Vol. 3

ISBN/EAN: 9783337778453

Printed in Europe, USA, Canada, Australia, Japan

Cover: Foto ©ninafisch / pixelio.de

More available books at **www.hansebooks.com**

THE BOOK OF ROBERT BURNS

GENEALOGICAL AND HISTORICAL MEMOIRS OF
THE POET HIS ASSOCIATES AND THOSE CELEBRATED
IN HIS WRITINGS

The Lineage of the Poet
BY THE LATE REV. CHARLES ROGERS, D.D., LL.D.

The Life of the Poet
BY REV. J. C. HIGGINS, A.M., B.D.,
TARBOLTON

IN THREE VOLUMES
VOL. III

EDINBURGH
PRINTED FOR THE GRAMPIAN CLUB
1891

PREFACE.

HAVING been asked, with a view to the completion of this Work, to prepare a short biography of Burns, I have aimed at writing a concise narrative, setting forth as many of the incidents of the Poet's career as the available space would allow, and at making as large use as possible of the Poet's own words.

For the purpose of writing a "Life of Burns," the late Dr. Charles Rogers had gathered a mass of notes; but these notes could have been advantageously utilised only by Dr. Rogers himself.

Every one knows that the subject of the Poet's Life and Writings has already been fully and powerfully dealt with by many eminent authors.

Having agreed, however, though not without misgivings, to complete Vol. III. of the *Book of Robert Burns*, I have tried to perform my task clearly, faithfully, and sympathetically.

J. C. H.

Is there a whim-inspired fool,
Owre fast for thought, owre hot for rule,
Owre blate to seek, owre proud to snool,
      Let him draw near;
And o'er this grassy heap sing dool,
      And drap a tear.

.   .   .   .   .   .

Is there a man whose judgments clear,
Can others teach the course to steer,
Yet runs himself life's mad career,
      Wild as a wave,
Here pause—and through the starting tear
      Survey this grave.

The poor inhabitant below
Was quick to learn and wise to know,
And keenly felt the friendly glow,
      And softer flame;
But thoughtless follies laid him low,
      And stained his name.
                  A Bard's Epitaph.

CONTENTS.

CHAPTER I.
The Poet's Lineage,   PAGE 1

CHAPTER II.
Birth and Early Environments, .   . 75

CHAPTER III.
From 1777-1784. Age 18-25. Tarbolton, Kirkoswald, Irvine,   91

CHAPTER IV.
From 1784-1786. Age 25-27. Mossgiel and Mauchline,   113

CHAPTER V.
First Winter in Edinburgh — November 28, 1786 - May 5, 1787. Age 27-28, ... 140

CHAPTER VI.
Border, West Highland, Northern, and Devon Valley Tours — May 5-October 20, 1787. Age 28,   .   . 161

CHAPTER VII.
More Edinburgh Life. Clarinda. Excise Appointment. Marriage. October 1787–June 1788. Age 28–29,   .   .   . 180

CHAPTER VIII.

Ellisland—June 1788–December 1791. Age 29–32,   194

CHAPTER IX.

Dumfries—1792–1795. Age 33–36,   226

CHAPTER X.

The Closing Year, July 1795–July 1796. Age 36–37,   274

APPENDICES.

Appendix A.—Concerning the Poet's Family,   307
Appendix B.—Manual of Religious Belief,   310
Appendix C.—The Poet's Commonplace Books,   315
Appendix D.—Burns and Freemasonry,   336
Appendix E.—The Ayr Burns Statue—1891,   346

ILLUSTRATION.

Silhouette of Robert Burns, taken by Miers in 1787.

THE BOOK OF ROBERT BURNS.

THE POET'S LINEAGE.

CHAPTER I.

> The land he trod
> Hath now become a place of pilgrimage;
> Where dearer are the daisies of the soil,
> That could his song engage.
> The hoary hawthorn, wreathed
> Above the banks on which his limbs he flung,
> While some sweet plaint he breathed;
> The streams he wandered near;
> The maidens whom he loved, the songs he sung—
> All, all are dear!
> Isa Craig Knox.

So early as the eleventh century the name of Burnes appears in the English records. In Domesday Book Godric de Burnes is named in the year 1050 as the owner of wide domains in Kent. In Rymer's *Fœdera* is recorded a bull of Pope Nicholas IV., whereby John de Burnes, knight, is in 1290 welcomed to Rome as envoy of Edward I. And according to Dugdale, in his *Monasticon*, William de Burnes is, in a charter of Edward II., included among the early benefactors of the hospital founded at Eastbridge, in Canterbury, by Thomas à Becket. Curious as pointing to the early origin of the surname, these notices do not otherwise avail our present inquiry, since it is certain that the family in which we are interested did not derive even remotely from an English source.

The Scottish surname, Burns or Burnes, is formed from the compound word Burn-house, signifying a dwelling or croft resting upon the margin of a rivulet or small stream. Farm homesteads and private dwellings styled Burnhouse are common in all the lowland counties, especially in the counties of Fife and Kincardine, while the family name Burnes or Burns is or was common in every district in which existed the territorial appellative.

In the parish and other registers of Kincardineshire the surname is variously spelt Burnes, Burnas, Burnase, Burnace, and Burness,[1] and members of the Kincardineshire stock seem to have derived from a common ancestor at or about the farm of Burnhouse, now called Kair, in the parish of Arbuthnot.[2] In the parish register of Arbuthnot are the following entries:—

> At the kirk of Arbuthnot, the 23rd May 1635, William Burness, in the parish of Kineff, and Janet Milne, in this parish, were married.
> On the 11th April 1617, John Burnace of Boghall, in Arbuthnot, and Margaret Stevinson, in the parish of Glenbervie, were proclaimed in order to marriage.

To John Burnace and his wife were baptized at Arbuthnot, Margaret, on the 15th October 1648; James, on the 22nd December 1650; and Robert, on the 20th January 1656.

At Arbuthnot, on the 23rd March 1656, the banns of marriage were proclaimed between Robert Burnes and Margaret Mill in

---

[1] In the Orkneys there are three places known as Burness—a small lake in the parish of Westray, an estate in the parish of Firth and Stenness, and the old parish of Burness, now annexed to that of Cross in the island of Sanday. But Burness or Burns, so far as we can ascertain, does not exist as a surname in any part of the Orkneys.

[2] There was another Burnhouse in the parish of Montrose, of which the name was abbreviated into Burnes at or prior to the middle of the seventeenth century. On the 20th February 1661 Alexander Turnbull, son of Peter Turnbull of Stracathro, gave infeftment in liferent to his wife Jean Hunter, daughter of David Hunter of Burnes, in the northmost fore-tenement of land on the east side of Murray Street, Montrose. —Burgh Records of Montrose, Seisins, vol. 1656–1670, p. 112.

THE POET'S LINEAGE.

Glenbervie, and on the 29th April of the same year John Burnes in Boghall of Arbuthnot and Agnes Jamie in Garvock were married. On the 26th of May 1664 Thomas Burnace and Mary Gib were married at Arbuthnot; and on the 6th September 1698 David Burness had baptized at Arbuthnot a daughter, Jean.

At or prior to the middle of the seventeenth century, George Burnace, from Arbuthnot, settled at Barnsen Hill, in the parish of Benholm. He had a son baptized on the 2nd April 1662, but his name is in the register incidentally omitted. Tradition affirms that he had a son Robert, who was father of Robert Burnes, solicitor in Stonehaven. The latter married Isabel Meldrum, by whom he had a son, Robert, who became Sheriff-Substitute of Kincardineshire. The Sheriff's wife was Anne Cushnie.

During the seventeenth century members of the Kincardineshire sept were variously employed. On the 5th April 1637 John Burnes, "servitor" or factor to Sir Alexander Strachan of Thornton, is named as a witness to an heritable bond granted by the Earl of Traquair, Treasurer of Scotland, to Alexander Straitoun of that Ilk.[1] Patrick Burness, "Clerk to the Presbytery of Brechin," attests a bond, whereby, on the 26th August 1659, John Lindsay of Edzell grants "ane hundreth merks and six bolls of oatmeal," etc., to the parish reader at Lochlea.[2] Colonel John Burnes is mentioned in the Act of 1690 for "rescinding the forefaultures and fynes since the year 1665."[3]

We have found members of the Burnes family at Arbuthnot intermarrying with parishioners of Glenbervie, a course perfectly natural, since these parishes are contiguous. An early Burnes settlement at Glenbervie becomes known to us in the following narrative.

---

[1] In his *Notes on the Name and Family of Burnes*, p. 13, Dr. James Burnes states that the instrument was in the possession of his father.

[2] *Ibid.* p. 17.

[3] Acta Parl. Scot., ix. 166.

David Stuart of Johnston near Laurencekirk, accompanied at the battle of Pinkie, on the 10th September 1547, his puissant neighbour, Sir Alexander Douglas of Glenbervie. Wounded in the conflict, Sir Alexander was by Stuart borne from the field; and, in acknowledgment of this service, Sir Alexander granted him the lands of Inchbreck, in his barony of Glenbervie, the gift being confirmed by a charter from the Regent, Mary of Guise, which is dated at Aberdeen in 1556.[1] And, according to Professor John Stuart of Aberdeen, who early in the present century owned the lands of Inchbreck, persons of the name of Burnes were farmers on the estate when his ancestor, David Stuart of Johnston, entered upon his grant.[2]

The early parish registers of Glenbervie have been lost—the extant record of births dating only from 1721, and that of marriages from 1748. The parish register of Arbuthnot, which is extant from 1631, contains the following important entry:—"At the kirk of Arbuthnot, the 27th of August 1633, the said day Robert Burnace presentit ane chyld to be baptizit, callit Robert. Witness thairto Robert Krow in Parkhead." According to the usual method, when a child was baptized publicly, the session-clerk named the congregation only as witnesses, while if a child was baptized privately, the names of two or more individuals were given as witnessing the solemnity. But at this time the minister of Glenbervie was Mr. James Douglas, second son of Sir Archibald Douglas of Glenbervie, who, admitting of a godfather, according to the episcopal mode, caused the godfather's name to be in the parish register entered as a witness. And Robert Krow, named as witness to the baptism of the 27th August, may probably have been the child's maternal

---

[1] Jervise's *Memorials of Angus and Mearns*, Edinb. 1861, 8vo. pp. 95–99; letter from Alexander Stuart, Esq., of Inchbreck, to the writer.
[2] Dr. James Burnes's "Notes," p. 14.

grandfather, since the infant evidently received his name. Krow is described as "in Parkhead," which implies that he rented the farm at the head of the slope or rising ground, on which is situated the demesne, or home park at Arbuthnot. Robert Krow, evidently a son of Robert Krow, farmer at Parkhead, "had a child baptized to him, by the name of Robert, at the kirk of Arbuthnot, on the 4th September 1646," and on the occasion, Sir Robert, afterwards first Viscount Arbuthnot, was present as godfather.[1] The presence of a territorial baron at a baptism in the family of a tenant betokened more than ordinary favour. And, as the name Robert was common in every generation of the Arbuthnot family from the close of the fourteenth century, and the bearers of it had latterly been persons of eminence,[2] it may be assumed that it was by the farmers Krow adopted in compliment to the family of their landlord. And we have remarked how that, apparently from one of the Krow family, it was introduced into that of Burnes.

The family of Krow, or Crow, can be traced to the parish of Arbuthnot only. During the eighteenth century members of the family rented farms in the parish of Brechin, and are found intermarrying in the families of the district landowners.[3]

Colonel John Crow, descended from the Brechin family, had a daughter and heiress, Helen Margaret, who in 1841 espoused Major-General Sir John Campbell, Bart.; her eldest son, Sir Archibald Ava Campbell, succeeded as third baronet on the death of his father in 1855.

Robert, son of Robert Burnace, baptized at Arbuthnot on the

---

[1] Arbuthnot Parish Register.
[2] Sir Robert Arbuthnot of that Ilk, a man of great ability and superior accomplishments, was employed in state service by James VI.; he died in 1615, and was succeeded by his nephew, Sir Robert Arbuthnot, who made a considerable figure in the reigns of James VI. and Charles I. His eldest son, also Sir Robert, was a man of authority and weight; he was created Viscount Arbuthnot in 1641, and died in 1659. His son, grandson, and great-grandson, successively Viscounts of Arbuthnot, each bore the Christian name of Robert.
[3] Brechin Parish Register.

27th August 1633, was by his father established in a farm in the parish of Glenbervie. In the Arbuthnot register a marriage proclamation is entered thus:—"June 10, 1665, Robert Burnace in the parische of Glenbervie, and Alspit [Elizabeth] Wise, lawfull daughter to Andrew Wise in Gyretsmire, gave in their names to be proclaimed for marriage."

The family of Wise rented lands in Kincardineshire; and synchronous with Andrew Wise, tenant in Gyretsmyre, there lived at Arbuthnot Richard Wise, also tenant at Gyretsmyre, and David Wise "in Bringieshill." Members of the sept intermarried with the families of Strachan of Thornton,[1] and of other landowners in Kincardineshire. The present representative is Thomas Alexander Wise, M.D., formerly Principal of the Hooghly and Dacca Colleges, and now of Hillbank, in the county of Forfar.

In leasing a farm at Glenbervie, Robert Burnes or Burnace joined a neighbourhood in which persons of his name and kin had rented portions of land for a series of generations.

Walter Burnes[2] of the parish of Glenbervie, who there died prior to the middle of the seventeenth century, had a son of the same Christian name.

Walter Burnes the younger held in lease on the estate of Inchbreck the farm of Bogjorgan,[3] extending to sixty acres, Scottish measure. He there resided till his death, which took place in November 1670.

---

[1] See *Memorials of the Scottish Families of Strachan and Wise*. Printed for private circulation, 1877.

[2] In his "Notes" Dr. James Burnes sets forth that the first Walter Burnes was traditionally represented as having been originally designated Walter Campbell, and as owner of a small farm styled Burnhouse, in the county of Argyle. He had, proceeded the tradition, given offence to his chief, the Earl of Argyle, by yielding support to the royal house of Stewart, and was consequently obliged to abandon his native country, and, as a fugitive, betake himself to the Lowlands, accompanied by his son Walter, who was then a boy. Finding his way to Glenbervie, he there dropped the name Campbell, substituting that of Burnes, as an abbreviation of Burnhouse, his former possession. The alleged tradition is utterly at variance with recorded facts.

[3] The present rent of Bogjorgan farm is £40.

His will, lately discovered by the present writer among the unrecorded testaments of the Commissariot of Brechin, is of the following purport:—

Testament Testamentar, Latter Will, Legacie, and Inventory of the goods, etc., pertaining to Walter Burnece in Bogjargan, and possessed in common betwixt him and Issobell Grig, his spous, the tyme of his deceis, who deceist in the month off November 1670, given up by himself at Bogjargan the 7th day of November 1670 years. Walter Burnece being sick of body and perfect of memorie, made his latter will befor thir witnesses, Robert Tailiour in Halkhill and John Greig in Halkhill.

INVENTOR.

Imprimis, two old oxen for 6 lib 13 4d. the peice.

Item, three stotes, 6 lib the peice.

Item, two kine, 6 lib the peice.

Item, three coyes [queys], 5 lib. the peice.

Item, two horses, the one 3 lib., the other 6 lib.

Item, eight wedders, 26s. 8d. the peice.

Item, ten ewes, 1 lib. the peice.

Item, beare and infield corne, a chalder, at 4 libs. ilk boll.

Item, Outfield corne, a chalder, at 3 libs. ilk boll.

Item, the houss, with the haill outsight and insight plenishing, 10 libs.

DEBTS RESTANED TO HIM.

Item, be David Wyse in Jaksbank, 6 lib. 10s.

DEBTS RESTANED DE HIM.

Item, the laird's duty, four score of merks.

Item, to the parson of teind silver, 5 libs.

Item, to William Neilson in Bogtoun, 6 libs.

Item, to Archibald Gellie in Lagevin, 2 libs.

Item, to two hooksfies, the one 8 merks, the other 4 libs.

Item, to John Greig in Halkhill, 20 merks.

Sum total, 91 lib.

LEGACY. *Item*, leaves his present wyffe Issobel Greig his executrix, and his debtors being paid, he leaves to his two youngest children, David and Jean Burnece, to ilk one fiftie merkis.

Item, he leaves John Greig in Halkhill to be tutor and overseer to them.

The will is attested by "Mr. John Irving," minister of Glenbervie.[1]

As Walter Burnes names Isobel Greig as his "present wyffe," the entry would imply that he had been espoused previously. And as he provides only for his two youngest children, David and Jean, it may be inferred that he had other children, and that these had already been provided for.

In the farm of Bogjorgan Walter Burnes was succeeded by two brothers, William and James, who may reasonably be regarded as his elder sons, and not improbably by a former wife. In 1705, when James, the younger brother, retired from the farm, the following memorandum as to the plenishing was drawn up, under sanction of the landlord, William Stuart of Inchbreck :—

> Ane note of the biging off Bogjorgine, belonging to William Stuart, heritor thereoff, given up be William Burnasse, present tenant of the sd. rowm, and James Burnasse, late possessore of the halff theroff, upon the seventainth day of Jully, 1705 years.
>
> *Imp.* (a ffyr) houss, consisting of thrie couplles, ffour horses, two taill postes, ane midle wall with ane post ffrom the ground, with ane rooff, two pares in the syd, with ane door bandet locked and bared, and with ane window of two lightes, bradet bandet and snecked, with ane loume, all to be sufficient.
>
> *Item,* ane barne, consisting of ffyve couplles, ffour horses, two taill postes, ane rooff, thrie pares in the syd, with ffor door locked and bandet, and back door bared and steepled, all to be sufficient.
>
> *Item,* ane byre, consisting of four couplles, two in the syd, ane rooff, with door and door cheikes bandet, all to be sufficient.
>
> It is declared be both parties that if ther be no other inventur ffound betwixt this and Whytsonday nixt, 1706 years, that this shall be ane tr[ue] inventur off the said William Burness at his removell from the said roum. In

---

[1] Mr. John Irving was parish minister of Glenbervie from 1636 till his death in November 1680.—*Fasti Eccl. Scot.* iii. 873.

THE POET'S LINEAGE.

witness . . . beffor these witnesses,—Robt. Middletoun in Broombank and David Watson in Polburn, wryter hereoff.

R. Midletoun, *Witnes.*
D. Watson, *witnes and wryter.*[1]

WILLIAM STUART,
1705.
"W. B."

On one of two recumbent tombstones in Glenbervie churchyard, commemorative of members of the Burnes family, are at the upper part engraved the initials W. B. and C. F., separated by the figure of a heart, indicating wedlock. These initials commemorate William Burnes, tenant in Bogjorgan, and his wife Christian Fotheringham. The tombstone is considerably defaced, but there are distinguishable the initials I. B., W. B., and R. B., evidently intended to indicate the names of three children of the family who had died young. Next follow the words, "And here lyes his son, John Burnes, who departed the 10th of April 17—, being of age 3—"

John Burnes may be historically recognised. In a work entitled "History of the Rebellion in the 1715, by the Rev. Mr. Robert Patten, formerly chaplain to Mr. Forster," published at London in 1745, there occurs, at page 121, the following entry: "Strathmore's Regiment. A great part of them were prevented from crossing the Forth by the King's ships, but there did John Burnes, Lieut., with fifteen others." On the outbreak of the insurrection under the Earl of Mar in 1715, the Earl Marischal was, by his relative and neighbour, William Stuart of Inchbreck, aided in forming a regiment in support of the Chevalier. And not improbably Lieutenant John Burnes was a member of the corps which, in December 1715, was reviewed at Stonehaven by the Chevalier, during his visit to the Earl Marischal at Fetteresso.

---

[1] The original of this inventory, with other documents relating to the Burnes family, was, about forty years ago, borrowed by one of the Poet's biographers from the late Mr. Stuart of Inchbreck, and was not returned to him.

On the Glenbervie tombstone, already described, is the further legend: "Here under lies —— Burnes, —— —— 1715," such being probably the date of William Burnes's death. The tombstone bears to have been erected in 1719.

Among the surviving children of William Burnes and Christian Fotheringham were William and James. William succeeded to the farm of Bogjorgan. He married Elspeth Taylor, by whom he had a son, William, also two daughters, Christian and Elspeth. Christian married James Kerr, and Elspeth became the wife of William Taylor, tenant in Whitebog, Kincardineshire.

William, son of William Burnes and Elspeth Taylor, married Helen, daughter of William Thomson, merchant at Drumlithie. He died in 1784, in his sixty-fifth year. He was father of four sons, William, James, Robert, and John; and of seven daughters, Jean (baptized 30th January 1752),[1] Janet, Margaret, Isobel, Jean, Sarah, and Mary. Of these, William, James, Jean, and Janet died in infancy. Margaret married Robert Dallas, merchant, Stonehaven. Robert settled in Stonehaven, and there died in 1816. He married, first, in November 1778, —— ——, when he paid as a proclamation fee the sum of £6, 6s. Scots; secondly, on the 8th February 1794, Anne Paul,[2] with issue a son, William, who established a manufactory at Stonehaven.[3]

John Burnes, youngest son of William Burnes and Helen Thomson, was born 23rd May 1771. After being a single year at school, he was apprenticed to a baker at Brechin at the age of thirteen. In 1794 he enlisted as a private in the Angus Fencibles, and while with his regiment stationed at Dumfries, he became known to his relative the Poet. At Dumfries, in 1796, he composed *Thrummy Cap*, a metrical tale, which was afterwards printed. On the dis-

---

[1] Fordoun Parish Register.   [2] Dunnottar Parish Register.
[3] Statement by William Burness, manufacturer, Stonehaven, to Dr. Burnes, dated 22nd August 1851.

banding of his corps, which took place at Peterhead on the 1st of April 1799, he proceeded to Stonehaven, where he entered into trade as a baker. In 1803 he joined the Forfarshire Militia, in which he served twelve years; he was discharged in June 1815. Thereafter employed as traveller by a publishing house, he, while prosecuting his duties, perished in a snowstorm, on the road between Stonehaven and Aberdeen, on the 12th January 1826. Besides his tale of *Thrummy Cap*, he, in 1819, published a volume containing "The Hermit, or, The Dead come to Life," a comic dramatic tale; "Rosmond and Isabella; or, The Persisting Penitent," a tragedy; "The Old Soldier," a comic drama; "Sir James the Rose," a tragedy; and "Charles Montgomerie," a tragedy. In his preface, dated "Stonehaven, May 5, 1819," he, in allusion to his compositions, remarks that "he leaves them to their fate," adding that "although the learned may condemn them as stubble to the flames, damning both them and the author for writing them; yet, if one good-natured fellow declare he has any pleasure in their perusal, the author has all he wishes for." Subsequently he published at Montrose "The Recruit," an interlude in one act. His plays were occasionally acted on the provincial stage, the author assisting in the performances. In his metrical writings John Burnes is a close imitator of his relative Robert Burns; but in his blank verse he is original and considerably powerful. He married, in 1801, Margaret Davidson, a native of Peterhead, by whom he had several children.

James Burnes, younger son of William Burnes and Christian Fotheringham, rented the farm of Brawlinmuir, in the parish of Glenbervie, and on the Inchbreck estate.[1] An anecdote illustrative of his sagacity has been preserved. Highland freebooters made

---

[1] The farms of Brawlinmuir and Mains of Inchbreck, which were usually let together, embrace about 200 acres, and might produce a present rental of £120. Both farms are now in the hands of the proprietor.

frequent incursions into Kincardineshire, snatching both money and goods. Learning that a body of these plunderers were hovering in his neighbourhood, he concealed his money in the nave of an old cart wheel which lay in front of his house. In this way the robbers were, on entering and quitting the dwelling, made to tread unconsciously upon the treasure they sought to plunder.[1]

On the 14th June 1740 James Burnes executed his will; it thus proceeds:—

> Be it known to all men by thir presents, Me, James Burnace, in Bralinmuir, that fforasmickle as I have thought fitt to setle my small worldly concern in my lifetime ffor preventing any disorder or confusion that may arise among my children after my death, I with the burden of my own liferent, sell and dispone from me and after death to and in ffavours of Robert Burnace, my eldest lawfull son, in Clochnahill; William Burnace, my second son, in Bralinmuir; James Burnace, in Halkhill, my third son; George Burnace, in Elphill, my fourth son; Margaret Burnace, spous to James Gawen, in Drumlithie, my only daughter; and the said James for his interest, my haill corns and croft and other moveables parteining to me at present or that may be the time of my decess in as ffar as extends to the soum of one hundred merks Scotts money to each of the saids Robert, William, James, and George Burnace, my sons; and ffifty merks money forsaid to the said Margret Burnace and James Gawen; and the like soum of ffifty merks to John Gawen, lawfull son to the said James Gawen, making in haill ffive hundred merks Scotts money divided and apointed to them in mener above exprest, with full power to them, agreeable to thir respective shares, to midle, intromitt with, sell, use, and dispose on my said croft and effects for payment to them of the said soum and shares, to each of them so due as above sett down and divided, always under the provision before of my liferent use, and what is over and above this payment as said is, I sett and dispon to my wife Margret ffalconer, to be by her liferented, and what remains after her death I recomend to be equally divided amongst my said ffive children free of any burden, except twenty merks to Margaret Scott Burnace, lawful daughter to the deceased Thomas Burnace, my fifth son, which, at discretion of my said children, I appoint to be payed either with themselves or

---

[1] Chambers's *Life and Works of Robert Burns*, Edin. 1851, vol. i. p. 334.

THE POET'S LINEAGE. 13

at the death of the said Margret ffalconer, my spous ; which disposition, with the burden and provision before mentioned, I bind and oblige me to warrend, acquit, and defend good and valid to my said children as above divided, with respect to the soums particularly above mentioned at all hands and against all deadly. Dispensing with the generality hereof, and with all nullities, imperfections, and objections in law, proponeable or prejudicial hereunto in any sort. I further recomend to my sons to be careful of, and dutiful to, my said spous and their mother, and to be assisting to bring to perfection my said goods so disponed, and the value of them aplyd for payt. of the forsaid soums as above apointed, and, more particularly, I recomend peace and unity among themselves and exact observance of what I herein above recomended ; and if any shall offer to contraveen or contradict this in any pairt, then the rest agreeing to and abiding by the same are hereby empowered to denude him or them of the share to them appointed, and to apply the same among themselves at discretion, and for the more security I consent to the registration hereof in the Books of Council and Session and others competent to have the strength of ane decreet, that letters of horning and other executorials necesser on ane charge of ten days may be direct hereon, I thereto constitut —— my procurators. In Witness wherof thir presents (written on this sheet of stampt paper by James Strachan, Writer in Stonhyve) are subscrived with my hand at Bralenmuir, the fourteen day of June, Seventeen hundred and ffourty years, Before thir witnesses—David Croll, in Whitbog; George Touch, in Inchbreck ; John Jellie, Subtenant in Bralenmuir ; and William Taillor, son to James Tailor, in Whitbog.

I. B.

David Croll, Witnes.
George Touch, Wittens.
John Jellie, Witnes.
William Tailyor, Witnes.[1]

The testator's signature is attested by
JAMES STRACHAN, *N.P.*

Margaret Falconer, wife of James Burnes, belonged to a family, ancient, and, in one of the branches, noble. Ranulph, son of Walter de Lunkyn, obtained from William the Lion, about the close of the twelfth century, the office of royal falconer, with a grant of lands in Kincardineshire, which, on account of the owner having charge of

---

[1] The original testament has been preserved in the sheriff-clerk's office, Stonehaven ; it bears to have been recorded on the 28th January 1743.

the king's hawks, were subsequently designated Halkerton. By the family was assumed the name of Falconer. Sir Alexander Falconer of Halkerton, a zealous adherent of Charles I., was appointed a Senator of the College of Justice, and in 1647 was raised to the peerage as Lord Falconer of Halkerton. He is now represented by Francis Alexander Keith Falconer, ninth Earl of Kintore.

James Burnes and his wife are in the churchyard of Glenbervie commemorated by a tombstone inscribed thus :—

> Here under lyes the body of James Burnes, who was tenant in Brawlinmuir, who died ye 23 of January 1743, aged 87 years. Also the body of Margaret Falconer, his spouse, who departed this life the 28th of December 1749, aged 90 years.
>
> Altho' our bodys worms destroy, our reins consumed be ;
> Yet in our flesh and with our eyes, shall our Redeemer see.
>
> Here is the grave of Thomas Burnes, son of the above, who departed this life June ye 8 1734, aged 29 years. Also his lawful and only daughter Margarett, who departed this life March ye 24th 1741, aged 8 years.

By his wife, Margaret Falconer, James Burnes had seven sons, of whom were Robert, William, James, George, and Thomas ; also a daughter, Margaret.

Margaret, only daughter of James Burnes and Margaret Falconer, married James Gavin, Drumlithie, Kincardineshire, with issue two sons, John and George.

John, the elder son, to whom James Burnes, his maternal grandfather, bequeathed the sum of fifty merks, rented the farm of West Bogtoun, in the parish of Glenbervie.

George Gavin, the second son, was born in 1736 ; he traded as a brewer at Drumlithie, and there died on the 28th of September 1800.[1] Having acquired considerable opulence, the succession to his estate was by his representatives keenly contested in the law

---

[1] Tombstone inscription in Glenbervie churchyard.

courts. By his first wife, Christian Bisset (who died in June 1770, at the age of thirty-four), he had two sons, James, who died in infancy, and Robert, who rented the farm of Collieston, and died 10th February 1805, aged forty-one; also a daughter, Isabella.

Isabella, only daughter of George Gavin and Christian Bisset, born in 1759, married in 1795 her cousin, George Greig,[1] farmer at Alpity, in the parish of Arbuthnot, and of Shepherdshaugh, in the parish of Fordoun, who died on the 1st of June 1840, at the age of seventy-seven. To the spouses, George Greig and Isabella Gavin (the latter died on the 9th of December 1837), were born six sons and a daughter, Catherine. Two of the sons, William and Alexander, died in infancy.

James, the eldest surviving son, born 14th April 1798, rented the farm of Mains of Kair, in Arbuthnot, and died on the 2nd July 1882. He married, 16th December 1821, Margaret Peat (who died 22nd December 1851), with issue three sons and three daughters.

John Kinloch, eldest son, born 22nd November 1822, is a banker at Leeds. He married, first, in 1850, Isabella, daughter of John M'Bean, Inverness, with issue three sons and two daughters, of whom survives —Duncan Macbean Greig, M.D., University College Hospital, London. He married, secondly, Elizabeth H. Tootall, without issue.

George, second son, born 14th April 1824, resides at 9 Argyle Place, Edinburgh. He married, in 1851, Catherine Smart, Arduthie, Stonehaven, with issue one son, Charles; also three daughters, Elizabeth, Maggie, and Norah.

James Booth, third son, born 22nd August 1838, is a banker at Laurencekirk. He married, in 1871, Margaret, daughter of James Stinson, Belfast, with issue two sons, John Reginald and James

---

[1] The family of Greig were extensively connected with the parish of Glenbervie, as is evidenced by the numerous tombstones commemorating persons of the name in the churchyard of that parish. In the Commissariot Register of Brechin is recorded the testament of Robert Greig in Nether Kinmonth, in the parish of Glenbervie, who died in March 1677.

Stephenson; also three daughters, Greta Kathleen, Eliza Stephenson, and Annie May.

Isabella, eldest daughter, born 6th February 1826, died in infancy.

Clementina, second daughter, born 30th December 1828, married, 13th May 1851, George Leghorn, merchant, Clones, Ireland, with issue five sons, John, William, George, Frederick, and Charles James; also four daughters, Margaret Peat, Elizabeth, Jane, and Primrose Leghorn.

Jane, third daughter, born 23rd July 1832, died 27th October 1847.

George, second son of George Greig and Isabella Gavin, rented the farm of Townhead of Arbuthnot; he afterwards settled in Tasmania, where he has acquired land and attained opulence. He married, and has a numerous offspring.

David, third son of George Greig, rented the farm of Harvieston, in the parish of Kinneff. He died young, and his remains are interred in the churchyard of Glenbervie, where he is commemorated by a granite tombstone.

John, fourth son, rented the farm of Grange of Kinneff; he married Elizabeth Burness of Cloch in the same parish, and died in 1889.

Catherine, only daughter of George Greig and Isabella Gavin, born 1804, married, in July 1827, Alexander Martin, who rented the farms of Hawhill and Mill of Garvock; he died at Aberdeen in 1887.

George Gavin married, secondly, Catherine Ley, who died 3rd December 1829, aged eighty-six. Of this marriage were born two sons, Thomas and John, and a daughter, Elizabeth. Thomas, the elder son, born 1782, died at St. George's, Granada, on the 23rd of January 1809. John, second son, born 1789, died in Jamaica 7th December 1818. Elizabeth, elder daughter, born 1778, died 15th July 1818.[1]

---

[1] Tombstone inscription in Glenbervie churchyard.

THE POET'S LINEAGE.

Thomas, fifth son of James Burnes, died 8th June 1734, at the age of twenty-nine;[1] his remains were committed to the churchyard of Glenbervie. He married, with issue a daughter, Margaret Scott, who died on the 24th March 1741, aged eight years; she is named in her grandfather's will as legatee for twenty merks.[2]

——, sixth son, rented the farm of Hawkhill of Glenbervie. He married Margaret Greig, and died in 1735, aged thirty-seven.[3]

William, the second son, succeeded his father in the lease of Brawlinmuir. He married, with issue, but his children seem to have died young or unmarried.

James Burnes, third son of James Burnes and Margaret Falconer, born in 1690, rented the farm of Hawkhill of Glenbervie, and, on the death of his elder brother William, succeeded to the lease of Brawlinmuir. He died 3rd April 1778, at the advanced age of eighty-eight.[4] He married, first, —— Christie, by whom he had four sons, James, Thomas, William first, and William second; also two daughters, Margaret and Catherine.

James, eldest son, was baptized 29th March 1724; he rented first, the farm of Auchtochter, in the parish of Fordoun, afterwards the farm of Higham, near Montrose. Thomas, second son, baptized 11th February 1729, was employed as a gardener in England; he returned to Scotland, where he died in 1804. William, first of the name, baptized 11th July 1731, died in infancy. William, second of the name, baptized 12th October 1735, settled in Montrose as an officer of excise; he spelt his name Burness.[5]

Margaret, elder daughter, was baptized 10th August 1722.

Catherine, younger daughter, was baptized 3rd May 1726.

James Burnes married, secondly, Catherine Beattie (a relative of

---

[1] Tombstone inscription in Glenbervie churchyard.
[2] Will of James Burnes, *supra*.
[3] *Ibid.*
[4] Tombstone inscription in Glenbervie churchyard.
[5] Glenbervie Parish Register.

Professor James Beattie, author of "The Minstrel"), by whom he had two sons, David and George. George, the younger son, died 16th October 1769, at the age of twenty-eight.[1]

David, the elder son, succeeded his father in the farm of Brawlinmuir.

In his instrument of lease, dated at Castleton,[2] 25th October 1788, the proprietor of his farm, Doctor John Stuart of Inchbreck,—

> agrees for himself, his heirs and successors, to sett to him and his heirs and executors the towns and lands of Mains of Inchbreck and Brawlinmoor, lying in the parish of Glenbervie, for the space of nineteen years while the lessee becomes bound to make residence, and to pay to the landlord an annual rent of £31, 18s. 10¾d. sterling; also to lead his peats from the Hill of Inchbreck, and to furnish shearers to him for one day in harvest.[3]

On the expiry of the lease of Brawlinmuir in 1807, David Burnes rented the larger farm of Boghead of Kintore.[4] About the year 1776 he married Catherine Milne, a native of Drumlithie, by whom he had five sons and five daughters.

Catherine Beattie, the eldest daughter, baptized 28th June 1775, married Archibald Falconer, with issue seven sons, David, Robert, William, John, who became a solicitor in Stonehaven, George, Archibald, and Alexander; also four daughters, Catherine, Margaret, Jean, and Isabel.

Jean, second daughter of David Burnes, baptized 18th May 1781, married John Reith, farmer at Tipperty, in the parish of Glenbervie, with issue five sons, David, John, Alexander, James, and

---

[1] Tombstone inscription in Glenbervie churchyard.
[2] Castleton of Mondynes, near Glenbervie, was then the residence of the proprietor of Inchbreck.
[3] For a copy of the lease we are indebted to Alexander Stuart, Esq., the present proprietor of Inchbreck.
[4] David Burnes was visited by the Poet at Brawlinmuir in September 1787. Aware of the Poet's celebrity, his wife sought to entertain him in the best manner, and accordingly produced on her table an infusion of tea, then a rare beverage in a farmer's dwelling.—Family Tradition.

William; also five daughters, Catherine, Margaret, Christian, Jean, and Louisa.

David Reith, the eldest son, rented the farm of Jackston, in the parish of St. Cyrus, and subsequently engaged in merchandise, first at St. Cyrus, afterwards at Auchenblae.

John Reith, second son, practised as a physician at Fettercairn, Banchory, Stonehaven, and St. Cyrus. His son, the Rev. John Reith, was in 1872 ordained minister of the Established Church at Rickarton, Banffshire.

Alexander Reith, third son, engaged in legal pursuits, and settled in Glasgow, where he died.

James Reith, the fourth son, succeeded his father as lessee of the farm of Tipperty; he now resides at Old Crombie, in the parish of Marnoch, Aberdeenshire.

William Reith, fifth son, farms land in Canada.

Catherine, eldest daughter of John Reith and Jean Burnes, is wife of John Smith, formerly farmer at Balmaladie, and subsequently at Pitgarvie, Kincardineshire.

Margaret, second daughter, espoused James Clark, farmer, Stoneyroo, Kincardineshire, with issue one son and two daughters.

Christian, third daughter, married Arthur Stephen, farmer at Jackston, parish of St. Cyrus, with issue four sons and two daughters.

Jean, fourth daughter, died young.

Louisa, fifth daughter, died unmarried.

Margaret, third daughter of David Burnes and Catherine Milne, was born 1st March 1782, and died at Aberdeen. She married first on the 3rd March 1802[1] Robert Ley, farmer, Knockback, in the parish of Fordoun, who died in 1815, aged thirty-four,[2] with issue three sons, David, James, and John; also four daughters, Catherine, Jane, Margaret, and Isabella.

[1] Tombstone inscription in Glenbervie churchyard.   [2] *Ibid.*

David, the eldest son, held a parochial office at Merton, in Surrey; he died at an advanced age, and a monument was, by his neighbours, erected to his memory in the parish church.

James, second son, succeeded his father as lessee of Knockback farm.

John, third son, died in childhood.

Catherine, the eldest daughter, married first William Collie, farmer, Tulloch, parish of Durris, Kincardineshire; secondly, Alexander Duthie, who rented the same farm.

Jane, second daughter, married John Masson, farmer, Hilton of Kinneff.

Margaret, third daughter, married William Don, farmer, Newlands, Kincardineshire.

Isabella, fourth daughter, died unmarried.

Margaret Burnes married, secondly, James Dickson, farmer at Knockback, who died in 1821, aged twenty-nine,[1] with issue a son, George, and a daughter, Mary.

George Dickson, son of James Dickson and Margaret Burnes, became a cattle-dealer in London; he died unmarried.

Mary Dickson married James Kesson, overseer at Drumtochty Castle, Kincardineshire, with issue a son, Edward, who died while prosecuting his studies for the ministry; also a daughter, Mary, wife of James Paton, superintendent of the Art Galleries, Glasgow, and who has issue four sons and two daughters.

Isabel, fourth daughter of David Burnes, baptized 13th May 1788, married George Brown, farmer, Wardhouse, parish of Kintore, with issue.

Mary, fifth and youngest daughter of David Burnes, baptized 4th June 1796, married William Urquhart, Woodside, Aberdeen, with issue.

---

[1] Tombstone inscription in Glenbervie churchyard.

THE POET'S LINEAGE. 21

James, eldest son of David Burnes, baptized 19th March 1777, rented the farm of East Mains of Barras, parish of Kinneff; he married Margaret Reith, sister of John Reith, farmer, Tipperty, with issue five sons, William, David, Alexander, John, and James; also six daughters, Catherine, born 25th April 1809; Jean, born 14th February 1815; Isabel; Margaret, born 5th August 1819; Nicholas, and Eliza.

George, second son of David Burnes, baptized 4th December 1784, succeeded his father in the lease of Boghead of Kintore. He married Nicholas, daughter of —— Tait, papermaker, Inverurie, with issue two sons, William and David; also a daughter, Elsie.

David, third son of David Burnes, baptized 11th August 1786, rented first the lands of Milltimber, and afterwards the farm of Knockquharn, in the parish of Kintore. He married Agnes Smith, a native of Kintore parish, with issue two sons, William and James. William perished in an insurrection at Fiji about the year 1870.

Alexander, fourth son of David Burnes, baptized 3rd July 1790, engaged in merchandise at Aberdeen, and, acquiring opulence, purchased the estates of Maestrick and Prospect Place in that county. By his wife, Mary Smith, he had a son, John, who died in childhood; also a daughter, Elizabeth Smith. Born in 1823, she became in 1842 the first wife of John Stuart, LL.D., advocate, Aberdeen. An accomplished antiquary, Mr. Stuart was in 1854 appointed one of the official searchers in the General Register House, Edinburgh; and in 1873 was promoted as principal keeper of the Register of Deeds. He died at Ambleside on the 19th July 1877, at the age of sixty-four. In 1866 he received from the University of Aberdeen the degree of LL.D., in recognition of his literary eminence. Of his many erudite works in relation to Scottish history and antiquities, his *Sculptured Stones of Scotland* holds a chief place. Dr. Stuart was twice married. By his first wife, Elizabeth Burnes, who died 1st March 1848, he had a son, Robert, who died in infancy; also two daughters. Mary, the elder daughter, is unmarried; Jane Gordon, the second daughter, born January 1847, married, in 1867, the Rev. John Woodward, incumbent of St. Mary's Episcopal Church, Montrose, with issue two sons, who died in childhood; also two daughters.

John, youngest son of David Burnes, prosecuted business as a distiller in Aberdeen; he died unmarried.

George Burnes, fourth son of James Burnes, farmer, Brawlinmuir, rented the farm of Elfhill, in the parish of Fetteresso. He married, with issue five sons and five daughters. James, the eldest son, was baptized 29th May 1729;[1] Robert, the second son, on the 14th August 1731;[2] John, the third son, on the 3rd June 1733;[3] George, fourth son, on the 22nd June 1746; and William, fifth son, on the 17th September 1749. Christian, the eldest daughter, was baptized 25th May 1735; Elizabeth, second daughter, on the 27th June 1737; Anne, third daughter, on the 6th May 1739; Jean, fourth daughter, on the 23rd April 1744; and Helen, fifth and youngest daughter, on the 5th April 1747.[4]

James, eldest son of George Burnes, farmer, Elfhill, succeeded to his father's lease, but latterly rented the farm of Midtoun of Barras, parish of Kinneff. He married, 25th November 1811, Elizabeth Wood, with issue three sons, George, Hugh, and James; also six daughters, Mary, Magdalene, Anne, Charlotte, Margaret, and Catherine. Mary, the eldest daughter, married William Fotheringham, farmer, Dubton, Glen of Cowton; Magdalene,

[1] One of the witnesses of the baptism was the child's paternal grandfather, described as "James Birnes, in Bralanmuire."—Fetteresso Parish Register.

[2] As witnesses to the baptism are "Robert Stewart, late Provost of Aberdeen," and "Robert Birness, in Clochanhill."—Fetteresso Parish Register.

[3] One of the witnesses to the baptism was "Mr. John Stewart, Professor of Mathematics in the Marischal College, Aberdeen."—Fetteresso Parish Register.

[4] Fetteresso Parish Register.

second daughter, married Alexander Mollison, farmer, Mergie; Anne, third daughter, married John Edward; Charlotte, fourth daughter, married David Taylor, farmer, Colliston; Margaret, fifth daughter, married Thomas Mitchell, Chapel of Barras; and Catherine, sixth daughter, married Andrew Duthie, farmer, Bog of Glaslaw.

Hugh, second son of James Burnes, settled in London. James, the third son, succeeded his father in the lease of Midtoun of Barras; he afterwards rented the farm of Cloch of Hilton, parish of Kinneff. He married, and had five sons, Hugh, David, John, Robert, and James; also three daughters, Elizabeth, Catherine, and Isabel.

Robert Burnes, eldest son of James Burnes, Brawlinmuir, by his wife, Margaret Falconer, rented the farm of Kinmonth in Glenbervie, from which he removed to the larger farm of Clochanhill, in the parish of Dunnottar, situated about four miles to the south-west of Stonehaven. Of this farm the rent was £10, 8s. 4d. sterling, with the payment as kain of two "reik hens" or domestic fowls, which, according to the usage of the period, implied a dwelling-house of four apartments. Along with the neighbouring farmers, he built a school at Clochanhill, and aided in supporting a teacher. Like the majority of the tenant-farmers of the North of Scotland, he was a severe sufferer from the inclement winter and spring of 1740, and the losses he then sustained he was unable to fully overcome. Along with his second son, Robert, he, on the 16th February 1744, granted to ex-Provost Stuart of Aberdeen the following obligation :—

> Mr. Robert Burnes, tenant in Clochanhill, in the parish of Dunnottar, and Robert Burness, his son there, grant us to have received in friendly borrowing, at the term of Martinmas last (notwithstanding of the date of thir presents), from Robert Stuart, Esq., Provost of Aberdeen, all and haill the sum of one

hundred and seventeen pounds one shilling Scots money, wherewith we hold ourselves well content, satisfied, and paid; and discharges him thereof, renouncing the exception of not numerate money, and all other exceptions and objections of law proponable in the contrary, the whole sum of one hundred and seventeen pounds one shilling money foresaid of principall, with one year's annual rent thereof from the said term of Martinmas last to the term of payment underwritten, we, the said Robert Burneses, elder and younger, bind and oblige us, conjunctly and severally, our heirs, executors, and successors, and intromitters with our goods and gear whatsomever, thankfully to content, repay, and again deliver to the said Robert Stuart, his heirs, executors, and assignees, and that at the term of Martinmas next to come, 1744 years, without any requisition or longer delay, with the sum of twenty-three pounds money above written of liquidate expenses in case of faillie, together also with the due and ordinary annual rent of the said principal sum yearly, termly, quarterly, and proportionally, so long as the same shall happen to remain unpaid after the foresaid term of payment, conform to the laws of the kingdom for the time being: And for the more security we consent to the registration hereof, and constitute Mr. William Grant, advocate, our procurator.—In witness whereof (written upon stamp paper by John Duncan, writer in Stonehyve) we have subscribed these presents with our hands at Stonehyve, the sixteenth day of February 1744 years, before these witnesses, William Ronald, merchant in Stonehyve, and the said John Duncan. ROBERT BURNES.
ROBERT BURNESS.[1]

With a view to the extension of agricultural business, Robert Burnes the elder obtained on the 15th January 1745, from George Kinloch of Kair, a lease for seven years of "the touns and lands of Fallside and Braiks," in the parish of Dunnottar. In the lease the rent of Fallside is specified as £63, 13s. 4d. Scots in money, and in grain to the value of £22, 7s. 4d., while the rent of Braiks is named as £26 Scots. Robert Burnes also became bound to pay the proportion of the minister's stipend and of the schoolmaster's salary due upon the lands. But, lacking capital, he

---

[1] General Register of Deeds, vol. clix. The younger Robert, it will be remarked, uses in his signature the double s.

THE POET'S LINEAGE.

fell into arrears to his new landlord. Accordingly, he granted to that gentleman,—Mr. Kinloch of Kair,—on the 13th December 1746, a promissory note for £155, 3s. 6d., and this instrument was on the 3rd August 1747 protested for non-payment.[1]

The date of the protested bill indicates the period when Robert Burnes was compelled to quit his several farms, including Clochanhill. He now retired to a cottage at Denside, in the parish of Dunnottar, his three unmarried daughters aiding by their industry to uphold the roof-tree.[2]

Robert Burnes married Isabella, daughter of Alexander Keith, tenant-farmer at Criggie, in the parish of Dunnottar.[3] Of the marriage were born four sons, James, Robert, William, and George; also six daughters, Margaret, Elspeth, Jean, Isabel, Mary, and a daughter who died in infancy.

Margaret, the eldest daughter, born in 1723, married Archibald Walker, residing at Crawton, Kincardineshire; with issue, a son, James, who rented the farm of Gallowton, Dunnottar, and, marrying, had a son, Alexander, iron merchant, Aberdeen; also a daughter, Isobel, who married James Knox, residing in Stonehaven.

Elspeth, second daughter of Robert Burnes, was baptized on the 18th August 1725. She married John Caird, who rented the farm of Woodhead, Fetteresso, and subsequently of Deeside of Dunnottar.[4] Of the marriage was born a daughter, Anna, baptized 26th April

---

[1] General Register of Deeds, vol. clxxii., part 2.
[2] Robert Burnes was helped by occasional remittances from his son William (the Poet's father); and there is a tradition that when, on one occasion, he received the remittance of a one-pound note, he was at a loss how to utilize it, since bank notes as an equivalent for coin were totally unfamiliar in the district of Dunnottar.
[3] "The Land of the Burnesses," by James Crabb Watt, F.S.A., article in the *Scots Magazine* for February 1890 (vol. v. pp. 176-188).

[4] In a letter addressed by the Poet to Mr. James Burnes of Montrose, dated 21st June 1783, John Caird is named as a correspondent of his brother Gilbert. Writing to Gilbert from Edinburgh on the 17th September 1787, the Poet, in referring to his movements in his northern tour, has these words, "John Caird, though born in the same year with our father, walks as vigorously as I can: they have had several letters from his son in New York."

1763,[1] who married Henry Watson, with issue two sons, James and Henry, also two daughters, Mary and Elspeth. By his wife, Elspeth Burnes, John Caird had also three sons. Robert, the eldest son, baptized 4th July 1753,[2] married Margaret Melvin, Stonehaven, with issue three daughters. Of these, Jean, the eldest, married James Sheritt, Aberdeen; Mary, the second daughter, married George Smith, a native of Stonehaven, who settled in London; and Margaret, the third daughter, married James Watson, residing at Aberdeen. James, the second son, baptized 20th June 1755, emigrated to New York. John, the youngest son, baptized 3rd January 1760, visited the Poet at Mossgiel during the summer of 1784. Respecting him the Poet writes, on the 3rd August 1784, to Mr. James Burness at Montrose:—"We were very happy with the unexpected favour of John Caird's company for nearly two weeks, and I must say it of him that he is one of the most agreeable, facetious, warm-hearted lads I was ever acquainted with." John Caird married Margaret Henderson, and settled at Markinch, Fifeshire.

Jean, third daughter of Robert Burnes, baptized 24th May 1727, married John Burnes, sub-tenant, Bogjorgan; she died at Fetteresso without issue. Isobel, fourth daughter, baptized 18th August 1730, became, in 1769, second wife of William Brand, manufacturer and dyer, Auchinblae, Kincardineshire.[3] Writing to his brother Gilbert from Edinburgh, 17th September 1787, the Poet remarks:—"I spent two days among our relations, and found our aunts Jean and Isobel still alive, and hale old women. . . . William Brand is a short old fellow."

Of the marriage of William Brand and Isobel Burnes was born

---

[1] Dunnottar Parish Register.
[2] Parish Register of Fetteresso.
[3] William Brand had issue by his first marriage. His progenitors were a race of yeomen of the name, who rented lands in Glenbervie for a course of centuries. Thomas Brand, tenant in Nether Kinmonth, parish of Glenbervie, died some time prior to March 1610. At the time of his death he was found largely indebted to Alexander Scott of Baldovie and another.—Brechin Commissariot Register. The family are believed to have been followers of the House of Douglas.

in 1770 a son James, who became a builder at Auchinblae. He married Rachel, daughter of James Guthrie, builder, Loanhead of Pitarrow, in the parish of Fordoun, with issue four sons, Charles, William, James, and David.

Charles Brand, the eldest son, was born at Auchinblae in 1805. After serving an apprenticeship in the building trade to James Guthrie, his maternal grandfather, he, in 1831 entered upon business at Montrose. Having satisfactorily executed some important building contracts in the neighbourhood, he, in connexion with the Scottish North-Eastern Railway, got several contracts, which included the construction of the viaducts over Drumlithie Glen and the Bervie Water. One of the syndicate who undertook the contract for the Great North of Scotland Railway, a part of the line was executed under his personal superintendence. Among his other works were the erection of the Central Station at Glasgow, and the completion of the Grangemouth Dock at the cost of £250,000. Interested in agricultural pursuits, he in 1857 leased the farm of Mains of Fordoun. He there died on the 8th January 1885. Charles Brand married, 27th November 1830, Margaret, daughter of William Falconer, farmer at Waters, parish of Glenbervie, by his wife Catherine Reith, eldest daughter of John Reith, farmer at Tipperty in the same parish; she was born in 1804, and died in 1881. Of the marriage were born two sons, James and David; also two daughters, Elizabeth and Anne Guthrie.

James Brand, the elder son, born 20th September 1831, was assumed by his father as a partner in the firm of Charles Brand & Son, railway contractors, Glasgow; he is now sole partner. From the firm which he represents, Mr. Arrol, the eminent constructor of the Forth Bridge, received his first commission as a bridge constructor. He married, 26th February 1862, Jane, daughter of William Robert Gordon, procurator-fiscal of Banffshire, by his wife, Margaret, daughter of James George, manufacturer, Keith, with issue six sons, Charles Joseph, James Gordon, Henry Francis, William Robert Joseph, David Guthrie, and Clement Ignatius; also five daughters, Margaret, Mary Louisa, Jane Agnes, Anne Elizabeth, and Gertrude Josephine.

David, younger son of Charles Brand, born 1849, died in 1885, without issue.

Elizabeth, elder daughter, born 1834, married James Catto, merchant, Aberdeen, with issue.

Anne Guthrie, younger daughter, born 1836, married William Jones, London; she died in 1879 without issue.

William, second son of James Brand and Rachel Guthrie, was born in 1807; he died in 1883, without issue.

James, third son, was born in 1808, and died in 1871. By his wife, Margaret Urquhart, a native of Dingwall, he had two sons, Kenneth and James; also four daughters, Rachel, Margaret, Jane, and Elizabeth.

David, fourth son, married Jane, daughter of Archibald Falconer, by his wife, Catherine Beattie, with issue, four sons, Archibald, William, Charles, and David Falconer; also two daughters, Jane Anne and Catherine.

Mary, fifth daughter of Robert Burnes, baptized 26th October 1732, died unmarried. The sixth daughter, whose name is unknown, died in infancy.

James Burnes, eldest son of Robert Burnes and Isabella Keith, was born in 1717. Apprenticed to a joiner at Montrose in 1732, he, on the 11th September 1751, became a burgess of that burgh, and was elected a town councillor on the 26th September 1753. He died on the 17th July 1761, at the age of forty-four. He married, in 1745, Margaret Grub (she died in 1795), by whom he had three sons and three daughters. One son and two daughters died young. Elizabeth, the surviving daughter, married, 8th

January 1768, George Hudson,[1] merchant, Bervie, and afterwards provost of that burgh, by whom she had three sons and eight daughters. Of these, two sons, George and William, and four daughters, Elizabeth, Margaret (first), Margaret (second), and Sarah Anne, died unmarried or without issue. John, the eldest son, married Jean Forster; Christian married Alexander Guthrie; Anne married John Pirie, without issue; Elizabeth married Dr. Douglas, surgeon, Elie; and Sarah married Dr. Davidson, physician at Edinburgh.

David, eldest son of James Burnes and Margaret Grub, born 30th July 1749, married, in December 1777, Jean M'Bean, with issue a son, Thomas, baptized 30th July 1783; also two daughters, Margaret, born 5th March 1780, and Jean, born 30th August 1781.[2]

James Burnes, second surviving son of James Burnes and Margaret Grub, was born on the 24th December 1750. In 1770 he was elected schoolmaster of Montrose, and on the 26th February 1771 he presented a petition to the town council of the burgh, representing that he had "commenced teacher of English, Writing, Arithmetic, and Church Music in the town, but as his circumstances were but narrow, and as he had been put to a considerable expense in acquiring these branches of education and some knowledge of the French language," he craved that he should be allowed a yearly salary. As the town council rejected his demand, he abandoned his office,[3] and, studying law, became a solicitor.[4] With his uncle, William Burnes, the Poet's father,[5] also with the Poet himself, he

---

[1] George Hudson was of English descent, his father and grandfather having come to Montrose in 1745 with Lord Robert Manners' regiment. His father married Elizabeth, daughter of William Carnegie, convener of the incorporated trades at Montrose.—Dr. James Burnes's "Notes," p. 35.

[2] Montrose Baptismal Register.

[3] Montrose Town Council Records.

[4] On the death of his father, James Burnes some time resided with his uncle William, and in deference to his wish adopted the double *s* in spelling his name. Subsequently he resumed the older form.

[5] A letter addressed by William Burnes, the Poet's father, to his nephew, Mr. James Burnes, dated Lochlie, 14th April 1781, is preserved in the Poet's monument at Edinburgh.

maintained a friendly correspondence; he was visited by the Poet in 1787, and, on the event of his death, offered to aid in maintaining his children. He died at Montrose on the 12th June 1837, aged eighty-seven; his remains were deposited near those of his father, in the old burgh churchyard. James Burnes married, on the 6th January 1777, Anne, daughter of John Greig, burgess of Montrose, by his wife, Jean, daughter of Robert Watson of Sheilhill, Forfarshire; she was born 16th July 1749, and died 12th February 1796. Of the marriage of James Burnes and Anne Greig were born four sons and four daughters. Anne, the eldest daughter, born 16th April 1783, died in infancy; Christian, second daughter, born 15th April 1785, died in 1815, unmarried; Elizabeth, third daughter, died in 1818, unmarried; Sarah, fourth daughter, died in 1814, unmarried. John, the eldest son, died in infancy in 1779; George, third son, born 30th September 1781, died in 1801, unmarried; and Robert, the youngest son, died in infancy.

James Burnes, second son of James Burnes and Anne Greig, was born on the 1st April 1780.[1] Articled to his father, he studied law, and became a solicitor in Montrose. As Dean of Guild, he, on the 11th December 1817, entered the town council of the burgh. On the 13th April 1818 he reported to the town council—

> That at a public meeting the Guildry had unanimously declared they had heard with satisfaction that Joseph Hume, Esq., a guild brother of the burgh, had, at the invitation of his townsmen, offered himself a candidate to represent the district of burghs in the next Parliament; and, taking into account the well-known talents, principles, and conduct of that gentleman for years past, they thought him a proper person to be their representative in Parliament, and therefore recommended him to the magistrates and town council for their votes on the occasion.

Mr. Burnes was, on the 23rd September 1818, elected provost;

[1] Montrose Parish Register.

he held the office for two years. He was re-elected provost on the 29th September 1824, and on the 2nd February 1825 was chosen to the office of joint town-clerk. Evincing a deep interest in municipal affairs, he corrected the abuses of the close burgh system, and has consequently been described as the father of Scottish burghal reform. A zealous agriculturist, he was, in recognition of service, appointed a J.P. for the county of Forfar. He latterly resided at Brunton Place, Edinburgh, where he died on the 15th February 1852, at the age of seventy-two. His remains were deposited in the cemetery at Dalry, where he is commemorated by a handsome tombstone.

Provost James Burnes married, 22nd April 1800, Elizabeth, sixth daughter of Adam Glegg, merchant burgess of Montrose, and provost of the burgh; she was born 5th April 1779, and died at Edinburgh on the 25th February 1851. The family of Gleg, Glegg, or Glyge, was connected with the Mearns. In 1694 Adam Glyge is commemorated in the church of Marykirk, on a tombstone thus inscribed:—

> Heir lyes Adam Glyge, smith in the hill . . . Morphye, some tyme howsband to Isobel Low, who departed the 10 of Awgwst. Adam Gle . . . died in April 1698, aged 86. John Gleig died May 15, 1737, aged 83. Isobel Gleig died March 4th, 1761, aged 78.

John Gleig, named in the epitaph, was grandfather of Provost Adam Glegg of Montrose, who was born in 1731, and died at London on the 1st June 1807. He married his cousin-german, Anne (born 8th November 1738, died 22nd December 1811), daughter of John Smith, provost of Brechin, by his wife, Christian Colvin, one of the three co-heiresses of Alexander Colvin, burgess of Montrose, by his wife, Christian Ramsay, descended from the old family of Ramsay of Balmain. By James Boswell, in his "Tour," he is mentioned as having conducted Dr. Samuel Johnson and himself to the Episcopal chapel at Montrose.

Among the descendants of Adam Glegg, blacksmith at Marykirk, were the Right Rev. George Gleig, LL.D., Bishop of Brechin, and Primus of the Scottish Episcopal Church, who died at Stirling on the 9th March 1840, aged eighty-seven; also his cousin, the Rev. George Gleig, parish minister of Arbroath, who died 19th June 1835, at the age of seventy-eight. Their fathers were blacksmiths, the bishop's father exercising his craft at Boghall, in the parish of Arbuthnot.

Of the marriage of James Burnes, provost of Montrose, and Elizabeth Glegg, were born nine sons and five daughters. Anne, the eldest daughter, and Margaret, died in infancy. Anne, second of the name, born on the 17th August 1808, married, 6th April 1833, at Bhooj, in India, Captain William Ward, who died at Tanna, near Bombay, 9th July 1845, without issue. Elizabeth, born 23rd August 1809, married at Bombay, 3rd March 1831, Lieutenant-General Richard Whish, son of the Rev. Richard Whish, rector of Northwold, Norfolk, and brother of Sir W. S. Whish, K.C.B., who commanded at Moultan; he died at Clifton, 10th November 1854.

Of the marriage of Lieutenant-General Richard Whish and Elizabeth Burnes were born five sons and six daughters. Frederick Alexander, the eldest son, born at Ahmedabad, 27th July 1833, died at Paunchgunny, India, in August 1872, a retired captain of the Royal Artillery. Albert William, second son, was born at Clifton, 11th July 1843. A commander in the Royal Navy, he was some time employed as inspecting officer of the coastguard, Montrose; he now resides at Woodcot, Allandale, in the Province of Ontario, Canada. He married, 30th October 1873, Louisa Emily, third daughter of Captain Charles Forbes, of the 17th Regiment, and widow of Captain T. M. Hewett, with issue four sons, Albert

Forbes, born 3rd January 1875, and died young; Cyril Beresford, born 3rd March 1876; Hugh Dudley, born 7th July 1877, and died young; and Arthur Burnes, born 1885; also three daughters, Lillian Theresa, born 1879, Beatrice Adelaide, born 1881, and Christabel Kathleen, born 1883.

Arthur Richard Lewis, third son of Lieutenant-General Whish and Elizabeth Burnes, was born at Clifton on the 1st March 1847; he is manager of the National Provincial Bank of England, Lincoln's Inn, London. In 1867 he married Agnes Cooke, with issue two daughters, Evelyn Mary, born 1871, and Ada Margaret, born 1874. Ernest Burnes, fourth son, born at Clifton, 12th September 1848, holds estates near Rosario, South America; he is unmarried. Cecil Holland, fifth and youngest son, was born at Clifton, 9th March 1850. As a lieutenant in the Royal Navy, he took part in the bombardment of Alexandria. Having retired from the navy, he now resides at Kinmount, Ontario, Canada. He married, in 1887, Mary St. George.

Matilda Emily, eldest daughter of Lieutenant-General Whish and Elizabeth Burnes, was born at Clifton on the 29th April 1835; she married, at Clifton, in August 1856, the Rev. Augustus Cooper, Greystoke, Upper Norwood, and has two children, Mabel and Augustus. Eliza Jane, second daughter, born at Clifton, 31st May 1836, married her cousin, Major Edward Burnes Holland, now deceased; she died 12th October 1882, leaving a son, Alexander Burnes, and a daughter, Constance Emily. Flora Thornborough, third daughter, born at Clifton, 11th January 1839, married in 1859 Major Daniel Eales, of the 25th Native Infantry, Bombay, who died in March 1874. Of the marriage were born a son, Lionel, and a daughter, Maud. She married, secondly, John Pollen, LL.D., of the Civil Service, Bombay. Annette Isabella, fourth daughter, born at Boulogne-sur-Mer, 21st July 1841, is unmarried; Clara Salter, fifth daughter, born at Clifton, 19th October 1844, and Kathleen White, the sixth daughter, born at Clifton, 3rd June 1851, are both unmarried, and are members of a "Sisterhood" in London.

Jane Glegg Burnes, fourth daughter of James Burnes and Elizabeth Glegg, was born at Montrose on the 11th October 1810. She married, on the 11th July 1833, at Ahmedabad, India, Colonel James Holland, quartermaster-general of the Bombay Army. Colonel Holland retired from active service on the 14th February 1857, and died on the 16th April 1889. By his wife, Jane Glegg Burnes, Colonel Holland had three sons and a daughter. Trevenen James, the eldest son, was born at Bombay on the 31st May 1834. Entering in 1851 the Indian Army, he became assistant quartermaster-general of the army at Bombay. On the 2nd June 1869, he was nominated C.B. He has composed a history of the Abyssinian campaign. In August 1871 he retired from the army with the rank of colonel; he is J.P. for Kent and Cornwall. He married Margaret Nicolson, with issue a son, Charles Trevenen Townsend, born 19th July 1882; also four daughters, viz. Emily Gertrude, born 15th October 1863, married, 30th June 1886, Andrew Noble Bertram of Clober, Stirlingshire; Mary Enid Margaret, born 18th October 1872; Lilian Elaine, born 9th June 1874; and Ethel May, born 16th April 1877.

Edward Burnes Holland, second son of Colonel James Holland by his wife, Jane Glegg Burnes, was born at Belgaum, India, on the 20th March 1836. In November 1850 he obtained by public competition at Cheltenham College the commission in the Indian Army awarded by Lieutenant-General Sir James Lushington, G.C.B. He became major of the Royal Engineers, and died at Bombay on the 12th March 1874. He married, at Clifton, in 1858, his cousin, Eliza Jane Whish, by whom he had a son and daughter.[1]

[1] See supra, p. 33.

Henry John Coode Holland, third son, born 28th October 1842, died in childhood.

Charles Wroughton Del Hoste Holland, fourth son of Colonel James Holland, was born at Bombay on the 20th January 1845. A stock and share broker in London, he resides at Wimbledon. He married, 25th February 1875, Margaret Riach, with issue two sons, Charles Stewart, born 28th December 1875, and James Burnes, born 3rd July 1883; also a daughter, Margaret Effie, born June 1886.

Cecilia Agnes Holland, only daughter of Colonel James Holland and Jane Glegg Burnes, was born at Bombay on the 22nd December 1846. She married, 3rd January 1870, George Dalton Hardy, underwriter, Lloyd's, with issue a son and four daughters.

Cecilia, fifth and youngest daughter of Provost James Burnes, was born at Montrose on the 10th November 1815. She married, on the 12th November 1839, at Bhooj, in India, John Philip Major, captain 11th Bombay Native Infantry, and died at Bombay on the 16th October 1840, eight days after her husband, who died off Gogo, in the Gulf of Cambay, 8th October 1840. Their only child, Francis Ward Major, was born at Ahmedabad, 12th August 1840. He is now a colonel in the Indian Staff Corps, and in the Paymaster-General's department, Madras. He married, 6th June 1863, Adelaide, second daughter of the late Captain Charles Forbes, of the 17th Regiment, with issue two sons, Francis Forbes, born 23rd December 1867, and Philip Charles, born 11th May 1873; also two daughters, Adelaide Louisa, born 21st July 1864, and Violet, born 24th October 1866.

Of the nine sons of Provost James Burnes, Robert, born 26th July 1803, William Maule, Edward Phillips, and George Patrick, died young.

James Burnes, the eldest son, was born at Montrose on the 12th

February 1801. Educated to the medical profession at the University of Edinburgh, and in Guy's and St. Thomas's Hospitals, London, he, in 1821, obtained a surgeon's commission in the East India Company's service. Distinguished as a linguist, he was authorized to explore the countries on the Bombay north-west frontier, and he prepared a valuable account of the southernmost of the Rajpootanah states, and of the vast dreary tract between Goozerat and the Indus. After holding various offices, he was posted in February 1823 to the 18th Native Infantry, stationed at Bombay, and in 1824 was preferred as surgeon to the Residency at Cutch. In 1827 his professional services were rendered to the Ameer of Scinde, with marked appreciation. His *Narrative of the Court of Scinde*, published in 1829, was generally esteemed. Returning to Britain in 1834, the University of Glasgow conferred upon him the degree of LL.D., and the Royal Society granted him a Fellowship. He also received the honour of Guelphic knighthood, and, at a public banquet given in his honour at Edinburgh, was presented with a silver vase with a commendatory inscription. A furlough of three years he improved by preparing a work on the history of the Knights Templars. In December 1837 he returned to Bombay, when he was appointed surgeon to the garrison. In 1841 he was elected secretary to the Medical Board, and in 1846 was promoted as superintending surgeon. With the rank of physician-general he was, in 1847, transferred to the Poonah division, and in 1848 he was nominated to a seat at the Medical Board of Bombay. Having served in India twenty-eight years, he, in July 1849, retired from his professional duties. Before leaving Bombay, he received complimentary addresses from various public bodies to which he had been helpful. Having held office as Grand Master of the Freemason lodges of Western India, the brethren, on his departure, presented him with several splendid gifts, and in his honour founded four medals, of which one was to be competed for in the academy of Montrose. On his return to this country, Dr. James Burnes occupied a portion of his time in preparing materials for a history of his family, which, in 1851, he printed for private circulation, in a thin duodecimo, under the title of *Notes on the Name and Family of Burnes*. He was appointed J.P. for the counties of Middlesex and Forfar. He died at Manchester on the 19th September 1862, and his remains were deposited at Swindon Church, near Cheltenham.

Dr. James Burnes married, first, on the 28th March 1829, Sophia, second daughter of Major-General Sir George Holmes, K.C.B., with issue seven sons and two daughters. He married, secondly, on the 17th June 1862, at St. Mary Abbot's, Kensington, Esther Price, a native of Wales, who now resides at 40 Ladbrook Square, Kensington.

Sophia Holmes, elder daughter of Dr. James Burnes, born at Bhooj, 6th September 1832, and Isabella Cecilia Holmes, younger daughter, born at Edinburgh on the 4th February 1835, died in infancy.

George James Holmes Burnes, eldest son of Dr. James Burnes, born at Bhooj on the 9th December 1829, held a commission in the 1st Bombay Fusiliers, and received medals for the Punjab, Moultan, and Guzerat. Consequent on his efforts to save a child from the violence of the mutineers, he was massacred at Lucknow on the 19th November 1857. In the vestibule of the parish church, Montrose, a monumental tablet, erected by his brother officers, commemorates his worth.

Fitz-James Holmes Burnes, second son of Dr. James Burnes, was born at Bhooj on the 6th September 1831. He served as an officer of the 33rd Regiment, Madras Native Infantry, and died in 1872.

Holland Ward Holmes Burnes, third son of Dr. James Burnes, was born at Bhooj on the 15th September 1833. An officer of the

Indian Navy, he died at Calcutta in 1873, when in command of the *Feroze*, the yacht of the Governor-General.

Hamilton Farquhar Holmes Burnes, fourth son of Dr. James Burnes, was born at Edinburgh on the 27th November 1836. Entering the army in 1855, he attained the rank of captain, and in November 1868 retired from active service. He died unmarried.

Dalhousie Holmes Burnes, fifth son of Dr. James Burnes, was born at Bombay on the 5th April 1839. He joined the army as an officer of Engineers, and died in 1872 unmarried.

Sidney Holmes Burnes, sixth son of Dr. James Burnes, was born at Bombay on the 13th August 1841; he died at London in 1871.

Alexander Holmes Burnes, seventh and youngest son of Dr. James Burnes, was born at Bombay on the 11th April 1843. He entered the Bombay Army in 1860, and, retiring on the 14th September 1867, settled in Australia. He died unmarried.

Adam Burnes, second surviving son of James Burnes, Provost of Montrose, was born on the 19th February 1802. He practised as a solicitor in Montrose, and there died on the 15th November 1872. He married, first, 3rd September 1827, Horatia, daughter of Harry Gordon, Esq., who died 2nd November 1834; secondly, 18th June 1838, Isabella, daughter of William Scott, Esq.

By his first wife Adam Burnes had two sons, Adam and Alexander Horatio. Adam, the elder son, born 12th June 1832, became manager of the Colonial Bank at Melbourne; he subsequently resided in New Zealand, and died at Sydney, New South Wales, on the 9th June 1876. He married, with issue six sons, Adam William Gray, James Henry, Napier Anderson, Alexander Plunkett, Ernest Blair, and George Douglas Inglis Scott; also a daughter, Mary Inglis.

Alexander Horatio, younger son of Adam Burnes by his first wife, was born 19th October 1834. He married Mary Jane Harris, with issue a daughter, Adamina Horatia, born October 1872. He resides in New Zealand.

By his second wife Adam Burnes had a son, James, born 24th May 1844, died 30th April 1873; also two daughters, Isabelle, who died 26th June 1848, aged nine years, and Annie Eliza Glegg, born 15th September 1842, married, 16th May 1866, John Smythe M'Cay, solicitor, Londonderry, with issue.

Alexander Burnes, third surviving son of Provost James Burnes, was born on the 16th May 1805. After a distinguished educational career at Montrose Academy, he entered the Indian Army. Arriving at Bombay on the 31st October 1821, he, in December 1822, was appointed interpreter in Hindostanee to the First Extra Battalion at Surat, and was afterwards employed by the judges of the Suddur Adawlut to translate the Persian documents of that court. He accompanied his regiment, the 21st Native Infantry, to Bhooj, in 1825, and during the disturbances at Cutch, in April of that year, was appointed quartermaster of brigade. A report on the statistics of Wagur, which he presented to Government in January 1827, was much commended and adequately acknowledged. A memoir on the eastern branch of the delta of the Indus, which he published in 1828, was also warmly approved. On the 18th March 1828 he was appointed assistant quartermaster-general. In September 1829, along with his brother-in-law, then Lieutenant Holland, he assisted the political agent at Cutch in conducting a survey of the north-west frontier. In 1830 he conveyed a gift of dray-horses from William IV. to Runjeet Sing, ruler of Lahore, using the occasion to procure more accurate details respecting the geography of the Indus. He completed a survey of the whole Indian delta.

Lieutenant Burnes conducted in 1832 an expedition into Central Asia. Returning to Bombay in January 1833, he received the thanks of the Governor-General; and, being authorized to bear his own despatches to England, he experienced a cordial reception at the India House. His *Travels in Bokhara* were published in 1834, and the work commanded a large sale, and was translated into French and German. Among various other public honours, he was admitted a Fellow of the Royal Society. Returning to India in 1835 with the rank of captain, he was in October despatched on a mission to Hyderabad, in Scinde. In November 1836 he was entrusted with a mission to Dost Mohammed, the ruler of Afghanistan, with a view of entering into commercial relations with him; he reached Cabool on the 20th September 1837. Meanwhile Mohammed, Shah of Persia, had besieged Herat with an army of 60,000 men, and the Indian Government began to apprehend that Persia and Russia might unite their forces with those of Afghanistan to make an attack on the Indian empire. From Herat the Persians were forced to retreat, but Captain Burnes requested Dost Mohammed to dismiss the Russian agent Vicovitch from his court. This he refused to do, and, on the contrary, dismissed Captain Burnes. Repairing to the Governor-General at Simla, Captain Burnes was knighted and promoted as lieutenant-colonel. From Scinde he proceeded to Beloochistan on a political mission, which proved unsuccessful. When Shah Shoojah was restored to the throne of Cabool, he was, in September 1839, appointed political resident at that capital, with a salary of £3000. He remained at Cabool not without a sense of insecurity, and, on the outbreak of an insurrection for restoring Dost Mohammed, he was set upon, and, along with his brother Charles and seven other officers, cruelly murdered. This sad event took place on the 2nd November 1841. Sir Alexander Burnes died unmarried, at the age of thirty-six. In 1842 his work entitled *Cabool: being a Narrative of a Journey to and Residence in that City in the years 1836-7-8*, was published at London.

THE POET'S LINEAGE.

Possessing a deep sagacity and marvellous powers of observation, Sir Alexander Burnes afforded promise of wide and varied usefulness. He opened up the Indus, and extended his researches to the shores of the Oxus, the ruins of Samarcand, and other territories which became the scenes of important events. A memoir of his career, published in the columns of the *Bombay Times* newspaper, was reproduced by his brother, Dr. James Burnes, in his *Notes on the Name and Family of Burnes.*

David Burnes, fourth surviving son of Provost James Burnes, was born at Montrose on the 6th September 1806. Having studied medicine and received the degree of M.D., he in 1826 entered the Royal Navy as a surgeon. After serving on board the *Asia* on the Mediterranean station for several years, he in 1835 retired from the navy owing to broken health. Subsequently he practised medicine in London. With an enfeebled constitution, he latterly settled in Montrose, and he there died on the 2nd February 1849. He married, on the 20th October 1838, Harriet Anne, second daughter of Alexander Anderson, M.D., surgeon R.N., London (she died 5th May 1873), with issue a son and daughter. The son, James Anderson Burnes, born 30th January 1845, served some years as a clerk in the Bank of Scotland, Dunfermline. He thereafter held appointments in connexion with the Oriental Bank at Madras, Calcutta, and the Mauritius. Since the suspension of the Bank in 1884, he has been in the employment, at London, of the Great Indian Peninsular Railway Company. He married, on the 14th December 1875, Emma, only daughter of the Rev. P. J. Jarbo, Ph.D., one of H.M. Bengal chaplains, with issue a daughter, May Violet, born May 1878. Charlotte Elizabeth, only daughter of Dr. David Burnes, was born 30th October 1842. She is unmarried, and is resident at Portsmouth.

Charles Burnes, youngest son of James Burnes, Provost of

Montrose, was born on the 12th January 1812. When lieutenant in the 17th Regiment, Bombay Native Infantry, he was murdered at Cabool, along with his elder brother, Sir Alexander Burnes, on the 2nd November 1841; he died unmarried.

We return to the younger sons of Robert Burnes, tacksman of Clochanhill. George, the youngest son, baptized on the 9th April 1729,[1] died young.

Robert, the second son, born in 1719, was, we found, associated with his father in February 1744 in borrowing from Provost Stuart of Aberdeen a sum of money to meet pressing engagements. His father being sequestrated in the autumn of 1747, he thereafter proceeded to England in quest of employment as an agricultural labourer. According to a family tradition, he and his brother William left Dunnottar together, and as, from a portion of rising ground by the way, they looked back on a scene associated with their progenitors, they were influenced by a deep emotion, as they severally reflected that they might not be privileged to return. At the nearest point Robert entered the stage-coach which proceeded to the north of England. In reference to this journey, Gilbert Burnes (son of William) wrote to Mrs. Dunlop long afterwards:—

> I have often heard my father describe his anguish of mind when they parted on the top of a hill, on the confines of their native place, each going off his several way in search of new adventures, and scarcely knowing whither they went.

In England Robert Burnes was many years employed as a gardener; he ultimately returned to Scotland, where he settled. His circumstances were considerably depressed. He died at Stewarton, in Ayrshire, on the 3rd of January 1789. He married,

[1] Dunnottar Parish Register.

with issue two sons and a daughter. John, the elder son, died young. William, the younger son, a builder by trade, died unmarried in 1850. Frances or Fanny, the only daughter, was, by her relative the Poet, described as the smartest of her kin. She married Adam Armour,[1] builder, Mauchline, brother of the Poet's wife, with issue five sons and four daughters. Robert, the eldest son, succeeded his father as a builder in Mauchline, and died in 1854. By his wife, Jean Wallace, daughter of the farmer at Mauchline Mains, he had several children. His son Thomas rents a farm in the parish of Stair ; another son, Robert, resides near Patna.

James, second son of Adam Armour and Frances Burnes, born 16th March 1793, died unmarried ; Adam, third son, born 9th March 1803, died unmarried ; John, born 24th December 1807, died young. William, the youngest son, inherited his mother's vivacity ; he died unmarried.

Of the daughters, Jean, first of the name, born 4th December 1794, died in infancy ; Jean, second of the name, born 24th February 1797, died unmarried ; Fanny, third daughter, born January 1801, died unmarried ; Mary Smith, fourth daughter, born 15th October 1805, died unmarried.

William Burnes, third son of Robert Burnes and Isabella Keith, was born at Clochanhill on the 11th November 1721. After some years assisting his father on the farm of Clochanhill, he was about the year 1740 apprenticed[2] to the gardener of Sir William Nicolson of Glenbervie, in whose employment he remained about five years. When his father in the autumn of 1747 quitted Clochanhill, William removed to Edinburgh, where, according to his son Gilbert, "he wrought hard, when he could get work, passing through a variety

---

[1] Adam Armour is the subject of the Poet's verses entitled "Adam Armour's Prayer."

[2] There is a family tradition that his relative, Alexander Greig, farmer at Brackla, in Glenbervie, was surety on the indenture. According to another account, William Burnes was apprenticed to the gardener at Monboddo.

of difficulties." According to tradition, he was one of the labourers employed under the magistrates and town council of Edinburgh in completing the drainage of the Meadows to the south of the city. From Edinburgh he migrated to the neighbourhood of Ayr. The cause of his proceeding thither has not been ascertained, but it is not without interest to remark that families of his name were long common in the district of Carrick. In the Burgh Records of Ayr, John Burnes appears in 1589, in a writ at the instance of George Campbell in Logan, charging him to remove from the lands of Freirland. And in the same Records, on the 24th November 1589, Hew Wallace adopted certain legal measures against William Burnes, his tenant at M'Knarustoun. In the Parish Registers of Ayr William Burnes in Burroughford is named in 1675 and 1679; John Burnes in Whinmoore in 1679 and 1683; and Robert Burnes and his wife, Isobel Campbell, in 1690 and 1695. The Carrick families changed their name from Burnes to Burns at a time somewhat antecedent to the change so made by the Poet.

Settling in the neighbourhood of Ayr, William Burnes became gardener to the proprietor of Fairlie, subsequently to Mr. Crawford of Doonside. At length he obtained in feu from Dr. Campbell, physician in Ayr, seven acres of land at Alloway, with the view of his establishing a nursery. On this portion of ground he reared with his own hand a mud cottage, and thither he conducted Agnes Broun, whom he wedded in December 1757.

The family of Broun is of Norman origin. Walterus le Brun was one of the Scottish barons who witnessed an inquisition on the Church lands of the see of Glasgow, made by Prince David in the year 1116, during the reign of his brother, Alexander I. Sir David, son of Walter le Brun, was one of those present at the founding of Holyrood Abbey in May 1128.[1]

[1] M'Kerlie's *Lands and their Owners in Galloway*, Edinb., 5 vols., 12mo.

THE POET'S LINEAGE.

Mary le Brun, daughter of Ingleram le Brun, was Queen of Alexander II. The name of le Brun was borne by the Counts of Lusignan and Valence in Poictou, one of whom, Hugh le Brun, married Isabel of Angouleme, widow of King John of England. David le Brun, his cousin, proceeded to Ireland in 1185, and became ancestor of the Lords Oranmore and Browne in that country. From his stock also derive the Lords Sligo, Kenmare, and Kilmaine.[1]

Among those who swore fealty to Edward I. in 1296 were " William Brun de Gamelscheles, del counte de Edinburgh, William le Broun de Laweder, del counte Berwyk, Gunnyd Brun, tenant le Roi, du counte de Edinburgh, Johan Broun, del counte de Berwyk, and Rauf Broun, de counte de Berwyk."[2]

During the reign of King Robert the Bruce, Robert Broun forfeited the lands of Auchindrane, in Ayrshire; and in the same reign Adie Broun forfeited a portion of land in the sheriffdom of Ayr. About the same period Adam Broun made a gift to St. Michael in the parish church of Ayr, and Thomas Broun had the grant of the foundation of an altarage in St. Nicholas' Church, Ayr.[3]

In the Burgh Records of Prestwick are named, in 1470, Alexander Broun, as owner of a portion of land; also along with him, " Jok Broun in stat of a porcinkle of commoun land, quhilk acht yerli, at the conceptioun of our ladi, ij^d till our ladi of Prestwic; ij^d to Sanct Nicholas lycht, and ij to St. Androis lycht in the said kirk."[4]

In a legal instrument dated at Irvine on the 27th January 1499, Adam Multrare, burgess of Irvine, becomes bound to deliver to John Broune, son and heir of John Broune, burgess of Ayr, before the next feast of St. John the Baptist, 300 bolls of salt, for which

---

[1] Marshall's *Ancient Scottish Families*. Privately printed at Perth, 1834, 4to, p. 129.
[2] Ragman Rolls, Bannatyne Club, 1834.
[3] Robertson's *Index of Charters*, 14, 100-102; 21, 39.
[4] Records of the Burgh of Prestwick, Maitland Club, 1834, 4to, p. 6.

he was to receive 6s. 8d. per boll, one-third part to be paid in money, a third in salted hides, and a further third in cloth.[1]

In a charter of the burgh of Ayr, dated 10th March 1454, James Broun is named as one of the magistrates.[2] In the Records of Ayr, under date 12th March 1581, is entered an inquisition at the instance of John Mure of Auchindrane, in which, with other tenants, are named Gilbert Broun and John Broun. Gilbert Broun appears on the 30th April 1582 as a member of the Burgh Court. On the 20th July of the same year he is named as protesting against an act of the town council respecting his removal from certain subjects; and on the 7th November 1589, he, being present in the council, was adjudged to settle a small debt; and on the 13th June 1593 he appears as defender in an action raised against him by Alexander Lockhart of Boghall, procurator for the burgh, in which he sought his removal "furth and from the cobill fischingis vpoun the wattir of Dwn" [Doon].

John Broun, "skinner burgess of Air," is named in the Burgh Records under 18th June 1582; and on the 12th August 1583, William and John Broun, skinners, are described as occupiers of property within the burgh. On the 2nd July 1582 "John Broun, skipper," was present as a member at the Burgh Court of Ayr. On the 5th November 1582 the town council ordered—

> John Payne, Inglisman, and owner of the ship Barkleys of Hippiswitch [Ipswich], in Ingland, to content and pay to Johnne Broun, maister of the ship called the Swallow of Air, the sum of £10, 10s. as dampnage and skayth sustenit by the said Johnne be breking of ane ankir and spilling of ane tow apperteining to the said Johnne Broun's schip throw ryding thairupoun be the said Johnne Payne's schip.

John Broun, skipper, is mentioned in the Ayr Records in 1584 and

---

[1] Protocol Register of Glasgow, 1499-1513, Grampian Club, ii. 27, 28.
[2] Charters of the Burgh of Ayr.

THE POET'S LINEAGE.

1585; he was at Michaelmas 1589 constituted one of the three councillors who discharged the office of Master of Works. On the 15th April 1594, he appears as served by the town council heir to a dwelling formerly belonging to Thomas Broun, burgess of Ayr, and Margaret Kennedy, his spouse. In the same Records, John Broun in Plenclay is named as having, on the 29th July 1583, raised a summons for the recovery of a debt before the Burgh Court of Ayr.

A subsequently prosperous trader in Ayr, William Broun is in the Burgh Records, under the 4th February 1582–83, described as a "tailor." On the 25th January 1590–91 he was created a burgess, and on the 22nd October 1600 he is named as William Broun, merchant. Elected a town councillor, he was chosen treasurer of the burgh at Michaelmas 1603, and again at Michaelmas 1609. In 1611 he was appointed collector of stent. He died in 1613. His will was executed on the 16th April of that year; the list of his debtors appended to it occupies six and a half pages of the Commissariot Register. He is described as owning the "lands of Brounhill and Newark in Carrik," and his moveable estate is estimated at £2003, 13s. 1d. To his mother, Agnes Wilson, he provides an annuity of fifty-two merks, specifies that his [second] wife, Margaret Cunningham, should retain "the money she brought with her," and bequeathes £40 to the poor of Ayr. He ordains his son William to pay to his daughters, Marcoun, Janet, Agnes, and Sara, the sum of 2500 merks, due to them at the death of their mother. Failing the survival of his children, he bequeathes his estate to his brother-in-law, Donald Smith, Dean of Guild of the burgh of Ayr.[1]

Janet Broun, second daughter of William Broun, and wife of John Mason, town-clerk of Ayr, executed her will on the 22nd

[1] Glasgow Com. Reg. Testaments.

September 1618, and died in October following. The administration of her estate (valued at £343, 2s. 2d.) she committed to David Garvan, her son by a former marriage, and Janet Dalrymple, daughter of Mr. Andrew Dalrymple.[1]

In the Burgh Records of Ayr are named, under the 20th May 1601, John Broun, merchant, and Thomas Broun, his son. On the 8th May 1611, James Broun, merchant, was created a burgess.

Alexander Broun, one of the magistrates of Newton-on-Ayr, acted as executor-dative of James Broun, merchant burgess of Ayr, who died in December 1647, and Margaret Blair, his wife, who died in October 1648; their united free gear was valued at £2902.[2]

John Broun, smith burgess of Ayr, died in October 1662; his inventory was produced by his relict, Janet Schaw.[3]

John Broun, shoemaker in Ayr, and Margaret Crauford, his spouse, had a son, John, born on the 21st, and baptized on the 30th August 1668.[4]

John Broun, litster in Ayr, was admitted a burgess of the burgh on the 15th November 1670.[5] By his wife, Margaret Smyth, he had three daughters, Margaret, born 24th April 1670; Bessie, born 3rd November 1671; and Agnes, born 3rd April 1676.[6]

Alexander Broun, litster in Ayr, had, by his wife, Janet Crauford, a son, John, who was born 22nd September 1674.[7]

Robert Broun, skipper in Ayr, married, 6th December 1699, Magdalen, daughter of the late John Crauford, one of the magistrates of Ayr. A son, Charles, was born at Ayr on the 19th October 1700; his baptism was witnessed by Captain Hugh Crauford, late Provost of Ayr, "his granduncle," and his uncle, Hugh Broun, writer in Edinburgh.[8]

---

[1] Glasgow Com. Reg. Testaments.
[2] Ibid.
[3] Ibid.
[4] Baptismal Register of Ayr.
[5] Ayr Burgh Records.
[6] Ayr Baptismal Register.
[7] Ibid.
[8] Ayr Burgh Records.

THE POET'S LINEAGE.

Members of the Broun family at Ayr effected settlements in the neighbouring parishes. At Loudoun, in the province of Cunningham, Hew Broun in Burneflat died in July 1604, leaving, by his wife, Agnes Young, two sons, Hew and Thomas; his testament dative is dated 26th July 1608.[1] At Loudoun, in February 1608, died Jonette Broun, wife of Alexander Broun, farmer at Tounflat, leaving three sons, Alexander, Hew, and John.[2] For being concerned in the rising at Bothwell, James Broun, son of James Broun, portioner in Newmilns, and Andrew Broun of Duncanziener at Cumnock, were by an assize at Ayr, in June 1683, pronounced guilty of rebellion, and sentenced to decapitation; the sentence was remitted.[3]

Of the Cumnock branch of the family a notable member was John Brown, described as "the Christian carrier." This devoted Presbyterian and ardent Covenanter resided at Priesthill, near Muirkirk. By order of John Graham of Claverhouse, Brown was seized while working in one of his fields, and, being borne to his dwelling, was called upon to renounce his creed. As he emphatically refused, he was, by Graham's own hand, shot dead in the presence of his wife and children. This cruel slaughter was perpetrated on the 1st of May 1685.[4]

At Townhead of Newmilns, in the parish of Loudoun, was born, on the 19th May 1799, Hugh Brown, the author of some graphic poetry.[5] In his poem of "The Covenanters" he has commemorated the martyrdom of "the Christian carrier" in these lines :—

> Far on the moor his lonely cot was placed,
> A rude, unpolished gem upon the waste;
> The smoke curled lonely, 'mid the air on high,
> A moment hung and melted in the sky;

---

[1] Glasgow Com. Reg. Testaments.
[2] Ibid.
[3] Wodrow's *History*, 1829, 8vo, iii. 490.
[4] Wodrow, iv. 245.
[5] Loudoun Parish Register.

Where the brook murmured, and the mountain frowned,
Through the far-stretching wilderness around;

. . . . . .

Summer's first morn had dawned upon the wild,
And Nature's fair and lovely features smiled,
When pious Brown, with day's first beam, arose,
And called his slumbering children from repose.
They gathered round the cottage hearth, to raise
The voice of psalms, the simple song of praise;
The holy, untaught melody of heart—
Dearer to Heaven than all the pomp of art;
Unheard by human ear the cadence dies,
Its last faint murmurs mingling with the skies.

. . . . . .

When, lo, a shriek!—the startled echoes rang
With neighing war-steeds, and the warriors' clang
Woke him to earth, and drew him from the sky,
To clasp his weeping family and die.
Firm in spirit of his prayer, he stood,
Resigned, yet fearless, calm, but unsubdued;
"Prepare!" the dark and fierce avenger cried;
"Prepare!" his language in his hour of pride.

The good man knelt upon the flowery heath,
Soon to be crimsoned with the tide of death;
His farewell prayer of triumph and repose;—
Heaven's glories dawning o'er his earthly woes—
In the true martyr's spirit pled with Heaven,
His death, his country's wrongs might be forgiven:
And more than angels' eloquence imparts—
It touched the tearless soldiers' iron hearts.
When loud and high, the leader's stern command
Rose fierce, but vain above that bloody band,
Though stained with slaughter's darkest, foulest hue,
No arm was raised, no death-winged bullet flew:—
The ruthless Clavers raised his hand on high,
Rage in his heart, and mockery in his eye;

> A moment—and the martyred hero lay
> Bedewed in blood—his soul has passed away!
> From death and insult springing to a throne,
> The guilt his foe's, the triumph all his own.

Robert Brown, merchant in Kilmarnock, died in January 1628. He had attained considerable opulence, his free gear amounting to £3866, 13s. 4d. The bulk of his estate he bestowed on his wife, Jonette Schoreswood, and his two daughters, Christian and Marcoune.[1] Matthew Brown, merchant in Kilmarnock, who died in June 1674, bequeathed one half of his estate to his wife, Janet Tailyor, and the other half to "his poorest friends." He also made provision for his "oy," Jonette Brown; and made bequests to the children of Matthew Brown in Byr of Bankhead; also to his nephew, Thomas Brown in Quarter House, and to his nieces, Jean Marion and Margaret Brown.[2]

A colony of the Brown family was planted at Dunlop, in the north of Ayrshire, where they were numerous during the eighteenth century.[3] To this parish belonged John Davidson Brown, author of "The Bard of Glazert," "Ballads founded on Ayrshire Traditions," and other poems. Born at Dunlop about the year 1820, he some time engaged in teaching. He afterwards emigrated to Canada. His poem, "My Native Land," is composed in Burns's own strain and with some measure of his power.[4]

A copy of the National Covenant, subscribed at Kirkoswald in 1639, has, by the kirk-session of that parish, been carefully preserved. Among the signatures is that of John Broun, his name being adhibited by a notary. From 1659 to 1694 there is a blank in the Kirkoswald register. In the register John Broun is named as having been ordained an elder on the 21st May 1701, and his death

---

[1] Glasgow Com. Reg. Testaments.
[2] Ibid.
[3] Dunlop Parish Register.
[4] *Modern Scottish Poets*, third series, pp. 55-59.

is recorded in 1724. In 1725 Thomas Broun in Drumgarloch and Samuel Broun in Craigentoun are named as elders.[1]

The baptismal register of Kirkoswald is extant from 1694. In that register there is, under the 5th of May 1695, an entry bearing that Edward, son to Hugh Broun in Balkenran, was baptized. The name Edward does not reappear, but during the first quarter of the eighteenth century we find living in the parish, and there marrying and obtaining baptism for their children, William Broun at Drumbeg, and Thomas Broun at Jamestoun; James Broun at Ardlochan; Samuel Broun at Craigentoun; also Henry Broun. In 1704 Robert Broun in Craigentoun is witness at a baptism. During the same period there also appear as parishioners of Kirkoswald, John Broun in Drummochrian; John Broun in Drummuscan; John Broun in Drumvaine; John Broun in Jamestoun; John Broun in Littleton; John Broun in Ardlochan; John Broun in Drumgarloch; John Broun in Turnberry; and John Broun in Craigentoun.

John Broun in Turnberry occupied a small croft near Turnberry Castle. In his holding he was succeeded by his son Thomas. John Broun, his grandson, became tacksman of the farm of Birniehill, in the same parish.

John Brown, one of the two sons of the farmer at Birniehill, engaged in merchandise at Glasgow, but, falling into social irregularities, he ultimately retired to the hamlet of Kirkoswald, where he died about the year 1850. A lover of song and ballad, he composed verses of considerable merit. In a print of forty-two duodecimo pages, entitled "The Carrick Muse," he has thus celebrated "The Woods of Culzean:"—

> When morning, smiling fresh and fair,
> Comes like a maid with flowing hair,

---

[1] Kirk-session Records of Kirkoswald.

An' rosy cheek and hazel eye,
Enough to make her lover sigh ;
The woods an' glens by music riven,
Are singing like the choir of heaven—
"Excelled by few, surpassed by nane,"
The bonny woods o' sweet Culzean.

In a poem entitled "The Kirkoswald Widow" Brown evinces considerable power :—

There's Correstown and Morristown,
　　Merkland and Minnabae,
Aul' Croftingie an' Craigintown,
　　Drumdow and mony mae.
Names 'tween Corra an' Abbey Mill,
　　Tradonock an' the sea,
That's aye the same sin' I was young—
　　But what are names to me ?

　.　　　.　　　.　　　.

They're dead an' gane wha made them dear
　　And left me here alane,
A wither'd leaf upon the tree,
　　When a' the lave are ta'en.

　.　　　.　　　.　　　.

The sun will rise 'yont Straiton hills ;
　　The heather on Craigdow
An' sea-pinks round auld Turnberry
　　Will aye be fair to view :
But folks, like mist in summer morn,
　　Or like an April shower,
Are here and gane, as nought had been,
　　They wither like the flower.

Auld Ballochniel and Ladyburns,
　　They aye will join the sea ;
And I maun join the silent grave,
　　I'm auld—I'm ninety-three.

John Brown published in 1830 "The Ploughing Humbug;" some satirical verses inspired by a challenge on the part of ploughmen at Dailly, ventilated in a local journal. Among his unprinted pieces, "an epitaph upon himself" contains the following stanza:—

> He whiles did right, he whiles did wrang,
> Whiles made a poem or a sang—
> This kept him just frae thinking lang
>   An' fools to fear him,
> For whiles in rhyme a loon he'd bang
>   Wha dar'd to steer him.

At the close of the seventeenth century there lived at Kirkoswald three brothers, Samuel, Robert, and John Broun, who succeeded jointly to the lease of John Broun, their father, in the farm of Craigentoun. John, one of the brothers, married, on the 24th December 1675, "Jennet M'Gren," also residing at Kirkoswald, but the nuptial rite was solemnized at Girvan.[1]

The family of M'Gren or M'Grean were scions of Grime or Graeme, a sept belonging to the old kingdom of Strathclyde, the name being derived from a Welsh word signifying strength. Prior to the twelfth century the sept of Graeme or Graham had acquired a settlement in that part of the western border included in the counties of Dumfries and Kirkcudbright. In 1321 Peter Graham appears as proprietor of the lands of Brakanwra in Annandale.[2] And in the reign of Queen Elizabeth there was a powerful colony of Grahams in Cumberland, including twenty head-men and their retainers. By the English Government under James VI. there was, on the 4th December 1603, issued a proclamation setting forth that, among other borderers, the Grahams had perpetrated sundry outrages, but that they were now at the king's peace, inasmuch as

---

[1] Kirkoswald Parish Register. [2] Robertson's Index, 6, 36.

they had acknowledged their offences. They had also sought the king's help in being removed to other localities, so that they might reform their lives. A large body of the sept were borne to Ireland.[1]

A branch of the Grahams penetrated into Carrick, and, on the province being disjoined from Galloway by William the Lion in 1186, they seem to have become known as the Grens, or M'Grens. Grenan, an estate in Kirkcudbrightshire, was an early possession of the clan. And within the parish of Maybole rests on the edge of a sea cliff Castle Grenan, which, latterly a stronghold of the Lord of the Isles, had originally accommodated a chief of the sept.

In the parish register of Ayr is, on the 13th August 1668, recorded the birth of Robert, son of William M'Grean, flesher burgess of Ayr.

To William M'Grean, at Maybole, was born, on the 17th May 1680, a son William.

In the parish register of Ayr is recorded, under the 8th February 1700, the marriage of William M'Graham, " milner in Grean, in the paroch of Maybole," and Elizabeth —— at Alloway. And in the parish register of Kirkoswald is entered, on the 24th November 1758, the marriage of Allan M'Grean and Jean Orr.

In his poem of "Hallowe'en," the Poet celebrates one of the sept thus :—

> Our stibble-rig[2] was Rab M'Graen,
> A clever, sturdy fallow.

John Broun seems to have remained at Girvan for several years subsequent to his marriage, for his name does not reappear in the Kirkoswald registers till 1706, when, as "John Broun in Craigen-

---

[1] See *The Debateable Land*, by T. J. Carlyle, Temple, Waterbeck, Dumfries, 1868. Privately printed.
[2] Leader of the reapers.

toun,"[1] he is named as a witness. Under the same designation he appears a witness in 1712, and again in 1717. According to the family tombstone, he died at Littletoun on the 3rd March 1724, in his fiftieth year; his wife, Janet M'Grean, died on the 28th March 1738, at the age of sixty. Of the marriage was born, in 1708, a son, Gilbert, who became lessee of the farm of Craigentoun, of which the area extends to about 160 imperial acres. On the 7th May 1731 Gilbert Broun was contracted at Kirkoswald to "Agnes Rennie," both parties being described as resident "in that parish."[2]

Rennie is, as a name, of territorial origin, derived from the Gaelic *Rinn*, signifying a point or promontory, also a district or division; various localities in Scotland are so designated. From the place styled Rhin, in Sutherlandshire, also from Rhynie, a parish in Aberdeenshire, the families of Rennie, in the north of Scotland, originally hailed.

In the parish of Saline, in the western extremity of Fifeshire, is the farm of Rhynd. Rhind is a parish in Perthshire, at the confluence of the Tay and Earn. The Rhind point indicates a sharp curve of the Forth near Alloa, and the Rhin marks a point at the confluence of the Earn and Blane in western Stirlingshire. In

---

[1] Craigentoun, a farm occupied by the Poet's maternal ancestors for several generations, is situated on the high ground about two miles to the south of Kirkoswald hamlet.

[2] Janet Brown, a sister of Gilbert, born in 1715, married, 5th June 1735, Alexander Hutchison in Burntown of Dalrymple. Of the marriage were born two sons, Samuel and John; also four daughters, Agnes, Janet, Helen, and Margaret. Janet, the second daughter, born in 1761, married, 27th April 1786, William Baird in Clachan of Dalrymple, with issue a son, Samuel, born 4th February 1787. Samuel Baird married Helen Kean. Their eldest son, Fullarton Baird, born at Dalrymple on the 24th June 1811, was some time assistant to the schoolmaster of Kirkoswald; he was afterwards appointed headmaster of St. John's school, Hamilton. He latterly became superintendent of the Free Church School, Portobello. He died on the 18th May 1880 at Portobello, and a handsome monument has been erected to his memory by the office-bearers of the Free Church of that place. William, eldest son of Fullarton Baird, is agent for the Clydesdale Bank at Portobello. Jane Baird, sister of Fullarton Baird, was the second wife of James Paterson, author of the *History of the Ayrshire Families*, and other historical works.

Stirlingshire families of the name have existed for a course of centuries. On the 8th October 1436, John Barbour, burgess of Stirling, granted to the chaplain performing divine service at the altar of St. Ninian in the church of Cambuskenneth an annual rent of two shillings, due to the granter from the tenement of John Rayny, skinner burgess of Stirling, as described in the charter.[1]

A member of the Stirlingshire family purchased, about forty years ago, the lands of Danevale, near Castle-Douglas. But the family of Rennie, now under special consideration, has a Gallovidian origin, and probably derived their name from the Rhynns, a peninsula resting between the Irish Channel and the bays of Luce and Loch Ryan. A tradition obtains that the Galloway sept were originally called Rhynsmen, and that they claimed descent from the Stewarts of Corswall, scions of Stewart of Garlies, a family which, through Sir John Stewart of Bonkill, sprang from the High Steward.

From the Rhynns of Galloway members of the sept of Rainie or Rennie spread to the east and west. Herbert Rainie or Rayning, merchant burgess and provost of Dumfries, sat in the Parliament of 1572. In 1578 he represented Dumfries in the Convention of Burghs. "Herbert Raynyng, younger in Dumfreis," is mentioned in 1579. His daughter married Francis Irving, merchant and chief magistrate of Dumfries, bringing him as dowry lands and heritages. Provost Irving, who in 1617 represented Dumfries in Parliament, obtained the favour of James VI., who gave him bailiary jurisdiction over the Crown property of the district. He died on the 6th November 1633. He is now represented by Wellwood Herries Maxwell, Esq., of Munches.[2]

John Rayning, eldest son of John Rayning, merchant in Dum-

---

[1] *Cartulary of Cambuskenneth*, edited by Sir William Fraser, Grampian Club, pp. 297, 395.
[2] *Scottish Arms*, by R. R. Stodart, Edinburgh, 1880, fol. ii. 365; Privy Seal Register, iii. 707; M'Dowall's *History of Dumfries*, pp. 239-244; M'Dowall's *Memorials of St. Michael's Churchyard, Dumfries*, pp. 11-13.

fries, died in October 1637. In his testament-dative are named his three brothers, Thomas, George, and William.[1]

Marion Rynnie, spouse to George Campbell in Aultitiber, in the parish of Maybole, died in November 1625, leaving a son, John.[2]

In 1639 Andrew Rinnie subscribed, by the hands of a notary, the National Covenant at Kirkoswald.[3] John Rynnie in Trabeoche, parish of Girvan, died in December 1641, leaving "free gear" to the value of £937, 8s.[4] To his wife, Margaret M'Fadzeane, he bequeathed the lease of his farm, so long as she should remain a widow, dividing the residue of his substance among his children. David Rinnie, farmer at Lunnochtie, in the parish of Girvan, died in November 1642, leaving free gear to the value of £477, 13s. 4d.[5] At Lunnochtie, Agnes Rynnie, wife of Patrick M'Alexander, died in April 1643, when John Rynnie, described as her brother-in-law, was appointed her executor-dative; her gear was valued at £675, 1s. 4d.[6]

William Rainy in Alloway had by his wife, Margaret Andrew, a daughter, named Susanna, born 28th September 1693.[7] William Rainy, son of the same parents, settled at Alloway. He married Agnes Morton, by whom he had a daughter, Katherine, born 25th February 1727. Captain John Renny, described as uncle of the child, was a witness to the baptism.[8]

William Rainy, described in the parish register as "baker in Air," married, 14th June 1704, "Jean Ramsay, servitrix to Agnes Boswall, widow in Air." Of this marriage a daughter, Elizabeth, was born on the 28th March 1705.[9] Subsequent to the birth of his

---

[1] Com. Reg. of Dumfries, Testaments, Vol. 1, 27th September, 1638.
[2] Glasgow Com. Reg. Testaments.
[3] Kirkoswald Kirk-session Records.
[4] Glasgow Com. Reg. Testaments.
[5] Ibid.
[6] Barr Parish Register.
[7] Ayr Parish Register.
[8] Ibid.
[9] Ibid.

daughter Elizabeth, William Rainy settled in Maybole, where was born to him, in 1708, a daughter, Agnes,[1] who, as is believed, espoused in 1731 Gilbert Broun at Craigentoun.

Agnes Rainy or Rennie, wife of Gilbert Broun, died in May 1742, at the age of thirty-four. She gave birth to four sons and two daughters. John, the eldest son, was baptized 26th September 1736; James, the second son, on the 18th February 1738; and David, the fourth son, on the 10th May 1741.[2]

Samuel, the third son, baptized 18th February 1739, became helper on the farm of Robert Niven, miller at Ballochneil, whose daughter Margaret he married on the 18th April 1765.[3] After his marriage he was accommodated in "the chalmer," an apartment usually connected with farm-offices for the occupancy of a married servant. Under his roof the Poet received his meals, when receiving instruction in mensuration and geometry at the parish school of Kirkoswald. Samuel Broun joined his brother-in-law, John Niven, in the business of wool-broking, but unsuccessfully.[4] Latterly he took charge of the cattle on Ballochneil farm. He died in October 1811. An account for "funeral bread" used on the occasion of his funeral is preserved in the family. It presents these items:—

"4 Pecks Plain Short Bread at 7s.,   £1 8
Loaf Bread,   2
                                           ─────
                                           £1 10"

Samuel Broun's wife survived till 1821. Their only child,

---

[1] The birth is not on record.
[2] Kirkoswald Parish Register.
[3] *Ibid*.
[4] Dr. Robert Chambers has fallen into error in describing Samuel Broun as having brewed and vended home-made ale; he also inaccurately describes him as a widower, which he never was.

Jenny, is named by the Poet in "Hallowe'en." Baptized on the 12th July 1765, she married Andrew Forsyth, a small trader in Maybole; she died without issue.

Of the two daughters born to Gilbert Broun by his first wife, Agnes Rennie, Agnes the elder became the Poet's mother; she will be noticed subsequently. Janet, the younger daughter, baptized 24th February 1734, married —— Rennie, a relative of her mother, by whom she had a son, David, and a daughter, Agnes, who both died unmarried.

Gilbert Broun married, secondly, 26th June 1744, Margaret Blain, of the parish of Barr, and member of a family which produced Sir Gilbert Blane, Bart., the eminent physician. She died in June 1751, aged thirty-six. Of the marriage were born two sons, Andrew and Hugh, also a daughter, Jean.

Andrew, the elder son, baptized 27th October 1745, became landlord of the Red Lion Inn, Maybole, the scene of the celebrated discussion between the Abbot of Crossraguel and John Knox. He married Jean Love, with issue several sons and one daughter.

Hugh, the second son, was baptized 23rd August 1747.

Jean, only daughter of Gilbert Broun and Margaret Blain, baptized 10th June 1750, married, in 1775, James Allan, a native of Stewarton, and joiner on the estate of Fairlie, parish of Dundonald. James Allan died in 1789, when his widow removed from Fairlie to the village of Old Rome, in the same neighbourhood. Her husband's savings amounted to only twenty pounds, and, without encroaching on this small capital, she, by a rigid frugality, contrived to maintain herself and her young children. After being many years a widow, she married, secondly, Adam Baird, a native of Dundonald; she died in 1821.

By her union with James Allan, her first husband, Jean Broun had four sons and three daughters.

THE POET'S LINEAGE.

James, the eldest son, settled as a joiner in Mauchline. He married, but died without issue.

Andrew, the second son, baptized at Dundonald 12th April 1778, engaged in handloom weaving at Greenholm, near Newmilns. He died about the year 1841, leaving considerable substance. He married and had five daughters: Anne, who married James Macpherson, Newmilns; Jean, who married Andrew Jack, Newmilns; Margaret, who married James Wylie; Janet, who married William Lambie, manufacturer, Newmilns; and Isabella, who married —— Smith.

Alexander, third son of James Allan and Jean Broun, was apprenticed to James Cunningham, shoemaker, College Wynd, Kilmarnock, and afterwards served his trade with James Nisbet, Loudoun Kirk. Abandoning his craft, he entered the workshop of a ship-carpenter at Saltcoats, and afterwards adopted a seafaring life. After a time he became captain of a sailing vessel, and subsequently he commanded ships trading between Glasgow and Montreal. Ultimately he laid the foundation of that great commercial undertaking known as the Allan Line of steamships. He died in 1854, at the age of seventy-four. By his wife, Jean Crawford, he had five sons, James, Hugh, Bryce, Andrew, and Alexander; also three daughters, Jean, who married Captain Greenhorn; Margaret, who married —— Service; and ——, who married —— Macfie of Liverpool.

Hugh, the second son, born in 1810, emigrated to Canada in 1826, and there in 1835 became a partner in the firm of Messrs. Millar and Edmonstone, shipowners in Montreal. In 1853 he obtained the Government contract for the first line of steamers from the river St. Lawrence to Liverpool. He afterwards established a line to Glasgow, and became the chief owner and principal manager of a large fleet of ships trading to various parts of the world. In the rebellions in Canada of 1837 and 1838 he served as a volunteer, with the rank of captain. In 1871 he received the honour of knighthood. Sir Hugh Allan resided at Ravenscraig, Montreal. He died at Edinburgh on the 9th December 1882, at the age of seventy-two.

John, fourth son of James Allan and Jean Broun, settled in Newmilns as a handloom weaver; he died in 1857, at the age of seventy-five. By his wife, Jean Richmond, he had eight sons and a daughter, Janet, who married Hugh Morton, Townhead, Newmilns, and is now a widow. Of the sons survive John and Alexander, weavers at Newmilns, and Andrew, who resides at West Troy, New York.

Margaret, eldest daughter of James Allan and Jean Broun, born 1784, married Hugh Jack, stone-dealer, Riccarton, with issue six sons, John, James, Hugh, Richard, Andrew, and Alexander; also four daughters, Jean, Fairlie, Elizabeth, and Margaret.

Janet Frances, the second daughter, born in 1788, married James Stevenson, church-officer at Riccarton; she died in 1840. Of the marriage were born six sons and four daughters. Alexander Allan, the youngest son, is lieutenant-colonel commanding the Field Battery of Artillery at Montreal.

Gilbert Broun married, thirdly, 16th April 1765, Catherine Moat. His banns were proclaimed in the parish church of Kirkoswald, on Sunday the 7th April 1765, at the same time that his third son, Samuel, then in his twenty-sixth year, had his banns proclaimed with his future wife, Margaret Niven. Of the marriage of Gilbert Broun and Catherine Moat were born Margaret, baptized 28th January 1766; James, baptized 25th August 1768; Christian, baptized 31st January 1771; and Helen, born 16th May 1772. Gilbert Broun left Craigentoun prior to 1768, and resided successively at Hallowshean and Broadshean in the same locality. He died on the 31st October 1774, aged sixty-six.

THE POET'S LINEAGE.

In Kirkoswald Churchyard, a few yards westward of the ruin of the old parish church, a plain upright tombstone commemorates the maternal grand and great-grandparents of the national Bard. It is thus inscribed :—

> Here lyes the corps of Iohn Broun in Litletown who died March 3d 1724 aged 50 and Jannet M'Grean his spouse, who died March 28 1738 aged 60 and Agnes Renie who died May 1742 aged 34 and Margret Blain, who died June 1751 aged 36 spouses to Gilbert Broun in Craigentoun. And Agnes Stien who died in 1748. Also James Broun in Riddelstown who died June 29th 1780 aged 65 years. Erected by John and Gilbert Broun and Robert and John and Samuel and William and John Broun in Roan and Jenet Banaktin his spouse. Also here lieth the body of Gilbert Broun, who died October 31 1774 aged 66 years.[1]

Three other tombstones in Kirkoswald Churchyard commemorate members of the Broun family. On one of these an uncle and cousin of the Poet are named in the following inscription :—" John Broun who died in 1774 aged 79 and his son Gilbert Broun, who died in 1786 aged 35."

Agnes, elder daughter of Gilbert Broun, by his wife Agnes Rennie, was born on the 17th March 1732. Ten years old at the time of her mother's death in 1742,[2] she, young as she was, took charge of the domestic concerns, till in 1744 her father contracted a second marriage. She now permanently left her father's house,

---

[1] Consequent on a public subscription, the tombstone of the Poet's maternal ancestors at Kirkoswald was in August 1883 suitably restored. The old stone was encased in a new setting of durable sandstone, and placed on an appropriate pedestal. See vol. ii. App. 3.

[2] When Mrs. Agnes Broun, the Poet's maternal grandmother (who suffered from a pulmonary ailment) was on her deathbed, she was visited by a sister, who, surprised to find her composed and cheerful, put to her the question, "Are you not grieved to leave your husband and children?" She answered meekly, "My children I leave to the care of God, and Gilbert will get another wife." This speech deeply impressed her daughter Agnes, who reported it to her own children.

first residing with her maternal grandmother, and afterwards with her paternal uncle, William Broun, at Maybole, then a widower, his wife, Agnes Stein or Steven, whom he married at Kirkoswald on 25th November 1717, having died in 1748. It was to William Broun that the Poet referred when writing to Mrs. Dunlop in these words :—

> I had an old granduncle, with whom my mother lived awhile in her girlish years ; the good old man, for such he was, was long blind ere he died ; during which time his highest enjoyment was to sit down and cry, while my mother would sing the simple old song of "The Life and Age of Man."

At an early age Agnes Broun had become betrothed to her grandmother's ploughman, but, learning that he had lapsed from virtue, she renounced him. Not long afterwards William Burnes met her at a Maybole fair, and afterwards offering her marriage, obtained her consent. In the parish register of Ayr their marriage is entered thus :—"Ayr, Dec. 2, 1757.—William Burns, gardener in this parish, and Agnes Broun in Maybole, gave in their names to be proclaimed in order for marriage, and after proclamation, were married accordingly." The marriage was solemnized on the 15th December.

Of the marriage of William Burnes and Agnes Broun were born four sons, Robert, Gilbert, William, and John ; also three daughters, Agnes, Annabella, and Isabella.

In the parish register of Ayr the birth of Agnes, the eldest daughter, is entered thus :—"Agnes Burns, daughter lawful of William Burns, gardener in Alloway, and Agnes Broun, his spouse, was born September 30, 1762. Baptized by Mr. W. Dalrymple." Agnes married, in 1804, William Galt, afterwards land-steward to Mr. Matthew Fortescue, on his estate in Ireland. She died, without issue, at Stephenstown, County Louth, Ireland, on the

THE POET'S LINEAGE.

17th October 1834, and her remains were conveyed to the churchyard of St. Nicholas Presbyterian Church, Dundalk. Her grave is reverently covered with a large pavement stone; while in a conspicuous part of the churchyard an obelisk about thirty feet in height has been raised to her memory. In front it presents the following legend :—

> As a tribute to the genius of Robert Burns, the national Bard of Scotland, and in respect for the memory of his eldest sister, Agnes, whose mortal remains are deposited in this churchyard, erected by the contributions of the Poet's numerous admirers in Dundalk and its vicinity, 25th January 1859.
>
> "Time but the impression deeper makes,
> As streams their channels deeper wear."

On the back of the obelisk are inscribed these words :—

> Sacred to the memory of Agnes Burns, eldest sister of Robert Burns, who departed this life at Stephenstown on the 17th October 1834, aged 72 years. Her mortal remains lie interred in the south-east corner of this churchyard.

William Galt, husband of Agnes Burns, died on the 1st March 1847.

Annabella, second daughter of William Burns, was born at Alloway on the 14th November 1764. She died unmarried at Grant's Braes, Haddingtonshire, on the 2nd March 1832. Her remains rest in the churchyard of Bolton.

Isabella, third daughter, is, in the parish register of Ayr, described as "lawful daughter of William Burns, farmer." Born on the 27th June 1771, she married at Mauchline, on the 9th December 1793, John Begg, described in the marriage register as "quarrier in Mossgiel." Mrs. Begg accompanied her husband to Dinning, in the parish of Closeburn, Dumfriesshire, when he became manager of that farm, in the absence of the lessee, his brother-in-law, Gilbert Burns, consequent on his accepting the factorship of the estate of Morham Muir, in the county of Haddington. Mr. Begg afterwards became land-steward on the estate of Blackwood, Lanarkshire, the property of Mr. James Hope Vere. He was killed by being thrown from his horse on the 26th April 1813. His remains were committed to the churchyard of Lesmahagow, where he is commemorated by a tombstone.

Subsequent to her husband's death, Mrs. Begg established her residence at Ormiston, Haddingtonshire. She afterwards occupied a cottage at Tranent, and in June 1843 she settled at Bridge House, Alloway. There, in the month of August 1857, she was visited by the present writer. She had passed her eighty-sixth birthday, but her faculties were unclouded and her memory perfect. Respecting the Poet she used words expressive of veneration; she remarked that "his countenance beamed with genius." She spoke of his respect for religion, and of his concern that she, his youngest sister, should read the Scriptures, and become familiar with the Shorter Catechism. Mrs. Begg indulged a pleasing jocundity; she had very dark eyes, and her features indicated a superior intelligence. Mrs. Begg died on the 4th December 1858, and her remains were consigned to the grave in Alloway Churchyard, in which, seventy-five years before, those of her father had been deposited.

Of the marriage of John Begg and Isabella Burns were born six sons, William, John, Robert Burns, Gilbert, James Hope, and Edward Hamilton; also three daughters, Agnes Brown, Jane Breckenridge, and Isabella.

William Begg, eldest son of John Begg and Isabella Burns, was born at Mossgiel on the 29th July 1794. In 1817 he was appointed parish schoolmaster of Ormiston, Haddingtonshire. This office he resigned in 1833, when he sailed for Canada; he resided at Clinton, Goderich, till his death, which took place on the 15th May 1864.

John Begg, second son of John Begg and Isabella Burns, was born at Mossgiel on the 27th April 1796. He worked as a joiner at

Kilmarnock, and there died on the 11th October 1867. He married, 14th November 1817, Agnes Wilson (born 1795, died 1851), with issue five sons and three daughters. John, the eldest son, born 21st March 1821, resides at Pudman Creek, New South Wales; twice married, he has four sons, John, Andrew, Robert, and Neil; also a daughter, Janet.

Robert Burns Begg, second son of John Begg and Agnes Wilson, was born 9th May 1823; he married in 1846 Winifred ——, with issue. Walter Wilson, the third son, born 16th July 1828, died in infancy. William, the fourth son, born 1st April 1833, married in 1852, with issue three sons and five daughters. James, the fifth son, born 19th September 1836, died unmarried on the 31st May 1874.

Marion Adams Begg, eldest daughter of John Begg and Agnes Wilson, was born 17th August 1818; she married Richard Johnstone, with issue a son and two daughters; she died 7th February 1871. Jane Breckenridge Begg, second daughter, born 8th March 1826, married David Campbell, with issue; she and her husband reside at Largs, in Ayrshire. Isabella Burns Begg, third daughter, born 27th April 1830, married George Preston; she died 3rd November 1856, leaving a son and daughter.

Robert Burns Begg, third son of John Begg and Isabella Burns, was born in the parish of Dundonald on the 9th of May 1798, and was educated at Wallace Hall Academy, parish of Closeburn. In 1818 he was appointed schoolmaster at Bent, on the estate of Blackwood; he afterwards assisted in the parish school of Dalmeny, and in 1822 was elected schoolmaster of Kinross, an office which he held for fifty-one years. He died at Kinross on the 25th July 1876. He married, 27th July 1825, Grace, daughter of Bruce Beveridge, and grand-daughter of James Beveridge, Esq. of Balado, with issue seven sons and three daughters.

John Begg, eldest son of Robert Burns Begg and Grace

Beveridge, born 25th May 1826, was manager and one of the owners of the Kinneil Ironworks, in the county of Linlithgow. He died 28th September 1878. He married, first, 10th April 1855, Eliza, daughter of Andrew Vannan, distiller, Borrowstounness; and, secondly, 3rd October 1865, Elizabeth Simpson, daughter of James Anderson, builder, Calcutta. He is survived by four sons, Robert Burns, Andrew Vannan, John, and James Beveridge Anderson; also by two daughters, Elizabeth Anderson and Grace Margaret.

Bruce Begg, second son of Robert Burns Begg, born 22nd December 1827, died 10th December 1836.

James Beveridge Begg, third son, born 24th October 1829, settled in Virginia. He married, first, 31st August 1857, Mary Haldane; secondly, 25th July 1863, Janet Haldane. He has a son, Robert, and two daughters, Isobel and Mary.

Robert Burns Begg, fourth son, born 1st May 1833, is Sheriff-Clerk of the county of Kinross. He has composed a history of Lochleven Castle, and is known as an antiquarian scholar. He married, first, 5th November 1861, Jane Hutchison; secondly, 17th March 1870, Mary Leburn, with issue a son, Robert Burns.

Bruce Beveridge Begg, fifth son, born 24th June 1837, studied at the University of Glasgow, and in 1865 was ordained minister of Abbotshall, Fifeshire. He married, 13th December 1871, Magdalene, daughter of Andrew Currie of Glassmount, with issue two sons, Robert Burns and Andrew Currie; also two daughters, Elizabeth and Grace.

William, sixth son, born 10th June 1839, settled in Newcastle as a naval engineer; he died in 1888. He married, 2nd June 1869, Eleanor Jane Hogg.

Gilbert Burns Begg, seventh son, born 17th May 1842, is a civil engineer, resident at Motherwell. He married, 27th September 1870, Annie Cuthbertson, with issue a son, Robert Burns, and a daughter, Grace.

THE POET'S LINEAGE.

Isabella, eldest daughter of Robert Burns Begg and Grace Beveridge, was born 28th May 1831; she married, 9th August 1866, Andrew Vannan, distiller, Borrowstounness.

Jane, second daughter, born 4th January 1844, died in infancy.

Grace Jane, youngest daughter, born 12th February 1846, is unmarried.

Gilbert Begg, fourth son of John Begg and Isabella Burns, was born on the 21st February 1802. Educated at Wallace Hall Academy, he served as apprentice to a joiner, but subsequently joined the navy. Discharged on a small pension, he was, on the outbreak of the Russian war in 1854, called up for coastguard service. He afterwards worked at his original trade, and when, owing to the infirmities of age, he was unable longer to exercise his calling, he became a boarder in the Old Men's Home at Glasgow. Subsequently he was received as a boarder in the Glasgow Poorhouse. But in July 1882 he was, at the instance of admirers of his uncle's genius, boarded at Pollokshaws. Gilbert died on the 11th January 1885, in his eighty-third year. His remains were deposited in the Old Vennel Churchyard, Pollokshaws.

James Hope, fifth son of John Begg and Isabella Burns, was born on the 2nd February 1809. He served in the 26th Regiment, and died unmarried at Chusan, in China, on the 2nd November 1840. He held a medal for "distinguished service."

Edward Hamilton, sixth son of John Begg and Isabella Burns, born 12th August 1811, died 2nd May 1824.

Agnes Brown, eldest daughter of John Begg and Isabella Burns, was born on the 17th April 1800. Acute and of a strong sagacity, she also indulged a generous humour. An ardent admirer of her uncle's genius, she rejoiced in every effort which was put forth to celebrate his memory. She died unmarried at Bridge House, Alloway, on the 1st May 1883, at the age of eighty-three.

Jane Breckenridge, second daughter, was born on the 16th April 1804; she died on the 7th July 1822, unmarried.

Isabella, third daughter, born 27th April 1806, died unmarried at Bridge House, Alloway, on the 27th December 1886, at the age of eighty-one. Her remains were deposited in Alloway Churchyard.

John Burnes, fourth and youngest son of William Burnes and Agnes Broun, was born on the 12th July 1769. He died in his fourteenth year, and his remains were interred in the churchyard of Mauchline.

William Burnes, third son of William Burnes and Agnes Broun, was born at Alloway on the 31st July 1767. A journeyman saddler, he prosecuted his craft, first at Newcastle, and afterwards in London. He died at London in July 1790, and his remains were deposited in St. Paul's Churchyard; the spot of his interment was unmarked, and is now unknown.

Gilbert Burns, second son of William Burnes and Agnes Broun, was born at Alloway on the 28th September 1760. Concerning him, his early preceptor, Mr. Murdoch, writes:—"Gilbert always appeared to me to possess a more lively imagination, and to be more of the wit than Robert."

By ranking as a creditor on his father's estate for his stipulated wages on Lochlea farm, Gilbert was, in conjunction with his brother the Poet, enabled to retain a portion of farm stock, and therewith, aided by the savings of other members of the family, to enter on the farm of Mossgiel, near Mauchline. This farm was at first held by the Poet on a sub-lease from Mr. Gavin Hamilton, who himself rented the farm from the Earl of Loudoun; but in March 1784 the Poet associated Gilbert with him in the lease. Three years later he retired personally from the concern, while from the proceeds of the second edition of his poems he granted Gilbert the loan of £180, which enabled him to discharge debt, and to struggle with an ungrateful soil till 1797, when he leased the farm of Dinning, in Nithsdale.

In 1800 Gilbert Burns was induced by Mrs. Dunlop to take temporary charge of Morham Muir, a farm in the neighbourhood of Haddington, which formed a part of her family estate. His own farm at Dinning, which he retained till 1810, he entrusted to the management of John Begg, husband of his sister Isabella. In 1804 he accepted the factorship of Lord Blantyre, and in the spring of that year established his residence at Grant's Braes, near Lethington, Haddingtonshire. As factor, he had, in reward of service, a free house, with a salary of £100, which was subsequently raised to £140. He died at Grant's Braes on the 8th April 1827, at the age of sixty-seven; his remains were deposited in the churchyard at Bolton.

Gilbert Burns facially resembled his brother the Poet, with this difference, that he had an aquiline nose, while Robert had a straight one. Possessed of a vigorous intelligence, and of no inconsiderable literary culture, he largely assisted Dr. Currie in preparing his brother's memoirs. He edited an edition of the Poet's works, published in 1820 by Cadell & Davies, adding a dissertation on the effect produced by Presbyterianism on the Scottish national character. For this edition he received from the publishers £500, which enabled him to discharge to the Poet's widow the debt of £180, contracted thirty-two years previously. Gilbert Burns married, 20th June 1791, Jean Breckenridge. Her mother, Janet Aird, was only child of John Aird, farmer at Sorn, and latterly a merchant in Kilmarnock. She married, first, James Breckenridge, farmer, Craigie, son of James Breckenridge, parish schoolmaster of Irvine, with issue a son, Thomas, and a daughter, Jean, afterwards Mrs. Gilbert Burns. She married, secondly, David Sillar,[1] farmer,

---

[1] Mauchline Marriage Register. Sir James Shaw, Bart., a native of Kilmarnock, Lord Mayor and Chamberlain of the city of London, was nephew of David Sillar. Sir

Heugh Mill, Symington, near Kilmarnock, by whom she had four children. Jean Breckenridge, wife of Gilbert Burns, inherited from her parents certain house property in Fore Street, Kilmarnock. She was born on the 6th February 1764, and died on the 6th February 1841; her remains rest in the churchyard of Erskine, Renfrewshire.

Of the marriage of Gilbert Burns and Jean Breckenridge were born six sons and five daughters. Janet, the eldest daughter, born 23rd May 1799, died 30th October 1816; Agnes, second daughter, born 16th November 1800, died 14th September 1815; Anne, third daughter, born 12th September 1805, died in August 1887; Jean, fourth daughter, born 8th June 1807, died 4th January 1827; Isabella, fifth daughter, born 17th May 1809, died 3rd July 1815.

William Burns, eldest son of Gilbert Burns and Jean Breckenridge, was born on the 15th May 1792, and died in 1880 at Portarlington in Ireland. Settling in Dublin in 1822, he married, in 1824, Jane, daughter of Peter Callanan of County Galway; she died in 1858. Of their marriage were born seven children, of whom four died young. Two sons, James and William, and a daughter, Helen, survive, all of whom are unmarried.

James Burns, second son of Gilbert Burns, born at Mossgiel on the 20th April 1794, became a writer, first at Haddington, and afterwards at Glasgow, where he was also surveyor of taxes. He latterly became factor to Lord Blantyre at Erskine, Renfrewshire, and there died on the 22nd June 1847.

Thomas Burns, third son of Gilbert Burns, was born at Mossgiel on the 10th April 1796. Having studied at the University of Edinburgh, he was licensed to preach by the presbytery of

---

James became an efficient patron of the Burns family. Through his exertions each of the Poet's three sons got a start in life. Robert, the eldest, got a post in the Stamp Office; James Glencairn was nominated to Christ's Hospital, where he received his education, and both he and his brother, William Nicol, obtained Indian cadetships.

THE POET'S LINEAGE.

Haddington on the 3rd December 1822, and on the 13th April 1826 was ordained minister of Ballantrae, in the county of Ayr. Translated to the parish of Monkton, in the same county, he was there settled on the 18th May 1830. He joined the Free Church in 1843, and, on the 25th June 1846, became minister of the Free Church congregation at Portobello, near Edinburgh. Having, along with Captain Cargill and others, projected the settlement of Otago, New Zealand, he relinquished his charge in the autumn of 1847, and, with the first body of settlers, sailed from Greenock as their pastor. He ministered at Otago till his death, which took place at Dunedin on the 23rd January 1871. He was D.D. of the University of Edinburgh.

Dr. Thomas Burns married Clementina, daughter of the Rev. James Francis Grant, rector of Merston, Sussex, son of Sir Alexander Grant of Monymusk, by whom he had one son, Arthur John, and six daughters.

Arthur John, only son of Dr. Thomas Burns, married Sarah, daughter of Thomas Dickson, merchant, Otago, with issue nine children.

Clementina, eldest daughter of Dr. Thomas Burns, married Andrew J. Elles, captain of the ship *Philip Laing*, which in 1847 took out the first settlers to Otago, and of the marriage there is issue three sons and one daughter. James, the eldest son, is resident at Amoy, in China; Gilbert, the second son, has settled at Oporto, and Malcolm Jamieson, the third son, is resident in London. The daughter, Clementina, resides with her father, who is now collector of customs at Invercargill, New Zealand.

Jane, second daughter of Dr. Thomas Burns, married the Rev. William Bannerman, minister of the Presbyterian Church, Otago, with issue.

Anne, third, and Frances, fourth daughter, married, at Dunedin,

Henry and Alexander Livingstone; both sisters have issue. Agnes, fifth daughter, is unmarried. Isabella, sixth daughter, married, at Dunedin, Alexander Stevenson. He died in 1876, leaving a son, Douglas.

Robert, fourth son of Gilbert Burns and Jean Breckenridge, was born at Mossgiel on the 22nd November 1797. He emigrated to South America in 1826, and there died about 1839. John, fifth son, born 6th July 1802, became a teacher of mathematics at Edinburgh, where he died on the 26th February 1827.

Gilbert Burns, sixth and youngest son of Gilbert Burns and Jean Breckenridge, was born at Morham Muir, Haddingtonshire, 24th December 1803. He studied at the High School of Edinburgh, when James Gray, formerly tutor in the Poet's family, was one of the masters. By Sir James Shaw, his mother's relative, he was offered an Indian cadetship, but, preferring the concerns of trade, he in 1824 proceeded to Dublin, where he became assistant in a merchant's office. In 1834 he joined Mr. William Todd, from Kinross, in establishing at Dublin the mercantile house of Todd & Burns, which became largely prosperous. Gilbert Burns died at his residence, Knockmaroon Lodge, Chapelizod, Dublin, on the 9th October 1881. He was much reputed for his benevolence. He married, in 1842, Jemima Georgiana, daughter of Alexander Ferrier, Dublin, with issue two sons, Robert and Theodore Gilbert Alexander, and two daughters, Mary and Isabella.

Robert, elder son of Gilbert Burns and Jemima Ferrier, resides at the Elms, Weybridge, Surrey. He married Sibylla, daughter of the Rev. Phillipps Donnithorne Dayman, vicar of Poundstock, Cornwall, with issue a son, Kenneth Glencairn, and a daughter, Edith Donnithorne.

CHAPTER II.

BIRTH AND EARLY ENVIRONMENTS.

> And love grew sweeter at his touch, for full in him there lay
> Its melting tones and sighs, and all its soft compelling sway ;
> He shaped its raptures of delight, for unto him was given
> The power to wed to burning words the sweetest gift of heaven.
> ALEXANDER ANDERSON.

ELDEST son of William Burnes, the Poet was born at Alloway on the 25th of January 1759. In the parish register of Ayr the event is recorded thus : " Robert Burns, son lawful to William Burns in Alloway, and Agnes Broun, his spouse, was born January 25th 1759. Baptized, 26th, by Mr. William Dalrymple. Witnesses— John Tennant and James Young."

In the preceding chapter has been detailed, from sources of information not available to the Poet himself, a narrative of his ancestry ; and at this point it is proper to refer to certain family traditions which the Bard at different times gave forth and insisted on. In his autobiographical letter to Dr. Moore of the 2nd August 1787,[1] he writes thus :—

> My forefathers rented lands of the famous noble Keiths of Marshal, and had the honour to share their fate. . . . I mention this circumstance because it threw my Father on the world at large ; where, after many years' wanderings and sojournings, he picked up a pretty large quantity of observation and experience.

---

[1] This letter, with others addressed by Burns to Dr. Moore, was borrowed from one of that gentleman's representatives by an editor of the Poet's works, and was not returned. At the sale of Mr. Peter Cunningham's effects by Sotheby, London, on the 26th February 1865, it constituted Lot 145, and was purchased for the Trustees of the British Museum.

Writing to Lady Winifred Maxwell Constable, in December 1789, the Poet remarks:—

> Though my fathers had not illustrious honors and vast properties to hazard in the contest; though they left their humble cottages only to add so many units more to the unnoted crowd that followed their leaders, yet what they could they did, and what they had they lost. With unshaken firmness, and unconcealed political attachments, they shook hands with ruin for what they esteemed the cause of their king and country.

And in his poetical address to William Tytler, the Bard refers to the same subject in these lines:—

> My fathers that name have rever'd on a throne,
> My fathers have fallen to right it;
> Those fathers would spurn their degenerate son,
> That name should he scoffingly slight it.

The fate of the Keiths, Earls Marischal, to which the Poet evidently refers, consisted in the forfeiture of their estates, subsequent to the rebellion of 1715. George, tenth Earl Marischal, proclaimed at Aberdeen, on the 28th September 1715, the Chevalier St. George as King of Great Britain. He commanded two squadrons of cavalry at the battle of Sheriffmuir, and in December thereafter re-proclaimed the Chevalier at the gate of his house at Fetteresso. For these and other acts of rebellion he was subjected to attainder. Now the Poet's progenitors were in 1715 and long subsequently tenants at Glenbervie, on the estate of the Stuarts of Inchbreck. And to the family of the Earls Marischal the Stuarts were nearly related, while Jacobite principles were common to both. In the light of the Poet's tradition, it may therefore be assumed that, in compliment to the laird of Inchbreck, John Burnes, eldest son of William Burnes, his tenant of Bogjorgan, served as a lieutenant in the Jacobite army of 1715.¹ But there is no evidence that the family of Burnes was, in connexion with the insurrection of 1715, involved in the attainder or other misfortunes of the Earl Marischal.

The Poet's family tradition may be otherwise accounted for. With their landlords, the Stuarts, the family of Burnes were privileged to maintain a degree of intimacy much in excess of ordinary tenants. Younger sons of the laird of Inchbreck, John Stuart was Professor of Mathematics in Marischal College, and Robert, merchant in Aberdeen, was some time Provost of that city. Now, in the register of Fetteresso parish, we find that these gentlemen witnessed—the former in 1731, the latter in 1733—the baptisms of John and Robert Burnes, grandsons of James Burnes, tenant at Brawlinmuir, on the Inchbreck estate. And further, we have found that when Robert Burnes, farmer at Clochnahill, the Poet's grandfather, was involved in pecuniary straits, he, in February 1744, received from ex-Provost Stuart of Aberdeen a considerable loan.²

Among those who actively espoused the cause of Prince Charles Edward in 1745 was Captain James Stuart, younger son of William Stuart of Inchbreck, who, after serving with the royal army in Holland, attached himself to Lord Ogilvie's Regiment on behalf of the Prince. He composed a journal or itinerary of the "March of the Highland Army," commencing at Holyrood-house on the 11th October 1745, and continuing till Monday, 21st April 1746, or five days after the defeat at Culloden.³ And that record, while it does not contain the names of his followers, affords evidence that by a

---

¹ *Supra*, p. 9.
² *Supra*, pp. 23, 24.
³ "March of the Highland Army in the years 1745-6, by Captain James Stuart, of Lord Ogilvie's Regiment," included in *The Miscellany* of the *Spalding Club*, vol. i., Aberdeen, 1841. After undergoing many privations, Captain Stuart succeeded in making his escape to France, where he was created a Knight of St. Louis; he died in 1776.

body of adherents he was accompanied to the capital. In his "Address to Edinburgh" the Poet writes :—

> Ev'n I, who sing in rustic lore,
> Haply my sires have left their shed,
> And fac'd grim danger's loudest roar,
> Bold following where your fathers led.

If these lines have any real meaning, there must be a reference to the only occasion when the burghers of Edinburgh evinced a disposition to support the Jacobite cause. They did so in September 1745, on the Prince's arrival in the city, and it may be assumed that the Poet refers to his progenitors having taken part in the affair. That his great-grandfather, Robert Burnes of Clochnahill farm, was somehow involved in the troubles of the Rebellion is attested by an undeviating tradition.

A question arises. From his advanced age, it is obvious that the farmer at Clochnahill was not personally concerned in the rising of 1745. Nor was his son William, the Poet's father,[1] for there was found among his papers, and still exists, a parochial certificate, testifying that he had no concern "in the late wicked rebellion." May not his uncle Robert, who was some time associated with his father in the management of Clochnahill farm, and who for nearly forty years worked as a gardener in England, have followed Captain James Stuart to Edinburgh, and so have been the indirect cause of the family impoverishment? May not Robert's departure into England be so accounted for?

The humble abode in which Burns was born stands on the high road to Maybole, and is distant about three miles from the ancient

---

[1] While it seems beyond reasonable doubt that Burns's ancestors were more or less actively concerned in the Jacobite cause, and that the family fortunes suffered in consequence, it seems also clear that the Poet's father did not personally take part in rebellion against the reigning house. He was not born till after 1715; and in 1745 he was engaged as a gardener in the vicinity of Edinburgh.

town of Ayr. The road runs close beside "Alloway's auld haunted kirk," and crosses the Doon at a lovely spot where stands that handsome memorial structure which has a primary claim to be specially spoken of as BURNS'S MONUMENT. From the new bridge (by which the river is now crossed in a straighter course) a fine view can be had of the "Auld Brig," the monument, and the "banks and braes" of the classic stream. There, if we call to mind the Poet's lines, as in Tam o' Shanter, *e.g.*, the place seems to live and move as of old at his immortalizing touch.

The "auld clay biggin'," where the Poet first saw the light, was for many years used as a wayside ale-house. Now, however, it is fittingly owned and cared for by the trustees of the monument. The *licence* is dispensed with, and in the neat little hall behind the cottage many interesting and valuable Burns relics are exhibited.[1] From all parts of our own country, and from many far-off lands, the throng of pilgrims to this natal scene yearly increases; until now, in the holiday season, the visitors number thousands weekly—a great and growing evidence that he who was born there spoke and still is speaking straight to the hearts of men and women everywhere.

A few days after the Poet's birth, the stability of the "clay biggin'" was so severely tried that mother and infant were removed for safety to a neighbouring dwelling—

> 'Twas then a blast o' Januar' wind
> Blew hansel in on Robin

—stormy presage of his uniquely rugged and passion-swayed

---

[1] William Burness, on leaving the neighbourhood in 1777, sold the cottage and the feu-right of his adjoining seven acres to the Ayr Shoemakers' Corporation. The hall was erected in 1847; and in 1881 the property was acquired by the trustees of the monument, at a cost of £4000.

career. The frail building having been repaired and strengthened, mother and child returned to their home, and there the family dwelt until Robert had reached his eighth year.

Of these childhood years very little is definitely known. As regards general worth and intelligence, William Burness and his wife were clearly above the average small farmers and cotters of their time. The Poet's mother is described by one who knew her intimately, as a woman of great sagacity, and pleasant, easy manner, having at her command a remarkable store of ballads and traditionary tales, by means of which she early kindled and fed the imagination of her wondrously-gifted eldest son. In this same direction, an aged relative of the family, Betty Davidson by name, exercised a lasting influence on the Poet's mind. Burns himself says of her :—

> In my infant and boyish days, I owed much to an old woman, who resided in the family, remarkable for her ignorance, credulity, and superstition. She had, I suppose, the largest collection in the country, of tales and songs concerning devils, ghosts, fairies, brownies, witches, warlocks, spunkies, kelpies, elf-candles, deadlights, wraiths, apparitions, cantraips, giants, enchanted towers, dragons, and other trumpery. This cultivated the latent seeds of poetry ; but had so strong an effect on my imagination, that to this hour, in my nocturnal rambles, I sometimes keep a sharp look-out in suspicious places ; and though nobody can be more sceptical than I am in such matters, yet it often takes an effort of philosophy to shake off these idle terrors.

Also, from the earliest dawn of intelligence, he was accustomed to those humble yet noble scenes of family industry, piety, and peace which he has depicted, *from the life*, in the "Cotter's Saturday Night."

In 1766, the family removed from their Alloway home, and entered the farm of Mount Oliphant, two miles inland. In his sixth year, Robert attended a small country school at Alloway Mill. In

BIRTH AND EARLY ENVIRONMENTS.

May 1765, William Burness and a few of his neighbours joined in starting a school nearer at hand, and employed one John Murdoch as master. Fortunately, Murdoch, though young, was already a man of well-cultured mind, and in many respects a born teacher. Compared with modern systems of *cramming*, his methods seem to have been far more truly educational—well suited, indeed, to draw out and develop the thinking powers of the children under his charge. He was a respected friend and frequent visitor of the Burness family, and has left a most interesting account of the school-days of his great pupil. He states that Robert and his younger brother Gilbert were by far his aptest pupils. They were generally at the upper end of their classes, even when competing with boys much older than themselves. It is remarkable that this able and worthy man then considered Gilbert the brighter of the two boys. Now, judging from his correspondence, Gilbert Burns was a clever, scholarly man for his station. At school he may have *seemed* brighter than his elder brother, while in Robert's mind and heart were greater, stronger thoughts and feelings—a deeper though more silently-flowing stream of rich imaginings. At this early stage, Murdoch was mistaken in his estimate of the youthful Poet's gifts, but William Burness was not so mistaken; he having early perceived in his eldest son promise of extraordinary powers of thought and feeling, which led him to say that " something wonderful would yet be seen and heard of that boy."

Murdoch further tells us that, along with the usual branches of elementary education, he tried to teach his pupils church music.

> Here they [Robert and Gilbert] were left far behind by all the rest of the school. Robert's ear, in particular, was remarkably dull, and his voice untunable. It was long before I could get them to distinguish one tune from another. . . . Certainly, if any person who knew the two boys had been

asked which of them was the most likely to court the muses, he would surely never have guessed that Robert had a propensity of that kind.

And yet this was he whose writings but a few years afterwards proclaimed him one of the greatest and sweetest of the world's song-makers.

In 1768, Robert's tenth year, Murdoch left the Alloway neighbourhood for a time; and now, while he ever carefully attended to the *home training* of his family, William Burness himself undertook and continued the general education of his boys. Of this period Gilbert says:—

> There being no school near us, and our little services being already useful on the farm, my father undertook to teach us arithmetic in the winter evenings by candle-light—and in this way my two elder sisters received all the education they ever received. . . . My father was for some time almost the only companion we had. He conversed familiarly on all subjects with us, as if we had been men; and was at great pains, while we accompanied him on the labours of the farm, to lead the conversation to such subjects as might increase our knowledge or confirm us in virtuous habits.

William Burness was also at pains to place in his boys' hands from time to time various volumes of a solidly educative kind; and Gilbert further states that "Robert read these books with an avidity and industry scarcely to be equalled, no book being so voluminous as to slacken his industry, or so antiquated as to damp his researches."

Thus for several years—he dutifully attending to the secular and religious instructions of his worthy father, eagerly perusing such books as were placed at his command, and, if possible, still more eagerly feasting his youthful fancy on the wealth of ballad and story sung and recited in the family circle—the Poet's education steadily proceeded.

In his fourteenth year, Robert and Gilbert attended week about during a summer quarter, for writing lessons, at Dalrymple parish

BIRTH AND EARLY ENVIRONMENTS.

school. About a year afterwards, Murdoch having returned to Ayr as English master, Robert spent three weeks with him, revising English grammar and learning French. At the three weeks' end master and pupil were reluctantly parted, Robert's services being required for harvesting at Mount Oliphant. During this brief term of study, he manifested gigantic powers of acquirement. Not only did he revise his English grammar, and learn some French, but he also acquired a smattering of Latin. Considering, however, how scant his opportunity, no one need be surprised when it is asserted that Burns knew little French and less Latin. Regarding the latter language he once remarked, "All I know of Latin is contained in three words—*Omnia vincit Amor.*"

Excepting the short time he afterwards spent at the Kirkoswald seminary, the foregoing is all the school training he received. It was not much; but obviously it was employed by a marvellous mind, with a spirit of keen inquiry and unflagging zeal.

There still lingers, in the minds of many, considerable misapprehension as to the quality and extent of Burns's education. While, on the one hand, we cannot altogether agree with the statement that "not a boy in Scotland was better educated;" on the other hand, we are bound to disagree with those who think our Poet's education was, in things essential to his great mission, a "poor indifferent affair."

His time at school was indeed brief and broken. To him the doors of no academy or college were open. Almost from childhood, his was a lot taxed by anxious cares and hard, engrossing toils. Nevertheless, he enjoyed not a few advantages of the best educational kind. Perhaps the first of these we take to be his upbringing in a Scottish peasant home of outstanding industry, intelligence, and integrity,—a home where he early imbibed his characteristic love of independence, and hatred of everything that partook of unthinking bigotry, cruel tyranny, or worldly meanness. He was taught, too, under the watchful care of a father of notable enlightenment,—a father who neglected no opportunity and grudged no trouble in cultivating the intelligence of his family, and particularly the soaring mind and spirit of his eldest son. Be it further remembered, the more impressionable years of Burns's youth were spent in a neighbourhood where "Nature's face is fair" indeed—a beautiful country-side—where, as with living forms and voices, his rich imagination learned to commune with hill and dale, wood and stream, fields and flowers. Nor should we forget that his daily duties in the farm-yard and the fields nurtured in his great kind heart that fellow-feeling which he has so sweetly manifested towards the humbler creation,—the "ourie cattle" and "silly sheep," the "hapless bird" and "hunted hare," his "pet ewe Mailie" and his "auld mare Meg." Lastly, in comparing his works with his opportunities, even the poverty and the grinding toil of his boyhood and youth are not to be undervalued. For by these he learned to know and sympathize with the stern realities and struggles of careworn human life, wherein

> Man's inhumanity to man
> Makes countless thousands mourn.

In further endeavouring to portray the early life and surroundings of the Poet, we cannot do better than follow the example of his best biographers, in quoting at length from the graphic and interesting records left by his teacher, John Murdoch, his brother Gilbert, and by Burns himself.

Speaking of the time when Robert was summoned home from his three weeks' term of study in Ayr, Murdoch says:—

> Thus was I deprived of my very apt pupil, and consequently agreeable companion. I did not lose sight of him, however, but was a frequent visitant

at his father's house, and very often went, accompanied by one or two persons more intelligent than myself, that good William Burness might enjoy a mental feast. The father and son sat down with us, when we enjoyed a conversation, wherein solid reasoning, sensible remark, and a moderate seasoning of jocularity were so nicely blended as to render it palatable to all parties. Robert had a hundred questions to ask me about French, etc.; and the father, who had always rational information in view, had still some question to propose to my more learned friends, upon moral or natural philosophy, or some such interesting subject. Mrs. Burness, too, was of the party as much as possible:—

> But still the house affairs would draw her thence,
> Which ever as she could with haste despatch,
> She'd come again, and with a greedy ear
> Devour up their discourse,

and particularly that of her husband. At all times, and in all companies, she listened to *him* with a more marked attention than to anybody else. This worthy woman, Agnes Brown, had the most thorough esteem for her husband of any woman I ever knew. I can by no means wonder that she highly esteemed him; for I myself considered William Burness as by far the best of the human race that ever I had the pleasure of being acquainted with— and many a worthy character I have known. . . . He was a tender and affectionate father; he took pleasure in leading his children in the path of virtue; not in driving them, as some parents do, to the performance of duties to which they themselves are averse. . . . As he was at no time overbearing to inferiors, he was equally incapable of that paltry, pitiful spirit which induces some people to keep *booing* and *booing* in the presence of a great man. He always treated superiors with a becoming respect, but he never gave the smallest encouragement to aristocratical arrogance. But I must not pretend to give you a description of all the manly qualities, the rational and Christian virtues of the venerable William Burness. Time would fail me. I shall only add that he carefully practised every known duty, and avoided everything that was criminal; or, in the apostle's words, "Herein did he exercise himself in living a life void of offence towards God and towards men." . . . I have often wished, for the good of mankind, that it were as customary to honour and perpetuate the memory of those who excel in moral rectitude, as it is to extol what are called heroic actions; then would the mausoleum of the friend of my youth overtop and surpass most of those I see in Westminster Abbey. Although I cannot do justice to the character of this worthy man, yet you will perceive, from these few particulars, what kind of person *had the principal hand in the education of our Poet*.[1]

Regarding the family life and work at Mount Oliphant, Gilbert Burness speaks clearly and fully in his communication to Dr. Currie. He tells us that nothing could be more retired than their general manner of living. The soil of the farm was of the very poorest kind, and, for the times, too highly rented.

> In consequence of this—he continues—my father soon came into difficulties which were increased by the loss of several of his cattle by accidents and disease. To the buffetings of misfortune we could only oppose hard labour and the most rigid economy. We lived very sparingly. For several years butcher's meat was a stranger in the house, while all the members of the family exerted themselves to the utmost of their strength, and rather beyond it, in the labours of the farm. My brother, at the age of thirteen, assisted in threshing the crop of corn, and at fifteen was the principal labourer on the farm, for we had no hired servant, male or female. The anguish of mind we felt at our tender years under these straits and difficulties was very great. To think of our father growing old (for he was now above fifty), broken down by the long fatigues of his life, with a wife and five other children, and in a declining state of circumstances; these reflections produced in my brother's mind and mine sensations of the deepest distress. I doubt not but the hard labour and sorrow of this period of his life was in a great measure the cause of that depression of spirits with which Robert was so often afflicted through his whole life afterwards. At this time he was almost constantly afflicted in the evenings with a dull headache, which, at a future period of his life, was exchanged for a palpitation of the heart, and a threatening of fainting and suffocation in the night-time.

In 1787, Burns penned his famous autobiographical sketch sent to Dr. Moore,[2] in which, as we might expect, he, best and most graphically of all, recounts the story of his early life.

---

[1] John Murdoch: see sketch of his career, vol. ii. p. 107.   [2] See vol. ii. p. 84.

At those years—he says—I was by no means a favourite with anybody. I was a good deal noted for a retentive memory, a stubborn sturdy something in my disposition, and an enthusiastic idiot piety. I say *idiot* piety, because I was then but a child. Though it cost the schoolmaster some thrashings, I made an excellent English scholar, and by the time I was ten or eleven years of age, I was a critic in substantives, verbs, and particles. . . . The earliest composition that I recollect taking pleasure in was "The Vision of Mirza," and a hymn of Addison's beginning, "How are thy servants blest, O Lord!" I particularly remember one stanza which was music to my boyish ear :—

> For though on dreadful whirls we hung
> High on the broken wave.

I met with these pieces in *Mason's English Collection*, one of my school-books. The two first books I ever read in private, and which gave me more pleasure than any two books I ever read since, were *The Life of Hannibal* and *The History of Sir William Wallace*. Hannibal gave my young ideas such a turn that I used to strut in raptures up and down after the recruiting drum and bagpipe, and wish myself tall enough to be a soldier ; while the story of Wallace poured a Scottish prejudice into my veins, which will boil along there till the flood-gates of life shut in eternal rest. . . . The farm [Mount Oliphant] proved a ruinous bargain ; and to clench the misfortune, we fell into the hands of a factor, who sat for the picture I have drawn of one in my tale of "Twa Dogs."[1] My father was advanced in life when he married ; I was the eldest of seven children ; and he, worn out by early hardships, was unfit for labour. My father's spirit was soon irritated, but not easily broken. There was a freedom in his lease in two years more, and to weather these two years we retrenched our expenses. We lived very poorly. I was a dexterous ploughman for my age ; and the next eldest to me was a brother [Gilbert] who could drive the plough very well, and help me to thrash the corn. A novel-writer might have viewed these scenes with some satisfaction ; but so did not I. My

---

[1] Puir *tenant bodies*, scant o' cash,
How they maun thole a *factor's* snash ;
He'll stamp an' threaten, curse an' swear
He'll *apprehend* them, *poind* their gear ;
While they maun stan' wi' aspect humble,
An' hear it a', an' fear an' tremble !

indignation yet boils at the recollection of the scoundrel factor's insolent threatening letters, which used to set us all in tears. This kind of life—the cheerless gloom of a hermit, with the unceasing moil of a galley-slave—brought me to my sixteenth year.

We are to think of Burns, then, at Mount Oliphant, as a hard-toiling farm lad, ungainly of manner, somewhat sullen of aspect, with little knowledge of the world, save what he acquired in the family circle, and from such books as he had by that time perused; his spirit already saddened and his bodily health impaired by the unusual cares and too heavy labours of his lot. So dragged along the weary years of his boyhood, until, amid his sorrows and toils, he was visited by that first bright dream of woman's love which warmed his care-chilled heart into song. Let the Poet himself tell about this interesting episode :—

> You know our country custom of coupling a man and woman together as partners in the labours of harvest. In my fifteenth autumn my partner was a bewitching creature a year younger than myself. My scarcity of English denies me the power of doing her justice in that language, but you know the Scotch idiom — she was a *bonnie, sweet, sonsie lass*. In short, she altogether, unwittingly to herself, initiated me in that delicious passion, which, in spite of disappointment, gin-horse prudence, and bookworm philosophy, I hold to be the first of human joys, our dearest blessing here below. How she caught the contagion I cannot tell; you medical people talk much of infection from breathing the same air, the touch, etc.; but I never expressly said I loved her. Indeed, I did not know myself why I liked so much to loiter behind with her when returning in the evening from our labours; why the tones of her voice made my heart-strings thrill like an Æolian harp; and particularly, why my pulse beat such a furious ratan, when I looked and fingered over her little hand to pick out the cruel nettle-stings and thistles. Among her other love-inspiring qualities she sang sweetly; and it was her favourite reel to which I attempted giving an embodied vehicle in rhyme. . . . Thus with me began Love and Poetry.

His youthful partner on the "hairst-rig" was Nellie Kilpatrick, daughter of the blacksmith who lent him *The Life of Wallace*, and the song he composed in honour of her charms was—

HANDSOME NELL.

Tune—"*I am a man unmarried.*"

O once I loved a bonnie lass,
    Ay, and I love her still;
And whilst that honour warms my breast,
    I'll love my handsome Nell.

As bonnie lasses I hae seen,
    And mony full as braw;
But, for a modest gracefu' mien,
    The like I never saw.

A bonnie lass, I will confess,
    Is pleasant to the e'e;
But, without some better qualities,
    She's no' the lass for me.

But Nellie's looks are blythe and sweet,
    And, what is best of a',
Her reputation is complete,
    And fair without a flaw.

She dresses aye sae clean and neat,
    Sae modest and genteel;
And then there's something in her gait
    Gars ony dress look weel.

A gaudy dress and gentle air
    May slightly touch the heart;
But it's innocence and modesty
    That polishes the dart.

> 'Tis this in Nellie pleases me,
> 'Tis this enchants my soul;
> For absolutely in my breast
> She reigns without control.

This song possesses a peculiar interest, being Burns's first. He afterwards said, "I composed it in a wild enthusiasm of passion; and to this hour, I never recollect it but my heart melts, and my blood sallies at the remembrance." He also spoke of it as a very "puerile and silly" performance. But, calling to mind that when he wrote it he was only a boy of fifteen, it may justly be considered no ordinary composition, but one giving, in some of its stanzas at least, rich promise of poetic grace and power.

Bearing generally on the foregoing period, and with more special reference to the question of the Poet's education, the following passage from his Autobiography may be quoted as showing what books, in addition to those used in school, he had read up to this stage :—"What I knew of ancient story was gathered from Salmon's and Guthrie's *Geographical Grammars;* and the ideas I had formed of modern manners, of literature and criticism, I got from the *Spectator.* These, with Pope's Works, some plays of Shakespeare, *Tull and Dickson on Agriculture, The Pantheon,* Locke's *Essay on the Human Understanding,* Stackhouse's *History of the Bible,* Justice's *British Gardener's Directory,* Boyle's *Lectures,* Allan Ramsay's Works, Taylor's *Scripture Doctrine of Original Sin, A Select Collection of English Songs,* and Hervey's *Meditations,* had formed the whole of my reading. The collection of songs was my *vade mecum.* I pored over them driving my cart, or walking to labour, song by song, verse by verse, carefully noting the true, tender, or sublime from affectation or fustian. I am convinced I owe to this practice much of my critic-craft, such as it is."

CHAPTER III.

FROM 1777-1784. AGE, 18-25. TARBOLTON, KIRKOSWALD, IRVINE.

The seven years we lived in Tarbolton parish were not marked by much literary improvements; but during this time the foundations were laid of certain habits in my brother's character which afterwards became but too prominent, and which malice and envy have taken delight to enlarge on. . . . Yet, I do not recollect, during these seven years, to have ever seen him intoxicated; nor was he at all given to drinking.

GILBERT BURNS.

HAVING spent eleven years of unsuccessful toil and struggle in Mount Oliphant, William Burness removed with his family to Lochlea, in the parish of Tarbolton. The farm then consisted of 130 acres of very indifferent soil, and was taken at twenty shillings an acre—a poor bargain, again, for the tenant. Lochlea is, in itself, somewhat bare and uninteresting, but from the hill-lands of the farm the outlook is both extensive and beautiful. Landward, there opens up some of the finest Ayrshire scenery; and seaward, the whole Firth of Clyde, with Arran, Cantyre, and Ailsa Craig for majestic background. The place probably owes its name to the little loch[1] which, though long since drained and cultivated, stood a few hundred yards from the farm-steading.

"It is," says the Poet, "during the time that we lived on this farm that my little story is most eventful." And, certainly, in these seven years he underwent several notable experiences.

---

[1] In 1878, when further operations for the better drainage of the site of the loch were being carried on, a very interesting discovery was made. The workmen came upon traces of an ancient lake-dwelling. Extensive excavations were executed, and the results were duly noted by antiquarian experts.

William Burness entered Lochlea at Whitsunday 1777; and, although there must have been much to do on the new farm, further proof of the father's anxious desire for Robert's education is found in the fact that, during this first summer, the Poet was sent to study at Kirkoswald, a rural village about a dozen miles south from Ayr. Of this, the last of his school-days, he says :—

> A circumstance in my life which made some alteration in my mind and manners was, that I spent my nineteenth summer on a smuggling coast, a good distance from home, at a noted school, to learn mensuration, surveying, dialling, etc., in which I made a pretty good progress; but I made a greater progress in the knowledge of mankind. The contraband trade was at this time very successful, and it sometimes happened to me to fall in with those who carried it on. Scenes of swaggering riot and roaring dissipation were till this time quite new to me; but I was no enemy to social life. Here, though I learnt to fill my glass, and to mix without fear in a drunken squabble, yet I went on with a high hand with my geometry, till the sun entered Virgo—a month which is always a carnival in my bosom—when a charming *fillette*, who lived next door to the school, overset my trigonometry, and set me off at a tangent from the sphere of my studies. I struggled on, however, with my sines and co-sines for a few days more; but stepping into the garden one charming noon, to take the sun's altitude, there I met my angel—
>
> "Like Proserpine gathering flowers—
> Herself a fairer flower."
>
> It was in vain to think of doing any more good at school. The remaining week I stayed I did nothing but craze the faculties of my soul about her, or steal out to meet her. And the two last nights of my stay in the country, had sleep been a mortal sin, the image of this modest and innocent girl had kept me guiltless.

The village of Kirkoswald is fully twenty miles distant from Lochlea; but two reasons may be given in explanation of Burns having been sent for instruction so far from his home. First, it was "a noted school"[1] he attended; and, second, he was boarded

---

[1] See vol. ii.: Hugh Roger, the noted Kirkoswald teacher.

at little cost with his uncle, Samuel Brown,[1] at the farm of Ballochneil, a mile out of the village. The parish takes up some six miles of rugged, rocky Ayrshire coast, well-suited for the purposes of the smuggler. During last century contraband trade with the Isle of Man and the Continent was largely and daringly carried on in this very neighbourhood in which the Poet spent his "nineteenth summer." At such an age, to a nature like his, the secret, dangerous, and romantic aspects of the smuggler's career would present a stirring interest. Even amongst the more settled farming class, the question with many was, not as to whether the traffic was right or wrong, but how best to share in its profits with impunity. In such circumstances, we can easily believe that our youthful Bard's impulsive spirit and keen curiosity sometimes led him to accompany the midnight expedition to lonely hiding-places among the hills or on the caverned coast, and brought him face to face with those scenes of "swaggering riot and roaring dissipation" of which he speaks. When, too, in after years, he filled the office of exciseman, his experiences among the Kirkoswald smugglers must have proved of much practical service to him. At Kirkoswald, Burns formed a close intimacy with a young man named Niven, whose family resided in the neighbourhood.[2] The two lads spent their spare time in rambling around the village, and engaging in friendly disputations on literary and social subjects, with a set view to sharpening each other's wits, and improving their powers of ready debate. According to Chambers, they asked several of their companions to come and take a side in these debates, but not one would do so; they only laughed at the young philosophers. The schoolmaster, hearing about these disputations, resolved to put a stop to them. He therefore, before the whole

---

[1] Brother of the Poet's mother, whose family belonged to Kirkoswald parish.
[2] See vol. ii. p. 143, on the Niven Family.

school, attempted to cast ridicule upon Burns and his companion on account of their pretentious debatings. The two, in answer, proceeded to justify their conduct, and at length enticed Roger to take a side in discussing, in presence of the scholars, the question, "Whether is a great general or a respectable merchant the most valuable member of society?" The schoolmaster confidently led off by taking the side of the "great general," Burns taking the opposite view. Roger is said to have been completely worsted in the controversy. "His hand," says Chambers, "was observed to shake; then his voice trembled, and he dissolved the house in a state of vexation pitiable to behold."

At Scottish farmhouses it was, and still is customary, after the labours of the day are over, for the sturdy youths of neighbouring farms to meet and engage in sundry trials of strength and agility, such as running, leaping, wrestling, etc. Burns took an active part in these exercises, and proved no mean antagonist in the friendly contest. Already, too, his sparkling wit and kindly ways made him the life of such humble rustic gatherings.

During his stay in this neighbourhood, long noted for its manly prowess, hard drinking, and lingering superstitions, he met with those characters which he afterwards sketched in "Tam o' Shanter" —Douglas Graham and his wife, tenants of Shanter Farm, "Souter Johnnie" and "Kirkton Jean," "the Miller" and "the Smith."

> O Tam! hadst thou but been sae wise
> As ta'en thy ain wife Kate's advice!
> She tauld thee weel thou was a skellum,
> A bletherin', blusterin', drunken blellum;
> That, frae November till October,
> Ae market-day thou wasna sober;
> That ilka melder, wi' the Miller,
> Thou sat as lang as thou had siller:

> That every naig was ca'd a shoe on,
> The Smith and thee gat roarin' fou on;
> That at the Lord's house, even on Sunday,
> Thou drank wi' Kirkton Jean till Monday.
> She prophesied that late or soon
> Thou would be found deep drowned in Doon;
> Or catched wi' warlocks in the mirk,
> By Alloway's auld haunted kirk.

We have seen how the Poet's brief and last school-term was abruptly ended. Peggy Thomson, the damsel who set him off at a tangent from the sphere of his studies, is the heroine of his song, "Now westlin winds and slaughtering guns." It is worthy of remark that this *love-fit* was not such a passing affair as it has been represented. Years afterwards he is known to have entertained the idea of making Peggy his wife; and, on a subsequent meeting with her, he revised this song into its published form.

> I returned home—he says—very considerably improved. My reading was enlarged by the very important additions of Thomson's and Shenstone's works. I had seen human nature in a new phasis; and I engaged several of my school-fellows to keep up a literary correspondence with me. This improved me in composition. I had met with a collection of letters by the wits of Queen Anne's reign, and I pored over them most devoutly. I kept copies of any of my own letters that pleased me; and a comparison between them and the compositions of most of my correspondents flattered my vanity. I carried this whim so far, that though I had not three-farthings' worth of business in the world, yet almost every post brought me as many letters as if I had been a plodding son of day-book and ledger.

He tells us that in his "seventeenth year, to give his manners a brush," he went, in defiance of his father's wish, to a country dancing-school. His statement that, because of this act of disobedience, his father took a kind of dislike to him, is contradicted by his brother Gilbert, who says:—

> I wonder how Robert could attribute to our father that lasting resentment of his going to a dancing-school, against his will, of which he was incapable. I believe the truth was, that about this time he began to see the dangerous impetuosity of my brother's passions, as well as his not being amenable to counsel, which often irritated my father, and which he would naturally think a dancing-school was not likely to correct. But he was proud of Robert's genius, which he bestowed more expense on cultivating than on the rest of the family; and he was equally delighted with his warmth of heart and conversational powers. He had, indeed, that dislike of dancing-schools which Robert mentions; but so far overcame it during Robert's first month of attendance, that he permitted the rest of the family, who were fit for it, to accompany him during the second month.

In these conflicting statements, Robert and Gilbert refer, in all likelihood, to different occasions—Robert to the Mount Oliphant, and Gilbert to the Lochlea, period. But, in any case, we cannot help thinking that in his use of the word *dislike* the Poet does a regrettable injury to his worthy father's memory. It is pleasing, however, to know that he felt a deep and lasting sorrow for this, his first act of rebellion against parental authority; and yet, it is sad to think that it is but one among so many instances in which we see Burns's nobler nature cast down in agonizing remorse, because of too easy yielding to the " witching voice " of his turbulent passions.

For all that is authentically known of his life for several years after his return from Kirkoswald, we are indebted to the narratives left by himself and his brother. The Poet's various love entanglements form the burden of both accounts.

> My heart—says the Poet—was completely tinder, and was eternally lighted up by some goddess or another. . . . At plough, scythe, or reap-hook I feared no competitor, and thus I set absolute want at defiance; and as I never cared further for my labours than while I was in actual exercise, I spent the evenings in the way after my own heart. A country lad seldom carries on a love-

adventure without an assisting confidant. I possessed a curiosity, zeal, and intrepid dexterity that recommended me as a proper second on these occasions; and I daresay I felt as much pleasure in being in the secret of half the loves of the parish of Tarbolton, as ever did statesman in knowing the intrigues of half the courts of Europe. The grave sons of science, ambition, or avarice, baptize these things by the name of follies; but to the sons and daughters of labour and poverty, they are matters of the most serious nature. To them the ardent hope, the stolen interview, the tender farewell, are the greatest and most delicious parts of their enjoyments.

After the above from his own pen, we are prepared to learn that the amorous genius of Burns produced songs on nearly all the handsome girls in Tarbolton; also one song, "The Tarbolton Lasses," in which he celebrates them as a body. Two courtships, however, which he himself at this time carried on, call for special notice. For over half a year he laid siege to the affections of the youthful housekeeper at Montgomerie Castle, at the end of which time he was driven off with the information that she was already betrothed to another. To this girl he inscribed the attractive little song, " Montgomerie's Peggy." He states in his Commonplace Book that he began this courtship in mere love-making frolic, but soon found himself holding Peggy in warm affection, and that it cost him " some heartaches to get rid of the affair,"—a statement which pleasantly reminds us of a fact which can be traced throughout his career, viz. that, amid all his impulsive waywardness, the *heart* of Robert Burns ever throbbed true to deep-rooted dictates of generous, manly feeling. The poet's passion for Ellison Begbie was a more prolonged and earnest matter. She was the daughter of a Galston farmer, and was at this time serving-maid to a family who resided at Cessnock, fully two miles from Lochlea. To this damsel he addressed, in 1780-81, four letters, notable for their sentiments of respect and admiration, notable also as being among the earliest of his letters which have been preserved to us. She is the heroine of two at least of his songs written at this juncture—"The Lass o' Cessnock Banks" and "Bonnie Peggy Alison."

Moved by his deep attachment to Ellison Begbie, and his anxious desire to find himself in a position to marry her, if she should finally accept his suit, he formed the plan of going to Irvine to learn the flax-dressing business. For some time previously, he and Gilbert had rented land from their father, and were growing flax on their own account. The brothers hoped that, by both growing the flax and dressing it for the market, they would make handsome profits. It was a prudent, sensible scheme; but it ended in failure. Robert went to Irvine to learn the trade of *heckling*, but went in a sadly dejected and unsettled frame of mind. For Ellison did not respond to his epistolary, lyrical, and personal advances. She would count him as a friend; but she would not accept him as her lover and prospective husband.

The Poet's Irvine episode is best told in his own words:—

> My twenty-third year was to me an important era. Partly through whim, and partly that I wished to set about doing something in life,[1] I joined a flax-dresser in a neighbouring town to learn his trade. This was an unlucky affair. My [here he charges his Irvine partner in trade with having defrauded him] and to finish the whole, as we were giving a welcome carousal to the New Year, the shop took fire and was burnt to ashes, and I was left, like a true poet, not worth a sixpence. I was obliged to give up this scheme: the clouds of misfortune were gathering thick round my father's head; and, what was worst of all, he was visibly far gone in consumption; and to crown my distresses, a *belle fille* whom I adored, and who had pledged her soul to meet me in the field of matrimony, jilted me, with peculiar circumstances of mortification. The finishing evil which brought up the rear of this infernal file was my constitutional melancholy being increased to such a degree, that for three months I was in a state of mind scarcely to be envied by the helpless wretches who have got their *mittimus*—"Depart from me, ye accursed."

---

[1] Gilbert speaks more explicitly on this point, stating that Robert's great desire at this time was to be in a position to marry.

> From this adventure I learned something of a town life; but the principal thing which gave my mind a turn was a friendship I formed with a young fellow, a very noble character, but a hapless son of misfortune. . . . His mind was fraught with independence, magnanimity, and every manly virtue. I loved and admired him to a degree of enthusiasm, and of course strove to imitate him. In some measure I succeeded. I had pride before, but he taught it to flow in proper channels. His knowledge of the world was vastly superior to mine, and I was all attention to learn. He was the only man I ever saw who was a greater fool than myself where woman was the presiding star; but he spoke of illicit love with the levity of a sailor, which hitherto I had regarded with horror. Here his friendship did me a mischief. . . .[1]

Truth to tell, the Poet's Irvine experiences seem to have had, in more ways than one, a baneful influence over his mind and conduct. Thither he repaired, gloomy and cast down because of disappointment in his ardent courtship of Ellison Begbie. Hitherto his habits were frugal and temperate, his mind reverent and pure. But in Irvine he was assailed by temptations on every hand; and in his dull, dejected state of mind, his principles became weakened by the taint of evil surroundings. Indeed, his situation was hapless in the extreme. Rejected by the idol of his love; swindled by his partner, Peacock; driven by his own passionate melancholy, and lured by boon companions into excitement and unwonted excesses; unsuccessful in his occupation; and worn down with ill health; finding no satisfaction in the present, and seeing only darkness in the future;—little wonder that among the older people in Irvine, whose grandfathers had seen and known the Poet, there lingered the tradition of him as a deeply-melancholy, strangely-gifted, erratic youth.

The account of Burns's stay in Irvine would be very incomplete without the following beautiful and touchingly suggestive letter which he, when but twenty-two years of age, penned to his father

[1] Richard Brown; see vol. ii. p. 332.

four days prior to that New Year's Day carousal in which the *heckling-shop* was burnt to the ground :—

IRVINE, *December* 27, 1781.

HONOURED SIR,—I have purposely delayed writing, in the hope that I should have the pleasure of seeing you on New Year's Day ; but work comes so hard upon us, that I do not choose to be absent on that account, as well as for some other little reasons, which I shall tell you at meeting. My health is nearly the same as when you were here, only my sleep is a little sounder ; and, on the whole, I am rather better than otherwise, though I mend by very slow degrees. The weakness of my nerves has so debilitated my mind, that I dare neither review past events nor look forward into futurity ; for the least anxiety or perturbation in my breast produces most unhappy effects on my whole frame. Sometimes, indeed, when for an hour or two my spirits are a little lightened, I *glimmer* a little into futurity ; but my principal, and indeed my only pleasurable employment, is looking backwards and forwards in a moral and religious way. I am quite transported at the thought that ere long, perhaps very soon, I shall bid an eternal adieu to all the pains, and uneasinesses, and disquietudes of this weary life, for I assure you I am heartily tired of it ; and, if I do not very much deceive myself, I could contentedly and gladly resign it.

"The soul, uneasy and confined at home,
Rests and expatiates in a life to come."

It is for this reason I am more pleased with the 15th, 16th, and 17th verses of the 7th chapter of Revelation[1] than with any ten times as many verses in the whole Bible, and would not exchange the noble enthusiasm with which they inspire me for all that this world has to offer. As for this world, I despair of ever making a figure in it. I am not formed for the bustle of the busy, nor the flutter of the gay. I shall never again be capable of entering into such

---

[1] 15. Therefore are they before the throne of God, and serve him day and night in his temple ; and he that sitteth on the throne shall dwell among them.
16. They shall hunger no more, neither thirst any more ; neither shall the sun light on them, nor any heat.
17. For the Lamb, which is in the midst of the throne, shall feed them, and shall lead them unto living fountains of waters ; and God shall wipe away all tears from their eyes.

scenes. Indeed I am altogether unconcerned at the thoughts of this life. I foresee that poverty and obscurity probably await me: I am in some measure prepared, and daily preparing to meet them. I have but just time and paper to return you my grateful thanks for the lessons of virtue and piety you have given me, which were too much neglected at the time of giving them; but which, I hope, have been remembered ere it is yet too late. Present my dutiful respects to my mother, and my compliments to Mr. and Mrs. Muir; and with wishing you a merry New Year's Day, I shall conclude. I am, honoured sir, your dutiful son,

ROBERT BURNS.

P.S.—My meal is nearly out; but I am going to borrow, till I get more.

The wild carousal and the blazing factory stand in strange, sad contrast with the almost simultaneous writing of such a letter as this. Only, the marvel is lessened, and the pity is deepened, when we remember that the contrast occurs in the life of Robert Burns.

Returning from Irvine in March 1782, the Poet manfully resumed his farm-work and his wonted steady and temperate manner of living. His brother states that at no period was Robert more kindly and attractive in the home circle or among his humble associates in daily toil.

> Rhyme—he says—except some religious pieces that are in print, I had given up; but meeting with Fergusson's Scottish Poems, I strung anew my wildly-sounding lyre with emulating vigour. The addition of two more authors to my library gave me great pleasure; Sterne and Mackenzie—*Tristram Shandy* and *The Man of Feeling*—were my bosom favourites. . . . I had usually half a dozen or more pieces on hand; taking up one or other, as it suited the momentary tone of my mind, and dismissing the work as it bordered on fatigue. My passions, when once lighted up, raged like very devils, till they got vent in rhyme; and then the conning over my verses, like a spell, soothed all into quiet.

The religious pieces referred to are "Winter—a Dirge," "A Prayer in the Prospect of Death," "A Prayer written under the Pressure of Violent Anguish," and paraphrases of the First Psalm and the

Nineteenth. These seem to have been for the most part written amid his gloom and misfortunes in Irvine. We cannot refrain from quoting some of those serious verses, as showing, in religious light, how deeply Burns at this time abased himself because of his aberrations, and with what sterling piety his penitent spirit trembled back to the God of mercy, yearned for the peace of holiness, and prayed for the strength of manly faith.

A PRAYER IN THE PROSPECT OF DEATH.

O Thou unknown, Almighty Cause
  Of all my hope and fear,
In whose dread Presence, ere an hour,
  Perhaps I must appear.

If I have wandered in those paths
  Of life I ought to shun;
As something, loudly, in my breast,
  Remonstrates I have done—

Thou know'st that Thou hast formed me
  With passions wild and strong;
And list'ning to their witching voice
  Has often led me wrong.

Where human weakness has come short,
  Or frailty stepped aside,
Do Thou, ALL-GOOD—for such Thou art—
  In shades of darkness hide.

Where with intention I have erred,
  No other plea I have,
But, Thou art good; and Goodness still
  Delighteth to forgive.

A PRAYER, WRITTEN UNDER THE PRESSURE OF VIOLENT ANGUISH.

O Thou great Being! what Thou art
 Surpasses me to know;
Yet sure I am, that known to Thee
 Are all Thy works below.

Thy creature here before Thee stands,
 All wretched and distrest;
Yet sure those ills that wring my soul
 Obey Thy high behest.

Sure Thou, Almighty, canst not act
 From cruelty or wrath!
O, free my weary eyes from tears,
 Or close them fast in death!

But if I must afflicted be
 To suit some wise design;
Then man my soul with firm resolves,
 To bear, and not repine!

It is notorious that several of these stanzas (particularly the third stanza of the former Prayer) have been by some people loudly objected to as *presumptuous, and unsound in doctrine*. Now, in that third stanza we *do not* find a " presumptuous excuse for sin " on the ground of overmastering passions; but we *do* find a sincere acknowledgment of sin, and the calm statement of a tremendous *fact* of the Poet's own great keen consciousness. It is perhaps uncharitable to characterize such objections as mere narrow-viewed, sanctimonious cavilling. Rather, remembering that Burns did not in these verses write as a cool-blooded, systematic theologian, but as a *man of bounding passions* writhing in wretchedness and remorse on account of his faults and misfortunes, the question may confidently be appealed to the opinion of the more generous and enlightened of the author's fellow-men, and judgment humbly left to the All-knowing and All-pitiful Tribunal, to which these prayers were, we venture to think, devoutly and trustfully addressed.

> Who made the heart, 'tis He alone
>   Decidedly can try us ;
> He knows each chord, its various tone,
>   Each spring, its various bias :
> Then at the balance let's be mute,
>   We never can adjust it ;
> What's *done* we partly may compute,
>   We know not what's *resisted*.

Moved by the fresh inspiration of which the Poet speaks, he produced various pieces, the most noteworthy of which is his "Death and Dying Words of poor Mailie"—a poem justly admired for its quaint conception and kindly, homely humour. It is probable that at this time he also gave forth in their well-known finished form the three famous songs, "Corn Rigs," "My Nannie, O," and "Mary Morrison." Critics may not agree as to who were the respective heroines of these songs ; but there is no question about the pre-eminent power and beauty of the songs themselves. Herein the matchless lyric genius of Burns already amply proclaimed itself. Professor Blackie, no ordinary authority on songs and song-makers, says :—

> In these poems, which were composed at Tarbolton, while his father still lived, and before the young lyrist had attained what the Scotch law calls the perfect age of five-and-twenty, we discover all the genuine warmth, unaffected simplicity, and easy grace of truthful nature, which will often be sought for in vain in the lyrical productions of the most accomplished poets of the most

THE BACHELORS' CLUB.

refined ages. Nothing conventional, nothing artificial, nothing affected or overstrained, here interferes to disturb the harmonious impression made by the utterance of the most finely modulated emotions, in an atmosphere and amid a scenery in which they seem to repose as naturally as a child in the bosom of its mother. They are a picture of rural nature, as much as they are the outpouring of an impassioned singer; they are not only eminently poetical and musical, but strikingly biographical; and stand here, therefore, as a scene in the life of the greatest love-poet of modern times, with a more vivid portraiture than the pen of the most finished master of descriptive eloquence could achieve.

Reverting to Burns's twenty-second year, the part he took in the Tarbolton Bachelors' Club again reminds us of his eager desire for social and intellectual excitement. From the record of the club's proceedings, we learn that in 1780 some half-dozen youths (among whom was Gilbert Burns) resolved, apparently at Robert's instigation, to form themselves into an association, under such rules and regulations that, while they should forget their cares and labours in mirth and diversion, they might not transgress the bounds of innocence and decorum.

At the first meeting, held on Halloween 1780, the Poet was elected president for the night, and the club proceeded to discuss this question:—

> Suppose a young man, bred a farmer, but without any fortune, has it in his power to marry either of two women, the one a girl of large fortune, but neither handsome in person, nor agreeable in conversation, yet who can manage the household affairs of a farm well enough; the other of them, a girl every way agreeable in person, conversation, and behaviour, but without any fortune: Which of them shall he choose?

The meetings were held monthly, and mental exercise was varied by social entertainment of a material kind. The members' indulgence in creature comforts was very moderate, however, no member being allowed to expend more than threepence per meeting.

Some of the other questions discussed were :—

> Whether is the savage man, or the peasant of a civilised country, in the most happy condition?
>
> Whether do we derive more happiness from love or friendship?
>
> Whether, between friends who have no reason to doubt each other's friendship, there should be any reserve?

In the fixing of such themes for debate, the mind and hand of Burns can be surely traced; more particularly so in the devising of Rule X. of the Club Regulations.

> RULE X.—Every man proper for a member of this society must have a frank, honest, open heart; above anything dirty or mean; and must be a professed lover of one or more of the female sex. No haughty, self-conceited person, who looks upon himself as superior to the rest of the club; and especially, no mean-spirited, worldly mortal, whose only will is to heap up money, shall upon any pretence whatever be admitted. In short, the proper person for this society is a cheerful, honest-hearted lad, who, if he has a friend that is true, and a mistress that is kind, and as much wealth as genteely to make both ends meet, is just as happy as this world can make him.

Among the Poet's papers there were found some notes showing that he had been at pains to prepare for the work of the society. One paper contains the heads of a speech on what several biographers have characterized as the *imprudent side* of the debate for the opening night. But, if we refrain, as Burns did, from attaching more importance to the "large fortune" than it really deserves in questions of this kind, we shall admit that, in supporting the claims of the "every way agreeable" though fortuneless lass, he advocated the more unselfish, unworldly, and *natural* choice.

To the Poet's marked social and friendly instincts, we may also attribute his early and enthusiastic participation in the booncompanionships and merry-makings of Freemasonry.[1]

From the Minutes of the Bachelors' Club we learn that in May

---

[1] See Appendix: on Burns and Freemasonry.

DAVID SILLARS.

1781 David Sillar[1] was admitted a member. He was for some years an intimate friend of Burns, and to him was addressed the "Epistle to Davie, a Brother Poet." To Sillar's pen we owe the following very interesting account of the Poet's personal appearance and general way of life during the closing years of the Lochlea period :—

> Mr. Robert Burns was some time in the parish of Tarbolton prior to my acquaintance with him. His social disposition easily procured him acquaintance; but a certain satirical seasoning, with which he and all poetical geniuses are in some degree influenced, while it set the rustic circle in a roar, was not unaccompanied by its kindred attendant, suspicious fear. I recollect hearing his neighbours observe he had a great deal to say for himself, and that they suspected his principles [meaning, we presume, his orthodoxy]. He wore the only tied hair in the parish; and in the church, his plaid, which was of a particular colour, I think fillemot, he wrapped in a particular manner round his shoulders. These surmises, and his exterior, had such a magical influence on my curiosity, as made me particularly solicitous of his acquaintance. Whether my acquaintance with Gilbert was casual or premeditated, I am not now certain. By him I was introduced not only to his brother, but to the whole of that family, where in a short time I became a frequent, and, I believe, not unwelcome visitant. After the commencement of my acquaintance with the Bard, we frequently met upon Sundays at church, when, between sermons, instead of going with our friends or lasses to the inn, we often took a walk in the fields. In these walks I have frequently been struck by his facility in addressing the fair sex; and many times, when I have been bashfully anxious how to express myself, he would have entered into conversation with them with the greatest ease and freedom; and it was generally a deathblow to our conversation, however agreeable, to meet a female acquaintance. Some of the few opportunities of a noontide walk that a country life allows her laborious sons he spent on the banks of the river, or in the woods in the neighbourhood of Stair, a situation peculiarly adapted to the genius of a rural bard. Some book (especially one of those mentioned in his letter to Mr. Murdoch) he always carried, and read when not otherwise employed. It was likewise his custom to read at table. In one of my visits to Lochlea, in time of a sowen supper, he was so

---

[1] David Sillar : see vol. ii. p. 200.

intent on reading, I think *Tristram Shandy*, that his spoon falling out of his hand, made him exclaim, in a tone scarcely imitable, "Alas, poor Yorick!" Such was Burns, and such were his associates, when, in May 1781, I was admitted a member of the Bachelors' Club.

It has been already noted that as early as 1782, when Robert returned from Irvine, the temporal prospects of the Burness family were becoming darkly clouded. The farm was not paying, and times were at a low ebb for the upland farmer. The father, too, was now quite unfit for labour, and fast breaking up. The woful situation at Lochlea is vividly sketched by a few lines in the *Autobiography*:—

> For four years we lived comfortably on this farm; but, a difference commencing between him [the Poet's father] and his landlord as to terms, after three years tossing and whirling in the vortex of litigation, my father was just saved from the horrors of a jail, by a consumption, which, after two years' promises, kindly stepped in, and carried him away to "where the wicked cease from troubling, and the weary are at rest."

Two letters which the Poet wrote during his last year in Lochlea possess, in many ways, a unique biographical interest. They are addressed to his cousin, James Burness, writer, Montrose :—

LOCHLEA, 21*st* June 1783.

DEAR SIR,—My father received your favour of the 10th current, and as he has been for some months very poorly in health, and is, in his own opinion (and indeed in almost everybody's else), in a dying condition, he has only, with great difficulty, written a few farewell lines to each of his brothers-in-law. For this melancholy reason, I now hold the pen for him, to thank you for your kind letter, and to assure you, sir, that it shall not be my fault if my father's correspondence in the north die with him. My brother writes to John Caird, and to him I must refer you for the news of our family.

I shall only trouble you with a few particulars relative to the wretched state of this country. Our markets are exceedingly high—oatmeal 17d. and

18d. per peck, and not to be got even at that price. We have indeed been pretty well supplied with quantities of white peas from England and elsewhere, but that resource is likely to fail us, and what will become of us then, particularly the very poorest sort, Heaven only knows. This country, till of late, was flourishing incredibly in the manufacture of silk, lawn, and carpet-weaving; and we are still carrying on a good deal in that way, but much reduced from what it was. We had also a fine trade in the shoe way, but now entirely ruined, and hundreds driven to a starving condition on account of it. Farming is also at a very low ebb with us. Our lands, generally speaking, are mountainous and barren; and our landholders, full of ideas of farming gathered from the English and the Lothians, and other rich soils in Scotland, make no allowance for the odds of the quality of land, and consequently stretch us much beyond what in the event we will be found able to pay. We are also much at a loss for want of proper methods in our improvements of farming. Necessity compels us to leave our old schemes, and few of us have opportunities of being well informed in new ones. In short, my dear sir, since the unfortunate beginning of this American war, and its as unfortunate conclusion, this country has been, and still is, decaying very fast. Even in higher life, a couple of our Ayrshire noblemen, and the major part of our knights and squires, are all insolvent. A miserable job of a Douglas, Heron, & Co's bank, which no doubt you have heard of, has undone numbers of them; and imitating English and French, and other foreign luxuries and fopperies, has ruined as many more. There is a great trade of smuggling carried on along our coasts, which, however destructive to the interests of the kingdom at large, certainly enriches this corner of it, but too often at the expense of our morals. However, it enables individuals to make, at least for a time, a splendid appearance; but Fortune, as is usual with her when she is uncommonly lavish of her favours, is generally even with them at the last; and happy were it for numbers of them if she would leave them no worse than when she found them.

My mother sends you a small present of a cheese; 'tis but a very little one, as our last year's stock is sold off. . . .

I shall conclude this long letter with assuring you that I shall be very happy to hear from you, or any of our friends in your country, when opportunity serves.

My father sends you, probably for the last time in this world, his warmest wishes for your welfare and happiness; and my mother and the rest of the family desire to enclose their kind compliments to you, Mrs. Burness, and the rest of your family, along with those of, dear sir, your affectionate cousin.

LOCHLEA, 17th *February* 1784.

DEAR COUSIN,—I would have returned you my thanks for your kind favour of the 13th of December sooner, had it not been that I waited to give you an account of that melancholy event which, for some time past, we have from day to day expected.

On the 13th current I lost the best of fathers. Though, to be sure, we have had long warning of the impending stroke, still the feelings of nature claim their part, and I cannot recollect the tender endearments and parental lessons of the best of friends and ablest of instructors, without feeling what perhaps the calmer dictates of reason would partly condemn.

I hope my father's friends in your country will not let their connection in this place die with him. For my part, I shall ever with pleasure, with pride, acknowledge my connection with those who were allied by the ties of blood and friendship to a man whose memory I shall ever honour and revere.

I expect, therefore, my dear sir, you will not neglect any opportunity of letting me hear from you, which will very much oblige, my dear cousin, yours sincerely.

Every unprejudiced reader will gladly agree with Lockhart when he says of these letters:—

> They are worthy of the strong understanding and warm heart of Burns; and, besides opening a pleasing view of the manner in which domestic affection was preserved between his father and the relations from whom the accidents of life had separated that excellent person in boyhood, they appear to me —written by a young and unknown peasant, in a wretched hovel, the abode of poverty, care, and disease—to be models of native good taste and politeness.

February 13, 1784, the day on which William Burness died, witnessed at Lochlea a truly touching and prophetic deathbed scene.

Mrs. Begg [the Poet's youngest sister, then in her fourteenth year]—says Chambers—remembers being at her father's bedside that morning, with no other company besides her brother Robert. Seeing her cry bitterly at the thought of parting with her dear father, he endeavoured to speak, but could only murmur a few words of comfort, such as might be suitable to a child, concluding with an injunction to her "to walk in virtue's paths, and shun every vice." After a pause, he said there was one of his family for whose future conduct he feared. He repeated the same expression, when the young Poet came up and said, "Oh, father, is it me you mean?" The old man said it was. Robert turned to the window, with the tears streaming down his manly cheeks, and his bosom swelling as if it would burst from the very restraint he put upon himself. The father had marked his son

"Misled by fancy's meteor ray,
By passion driven."

All the world knows that the dying parent's fears were only too well grounded. But, be it remembered, if William Burness lived long enough to tremble for Robert's future amid life's snares and pitfalls, he also lived long enough to experience bright hope in the rich promise, and joyous admiration in the actual perusal, of some of the unsurpassed early productions of his marvellously gifted eldest son.

Over the mortal remains of his beloved and venerated father, which were conveyed to their resting-place in Alloway Kirkyard, Robert reared a simple tombstone, and for an epitaph he wrote the well-known lines inscribed thereon :—

O ye whose cheek the tear of pity stains,
  Draw near with pious rev'rence, and attend!
Here lie the loving husband's dear remains,
  The tender father, and the gen'rous friend;
The pitying heart that felt for human woe;
  The dauntless heart that fear'd no human pride;
The friend of man—to vice alone a foe:
  For "even his failings lean'd to virtue's side."

May we not regard Burns as herein imparting to his father a share in his own deathless fame—a share well-merited, indeed, by the essential worth of the man, and because of the unwearying pains and ungrudging self-sacrifices he underwent to help Robert, through training of head and heart, to be what he is, as a Poet, to Scotland and the world.

CHAPTER IV.

FROM 1784–1786. AGE, 25–27. MOSSGIEL AND MAUCHLINE.

> I mind it weel in early date,
> When I was beardless, young, and blate,
> And first could thresh the barn, ...
> E'en then a wish, I mind its power,
> A wish that to my latest hour
> Shall strongly heave my breast;
> That I, for puir auld Scotland's sake,
> Some useful plan or book could make,
> Or sing a sang at least.
> *Epistle to the Guidwife o' Wauchope House.*

SHORTLY before the death of their father, Robert and Gilbert had leased the farm of Mossgiel, situated on the parish road between Tarbolton and Mauchline, distant about two miles from Lochlea and one mile from Mauchline village. The farm consisted of 118 acres of clayey upland, and, in its then undrained condition, must have been a very cold and backward subject for cultivation. During the latter years at Lochlea, the affairs of William Burness were, as already noticed, sorely embarrassed; hence Mossgiel was but indifferently stocked with what remained after settlement with the creditors at Lochlea.

In March 1784, however, the family entered the new farm, which was a joint concern among them, with a united determination toward frugal industry, and not without considerable prospect of success. Robert was strong and skilful in all kinds of farm-work;

Gilbert was steady and prudent in business affairs; while Mrs. Burness and her daughters were available for the duties of the household and dairy. But, in little over a year, the family was again confronted with disheartening failure and harassing poverty. The Poet himself thus sketches the situation :—

> I entered this farm with a full resolution—*Come, go to, I will be wise!* I read farming books, I calculated crops, I attended markets; and, in short, in spite of "the devil, and the world, and the flesh," I believe I should have been a wise man; but the first year, from unfortunately buying bad seed, and the second, from a late harvest, we lost half our crops. This overset all my wisdom, and I returned like "the dog to his vomit, and the sow that was washed to her wallowing in the mire." My brother wanted my hare-brained imagination, as well as my *social and amorous madness;* but in good sense, and every sober qualification, he was far my superior.

Notwithstanding these resolutions, no doubt sincere at the time, it might have been suspected that, so far as success on the farm depended on Robert, it rested on an unstable foundation. It is indeed conceivable that such an one as he was as a poet might also prove, in backward times, a drudging successful farmer on a fully-rented farm such as Mossgiel. But experience has nearly always pointed the other way. His gifts and destinies were those of an unrivalled national poet, and for this let us be duly and deeply thankful. The lives of not a few famous votaries of the muse join with Burns's life in lending point to his facetious, truth-laden lines—

> Of a' the thoughtless sons o' man,
> Commen' me to the bardie clan;
> Except it be some idle plan
>   O' rhymin' clink,
> The devil hae't, that I sud ban,
>   They ever think.

MOSSGIEL.

>Nae thought, nae view, nae scheme o' livin',
>Nae cares to gie us joy or grievin';
>But just the pouchie put the nieve in,
>   And while ought's there,
>Then hiltie skiltie we gae scrievin',
>   And fash nae mair.[1]

In this connexion, Allan Cunningham has made the following appropriate remark :—

> Burns was attentive as far as ploughing, sowing, harrowing, reaping, threshing, winnowing, and selling went : he did all this by a sort of mechanical impulse; but success in farming demands more. The farmer should know what is doing in his way in the world around; he must learn to anticipate demand, and, in short, to *time* everything. But he who pens an ode on his sheep when he should be driving them forth to pasture—who sees visions on his way home from market, and makes rhymes on them—who writes an ode on the horse he is about to yoke, and a ballad on the girl who shows the brightest eyes among his reapers—has no chance of ever growing opulent, or of purchasing the field on which he toils.

Burns had then—1784—reached his twenty-sixth year, and so far, his career fully bears out his own statement, that the great misfortune of his earlier years was the want of any fixed aim in life. But, though he continued to the end the same fitful, glowing, wayward being, he at length bethought him of his towering gift as poet, and set himself to base thereon a distinct life-purpose. This is unmistakably attested by various allusions in his letters and poems of this time, and more particularly so by the following noteworthy entry in his Commonplace Book :—

> However I am pleased with the works of our Scotch poets, particularly the excellent Ramsay, and the still more excellent Fergusson, yet I am hurt to see

---

[1] Robert's personal expenditure at this period cannot be deemed in any sense lavish ; for we are emphatically assured by Gilbert that his own and Robert's allowance was but £7 a year each, and that at no time during the Lochlea and Mossgiel periods did the Poet's expenditure (for clothing included) exceed the above-mentioned modest sum.

other places of Scotland, their towns, rivers, woods, haughs, etc., immortalized in such celebrated performances, while my dear native country, the ancient bailieries of Carrick, Kyle, and Cunningham, famous both in ancient and modern times for a gallant and warlike race of inhabitants—a country where civil, and particularly religious liberty, have ever found their first support, and their last asylum—a country, the birthplace of many famous philosophers, soldiers, and statesmen, and the scene of many important events recorded in Scottish history, particularly a great many of the actions of the glorious Wallace, the saviour of his country; yet we have never had one Scotch poet of any eminence to make the fertile banks of Irvine, the romantic woodlands and sequestered scenes on Ayr, and the heathy mountainous source and winding sweep of Doon, emulate Tay, Forth, Ettrick, Tweed, etc. This is a complaint I would gladly remedy, but, alas! I am far unequal to the task, both in native genius and education. Obscure I am, and obscure I must be, though no young poet nor young soldier's heart ever beat more fondly for fame than mine—

> And if there is no other scene of being
> Where my insatiate wish may have its fill—
> This something at my heart that heaves for room,
> My best, my dearest part, was made in vain.

There is a noble sublimity, a heart-melting tenderness, in some of our ancient ballads, which show them to be the work of a masterly hand. And it has often given me many a heartache to reflect that such glorious old bards—bards who probably owed all their talents to native genius, yet have described the exploits of heroes, the pangs of disappointment, and the meltings of love, with such fine strokes of nature — that their very names (oh, how mortifying to a bard's vanity!) are now "buried among the wreck of things which were."

Oh, ye illustrious names unknown! who could feel so strongly, and describe so well: the last, the meanest of the muse's train—one who, though far inferior to your flights, yet eyes your path, and with trembling wing would sometimes soar after you—a poor rustic bard unknown—pays this sympathetic pang to your memory! Some of you tell us, with all the charms of verse, that you have been unfortunate in the world—unfortunate in love; he, too, has felt the loss of his little fortune, the loss of friends, and, worse than all, the loss of the woman he adored. Like you, all his consolation was his muse: she taught him in rustic measures to complain. Happy could he have done it with your strength of imagination and flow of verse! May the turf lie lightly on your bones!—and may you now enjoy that solace and rest which this world rarely gives to the heart tuned to all the feelings of poesy and love!

The glowing aspirations thus so carefully and beautifully recorded were not to remain long unfulfilled. Soon there burst from him a stream of poesy, which for richness and impetuosity of flow is scarcely equalled in the annals of literature. During his two years' sojourn at Mossgiel, he was constantly weighted with toil, worried by ill-success on the farm, distracted by his own luckless conduct, and borne down by ill-health.[1] Yet against all this he struggled, and triumphed in producing at this time most of those poems, on which his fame at first was based, and still stands secure, growing and spreading from generation to generation.

While in all likelihood Burns's friends and neighbours in those days looked upon his farming prospects with shrewd misgivings, he entered Mossgiel with no ordinary reputation for bookish knowledge, quick powers of observation, rhyming, and debate; and, withal, very keen social and amorous tendencies. We also know that he still constantly and eagerly perused whatever newspaper, periodical, or book came his way; revelling, above all, in the study of nature and life. Mossgiel stands on a ridge overlooking the valley of the Ayr, and from his own door the Poet commanded a wide and splendidly varied landscape. The farmhouse consisted of a room and kitchen, with three small garret-rooms above. The mid-attic was occupied by Robert and Gilbert as bedroom. It also served as the Poet's *study*, where, on a little table placed beneath the small roof-light,

---

[1] For over a year (1784-85) he was subject to depressing languor and alarming fainting fits, arising from irregular action of the heart, and had often during the night-time to seek relief from nervous spasms, by plunging into a tub of cold water which he kept in readiness at his bedside.

he revised and transcribed his immortal poems. His favourite time for composition was when guiding the plough; but he loved to wander in solitary musing along the banks of the "gurgling Ayr."

> Robert—says Gilbert—often composed without any regular plan. When anything made a strong impression on his mind, so as to rouse it to any poetic exertion, he would give way to the impulse, and embody the thought in rhyme. If he hit on two or three stanzas to please him, he would then think of proper introductory, connecting, and concluding stanzas; hence the middle of a poem was often first produced.

To this period belong a set of pieces of great biographical interest, viz. the Poet's poetical epistles sent to various correspondents. Through these epistles we obtain most interesting glimpses into the innermost recesses of Burns's thought and feeling. Reference has already been made to David Sillar, that intimate friend and companion, to whom Burns addressed two rhyming letters. From the first and more noteworthy of these we quote the following lines:—

> It's hardly in a body's power
> To keep, at times, frae being sour,
>   To see how things are shared;
> How best o' chiels are whiles in want,
> While coofs on countless thousands rant,
>   And ken na how to wair't;
> But, Davie, lad, ne'er fash your head,
>   Though we hae little gear,
> We're fit to win our daily bread,
>   As lang's we're hale and fier:
>   "Mair spier na, nor fear na,"
>   Auld age ne'er mind a feg,
>   The last o't, the warst o't,
>   Is only but to beg.

It's no' in titles nor in rank ;
It's no' in wealth like Lon'on bank,
  To purchase peace and rest ;
It's no' in making muckle mair ;
It's no' in books ; it's no' in lear,
  To make us truly blest ;
If happiness hae not her seat
  And centre in the breast,
We may be wise, or rich, or great,
  But never can be blest :
    Nae treasures nor pleasures
      Could make us happy lang ;
    The heart aye's the part aye
      That makes us richt or wrang.

Think ye, that sic as you and I,
Wha drudge and drive through wet and dry,
  Wi' never-ceasing toil ;
Think ye, we are less blest than they,
Wha scarcely tent us in their way,
  As hardly worth their while ?
Alas ! how aft, in haughty mood,
  God's creatures they oppress !
Or else, neglecting a' that's guid,
  They riot in excess !
    Baith careless and fearless
      Of either heaven or hell !
    Esteeming and deeming
      It's a' an idle tale !

Then let us cheerfu' acquiesce ;
Nor make our scanty pleasures less,
  By pining at our state ;
And even should misfortunes come,
I, here wha sit, hae met wi' some,
  An's thankfu' for them yet.

> They gie the wit of age to youth ;
> They let us ken oursel' ;
> They make us see the naked truth,
> The real guid and ill.
> Though losses and crosses
> Be lessons right severe,
> There's wit there, ye'll get there,
> Ye'll find nae other where.

Here we find one kind of pride—which was very marked in Burns—querulously *banning* another form of pride in others more favoured by worldly fortune, yet amid his querulous and scathing complainings it is easy to note a deeper strain of kindly, noble feeling. His apprehensions of worldly adversity were far from groundless. He himself knew well his own erratic disposition and his lack of worldly push or method ; and he gives voice to a characteristic consolation in his reflection that, at the worst, he could go *a-begging*.

It may also be asked, Who could better think and teach " braw sober lessons " of practical philosophy and far-reaching truth than he has done throughout this poem, and more especially in that stanza which ends with the well-known immortal couplet—

> The heart aye's the part aye
> That makes us richt or wrang.

To this same period belong the epistles sent to John Lapraik, a rhymer hailing from Muirkirk. At a *rocking* or social gathering one evening in Mossgiel, a song, said to have been composed by Lapraik, was sung in Burns's hearing, and so attracted his notice that he resolved to write and compliment the author. Hence the correspondence to which we owe those three poetical letters, from which we quote as follows :—

POETICAL EPISTLES.

FIRST EPISTLE TO LAPRAIK.

. . . .

But first and foremost, I should tell,
Amaist as soon as I could spell
I to the crambo-jingle fell,
    Though rude and rough;
Yet crooning to a body's sel'
    Does weel enough.

I'm nae a poet in a sense,
But just a rhymer, like, by chance,
And hae to learning nae pretence,
    Yet what the matter?
Whene'er my muse does on me glance,
    I jingle at her.

Your critic folk may cock their nose,
And say, "How can you e'er propose,
You, wha ken hardly verse frae prose,
    To mak' a sang?"
But, by your leaves, my learned foes,
    Ye're maybe wrang.

What's a' your jargon o' your schools,
Your Latin names for horns and stools?
If honest nature made you fools,
    What sairs your grammars?
Ye'd better taen up spades and shools,
    Or knappin'-hammers.

A set o' dull conceited hashes,
Confuse their brains in college classes;
They gang in stirks, and come out asses,
    Plain truth to speak;
And syne they think to climb Parnassus
    By dint o' Greek.

> Gie me ae spark o' nature's fire!
> That's a' the learning I desire;
> Then though I drudge through dub and mire
>   At pleugh or cart,
> My muse, though hamely in attire,
>   May touch the heart.

Chambers says:—

> Lapraik was not slow to apprehend the value of the offered correspondence. He sent an answer by the hands of his son, who lately lived to relate the circumstances attending its delivery. He found the goodman of Mossgiel in a field engaged in sowing. "I'm no' sure if I ken the hand," said Burns, as he took the letter; but no sooner had he glanced at its contents than, unconsciously letting go the sheet containing the grain, it was not till he had finished reading that he discovered the loss he had sustained. Does not the reader delight in this anecdote, so significant of the character of Burns, ever ready and apt to sacrifice the worldly and the professional to the spirits of poetry and of friendship!

Students and admirers of Burns are ever offering, in speech or essay, opinions regarding the secret of his power and charm as a poet. Is not the secret revealed by Burns himself in the last stanza of the above quotation? It is by virtue of his bright pure spark of "nature's fire," that he so touches and enlightens and warms the heart of mankind.

Again, in the second epistle, written in reply to Lapraik, Burns's deliberate estimate of the relative merits of temporal success and poetic fame is thus indicated:—

> Now comes the sax-and-twentieth simmer
> I've seen the bud upo' the timmer,
> Still persecuted by the limmer,
>   Frae year to year;
> But yet, despite the kittle kimmer,
>   I, Rob, am here.

Do ye envy the city gent,
Behint a kist to lie and sklent,
Or, purse-proud, big wi' cent. per cent.
    And muckle wame,
In some bit brugh to represent
    A bailie's name?

Or is't the paughty feudal thane,
Wi' ruffled sark and glancin' cane,
Wha thinks himsel' nae sheep-shank bane,
    But lordly stalks,
While caps and bonnets aff are taen,
    As by he walks?

O Thou wha gies us each guid gift!
Gie me o' *wit and sense* a lift,
Then turn me, if Thou please, adrift
    Through Scotland wide;
Wi' cits nor lairds I wadna shift,
    In a' their pride!

Were this the charter of our state,
"On pain o' hell be rich and great,"
Damnation then would be our fate,
    Beyond remead;
But, thanks to Heaven, that's no' the gate
    We learn our creed.

For thus the royal mandate ran,
When first the human race began,
"The social, friendly, honest man,
    Whate'er he be,
'Tis he fulfils great Nature's plan,
    And none but he!"

O mandate glorious and divine!
The followers o' the ragged Nine,

> Poor thoughtless devils! yet may shine
>   In glorious light,
> While sordid sons o' Mammon's line
>   Are dark as night.

Then, in his epistle to William Simpson, schoolmaster, Ochiltree (written in May 1785), the Poet gives glowing expression to his love of nature in all its phases; also to the growing idea of his genius, and his fixed resolve to be the "patriot bard" of his native land:—

> Ramsay and famous Fergusson
> Gied Forth and Tay a lift abune;
> Yarrow and Tweed, to monie a tune
>   Owre Scotland rings,
> While Irvine, Lugar, Ayr, and Doon,
>   Naebody sings.
>
> Th' Illissus, Tiber, Thames, and Seine,
> Glide sweet in mony a tunefu' line;
> But, Willie, set your fit to mine,
>   And cock your crest,
> We'll gar our streams and burnies shine
>   Up wi' the best.
>
> We'll sing auld Coila's plains and fells,
> Her moors red-brown wi' heather bells,
> Her banks and braes, her dens and dells,
>   Where glorious Wallace
> Aft bure the gree, as story tells,
>   Frae Southron billies.
>
> At Wallace' name what Scottish blood
> But boils up in a spring-tide flood!
> Oft have our fearless fathers strode
>   By Wallace' side,
> Still pressing onward, red-wat shod,
>   Or glorious died!

O sweet are Coila's haughs and woods,
When lintwhites chant amang the buds,
And jinkin' hares, in amorous whids,
  Their loves enjoy,
While through the braes the cushat croods
  With wailfu' cry!

Even winter bleak has charms to me,
When winds rave through the naked tree;
Or frosts on hills of Ochiltree
  Are hoary grey;
Or blinding drifts wild furious flee,
  Darkening the day!

O nature! a' thy shows and forms
To feeling, pensive hearts hae charms!
Whether the summer kindly warms
  Wi' life and light,
Or winter howls, in gusty storms,
  The lang, dark night!

The muse, nae poet ever fand her,
Till by himsel' he learned to wander
Adown some trotting burn's meander,
  And no' think lang;
O sweet to stray and pensive ponder
  A heartfelt sang!

The war'ly race may drudge and drive,
Hog-shouther, jundie, stretch, and strive;
Let me fair nature's face descrive,
  And I wi' pleasure
Shall let the busy grumbling hive
  Bum owre their treasure.

From yet another of this class of composition we quote these verses :—

> The sacred lowe o' weel-placed love,
>   Luxuriantly indulge it ;
> But never tempt th' illicit rove,
>   Though naething should divulge it :
> I waive the quantum o' the sin,
>   The hazard of concealing ;
> But och ! it hardens a' within,
>   And petrifies the feeling !
>
> To catch dame Fortune's golden smile,
>   Assiduous wait upon her ;
> And gather gear by every wile
>   That's justified by honour ;
> Not for to hide it in a hedge,
>   Nor for a train-attendant,
> But for the glorious privilege
>   Of being independent.
>
> The fear o' hell's a hangman's whip
>   To haud the wretch in order ;
> But where ye feel your honour grip,
>   Let that aye be your border :
> Its slightest touches, instant pause—
>   Debar a' side pretences ;
> And resolutely keep its laws,
>   Uncaring consequences.
>
> When ranting round in pleasure's ring,
>   Religion may be blinded ;
> Or if she gi'e a random sting,
>   It may be little minded ;
> But when on life we're tempest-driven,
>   A conscience but a canker ;
> A correspondence fixed wi' Heaven
>   Is sure a noble anchor.

> Adieu, dear amiable youth!
> Your heart can ne'er be wanting!
> May prudence, fortitude, and truth
> Erect your brow undaunting.
> In ploughman phrase, "God send you speed"
> Still daily to grow wiser,
> And may you better reck the rede
> Than ever did the adviser.

These lines from the "Epistle to a Young Friend," written in May 1786, have, in addition to their own weight and beauty, a very significant bearing upon the Poet's circumstances and feelings at the time of writing; for then, alas! he was speaking straight from his own bitter experiences as one who had tempted "the illicit rove," and been branded as a profane person because of his contributions to the religious controversy which was at that time raging in Ayrshire and the west country.

The notable part Burns played in this controversy now claims our attention. The south-west of Scotland—Ayrshire in particular—is well known to have been a centre of the Covenanting spirit, and an outstanding stronghold of stern, unbending Calvinism. But in the Poet's day a great change had taken place in the aspect of religious affairs in Ayrshire. A wide divergence in belief was manifest both among clergy and laity. Of course, because of their public office and their education, this divergence was more distinctly marked among the clergy, who had, indeed, more or less ranged themselves into two parties, to which the terms *Evangelical* and *Moderate*, or *Auld Licht* and *New Licht*, were applied, in Burns's writings the latter terms being usually employed. The "Auld Lichts" stuck to Genevan theology, preached hard and fast Puritanic doctrine, and gained the greater favour among the common people, because of greater apparent religious zeal, more ascetic manner of life, and strong denunciation of patronage in Church affairs. On the other hand, the "New Lichts" were more free and rational in their creed and teaching, and less sour in their personal walk and conversation. They also approved of the law and custom of patronage. Considering the mind and disposition of the Poet, we can discover but one reason why he might have been expected to take the "Auld Licht" side; whereas several reasons may be adduced for his taking the opposite side. It might have been expected that such an one as Burns, so strongly democratic in his nature, would, on the question of patronage, have assisted the people to

> "Join their counsel and their skills
> To cowe the lairds."

But when we call to mind the intelligent religious teaching which William Burness took pains to impart to his family, and the narrowness of view and unnatural stiffness of practice which characterized the "Auld Licht" party—when we remember, too, that the "rigid feature" and the "preaching cant" were not seldom found in conjunction with, and were sometimes even a flaunting hypocritical cloak for, envy, malice, pride, and uncharity, we need hardly marvel that Burns—so great and full of thought, so far beyond his age in perception, so social and generous of impulse, so hateful of all forms of moral sham and religious pretence—should have ardently espoused the "New Licht" cause. Some more personal considerations are said to have influenced and embittered his bearing in this remarkable controversy.

In the matter of Church discipline[1] he had come under the

---

[1] Soon after entering Mossgiel, a child was born to Burns, by Elizabeth Paton, his "bonnie Betty," who had been servant for some time in Lochlea. This child, who was brought up by the Poet's mother, married a Mr. John Bishop, Polkemmet, and survived till 1817. Nothing definite is known of the subsequent history of Elizabeth Paton. The incident was the subject of the songs, "The rantin' dog, the daddie o't," "The Poet's Welcome to his Illegitimate Child," and the "Epistle to John Rankine."

censure of Mr. Auld, minister of Mauchline, who was an uncompromising "Auld Licht," his elders being moved by a like spirit, only with less intelligence and far more bigotry.

Gavin Hamilton, too, the Poet's landlord, patron, and genial friend, had, as Burns thought, and as the Church courts at length decided, been wrongously meddled with and spitefully harassed by the Mauchline kirk-session, of which body "Holy Willie" was an active member.

Such, in brief, were the leading circumstances amid which Burns rushed into the fray. He himself says :—

> The first of my poetic offspring that saw the light was a burlesque lamentation on a quarrel between two reverend Calvinists, both of them *dramatis personæ* in my "Holy Fair." With a certain description of the clergy, as well as the laity, it met with a roar of applause.

The poem referred to is the "Twa Herds, or the Holy Tulzie," through which the "New Lichts" at once recognised that in the author they had found an invaluable ally, and for encouragement to further effort of this kind they readily gave Burns their countenance and applause. Then followed from the Poet's pen satire after satire, in quick succession and with deadly, scathing effect— as in "Holy Willie's Prayer," "An Epistle to John Goudie," "The Holy Fair," "The Unco Guid," "The Ordination," etc. Now, no one who reads these extraordinary satires can altogether acquit Burns of the bitterness of partisanship, nor of a very daring and headlong rushing upon matters of the most venerable and sacred character. Still, in recollection of the times and circumstances, and pleading, as we venture to do, that in him, amid all his aberrations, there was a deep sense of personal religion, and an instinctive admiration of all that was real and worthy in men and customs, we cannot shake off the conviction that, writing as he did, he aimed not at injuring true morals or religion, but at exposing and lashing sham or hypocrisy in human conduct and superstition or abuse in religious observance. But, in any case, in view of things as they then were and now are in the matters dealt with, if it be asserted that Burns assailed with ruthless hand and unsparing voice, it may be justly replied that his was the hand of a reformer, and the voice of a prophet.

From allusions in several pieces written in 1784, we gather that, very shortly after entering Mossgiel, Burns had formed acquaintance with Jean Armour, daughter of a well-to-do Mauchline mason. On their first and casual meeting, some rustic banter was exchanged, and very soon they were lovers. Like most of Burns's heroines, she was not reckoned a great beauty; but was, withal, a comely, sweet-natured lass, of frank, taking manner, possessed of a fine musical voice, and natural taste in singing. Obviously, what her lover lacked in worldly station and substance was, in her eyes, more than made up by his great personal charm of manner, mind, and heart. The situation in which Burns and Jean Armour found themselves is briefly and delicately stated in Gilbert's narrative. After alluding to the family disappointments in the farming of Mossgiel during 1784-5, he says:—

> It was during these years that Robert formed his connexion with Jean Armour, afterwards Mrs. Burns. This connexion could no longer be concealed, about the time we resolved to quit the farm. Robert durst not engage with a family in his poor, unsettled state, but was anxious to shield his partner, by every means in his power, from the consequences of their imprudence. It was agreed, therefore, between them, that they should make a legal acknowledgment of their marriage; that he should go to Jamaica to push his fortune, and that she should remain with her father, till it might please Providence to put the means of supporting a family in his power. Mrs. Burns was a great favourite of her father's. The intimation of a marriage was the first suggestion he received of her real situation. He was in the greatest distress, and fainted away. A husband in Jamaica appeared to him and his wife little better than

none. . . . They therefore expressed a wish to their daughter that the written papers respecting the marriage should be cancelled and the marriage thus rendered void. Jean, in her melancholy state, felt the deepest remorse at having brought such heavy affliction on her parents, and submitted to their entreaties.

Burns had, so far, made that amends which the ideas of the times recognised in an irregular marriage; and as we are bound to consider this secret engagement an act of faithfulness and affection on the Poet's part towards Jean Armour, so we can conceive how the destruction of the marriage lines was to him a terrible blow, under which he staggered with mingled feelings of sorrow, shame, and anger. To these feelings he gave vent in "The Lament" and "Despondency—an Ode," poems full of the sadness and bitterness of the life of Burns, then but twenty-seven years of age.

At this point, the romantic "episode" of the Poet's attachment to Highland Mary emerges as "an underplot in the drama of his love." This oft-told and fascinating story is briefly narrated in vol. i. of this work (see "Mary Campbell"). For aught that is known to the contrary, we cling to the simple explanation and charitable opinion that it was when he deemed himself cast off by Jean Armour and flouted and disowned by her connexions, that Burns turned away to seek consolation from his "Highland lassie—a warm-hearted, charming young creature as ever blessed a man with generous love." Here, in the remembrance of all the "amorous madness" of his tremendously impassioned nature,—a nature how different from that of ordinary mortals,—the voice of condemnation may well be hushed. That Burns's love for Mary Campbell was deep and true, and that his intention to make her his wife and take her with him to the Indies was faithful and sincere, cannot be gainsaid. And so, rather than blaming, we would, in consideration of all the hard, trying circumstances, plead for sympathy with our hapless, distracted Bard, whose great, kind, sensitive soul cried out so loudly, in the chill desolation of his disappointment, for some other woman's gentle heart into which he might pour the mighty pent-up tide of his glowing passion. While the Poet was still in gloom and difficulty, and seeing no way save to emigrate, news reached him that Mary had died in Greenock on 20th October. To his troubled spirit, this sad ending of Mary's young and lovely life was an added pang of misery. In all probability, her decease changed the after-current of Burns's career. Had she lived on, who can tell what might have resulted?

According to his brother's narrative, the Poet's determination to emigrate was taken in March or April, about which time his troubles with the Armour family reached a crisis. In the *Autobiography* he reviews his life during the ensuing months from May till August. Alluding to his difficulties and disappointments in connexion with his "bonnie Jean," whom, notwithstanding all that had happened, he still ardently loved,[1] he says :—

> This was a most melancholy affair, which I cannot yet bear to reflect on, and had very nearly given me one or two of the principal qualifications for a place among those who have lost the chart and mistaken the reckoning of rationality. I gave up my part of the farm to my brother,—in truth it was only nominally mine,—and made what little preparation was in my power for Jamaica. But before leaving my native country for ever, I resolved to publish my poems. I weighed my productions as impartially as was in my power; I thought they had merit; and it was a delicious idea that I should be called a clever fellow, even though it should never reach my ears—a poor negro-driver; or perhaps a victim to that inhospitable clime, and gone to the world of spirits. I can truly say that, *pauvre inconnu* as I then was, I had pretty nearly as high an idea of myself and of my works as I have at this moment, when the public has decided in their favour. It ever was my opinion that the mistakes and blunders, both

---

[1] "What Jean thinks of her conduct now, I don't know; one thing I do know, she has made me completely miserable. Never man loved, or rather adored, a woman, more than I did her; and to confess a truth between you and me, I do still love her to distraction after all." (From letter to David Brice, Glasgow.)

in a rational and religious point of view, of which we see thousands daily guilty, are owing to their ignorance of themselves. To know myself had been all along my constant study. I weighed myself alone—I balanced myself with others—I watched every means of information, to see how much ground I occupied as a man and as a poet—I studied assiduously Nature's design in my formation—where the lights and shades in my character were intended. I was pretty confident my poems would meet with some applause; but, at the worst, the roar of the Atlantic would deafen the voice of censure, and the novelty of West Indian scenes make me forget neglect. I threw off six hundred copies, of which I had got subscriptions for about three hundred and fifty. My vanity was highly gratified by the reception I met with from the public; and besides, I pocketed, all expenses deducted, nearly twenty pounds. This sum came very seasonably, as I was thinking of indenting myself, for want of money to procure my passage. As soon as I was master of nine guineas, the price of wafting me to the torrid zone, I took a steerage passage in the first ship that was to sail from the Clyde; for

"Hungry ruin had me in the wind."

In the hope of bettering his fortune, he had reluctantly made up his mind to go to the Indies. But he was penniless, and money was needed to carry out this plan. It was then that his friend Gavin Hamilton suggested that, to overcome the difficulty, he should publish by subscription a volume of his poems. The suggestion readily fell in with Burns's deep-rooted yearning for fame, and his clear consciousness of poetic genius. By this time he had written, in addition to those already mentioned, not a few of his other more noted poems,—"Death and Dr. Hornbook," "Man was made to Mourn," "Hallowe'en," "The Vision," "To a Mouse," "The Cotter's Saturday Night," etc.

There was thus good ground for expecting that the poems would meet with considerable sale, and yield some little profit to the author. Burns accordingly set eagerly to work; and, notwithstanding his distressful situation, succeeded in revising a selection of pieces already produced, in composing several new pieces, and in carrying on a large amount of canvassing and correspondence in connexion with the preparation and sale of the projected volume.

On 31st July 1786 the book was issued from the press of John Wilson, Kilmarnock. The entire issue, consisting of 600 copies, was taken up as quickly as the printers and binders could get through the work. So scarce did the copies become, that the family at Mossgiel had to wait until the Edinburgh edition was published, ere they were privileged to peruse the poems in printed form. The volume was instantly successful, and very soon the whole country-side literally rang in its praise. The genius of Burns was thus made widely known, and his fame enthusiastically spread. In his "Memoir of Burns," the hapless Robert Heron, speaking of the reception accorded to the Kilmarnock edition, says :—

> Old and young, high and low, grave and gay, learned or ignorant — all were alike delighted, agitated, transported. I was at that time resident in Galloway, contiguous to Ayrshire; and I can well remember how that even ploughboys and maidservants would have gladly bestowed the wages which they earned the most hardly, and which they wanted for necessary clothing, if they might but procure the works of Burns. A friend in my neighbourhood put a copy into my hands on a Saturday evening. I opened the volume while I was undressing to go to bed, and closed it not till a late hour on the rising Sunday morn, after I had read over every syllable it contained.

Burns began his book with a short preface of fine manly tone, and closed it with "The Bard's Epitaph," that startlingly vivid and prophetic portraiture of his own character and career :—

> Is there a whim-inspired fool,
> Owre fast for thought, owre hot for rule,
> Owre blate to seek, owre proud to snool,
>   Let him draw near ;
> And owre this grassy heap sing dool,
>   And drap a tear.

> Is there a bard of rustic song,
> Who, noteless, steals the crowds among,
> That weekly this area throng,
>   Oh, pass not by!
> But, with a frater-feeling strong,
>   Here heave a sigh.
>
> Is there a man, whose judgment clear,
> Can others teach the course to steer,
> Yet runs himself life's mad career,
>   Wild as the wave;
> Here pause—and, through the starting tear,
>   Survey this grave.
>
> The poor inhabitant below
> Was quick to learn, and wise to know,
> And keenly felt the friendly glow,
>   And softer flame;
> But thoughtless follies laid him low,
>   And stained his name.
>
> Reader, attend—whether thy soul
> Soars fancy's flights beyond the pole,
> Or darkly grubs this earthly hole,
>   In low pursuit;
> Know, prudent, cautious self-control
>   Is wisdom's root.

The remarkable popularity of the Kilmarnock volume did not, however, immediately bring peace to the vexed heart of the Poet. His wretchedness was too deep and complicated to be so easily or quickly relieved. But at length the heavy clouds of misfortune and shame, under which, for months, he had sorrowed and chafed, began to clear away. At the very time when his immortal poems were being issued from the press, he was lurking in concealment from the grasp of the law. For Jean Armour's father had out a warrant against him for a large sum of money,—as security,—which it was out of his power to pay. The fame of his poems, however, somewhat appeased the wrath of the Armours; and no longer in fear from the warrant, he was at liberty to return to Mossgiel. During the latter half of August he was occupied collecting the subscriptions due for his volume, a task which led him into a good deal of company and merrymaking with numerous admirers, and served to further distract his attention from any fixed purpose. It was at this period he made the acquaintance of Mrs. Dunlop of Dunlop, his lifelong friend and correspondent, and of Professor Dugald Stewart, then resident in his summer resort at Catrine House. Professor Stewart's description of the Poet as he appeared in the autumn of 1786 runs as follows :—

> His manners were then, as they continued ever afterwards, simple, manly, and independent; strongly expressive of conscious genius and worth, but without anything that indicated forwardness, arrogance, or vanity. He took his share in conversation, but not more than belonged to him; and listened with apparent attention and deference on subjects where his want of education deprived him of the means of information. If there had been a little more of gentleness and accommodation in his temper, he would, I think, have been still more interesting; but he had been accustomed to give law in the circle of his ordinary acquaintance, and his dread of anything approaching to meanness or servility rendered his manner somewhat decided and hard. Nothing perhaps was more remarkable among his various attainments than the fluency, and precision, and originality of his language, when he spoke in company; more particularly as he aimed at purity in his turn of expression, and avoided, more successfully than most Scotchmen, the peculiarities of Scottish phraseology. At this time, Burns's prospects in life were so extremely gloomy, that he had seriously formed a plan of going out to Jamaica in a very humble situation, not, however, without lamenting that his want of patronage should force him to think of a project so repugnant to his feelings, when his ambition aimed at no higher an object than the station of an exciseman or gauger in his own country.

THE EXCISE.

With reference to the above allusion to the Poet's anxiety to obtain a situation as exciseman, it is due to Burns's friends to state that at this time some of them were doing what they could in the direction of his desire for such an appointment. This fact may in some measure explain the delay in carrying out his plan of repairing to Jamaica. "The feelings of a father" also operated in keeping him at home, for, in the beginning of September, Jean Armour brought forth twins—"a fine boy and girl," he remarks. "God bless them, poor little dears." The following notable letter, written to Mr. Aiken, Ayr, early in October, casts a sad light upon the Poet's sorely complicated situation and distracted state of mind at this time :—

TO MR. ROBERT AIKEN.

Sir,—I was with Wilson my printer t'other day, and settled all our bygone matters between us. After I had paid all demands, I made him the offer of the second edition, on the hazard of being paid out of the first and readiest, which he declines. By his account the paper of 1000 copies would cost about twenty-seven pounds, and the printing about fifteen or sixteen: he offers to agree to this for the printing if I will advance for the paper, but this, you know, is out of my power; so farewell hopes of a second edition till I grow richer! an epocha which I think will arrive at the payment of the British national debt. . . .

I have been feeling all the various rotations and movements within respecting the Excise. There are many things plead strongly against it ; the uncertainty of getting soon into business; the consequences of my follies, which may perhaps make it impracticable for me to stay at home ; and, besides, I have for some time been pining under secret wretchedness, from causes which you pretty well know — the pang of disappointment, the sting of pride, with some wandering stabs of remorse, which never fail to settle on my vitals like vultures, when attention is not called away by the calls of society or the vagaries of the muse. Even in the hour of social mirth, my gaiety is the madness of an intoxicated criminal under the hands of the executioner. All these reasons urge me to go abroad, and to all these reasons I have only one answer—the feelings of a father. This, in the present mood I am in, overbalances everything that can be laid in the scale against it.

You may perhaps think it an extravagant fancy, but it is a sentiment which strikes home to my very soul; though sceptical in some points of our current belief, yet I think I have every evidence for the reality of a life beyond the stinted bourne of our present existence: if so, then how should I, in the presence of that tremendous Being, the Author of existence, how should I meet the reproaches of those who stand to me in the dear relation of children, whom I deserted in the smiling innocency of helpless infancy? Oh, thou great unknown Power!—thou Almighty God! who hast lighted up reason in my breast, and blessed me with immortality!—I have frequently wandered from that order and regularity necessary for the perfection of thy works, yet thou hast never left me nor forsaken me!

Since I wrote the foregoing sheet, I have seen something of the storm of mischief thickening over my folly-devoted head. Should you, my friends, my benefactors, be successful in your applications for me, perhaps it may not be in my power in that way to reap the fruit of your friendly efforts. What I have written in the preceding pages is the settled tenor of my present resolution; but should inimical circumstances forbid me closing with your kind offer, or enjoying it only threaten to entail further misery——

To tell the truth, I have little reason for complaint, as the world, in general, has been kind to me fully up to my deserts. I was, for some time past, fast getting into the pining, distrustful snarl of the misanthrope. I saw myself alone, unfit for the struggle of life, shrinking at every rising cloud in the chance-directed atmosphere of fortune, while, all defenceless, I looked about in vain for a cover. It never occurred to me, at least never with the force it deserved, that this world is a busy scene, and man a creature destined for a progressive struggle; and that, however I might possess a warm heart and inoffensive manners (which last, by the bye, was rather more than I could well boast), still, more than these passive qualities, there was something *to be done*. When all my schoolfellows and youthful compeers (those misguided few excepted who joined, to use a Gentoo phrase, the "hallachores" of the human race) were striking off with eager hope and earnest intent in some one or other of the many paths of busy life, I was "standing idle in the market-place," or only left the chase of the butterfly from flower to flower, to hunt fancy from whim to whim.

You see, sir, that if to know one's errors were a probability of mending

EDINBURGH PROSPECTS.

them, I stand a fair chance; but, according to the reverend Westminster divines, though conviction must precede conversion, it is very far from always implying it.

The phenomenal success and quick disposal of his first edition naturally prompted the Poet to think of issuing a second; but, disappointed in this proposal, and with the prospect of self-exile still looming ahead, the months of September and October found him, notwithstanding the fame and flattering notice he received from many quarters, still restless and undecided, pining under secret wretchedness, suffering from "the pang of disappointment, the sting of pride, and some wandering stabs of remorse." The weeks of that autumn dragged along darkly and wearily for poor Burns, until glad light and cheer broke upon him from an unlooked-for and highly influential source.

> I had—he tells us—taken the last farewell of my friends; my chest was on the road to Greenock. I had composed the last song I should ever measure in Caledonia—"The gloomy night is gathering fast"—when a letter from Dr. Blacklock to a friend of mine overthrew all my schemes, by opening new prospects to my poetic ambition.[1] The doctor belonged to a set of critics for whose applause I had not dared to hope. His opinion that I should meet with encouragement in Edinburgh for a second edition fired me so much, that away I posted for that city, without a single acquaintance or a single letter of introduction. The baneful star that had so long shed its blasting influence in my zenith, for once made a revolution to the nadir; and a kind Providence placed me under the patronage of one of the noblest of men—the Earl of Glencairn.
>
> Oublie moi, Grand Dieu, si jamais je l'oublie.

His arrival in Edinburgh on the 28th of November 1786, clearly marks a new phase of the Poet's career.

---

[1] The friend here mentioned was the Rev. Mr. Lawrie, minister of Loudon parish. For full account of this memorable turning-point in Burns's life, see vol. i. p. 46 and vol. ii. p. 1.

CHAPTER V.

FIRST WINTER IN EDINBURGH—NOVEMBER 28, 1786-MAY 5, 1787.
AGE 27-28.

> Edina ! Scotia's darling seat !
>   All hail thy palaces and towers,
> Where once beneath a monarch's feet
>   Sat Legislation's sovereign powers !
> From marking wildly-scattered flowers,
>   As on the banks of Ayr I strayed,
> And singing, lone, the lingering hours,
>   I shelter in thy honoured shade.
>
> *Address to Edinburgh*

> It needs no effort of imagination to conceive what the sensations of an isolated set of scholars (almost all either clergymen or professors) must have been in presence of this big-boned, black-browed, brawny stranger, with his great flashing eyes, who, having forced his way among them from the plough-tail at a single stride, manifested in the whole strain of his bearing and conversation a most thorough conviction that, in a society of the most eminent men of his nation, he was exactly where he was entitled to be. . . .
>
> LOCKHART's *Life of Burns.*

BIDDING a kindly good-bye to his mother and brothers and sisters, and remembering, we may be sure, to leave a fond paternal kiss on the cheek of the "wee image of his bonnie Betty," Burns set out from Mossgiel for Edinburgh on the morning of November 27. After a hard day's ride, he halted, and spent a memorable and joyous night at Covington Mains (a farm in the Lanarkshire parish of Covington and Thankerton), his hospitable entertainer, Mr. Prentice, being an enthusiastic admirer of the Poet.

ARRIVAL IN EDINBURGH.

According to an account written many years afterwards by a son of this worthy farmer,—

> It was arranged that Burns should, on his journey to Edinburgh, make the farm-house at Covington Mains his resting-place on the first night. All the farmers in the parish had read with delight the Poet's then published works, and were anxious to see him. They were all asked to meet him at a late dinner, and the signal of his arrival was to be a white sheet attached to a pitchfork, and put on the top of a corn-stack in the barn-yard. The parish is a beautiful amphitheatre, with the Clyde winding through it, with Wellbrae Hill to the west, Tinto and the Culter Fells to the south, and the pretty, green, conical hill, Quothquan Law, to the east. My father's stackyard, lying in the centre, was seen from every house in the parish. At length Burns arrived, mounted on a *pownie* borrowed of Mr. Dalrymple, near Ayr. Instantly was the white flag hoisted, and as instantly were seen the farmers issuing from their houses, and converging to the point of meeting. A glorious evening, or rather night, which borrowed something from the morning, followed, and the conversation of the Poet confirmed and increased the admiration created by his writings.

Next morning, after breakfasting with a large party at the neighbouring farm-house, he resumed his journey. That same night, feeling very weary and lonely, and weighted with those galling chains which misfortune and his own wayward conduct had bound around him, yet conscious of a mighty poetic genius, with many an earnest resolve toward steadier purpose, and not without some gladdening hopes of brighter destiny, he entered the ancient queenly city. His Mauchline friend and correspondent, John Richmond,[1] law clerk, was then residing in Baxter's Close in the Lawnmarket. Thither the way-worn Poet repaired, thankful to share Richmond's humble bed and board, in that single room, famous ever since as Burns's lodging-place throughout his first winter in Edinburgh.

[1] See vol. ii. p. 103.

The Scottish capital, with its quaint beauty, majestic natural surroundings, and grand old associations, never fails to excite the interest and admiration of those who are visiting it for the first time. To the keenly observant eye and patriotic spirit of Burns its attractiveness must have been peculiarly great. And yet it is not hard to conceive how, during the first day or two, he felt lonely enough amid the city throng—all strangers to him, whose kindly heart ever panted for friendly communion with his fellow-creatures. In this connexion Allan Cunningham made the following likely enough statement :—

> Though he had taken a stride from the furrowed field into the land of poetry, and abandoned the plough for the harp, he seemed for some days to feel, as in earlier life, unfitted with an aim, and wandered about looking down from Arthur's Seat, surveying the Palace, gazing at the Castle, or contemplating the windows of the booksellers' shops, where he saw all works save the poems of the Ayrshire Ploughman. He found his way to the lowly grave of Fergusson, and, kneeling down, kissed the sod ; he sought out the house of Allan Ramsay, and, on entering it, took off his hat ; and when he was afterwards introduced to Creech, the bibliopole remembered that he had before heard him inquiring if this had been the shop of the author of " The Gentle Shepherd." [1]

The Poet did not, however, hurry away to Edinburgh without having some kindly and effective influence in view. During

---

[1] Burns repeatedly expressed enthusiastic admiration of the works of "Ramsay and famous Fergusson," and avowed his own indebtedness to and inferiority compared with these two authors, neither of whom possessed a twentieth part of his own soaring genius. Some explanation may be found in calling to mind that, when but a youth, Burns had read and fondly admired these writings. Further, it is not hard to conceive how *he* sorrowed so deeply over the darkly-chequered career of poor Fergusson, and hastened to rear a lasting memorial over the lowly, neglected grave of one whom he counted his master in the field of Scottish poesy. The following minute sets forth his actions in this matter :—

Session-house within the parish of Canongate, the twenty-second day of February, one thousand seven hundred eighty-seven years.

Sederunt of the Managers of the Kirk and Kirkyard Funds of Canongate ;

Which day, the treasurer to the said funds produced a letter from Mr. Robert Burns, of date the 6th current, which was read and the previous autumn, the fame of his Kilmarnock edition had brought him in contact with several Ayrshire men of good position, who had also high influence in the capital. Professor Stewart and Dr. Blacklock, too, were there, and on their aid he could fairly reckon. One of his Ayrshire friends was the frank, liberal-minded Mr. Dalrymple of Orangefield, a gentleman having high and powerful family connexions in Edinburgh. This was the man whom Burns first approached, and by whom he was courteously and encouragingly received. Dalrymple at once introduced Burns to the Earl of Glencairn, a nobleman alike by station, culture, and temperament, who so exerted himself that, in the course of a few days, the doors of the highest society were thrown open to the Ayrshire Peasant Bard. But still more effective on Burns's behalf than the countenance of the learned and noble ones of Edinburgh, was the review of his poems which appeared in *The Lounger* of December 9. In this article—written by Mr. Henry Mackenzie, the elegant author of the *Man of Feeling*—the genius of "the heaven-taught ploughman" was emphatically pronounced to be "of

appointed to be engrossed in their sederunt-book, and of which letter the tenor follows:—

"To the honourable bailies of Canongate, Edinburgh,—Gentlemen, I am sorry to be told that the remains of Robert Fergusson, the so justly celebrated poet, a man whose talents for ages to come will do honour to our Caledonian name, lie in your churchyard among the ignoble dead, unnoticed and unknown.

"Some memorial to direct the steps of the lovers of Scottish song, when they wish to shed a tear over the 'narrow house' of the bard who is no more, is surely a tribute due to Fergusson's memory—a tribute I wish to have the honour of paying.

"I petition you, then, gentlemen, to permit me to lay a simple stone over his revered ashes, to remain an unalienable property to his death-less fame.—I have the honour to be, gentlemen, your very humble servant, ROBERT BURNS."

Therefore the said managers, in consideration of the laudable and disinterested motion of Mr. Burns, and the propriety of his request, did, and hereby do, unanimously, grant power and liberty to the said Robert Burns to erect a head-stone at the grave of the said Robert Fergusson, and to keep up and preserve the same to his memory in all time coming. Extracted forth of the records of the managers by
WILLIAM SPROTT, *Clerk.*

To whomsoever this incident is known, it speaks, in its own sweet way, of the generous impulse—the noble, unselfish spirit of Robert Burns.

no ordinary rank," and Scotland was called upon to recognise, and welcome, and cherish in Burns a great national poet. Following up his lengthened review of the Kilmarnock edition, Mackenzie went on to say :—

> Burns possesses the spirit as well as the fancy of a poet. That honest pride and independence of soul, which are sometimes the Muse's only dower, break forth on every occasion in his works. It may be, then, I shall wrong his feelings while I indulge my own, in calling the attention of the public to his situation and circumstances. That condition, humble as it was, in which he found content and wooed the muse, might not have been deemed uncomfortable; but grief and misfortune have reached him there; and one or two of his poems hint, what I have learned from some of his countrymen, that he has been obliged to form the resolution of leaving his native land, to seek, under a West Indian clime, that shelter and support which Scotland has denied him. But I trust that means may be found to prevent this resolution from taking place, and that I do my country no more than justice when I suppose her ready to stretch out her hand to cherish and retain this native poet, whose "wood-notes wild" possess so much excellence. To repair the wrongs of suffering or neglected merit, to call forth genius from the obscurity in which it had pined indignant, and place it where it may profit or delight the world—these are exertions which give to wealth an enviable superiority, to greatness and to patronage a laudable pride.

So favourable a criticism from such an authoritative quarter went far to exalt the name and fame of Burns beyond reach of the petty meddlings of bigotry or pharisaism, and to make abundantly secure the financial success of the Edinburgh edition.

Turning to the Poet's letters to his Ayrshire correspondents, we extract the following passages in reference to his reception and situation in Edinburgh at this stage. To Gavin Hamilton he writes on December 7th :—

> For my own affairs, I am in a fair way of becoming as eminent as Thomas à Kempis or John Bunyan; and you may expect henceforth to see my birthday inserted among the wonderful events in the Poor Robin's and Aberdeen

Almanacs, along with the Black Monday and the battle of Bothwell Bridge. My Lord Glencairn and the Dean of Faculty, Mr. H. Erskine, have taken me under their wing; and by all probability I shall soon be the tenth worthy and the eighth wise man of the world. Through my lord's influence, it is inserted in the records of the Caledonian Hunt that they universally, one and all, subscribe for the second edition. My subscription bills come out to-morrow, and you shall have some of them next post. I have met in Mr. Dalrymple of Orangefield what Solomon emphatically calls "a friend that sticketh closer than a brother." The warmth with which he interests himself in my affairs is of the same enthusiastic kind which you, Mr. Aiken, and the few patrons that took notice of my earlier poetic days, showed for the poor unlucky devil of a poet.

And to John Ballantyne, on December 13th :—

I arrived here on Tuesday se'night, and have suffered ever since I came to town, with a miserable headache and stomach complaint; but am now a good deal better. . . . Mr. Dalrymple of Orangefield introduced me to Lord Glencairn, a man whose worth and brotherly kindness to me I shall remember when time shall be no more. By his interest it is passed in the Caledonian Hunt, and entered in their books, that they are to take each a copy of the second edition, for which they are to pay one guinea.[1] I have been introduced to a good many of the *noblesse*, but my avowed patrons and patronesses are, the Duchess of Gordon — the Countess of Glencairn, with my Lord and Lady Betty—the Dean of Faculty—Sir John Whitefoord. I have likewise warm friends among the literati: Professors Stewart, Blair, and Mr. Mackenzie, the "Man of Feeling." An unknown hand left ten guineas for the Ayrshire bard with Mr. Sibbald, which I got. I since have discovered my generous unknown friend to be Patrick Miller, Esq., brother to the Justice Clerk ; and drank a glass of claret with him by invitation at his own house yesternight. I am nearly agreed with Creech to print my book, and I suppose I will begin on

---

[1] However Burns was led to believe that the society here mentioned intended to pay a guinea a volume, he was obviously misinformed. The resolution come to by the meeting at which the matter was dealt with was "that in consideration of his superior merit, as well as of the compliment paid to them, Mr. Haggart should be directed to subscribe for one hundred copies in their name, for which he should pay to Mr. Burns £25 upon the publication of his book,"—that is to say, the volumes were to be paid for at the ordinary rate to subscribers.

Monday. I will send a subscription bill or two next post, when I intend writing my first kind patron, Mr. Aiken. I saw his son to-day, and he is very well.

Dugald Stewart, and some of my learned friends, put me in the periodical paper called the *Lounger*, a copy of which I here enclose you. I was, sir, when I was first honoured with your notice, too obscure; now I tremble lest I should be ruined by being dragged too suddenly into the glare of polite and learned observation.

The Edinburgh society into which the Poet was thus speedily introduced was, in many respects, a brilliant one. Of men of letters who flourished there, the following are noteworthy:—Dr. Dugald Stewart, Professor of Moral Philosophy; Dr. Hugh Blair, Professor of Belles Lettres; Dr. Blacklock, the blind poet; Dr. Robertson, the historian; Mr. Alison, author of a famous "Essay on Taste;" and Mr. Mackenzie, the "Man of Feeling."

In the legal circle, two names stand out prominently in connexion with Burns's career in Edinburgh,—Henry Erskine, the witty and eminent advocate, and Lord Monboddo, the genial Lord of Session, whose lovely daughter's charms Burns has so enthusiastically celebrated both in prose and verse.[1]

Besides those men of literary and legal note, not a few persons of high rank still deigned to find town-residence in Edinburgh; amongst which notables Jane, Duchess of Gordon, was the leading star.

---

[1] To this Edinburgh beauty, Burns thus refers in his "Address to Edinburgh:—

Fair Burnet strikes the adoring eye,
Heaven's beauties on my fancy shine;
I see the Sire of Love on high,
And own His work indeed divine.

And in a letter to Wm. Chalmers, Ayr, this glowing passage occurs:—

"Heavenly Miss Burnet, daughter to Lord Monboddo, at whose house I have had the honour to be more than once. There has not been anything like her in all the combinations of beauty, grace, and goodness the great Creator has formed since Milton's Eve on the first day of her existence."

We saw how within a few weeks Burns found himself lionized by the highest and most learned of the city; and we know how, by virtue of his native genius and strong good sense, he managed, for a time, to acquit himself nobly among the noblest and most scholarly with whom he was so suddenly brought into unwonted contact. In one sense, it was a marvellous achievement for him, the rustic son of rustic toils and experiences, to command and fill, as he did, a place in such a brilliant and cultured circle. Yet in another sense it was not strange; for in all that circle there was, after all, none so great and gifted as he.

> While spending his evenings—says Chambers—with beauty, rank and talent, Burns continued content with the share of John Richmond's room and bed. John helped him to transcribe his poems for the press, and, when he came in at night, jaded and excited, would read to him till he fell asleep. Richmond testified that he kept good hours, and observed the rules of sobriety. After a brief residence in town, his plain rustic garb gave way to a suit of blue and buff, the livery of Mr. Fox, with buckskins and top-boots. He continued to wear his hair tied behind, and spread upon his forehead, but without the powder which was then nearly universal. On the whole, his appearance was modest and becoming. It was remarked that he showed no sign of embarrassment in refined society, and that he took his part in conversation with freedom and energy, but without the least forwardness. The literati were surprised to find in what pure English and with how much eloquence he could express his ideas, and how glowing and brilliant these ideas often were. Principal Robertson declared that he had "scarcely ever met with any man whose conversation displayed greater vigour than that of Burns." His poems had, he acknowledged, surprised him; his prose compositions appeared even more wonderful; but the conversation was a marvel beyond all. We are thus left to understand that the best of Burns has not been, and was not of a nature to be, transmitted to posterity.

The unique power and charm of the Poet's conversation are alluded to by many who were privileged to converse with him, strikingly, amongst others, by the witty and accomplished Duchess of Gordon, who once confessed that in all her experience in the most brilliant society, no conversation had ever "so set her off her feet" as that of Burns. It is no great matter for surprise that he was able to fascinate as he did the rustic maidens of Tarbolton and Mauchline; but to astonish and captivate those high-born ladies in Edinburgh was indeed an amazing accomplishment. The secret of it we take to have been the same in both cases. By nature, he, with all his great passionate soul, simply worshipped the sex, and freely offered his unstinted homage. To his wondrous mind and imagination, his whole manner, his thrilling voice, his great dark flashing eye, all lent their aid in proclaiming his adoration; and so Burns—ever gentle and deferential towards the ladies—with gleaming wit and melting pathos, with glowing imagination and irresistible power, stormed the hearts of "the lovely dears."

Various contemporary sketches of his appearances in Edinburgh society afford information so thoroughly interesting and reliable as to command a prominent place in his biography.

In a communication to Dr. Currie, Professor Stewart, who, it will be remembered, had met with and entertained the Poet at Catrine House, in October 1786, says:—

> The attentions he received during his stay in town from all ranks and descriptions of persons, were such as would have turned any head but his own. I cannot say that I could perceive any unfavourable effect which they left on his mind. He retained the same simplicity of manners and appearance which had struck me so forcibly when I first saw him in the country; nor did he seem to feel any additional self-importance from the number and rank of his new acquaintance. His dress was perfectly suited to his station, plain and unpretending, with a sufficient attention to neatness.
>
> The variety of his engagements, while in Edinburgh, prevented me from seeing him so often as I could have wished. In the course of the spring he called on me once or twice, at my request, early in the morning, and walked

with me to Braid Hills, in the neighbourhood of the town, when he charmed me still more by his private conversation than he had ever done in company. He was passionately fond of the beauties of nature; and I recollect once he told me, when I was admiring a distant prospect in one of our morning walks, that the sight of so many smoking cottages gave a pleasure to his mind, which none could understand who had not witnessed, like himself, the happiness and the worth which they contained. All the faculties of Burns's mind were, as far as I could judge, equally vigorous; and his predilection for poetry was rather the result of his own enthusiastic and impassioned nature, than of a genius exclusively adapted to that species of composition. From his conversation, I should have pronounced him to be fitted to excel in whatever walk of ambition he had chosen to exert his abilities.

Professor's Walker's first meeting with Burns took place at breakfast in the house of Dr. Blacklock. Of that meeting he wrote as follows:[1]—

I was not much struck with his first appearance, as I had previously heard it described. His person, though strong and well knit, and much superior to what might be expected in a ploughman, was still rather coarse in its outline. His stature, from want of setting up, appeared to be only of the middle size, but was rather above it. His motions were firm and decided, and though without any pretensions to grace, were at the same time so free from clownish constraint, as to show that he had not always been confined to the society of his profession. His countenance was not of that elegant cast which is most frequent among the upper ranks, but it was manly and intelligent, and marked by a thoughtful gravity which shaded at times into sternness. In his large dark eye the most striking index of his genius resided. It was full of mind, and would have been singularly expressive, under the management of one who could employ it with more art, for the purpose of expression.

He was plainly, but properly dressed, in a style midway between the holiday costume of a farmer and that of the company with which he now associated. His black hair, without powder, at a time when it was very generally worn, was tied behind, and spread upon his forehead. Upon the whole, from his person,

---

[1] Professor Walker. See vol. ii. p. 301.

physiognomy, and dress, had I met him near a seaport, and been required to guess his condition, I should have probably conjectured him to be the master of a merchant vessel of the most respectable class.

In no part of his manner was there the slightest degree of affectation; nor could a stranger have suspected, from anything in his behaviour or conversation, that he had been for some months the favourite of all the fashionable circles of a metropolis.

In conversation he was powerful. His conceptions and expression were of corresponding vigour, and on all subjects were as remote as possible from commonplaces. Though somewhat authoritative, it was in a way which gave little offence,[1] and was readily imputed to his inexperience in those modes of smoothing dissent and softening assertion which are important characteristics of polished manners. After breakfast I requested him to communicate some of his unpublished pieces, and he recited his farewell song to the "Banks of Ayr," introducing it with a description of the circumstances in which it was composed, more striking than the poem itself. I paid particular attention to his recitation, which was plain, slow, articulate, and forcible, but without any eloquence or art. He did not always lay the emphasis with propriety, nor did he humour the sentiment by the variations of his voice. He was standing, during the time, with his face towards the window, to which, and not to his auditors, he directed his eye; thus depriving himself of any additional effect which the language of his composition might have borrowed from the language of his countenance. In this he resembled the generality of singers in ordinary company, who, to shun any charge of affectation, withdraw all meaning from

---

[1] Burns certainly did give offence in one incident narrated by Cromek:—At a private breakfast party, in an Edinburgh literary circle, the conversation turned on the poetical merit and pathos of Gray's *Elegy*, a poem of which he was enthusiastically fond. A clergyman present, remarkable for his love of paradox and for his eccentric notions upon every subject, distinguished himself by an injudicious and ill-timed attack on this exquisite poem, which Burns, with generous warmth for the reputation of Gray, manfully defended. As the gentleman's remarks were rather general than specific, Burns urged him to bring forward the passages which he thought exceptionable. He made several attempts to quote the poem, but always in a blundering, inaccurate manner. Burns bore all this for a good while with his usual good-natured forbearance, till at length, goaded by the fastidious criticisms and wretched quibblings of his opponent, he roused himself, and, with an eye flashing contempt and indignation, and with great vehemence of gesticulation, he thus addressed the cold critic: "Sir, I now perceive a man may be an excellent judge of poetry by square and rule, and after all be a d—— blockhead."

their features, and lose the advantage by which vocal performers on the stage augment the impression and give energy to the sentiment of the song.

In a letter written to Lockhart some forty years after the event, Sir Walter Scott embodied his reminiscences of that single occasion on which he met with Burns. A special interest attaches to what the world-famed novelist tells us about him whose name stands alongside his own at the head of the roll of Scottish literary greatness.

> As for Burns, I may truly say, *Virgilium vidi tantum.* I was a lad of fifteen in 1786-87, when he came first to Edinburgh, but I had sense and feeling enough to be much interested in his poetry, and would have given the world to know him. . . . As it was, I saw him one day at the late venerable Professor Fergusson's, where there were several gentlemen of literary reputation, among whom I remember the celebrated Dr. Dugald Stewart. Of course we youngsters sat silent, looked, and listened. The only thing I remember which was remarkable in Burns's manner was the effect produced upon him by a print of Bunbury's, representing a soldier lying dead on the snow, his dog sitting in misery on one side—on the other his widow, with a child in her arms. These lines were written underneath :—
>
>> Cold on Canadian hills, or Minden's plain,
>> Perhaps that parent wept her soldier slain—
>> Bent o'er her babe, her eye dissolved in dew,
>> The big drops mingling with the milk he drew,
>> Gave the sad presage of his future years,
>> The child of misery baptized in tears.
>
> Burns seemed much affected by the print, or rather the ideas which it suggested to his mind. He actually shed tears. He asked whose the lines were, and it chanced that nobody but myself remembered that they occur in a half-forgotten poem of Langhorne's, called by the unpromising title of "The Justice of Peace." I whispered my information to a friend present, who mentioned it to Burns, who rewarded me with a look and a word which, though in mere civility, I then received, and still recollect, with great pleasure. His person was strong and robust ; his manners rustic, not clownish ; a sort of dignified plainness and

simplicity, which received part of its effect perhaps from one's knowledge of his extraordinary talents. His features are represented in Mr. Nasmyth's picture; but to me it conveys the idea that they are diminished, as if seen in perspective. I think his countenance was more massive than it looks in any of the portraits. I would have taken the Poet, had I not known what he was, for a very sagacious country farmer of the old Scotch school; that is, none of your modern agriculturists, who keep labourers for their drudgery, but the *douce gudeman* who held his own plough. There was a strong expression of sense and shrewdness in all his lineaments: the eye alone, I think, indicated the poetical character and temperament. It was large, and of a cast which glowed (I say literally *glowed*) when he spoke with feeling or interest. I never saw such another eye in a human head, though I have seen the most distinguished men of my time. His conversation expressed perfect self-confidence, without the slightest presumption. Among the men who were the most learned of their time and country, he expressed himself with perfect firmness, but without the least intrusive forwardness. . . . I have only to add that his dress corresponded with his manner. He was like a farmer dressed in his best to dine with the laird. I do not speak in *malem partem* when I say I never saw a man in company with his superiors in station and information, more perfectly free from either the reality or the affectation of embarrassment. I was told, but did not observe it, that his address to females was extremely deferential, and always with a turn either to the pathetic or humorous, which engaged their attention particularly. I have heard the late Duchess of Gordon remark this. I do not know anything I can add to these recollections of forty years since.

No student of Burns need fail to gather from the above a pretty clear idea of how the Poet looked and played what may be termed his more public part among the eminent literati and the social grandees of that time in Edinburgh. We turn now to look at him as he walked and talked on a somewhat lower social plane, more in the way of private acquaintance and boon-companionship. Early in 1787 a personal intimacy was formed between Burns and Alexander Nasmyth,[1] the young artist who, in expression of his admiration, gratuitously executed the famous painting of the

---

[1] Alexander Nasmyth. See vol. ii. p. 121.

Poet.[1] The preparation of this work brought Burns and Nasmyth a good deal together. From reliable information, which he personally fell in with, Chambers tells us that—

> After the sittings for that original, Mr. Nasmyth and the Poet would take a ramble together, not unfrequently to the King's Park, where Burns delighted to climb Arthur's Seat, and, lying on the summit, gaze at its grand panorama of twelve of the principal Scottish counties. Having one night transgressed the rules of sobriety, and sat up till an early hour in the morning, they agreed not to go home at all, but commence an excursion to the Pentland Hills. Passing a cottage a few miles out of town, they heard a frightful noise within, and, going up to learn what was the matter, found that the sounds proceeded from a poor man whose reason had given way. Mr. Nasmyth used afterwards to describe in thrilling terms the appalling exclamations of the lunatic, and the effect which they had upon Burns. The two friends afterwards continued their walk to the hills, had a fine morning ramble, and, having thus cleared off the effects of their dissipation, came down to Roslin to breakfast. Burns, who was now extremely hungry, found in Mrs. David Wilson's little inn such ample solacement, that in a fit of gratitude he scrawled a couple of verses on the reverse side of a wooden platter :—

> My blessings on ye, honest wife,
>   I ne'er was here before ;
> Ye've wealth o' gear for spoon and knife—
>   Heart could not wish for more.
>
> Heaven keep you clear of sturt and strife,
>   Till far ayont fourscore ;
> And by the Lord o' death and life,
>   I'll ne'er gae by your door ![2]

Another associate with whom the Poet was necessarily brought into contact was William Smellie,[3] printer, to whom the typography

---

[1] From Nasmyth's painting there was taken (also gratuitously) by John Beugo the engraving which was reproduced in the Edinburgh edition. In his letter to John Ballantyne of February 24, the Poet refers to this excellent and generally accepted likeness : "I am getting my *phiz* done by an eminent engraver, and if it can be ready in time, I shall appear in my book, looking like other fools, to my title-page."

[2] See Vol. ii. p. 123.

[3] See Vol. ii. p. 239.

of the Edinburgh edition was entrusted. Burns spent a good deal of time revising his proof-sheets at Smellie's place of business, and some amusing anecdotes are told of his appearances there. He used to walk up and down the composing-room, vigorously cracking a whip which he often carried with him; and when in the office working at his proofs, he insisted on occupying a particular seat, which came to be known in the place as "Burns's Stool."

Burns was introduced by Smellie to the Crochallan Fencibles, a convivial club of a kind then common enough in the city. There the Poet met with company more on his own social level, and found a species of entertainment more to his liking, unfortunately, than among his learned and noble patrons.

In such-like jovial spheres, he made the acquaintance of Heron, Dunbar, Nicol, Ainslie, and others; for it seems beyond doubt that the Poet mingled a good deal in the tavern-revels of middle-class tradesmen, writers, and kindred Edinburgh cronies.

Meanwhile, notwithstanding so many new and hazardous social distractions, he had pushed forward with his second edition, which was at length issued by Creech, the noted publisher, on the 21st of April. Three well-known poems, which had been withheld from the Kilmarnock edition, now appeared in this—"The Address to the Unco Gude," "The Ordination," and "Death and Doctor Hornbook."

Among other new pieces, there appeared the "Address to Edinburgh," "Tam Samson's Elegy," and the "Twa Brigs." The Kilmarnock Preface was displaced by the Author's Dedication,— "To the Noblemen and Gentlemen of the Caledonian Hunt,"—which is here reproduced in full :—

> MY LORDS AND GENTLEMEN —A Scottish bard, proud of the name, and whose highest ambition is to sing in his country's service—where shall he so properly look for patronage as to the illustrious names of his native land, those who bear the honours and inherit the virtues of their ancestors? The poetic

EDINBURGH EDITIONS. 155

genius of my country found me, as the prophetic bard Elijah did Elisha, at the plough, and threw her inspiring mantle over me. She bade me sing the loves, the joys, the rural scenes and rural pleasures of my native soil, in my native tongue. I tuned my wild, artless notes as she inspired. She whispered me to come to this ancient metropolis of Caledonia, and lay my songs under your honoured protection. I now obey her dictates.

Though much indebted to your goodness, I do not approach you, my Lords and Gentlemen, in the usual style of dedication, to thank you for past favours; that path is so hackneyed by prostituted learning, that honest rusticity is ashamed of it. Nor do I present this address with the venal soul of a servile author, looking for a continuation of those favours—I was bred to the plough, and am independent. I come to claim the common Scottish name with you, my illustrious countrymen, and to tell the world that I glory in the title. I come to congratulate my country that the blood of her ancient heroes still runs uncontaminated, and that from your courage, knowledge, and public spirit, she may expect protection, wealth, and liberty. In the last place, I come to proffer my warmest wishes to the great Fountain of honour, the Monarch of the Universe, for your welfare and happiness.

When you go forth to awaken the echoes, in the ancient and favourite amusement of your forefathers, may pleasure ever be of your party, and may social joy await your return! When harassed in courts or camps with the justlings of bad men and bad measures, may the honest consciousness of injured worth attend your return to your native seats; and may domestic happiness, with a smiling welcome, meet you at your gates! May corruption shrink at your kindling, indignant glance; and may tyranny in the ruler, and licentiousness in the people, equally find you an inexorable foe! I have the honour to be, with the sincerest gratitude and highest respect, my Lords and Gentlemen, your most devoted, humble servant, ROBERT BURNS.

EDINBURGH, *April* 4, 1787.

In the volume there also appeared a list of the subscribers, covering thirty-eight pages, showing fifteen hundred subscribers, taking up two thousand eight hundred copies, and containing the names of many persons of the highest literary and social status in the country.

With the issuing of this second edition of his poems, the Poet's avowed mission to Edinburgh was accomplished. Early in the ensuing month of May he left the city for a tour in the Border country. But ere we pass from this strange eventful period,—the hey-day of Burns's lifetime,—let us try to gather, from his own pen, some further idea of what he himself thought about his bright adventure and its probable results. That he all along considered that his Edinburgh blaze of popularity would not and could not last, is made very evident by various letters penned by him in the midst of that "meteoric glow."

As early as January 15 he wrote to Mrs. Dunlop as follows :—

> You are afraid I shall grow intoxicated with my prosperity as a poet. Alas! madam, I know myself and the world too well. I do not mean any airs of affected modesty; I am willing to believe that my abilities deserve some notice; but in a most enlightened, informed age and nation, when poetry is, and has been, the study of men of the first natural genius, aided with all the powers of polite learning, polite books, and polite company—to be dragged forth to the full glare of learned and polite observation, with all my imperfections of awkward rusticity and crude, unpolished ideas on my head—I assure you, madam, I do not dissemble when I tell you I tremble for the consequences. The novelty of a poet in my obscure situation, without any of those advantages which are reckoned necessary for that character, at least at this time of day, has raised a partial tide of public notice which has borne me to a height where I am absolutely, feelingly certain, my abilities are inadequate to support me; and too surely do I see that time when the same tide will leave me, and recede perhaps as far below the mark of truth. I do not say this in the ridiculous affectation of self-abasement and modesty. I have studied myself, and know what ground I occupy; and, however a friend or the world may differ from me in that particular, I stand for my own opinion, in silent resolve, with all the tenaciousness of property. I mention this to you once for all, to disburden my mind, and I do not wish to hear or say more about it. But,
>
> "When proud fortune's ebbing tide recedes,"
>
> you will bear me witness, that when my bubble of fame was at the highest, I stood unintoxicated, with the inebriating cup in my hand, looking forward with

rueful resolve to the hastening time when the blow of calumny should dash it to the ground with all the eagerness of vengeful triumph.

In a similar strain he wrote to the Rev. Mr. Lawrie, of Loudon, on February 5th; and on the eve of his departure from the city, he sent the following to Dr. Blair:—

> I leave Edinburgh to-morrow morning, but could not go without troubling you with half a line, sincerely to thank you for the kindness, patronage, and friendship you have shown me. I often felt the embarrassment of my singular situation: drawn forth from the veriest shades of life to the glare of remark, and honoured by the notice of those illustrious names of my country whose works, while they are applauded to the end of time, will ever instruct and mend the heart. However the meteor-like novelty of my appearance in the world might attract notice, and honour me with the acquaintance of the permanent lights of genius and literature, those who are truly benefactors of the immortal nature of man, I knew very well that my utmost merit was far unequal to the task of preserving that character when once the novelty was over: I have made up my mind that abuse, or almost even neglect, will not surprise me in my quarters.

It is impossible to read these passages, written in the shadows of that bright public glare, without feeling deeply for poor Burns, haunted, amid so splendid an outward show, by such gloomy forebodings, and still inly writhing from the "wandering stabs of remorse." Making large allowance, however, for his situation in Edinburgh (so terribly trying in many a way), it must be admitted that the results of that time of fame might have been far different from what they turned out to be, had he succeeded better in exercising that "prudent, cautious *self-control*" of which he elsewhere speaks. Scanning his own ways in Edinburgh, Burns clearly saw and fully acknowledged all this, and more: witness, *e.g.*, that remarkable letter, with its sad, heart-searching allegory, which he wrote in February to the Earl of Buchan:—

The honour your lordship has done me, by your notice and advice in yours of the 1st instant, I shall ever gratefully remember—

"Praise from thy lips 'tis mine with joy to boast,
They best can give it who deserve it most."

Your lordship touches the darling chord of my heart, when you advise me to fire my muse at Scottish story and Scottish scenes. I wish for nothing more than to make a leisurely pilgrimage through my native country; to sit and muse on those once hard-contended fields, where Caledonia, rejoicing, saw her bloody lion borne through broken ranks to victory and fame; and, catching the inspiration, to pour the deathless names in song. But, my lord, in the midst of these enthusiastic reveries, a long-visaged, dry, moral-looking phantom strides across my imagination, and pronounces these emphatic words:—

"I, Wisdom, dwell with Prudence. Friend, I do not come to open the ill-closed wounds of your follies and misfortunes, merely to give you pain: I wish through these wounds to imprint a lasting lesson on your heart. I will not mention how many of my salutary advices you have despised; I have given you line upon line, and precept upon precept; and while I was chalking out to you the straight way to wealth and character, with audacious effrontery you have zig-zagged across the path, contemning me to my face. You know the consequences. It is not yet three months since home was so hot for you, that you were on the wing for the western shore of the Atlantic, not to make a fortune, but to hide your misfortune.

"Now that your dear-loved Scotia puts it in your power to return to the situation of your forefathers, will you follow these will-o'-wisp meteors of fancy and whim, till they bring you once more to the brink of ruin? I grant that the utmost ground you can occupy is but half a step from the veriest poverty; but still it is half a step from it. If all that I can urge be ineffectual, let her who seldom calls to you in vain, let the call of pride prevail with you. You know how you feel at the iron gripe of ruthless oppression: you know how you bear the galling sneer of contumelious greatness. I hold you out the conveniences, the comforts of life, independence, and character, on the one hand; I tender you servility, dependence, and wretchedness on the other. I will not insult your understanding by bidding you make a choice."

This, my lord, is unanswerable. I must return to my humble station, and woo my rustic muse in my wonted way, at the plough-tail. Still, my lord, while the drops of life warm my heart, gratitude to that dear-loved country in which I boast my birth, and gratitude to those her distinguished sons who have honoured me so much with their patronage and approbation, shall, while stealing through my humble shades, ever distend my bosom, and at times, as now, draw forth the swelling tear.

It need occasion little or no surprise that, during these five months, Burns produced very little poetry. He had his new edition to complete and supervise for publication, and endless social engagements to engross his time and tax his powers. Besides, he wrote a goodly number of letters (some of them of outstanding excellence), and began his second Commonplace Book.[1]

Among the few poetical pieces composed in Edinburgh, the following may be noted—"Epistle to the Gudewife of Wauchope House," "Address to Edinburgh," and the original and more balladlike version of "Ye Banks and Braes":—

> Ye flowery banks o' bonnie Doon,
>   How can ye bloom sae fair?
> How can ye chant, ye little birds,
>   And I sae fu' o' care?
>
> Thou'll break my heart, thou bonnie bird,
>   That sings upon the bough;
> Thou minds me o' the happy days
>   When my fause luve was true.
>
> Thou'll break my heart, thou bonnie bird,
>   That sings beside thy mate;
> For sae I sat, and sae I sang,
>   And wistna o' my fate.
>
> Aft hae I roved by bonnie Doon,
>   To see the woodbine twine,

---

[1] For Burns's Commonplace Books, see Appendix.

And ilka bird sang o' its luve ;
   And sae did I o' mine.

Wi' lightsome heart I pu'd a rose
   Frae aff its thorny tree ;
But my fause luver staw the rose,
   And left the thorn wi' me.

CHAPTER VI.

BORDER, WEST HIGHLAND, NORTHERN, AND DEVON VALLEY TOURS- MAY 5-OCTOBER 20, 1787. AGE 28.

> We'll sing auld Coila's plains and fells,
> Her moors red-brown wi heather bells,
> Her banks and braes, her dens and dells,
>   Where glorious WALLACE
> Aft bure the gree, as story tells,
>   Frae Southron billies.
>
> . . . .
>
> O sweet are Coila's haughs an' woods,
> When lintwhites chant among the buds,
> And jinkin' hares, in amorous whids,
>   Their loves enjoy ;
> While thro' the braes the cushat croods
>   With wailfu' cry.
>   *Epistle to William Simpson.*
>
> Admiring nature in her wildest grace,
> These northern scenes with weary feet I trace.
>
> . . . .
>
> Here Poesy might wake her heaven-taught lyre
> And look through nature with creative fire.
>   *Lines pencilled at Kenmore, Taymouth.*

ESCAPING from the wearing strain of society engagements and club convivialities, Burns set out on 5th May, in company with Mr. Robert Ainslie[1] for a tour in the Border country,[2] and arrived that

---

[1] See vol. i. p. 9.

[2] Throughout this tour, Burns rode his famous mare "Jenny Geddes," so called by him in memory of the plucky old Scotch worthy of that name, of whom tradition states that she threw her stool at the head of the clergyman who, in 1637, first attempted to read the obnoxious Liturgy in St. Giles' Cathedral.

same (Saturday) evening at Ainslie's home at Berrywell, near Dunse. Next day he went with the family to church, where, in course of the sermon, the minister having quoted Scripture in stern denunciation of the sinful, according to a good old custom Miss Ainslie hastened to search out the passage quoted. On observing this, Burns, taking pencil and paper, wrote off-hand and presented to Miss Ainslie the following neat little product of his extraordinary *impromptu* gift :—

> Fair maid, you need not take the hint
> Nor idle texts pursue,
> 'Twas *guilty sinners* that he meant,
> Not *angels* such as you.

On Monday the travellers passed on to Coldstream, and there crossing the Tweed, Burns set foot for the first time on English soil. The occasion strongly excited in the breast of Scotland's great national Bard those deep-rooted feelings of patriotism which he ever cherished for the land of his birth. From an account of the scene, communicated many years afterwards by Ainslie, Chambers gives an interesting passage :—

> When they arrived at Coldstream, where the dividing line between England and Scotland is the Tweed, Mr. Ainslie suggested going across to the other side of the river by the Coldstream bridge, that Burns might be enabled to say he had been in England. They did so, and were pacing slowly along on English ground, enjoying their walk, when Mr. Ainslie was surprised to see the Poet throw away his hat, and, thus uncovered, kneel down with uplifted hands, and apparently rapt in a fit of enthusiasm. Mr. Ainslie kept silence, uncertain what was next to be done, when Burns, with extreme emotion, and an expression of countenance which his companion could never forget, prayed for and blessed Scotland most solemnly, by pronouncing aloud, in tones of the deepest devotion, the two concluding stanzas of the "Cotter's Saturday Night" :—
>
> > O Scotia! my dear, my native soil!
> > For whom my warmest wish to Heaven is sent!
> > Long may thy hardy sons of rustic toil

> Be blest with health, and peace, and sweet content!
>   And O! may Heaven their simple lives prevent
> From luxury's contagion, weak and vile!
>   Then, howe'er crowns and coronets be rent,
>   A virtuous populace may rise the while,
> And stand a wall of fire around their much-loved Isle.
>
> O Thou! who poured the patriotic tide
>   That streamed through Wallace's undaunted heart,
> Who dared to nobly stem tyrannic pride,
>   Or nobly die, the second glorious part,
>   (The patriot's God, peculiarly Thou art,
> His friend, inspirer, guardian, and reward!)
>   O never, never Scotia's realm desert;
> But still the patriot, and the patriot bard,
> In bright succession raise, her ornament and guard!

The next places visited were Kelso and Jedburgh, at the latter of which towns he carried on a lively flirtation with a certain Miss Lindsay, to whom he presented his likeness, and of whom he thus (in his Diary) takes farewell:—"Sweet Isabella Lindsay, may peace dwell in thy bosom, uninterrupted, except by the tumultuous throbbings of love! That love-kindling eye must beam on another, not on me—that graceful form must bless another's arms, not mine!"

Spending Sunday, 13th May, at Selkirk, he wrote (enclosing that racy panegyric entitled "Willie's Awa',") to his publisher, Creech, then on a visit to London. Monday he spent at Innerleithen, and "saw Elibanks and Elibraes, on the other side of the Tweed." Returning to Berrywell on Tuesday, he sojourned there until Friday, when he set out for Berwick. On Saturday, he and Ainslie were admitted Royal Arch Masons of St. Abbs' Lodge, Eyemouth. Dunbar was next visited; then Berrywell and Kelso again.

His Diary shows this note of Thursday (24th May):—

> I am taken extremely ill with strong feverish symptoms, and take a servant of Mr. Hood's [at whose house Burns dined that evening] to watch me all night. Embittering remorse scares my fancy at the gloomy forebodings of death. I am determined for the future to live in such a manner as not to be scared at the approach of death. I am sure I could meet him with indifference, but for "the something beyond the grave."

Having quickly recovered from this sharp illness, he again crossed the Border, and in course of the ensuing few days saw Alnwick, Warkworth, Morpeth, Newcastle, Hexham, Longtown, and Carlisle. From Carlisle he returned by the coast to Annan; thence on to Dumfries, where he stayed about a week, and visited Dalswinton, the estate of Mr. Patrick Miller, who had already expressed a wish to have the Poet as tenant of one of his farms. On 9th June, after nearly five weeks' sight-seeing, he arrived, quite unlooked for, at Mossgiel. It is said that his mother welcomed him with the simple, heart-full exclamation, "Oh, Robbie!" When six months before, he rode away to Edinburgh, his fortunes were low, and his prospects, to say the least, very uncertain; but he now returned home with the laurels of high poetic fame on his brow, and with the ball of bright fortune apparently at his foot. It is needless to speculate on the feelings of the Mossgiel family at such a return. These may be in some measure imagined, but can in no adequate way be put into words. Our thoughts on this subject, however, may be pleasantly helped by remembering that, notwithstanding his passionate errors, Burns had ever borne himself to his mother and brothers and sisters, as an affectionate, generous-hearted son and brother.

On the evening of the day on which he arrived at Mossgiel, he went to Mauchline to visit his more intimate associates. Calling at Jean Armour's home, ostensibly to see his infant daughter, he seems to have been received in an almost fawning way by Jean's father and mother. Recollecting the *fugæ warrant* of the preceding summer, the altered reception irritated his proud spirit, as we gather from a letter written at Mauchline, on 11th June, to Mr. James Smith, Linlithgow, in which the following passage occurs:—

> If anything had been wanting to disgust me completely at Armour's family, their mean, servile compliance would have done it. Give me a spirit like my favourite hero, Milton's Satan—
>
> > Hail! horrors, hail!
> > Infernal world! and thou profoundest hell
> > Receive thy new possessor! one who brings
> > A mind not to be changed by *place* or *time!*
>
> I cannot settle to my mind. Farming—the only thing of which I know anything, and Heaven knows but little do I understand even of that—I cannot, dare not risk, on farms as they are. If I do not fix, I will go for Jamaica. Should I stay in an unsettled state at home, I would only dissipate my little fortune, and ruin what I intend shall compensate my little ones for the stigma I have brought on their names.

As also from that written to William Nicol,[1] in which still more of this chafing pride and bitterness appear:—

> I never, my friend, thought mankind very capable of anything generous; but the stateliness of the patricians in Edinburgh, and the civility of my plebeian brethren (who perhaps formerly eyed me askance) since I returned home, have nearly put me out of conceit altogether with my species. I have bought a pocket Milton, which I carry perpetually about with me, in order to study the sentiments, the dauntless magnanimity, the intrepid, unyielding independence, the desperate daring, and noble defiance of hardship, in that great personage, Satan. 'Tis true I have just now a little cash; but I am afraid the star that hitherto has shed its malignant, purpose-blasting rays full in my zenith; that noxious planet, so baneful in its influences to the rhyming tribe, I

---

[1] See vol. ii. p. 128.

much dread is not yet beneath my horizon. Misfortune dodges the path of human life; the poetic mind finds itself miserably deranged in, and unfit for, the walks of business; add to all, that thoughtless follies and harebrained whims, like so many *ignes fatui* eternally diverging from the right line of sober discretion, sparkle with step-bewitching blaze in the idly-gazing eyes of the poor heedless bard, till pop, "he falls like Lucifer, never to hope again." God grant this may be an unreal picture with respect to me!

It has already been mentioned that even in his angriest mood against the Armour family in general, he never lost notion of bonnie Jean in particular. So now, when back to his "rural shades," though during the bygone winter and spring he had been smiled upon by so many high-born beauties, his heart glowed afresh with the old love for that simple-mannered, warm-hearted, sweet-tempered country lass. Their intimacy was renewed as formerly, and, as it transpired, with a like result.

Towards the end of the month, he went on a short trip to the West Highlands. On his way he visited Glasgow, from whence he sent to his mother and three sisters a present of silk sufficient to make dresses and cloaks for them all. At Inverary, his entertainment not proving quite to his liking, drew from him the petulant and somewhat irreverent epigram :—

> Whoe'er he be that sojourns here,
>   I pity much his case,
> Unless he come to wait upon
>   The Lord their God—his Grace.
> There's naething here but Highland pride,
>   And Highland scab and hunger;
> If Providence has sent me here,
>   'Twas surely in an anger.

Before this trip was over, however, he made some amends for

the above by penning that other more just and kindly estimate of Highland hospitality :—

> When death's dark stream I ferry o'er—
> A time that surely shall come—
> In heaven itself I'll ask no more,
> Than just a Highland welcome.

Returned home, he wrote on 30th June a long letter to James Smith, describing a few of his West Highland experiences, and making mention of a certain love affair with an Ayrshire lady, whose identity has to this day remained a mystery. After telling of a very merry all-night entertainment at some hospitable Highland mansion, and of a day spent on Loch Lomond, the letter goes on to say :—

> We dined at another good fellow's house, and consequently pushed the bottle; when we went out to mount our horses, we found ourselves "No vera fou, but gaylie yet." My two friends and I rode soberly down the loch side, till by came a Highlandman at the gallop, on a tolerably good horse, but which had never known the ornaments of iron or leather. We scorned to be out-galloped by a Highlandman, so off we started, whip and spur. My companions, though seemingly gaily mounted, fell sadly astern; but my old mare, Jenny Geddes, one of the Rosinante family, strained past the Highlandman in spite of all his efforts with the hair-halter. Just I was passing him, Donald wheeled his horse, as if to cross before me, to mar my progress, when down came his horse, and threw his breckless rider in a clipt hedge; and down came Jenny Geddes over all, and my bardship between her and the Highlandman's horse. Jenny Geddes trode over me with such cautious reverence, that matters were not so bad as might well have been expected; so I came off with a few cuts and bruises, and a thorough resolution to be a pattern of sobriety for the future.
>
> I have yet fixed on nothing with respect to the serious business of life. I am, just as usual, a rhyming, mason-making, raking, aimless idle fellow. However, I shall somewhere have a farm soon. I was going to say a wife too; but that must never be my blessed lot. I am but a younger son of the house of

Parnassus, and, like other younger sons of great families, I may intrigue, if I choose to run all risks, but must not marry.

I am afraid I have almost ruined one source, the principal one, indeed, of my former happiness—that eternal propensity I always had to fall in love. My heart no more glows with feverish rapture. I have no paradisiacal evening interviews stolen from the restless cares and prying inhabitants of this weary world. I have only——. This last is one of your distant acquaintances, has a fine figure and elegant manners, and, in the train of some great folks whom you know, has seen the politest quarters in Europe. I do like her a good deal; but what piques me is her conduct at the commencement of our acquaintance. I frequently visited her when I was in ——; and after passing regularly the intermediate degrees between the distant formal bow and the familiar grasp round the waist, I ventured, in my careless way, to talk of friendship in rather ambiguous terms; and after her return to ——, I wrote to her in the same style. Miss, construing my words further, I suppose, than even I intended, flew off in a tangent of female dignity and reserve, like a mounting lark in an April morning; and wrote me an answer which measured me out very completely what an immense way I had to travel before I could reach the climate of her favour. But I am an old hawk at the sport; and wrote her such a cool, deliberate, prudent reply, as brought my bird from her aerial towerings pop down at my foot like Corporal Trim's hat.

During the month of July, which he spent at Mossgiel, he composed his elegy on Mr. John M'Leod of Raasay, and drew up for Dr. Moore the famous *Autobiographical Sketch*, from which we have repeatedly quoted in former chapters. On the 7th of August he returned to Edinburgh. There were accounts to settle with his publisher, Wm. Creech; besides, he purposed making the city his starting-point on a tour to the north. Share of John Richmond's room not being at this time available, he took up quarters with William Nicol. A matter of a very disagreeable nature now demanded urgent attention—a matter which may go a good way to explain those gloomy, self-upbraiding passages which we find in some of his letters of this period. In brief, a woman, named Jenny Clow, then "under a cloud" on his account, had taken out an *in meditatione fugæ* warrant against him. On 15th August he furnished the necessary security, and was thus free from apprehension. Ten days afterwards, he set out on his tour in the north country, in company with Nicol. They travelled in a *chaise*, the dominie being but an indifferent horseman. From the journal which Burns kept, we gather that the tour comprised visits to (among other places) Linlithgow, Falkirk, Stirling, Bannockburn, Devon Valley, Harvieston Castle, Crieff, Taymouth, Dunkeld, Aberfeldy, Blair Castle, Inverness, Gordon Castle, Cullen, Banff, Duff House, Aberdeen, Stonehaven, Laurencekirk, Arbroath, Dundee, and Kinross; thence, *via* Queensferry, back to Edinburgh. The Poet's notes of this extensive tour show that, though the time was short for so much travelling, he contrived to see a great variety of Scotland's finest inland scenery, and to personally visit, with set purpose and peculiar delight, many places identified with ancient Scottish warfare and romance, tradition, and song.

Before passing from this tour, more particular notice must be taken of some of its outstanding incidents.

On the windows of the room which Burns occupied at Stirling he inscribed these lines reflecting on the then reigning dynasty:—

> Here Stuarts once in glory reigned,
> And laws for Scotland's weal ordained;
> But now unroofed their palace stands,
> Their sceptre's swayed by other hands.
> The injured Stuart line is gone,
> A race outlandish fills their throne—
> An idiot race, to honour lost;
> Who know them best, despise them most.

To this imprudent action he was tempted on viewing the neglected state of the old hall at the castle, where, in Stuart times, the Parliament of Scotland sometimes assembled. The rude, harsh satire gave rise to considerable comment, from which the Poet suffered for a time.

Standing on the field of Bannockburn, his fancy took a nobler, happier flight.

> Here—he wrote in his Diary—no Scot can pass uninterested. I fancy to myself that I see my gallant, heroic countrymen, coming o'er the hill and down upon the plunderers of their country, the murderers of their fathers; noble revenge and just hate glowing in every vein, striding more and more eagerly as they approach the oppressive, insulting, bloodthirsty foe! I see them meet in gloriously-triumphant congratulation on the victorious field, exulting in their heroic royal leader, and rescued liberty and independence!

—which glowing prose might be set as a preface worthy of his grandest of all patriotic war-songs, "Scots wha hae."

From Stirling he went on his first visit to Harvieston Castle, where resided Mrs. Hamilton and Mrs. Chalmers (relatives of Gavin Hamilton) and their lovely daughters Charlotte Hamilton[1] and Peggy Chalmers,[2] with whom he afterwards carried on a peculiarly interesting correspondence.

Of his two days' sojourn at Blair Athole, an admirable sketch by Professor Walker is again available. The Professor, who was at this period tutor to the ducal family, and spent most of that Saturday and Sunday in the Bard's company, says:—

> On reaching Blair, he sent me notice of his arrival (as I had been previously acquainted with him), and I hastened to meet him at the inn. The Duke, to whom he brought a letter of introduction, was from home; but the Duchess, being informed of his arrival, gave him an invitation to sup and sleep at Athole House [Blair]. He accepted the invitation; but as the hour of supper was at some distance, begged I would, in the interval, be his guide through the grounds. It was already growing dark; yet the softened though faint and

---

[1] See vol. i. 304. [2] See vol. i. 94.

uncertain view of their beauties, which the moonlight afforded us, seemed exactly suited to the state of his feelings at the time. I had often, like others, experienced the pleasures which arise from the sublime or elegant landscape, but I never saw those feelings so intense as in Burns. When we reached a rustic hut on the river Tilt, where it is overhung by a woody precipice, from which there is a noble waterfall, he threw himself on the heathy seat, and gave himself up to a tender, abstracted, and voluptuous enthusiasm of imagination. I cannot help thinking it might have been here that he conceived the idea of the following lines, which he afterwards introduced into his poem on Bruar Water, when only fancying such a combination of objects as were now present to his eye :—

>Or, by the reaper's nightly beam,
>Mild-chequering through the trees,
>Rave to my darkly-dashing stream,
>Hoarse-swelling on the breeze.

It was with much difficulty I prevailed on him to quit this spot, and to be introduced in proper time to supper.

My curiosity was great to see how he would conduct himself in company so different from what he had been accustomed to. His manner was unembarrassed, plain, and firm. He appeared to have complete reliance on his own native good sense for directing his behaviour. He seemed at once to perceive and to appreciate what was due to the company and to himself, and never to forget a proper respect for the separate species of dignity belonging to each. He did not arrogate conversation, but, when led into it, he spoke with ease, propriety, and manliness. He tried to exert his abilities, because he knew it was ability alone gave him a title to be there. The Duke's fine young family attracted much of his admiration ; he drank their healths as *honest men and bonnie lasses*, an idea which was much applauded by the company, and with which he has very felicitously closed his poem.

This visit, which Burns looked upon as one of the happiest he had ever made, was cut short by Nicol's imperious desire to hurry forward. Short as it was, however, he was fortunate enough then to make the acquaintance of Mr. Graham of Fintry, who afterwards proved, in connexion with Excise and other matters, a friend kind and true.

At Castle Gordon, too, the Poet was received with the greatest cordiality by the Duke and Duchess. His note on this point says:—"The Duke makes me happier than ever great man did; noble, princely, yet mild and condescending and affable, gay and kind. The Duchess, charming, witty, kind, and sensible. God bless them!"

In such pleasant circumstances, Burns naturally wished to prolong his stay. But here again his travelling companion marred his happiness, and rudely broke up his visit. Quite inadvertently, the irascible Nicol had not been invited to dine at the castle; and, though the omission was at once corrected by a pressing invitation, his wrath was not appeased. To back up the invitation, Burns himself accompanied the Duke's messenger. They found Nicol in a towering passion at what he regarded as a deadly affront to his pedagogic majesty. Explanation and apology availed not. He had already ordered out the horses, and was stamping up and down in front of the village inn, rudely chiding the grooms for delaying to carry out his commands. The Poet had to choose between prolonging his auspicious visit to Castle Gordon, or at once proceeding on the journey with his highly-incensed fellow-traveller. He adopted the latter alternative. Driving away from Fochabers, his experience of Nicol's temper would fully justify the remark that travelling in such company was like "travelling with a loaded blunderbuss, full cock, at one's head."

From the narrative of one who, as a boy of thirteen, accompanied Burns and Nicol on a drive from Banff to Duff House, we reproduce the following:—

> In driving through the park, Mr. Nicol asked me whether I was aware that the gentleman who was speaking to me about the park was the author of the

poems I had no doubt heard of. "Yes," I replied. "Then have you read the poems?" "Oh yes! I was glad to do that," was my reply. "Then which of them did you like best?" Nicol asked. I said, "I was much entertained with the 'Twa Dogs,' and 'Death and Dr. Hornbook ;' but I like best by far the 'Cotter's Saturday Night,' although it made me *greet* when my father had me to read it to my mother."

Burns, with a sort of sudden start, looked in my face intently, and, patting my shoulder, said, "Well, my callant, I don't wonder at your *greeting* at reading the poem ; it made me *greet* more than once when I was writing it at *my* father's fireside."

I recollect very well that while Mr. Nicol loitered in the library, looking at the fine collection of old classics there, Burns, taking me with him for a guide, went a second time through some of the rooms to look at the old paintings, with the catalogue in his hand, and remarked particularly those of the Stuart family in the great drawing-room, on which he seemed to look with intense interest, making some remarks on them to his *boy*-guide, which the *man* fails to recollect. But the face and look of Robert Burns were such as, either boy or man, I never could forget.

In the neighbourhood of Montrose the Poet found himself among his paternal relations, concerning whom he wrote to his brother Gilbert in a letter which may fitly close our notes on this north-country tour :—

EDINBURGH, 17*th September* 1787.

I arrived here safe yesterday evening, after a tour of twenty-two days, and travelling nearly six hundred miles, windings included. My farthest stretch was about ten miles beyond Inverness. I went through the heart of the Highlands, by Crieff, Taymouth, the famous seat of Lord Breadalbane, down the Tay, among cascades and Druidical circles of stones, to Dunkeld, a seat of the Duke of Athole ; thence across Tay, and up one of his tributary streams to Blair of Athole, another of the Duke's seats, where I had the honour of spending nearly two days with his Grace and family ; thence many miles through a wild country, among cliffs grey with eternal snows and gloomy, savage glens, till I crossed Spey, and went down the stream through Strathspey, so famous in Scottish music, Badenoch, etc., till I reached Grant Castle, where I spent half a day with Sir James Grant and family ; and then crossed the country for Fort-

George, but called by the way at Cawdor, the ancient seat of Macbeth; there I saw the identical bed in which tradition says King Duncan was murdered; lastly, from Fort-George to Inverness.

I returned by the coast, through Nairn, Forres, and so on, to Aberdeen, thence to Stonehive [Stonehaven], where James Burnes, from Montrose, met me by appointment. I spent two days among our relations, and found our aunts, Jean and Isabel, still alive, and hale old women. John Caird, though born the same year with our father, walks as vigorously as I can. They have had several letters from his son in New York. William Brand is likewise a stout old fellow. But further particulars I delay till I see you, which will be in two or three weeks. The rest of my stages are not worth rehearsing: warm as I was from Ossian's country, where I had seen his very grave, what cared I for fishing-towns or fertile carses? I slept at the famous Brodie of Brodie's one night, and dined at Gordon Castle next day with the Duke, Duchess, and family. I am thinking to cause my old mare to meet me, by means of John Ronald, at Glasgow; but you shall hear further from me before I leave Edinburgh. My duty and many compliments from the north to my mother; and my brotherly compliments to the rest. I have been trying for a berth for William,[1] but am not likely to be successful. Farewell.

After spending a few weeks in Edinburgh, Burns made his final excursion in October. His companion on this occasion was a young doctor, James M'Kittrick Adair,[2] who had requested the Poet to introduce him to the family group at Harvieston, and who, it may be remarked, made such effective use of his introduction that in a short time Charlotte Hamilton consented to become Mrs. Adair. On the way to Harvieston, Stirling was revisited, when Burns summarily smashed the pane on which he had scrawled the revolutionary lines already referred to. Eight or ten days were joyously spent at Harvieston Castle, amid the splendid scenery of the winding vale of Devon; Rumbling Brig, Cauldron Linn, and weird old gloomy Castle Campbell being notable among the places visited.

[1] William Burns, the Poet's younger brother, a saddler to trade.
[2] See vol. i. p. 1.

But above and beyond all else that charmed the Poet in and around Harvieston was the fascination of his sweet, kindly, accomplished friend and correspondent, Peggy Chalmers.

Going on from Harvieston, he was warmly welcomed and entertained by Mr. Ramsay of Auchertyre, on the Teith, and by Sir William Murray of Auchertyre, in Strathearn. In a communication to Dr. Currie, the first-named gentleman gave his impressions of Burns as he saw and conversed with him at Auchertyre:—

> I have been in the company of many men of genius, some of them poets, but never witnessed such flashes of intellectual brightness as from him—the impulse of the moment, sparks of celestial fire! I never was more delighted, therefore, than with his company for two days, tête-à-tête. . . . I not only proposed to him the writing of a play similar to the "Gentle Shepherd," *qualem decet esse sororem*, but Scottish Georgics, a subject which Thomson has by no means exhausted in his "Seasons." What beautiful landscapes of rural life and manners might not have been expected from a pencil so faithful and forcible as his, which could have exhibited scenes as familiar and interesting as those in the "Gentle Shepherd," which every one who knows our swains in their unadulterated state instantly recognises as true to nature! But to have executed either of these plans, steadiness and abstraction from company were wanting, not talents. When I asked him whether the Edinburgh literati had mended his poems by their criticisms, "Sir," said he, "these gentlemen remind me of some spinsters in my country who spin their thread so fine that it is neither fit for weft nor woof."

A grotesquely interesting incident occurred at Clackmannan Tower, then tenanted by a Mrs. Bruce, who claimed royal descent from Robert the Bruce. Wielding the sword of her great ancestor (so she maintained), this Jacobite dame of ninety years conferred on the Poet and Adair the honour of Scottish knighthood, remarking that she had a better right to do so than *some people*. Her after-dinner toast, "*Hooi Uncos*" (away with the strangers), greatly interested Burns, who, essaying to respectfully kiss the hand of this eccentric and worthy old lady at parting, was met by the question " What ails thee at my lips, Robin ? "

In the old churchyard at Dunfermline the travellers reverently viewed the grave of the Bruce; and in the Abbey Church they irreverently made a mock of a well-known, and, in its time, salutary form of Church discipline. Adair mounted the *cutty stool*, assuming the character of a penitent for fornication; while Burns from the pulpit addressed to him a ludicrous reproof and exhortation, by way of a parody on what the Poet had undergone in the kirk at Mauchline.

Returning to Edinburgh on 20th October, he took up his abode with William Cruikshank, who was, like Nicol, a teacher in the High School.

The desirability of settling down as farmer seems to have been occupying the Poet's mind at this time; for on the very day of his return to Edinburgh he wrote on this subject to Mr. Miller of Dalswinton :—

> I want—the letter goes on to say—to be a farmer in a small farm, about a plough-gang, in a pleasant country, under the auspices of a good landlord. I have no foolish notion of being a tenant under easier terms than another. To find a farm where one can live at all, is not easy—I only mean living soberly, like an old-style farmer, and joining personal industry. The banks of the Nith are as sweet poetic ground as any I ever saw; and besides, sir, it is but justice to the feelings of my own heart and the opinion of my best friends, to say that I would wish to call you landlord sooner than any landed gentleman I know.

But, though he viewed and reviewed the Dalswinton lands, and thought and wrote a good deal during this winter about taking one of Mr. Miller's farms, not till March of the ensuing year did he finally make up his mind and close the bargain for Ellisland.

During his first winter in the capital, he had made the acquaintance of James Johnson, engraver, who was then editing the *Scots*

SONG ENTHUSIASM. 177

Musical Museum, a collection of songs, old and new, with appropriate melodies set for instrumental accompaniment. To this work our Poet heartily lent his unrivalled services. To him such a task was naturally a most congenial one. With what loving eagerness he entered into co-operation with Johnson is seen, *e.g.*, in his correspondence with the venerable Rev. John Skinner, author of "Tullochgorum," "The Ewie wi' the Crookit Horn," and other popular songs. We give Burns's letter to Mr. Skinner, of date 25th October, 1787 :—

> REVEREND AND VENERABLE SIR,—Accept in plain, dull prose my most sincere thanks for the best poetical compliment I ever received. I assure you, sir, as a poet, you have conjured up an airy demon of vanity in my fancy, which the best abilities in your other capacity would be ill able to lay. I regret, and while I live I shall regret, that when I was in the north I had not the pleasure of paying a younger brother's dutiful respect to the author of the best Scotch song ever Scotland saw—"Tullochgorum's my delight!" The world may think slightingly of the craft of song-making if they please; but, as Job says, "Oh that mine adversary had written a book!" Let them try. There is a certain something in the old Scotch songs, a wild happiness of thought and expression, which peculiarly marks them, not only from English songs, but also from the modern effects of song-wrights in our native manner and language. The only remains of this enchantment, these spells of the imagination, rest with you. Our true brother, Ross of Lochlee, was likewise "owre cannie"—"a wild warlock"—but now he sings among the "sons of the morning."
>
> I have often wished, and will certainly endeavour, to form a kind of common acquaintance among all the genuine sons of Caledonian song. The world, busy in low, prosaic pursuits, may overlook most of us; but "reverence thyself." The world is not our *peers*, so we challenge the jury. We can lash that world, and find ourselves a very great source of amusement and happiness independent of that world.
>
> There is a work going on in Edinburgh just now which claims your best assistance. An engraver in this town has set about collecting and publishing all the Scotch songs, with the music, that can be found. Songs in the English language, if by Scotchmen, are admitted, but the music must all be Scotch.

Drs. Beattie and Blacklock are lending a hand, and the first musician in town presides over that department. I have been absolutely crazed about it, collecting old stanzas, and every information remaining respecting their origin, authors, etc., etc. This last is but a very fragment business; but at the end of his second number—the first is already published—a small account will be given of the authors, particularly to preserve those of latter times. Your three songs, "Tullochgorum," "John of Badenyon," and "Ewie wi' the Crookit Horn," go in this second number. I was determined, before I got your letter, to write you, begging that you would let me know where the editions of these pieces may be found, as you would wish them to continue in future times; and if you would be so kind to this undertaking as send any songs, of your own or others, that you would think proper to publish, your name will be inserted among the other authors—"Nill ye, will ye." One-half of Scotland already give your songs to other authors. Paper is done. I beg to hear from you; the sooner the better, as I leave Edinburgh in a fortnight or three weeks. I am, with the warmest sincerity, sir, your obliged humble servant.

In this connection, Chambers most appropriately and justly observes :—

> The zeal of Burns for the collection, illustration, and extension of the body of Scottish song was at this season a conspicuous feeling in his bosom. He entered into the views of Johnson with an industry and earnestness which despised all money considerations, and which money could not have purchased. The character of our Bard is seen strongly here. He adored his native muse, and held the codex of her effusions as a sacred volume. He was also wholly above the idea of mercenary verse. Numbers he gave forth because "the numbers came." Though he had published a volume of these, and consented to realize a profit by it, he had no idea of composing either poems or songs with a view to a pecuniary recompense for them. Above all, he was incapable of writing a *song* directly for money. There may have been something of over-fastidiousness in this feeling of Burns; and yet it was, on the whole, in high consonance with the poetical character which he bore.

As in the preceding chapter, so in this—the actual poetic results must again be described as meagre. Still, in these hurried tours the Poet sought and found rich springs of inspiration for that grand song-making enthusiasm which was destined to henceforth almost entirely engross his muse, and under which he gave to mankind the many priceless fruits of his peerless lyric genius. Among the dozen or so of pieces produced during this period of hard, fatiguing travel, hasty sight-seeing, and widely varied, unsettling experiences, these may be specially noted:—"Lines at Kenmore," "Bruar Water," "Macpherson's Farewell," "The Banks of Devon," and, best of all, that lovely, lightsome lyric, "The Birks o' Aberfeldy."

CHAPTER VII.

MORE EDINBURGH LIFE. CLARINDA. EXCISE APPOINTMENT. MARRIAGE. OCTOBER 1787–JUNE 1788. AGE 28–29.

> Had we never loved so kindly,
> Had we never loved so blindly,
> Never met or never parted,
> We had ne'er been broken-hearted.
> *Burns to Clarinda.*

Without claiming for Burns the praise of perfect sagacity, we must say that his Excise and farm scheme does not seem to us a very unreasonable one; that we should be at a loss, even now, to suggest one decidedly better. . . . It reflects credit on the manliness and sound sense of Burns, that he felt so early on what ground he was standing, and preferred self-help, on the humblest scale, to dependence and inaction, though with hope of far more splendid possibilities.
CARLYLE.

Had Burns deserted her (Jean Armour), he had merely been a heartless villain. In making her his lawful wedded wife, he did no more than any other man, deserving the name of man, would have done, and had he not, he would have walked in shame before men, and in fear and trembling before God.
PROFESSOR WILSON.

WHAT is known as the Poet's *Second Winter in Edinburgh* began on his return, October 20, from the Devon Valley excursion. He found a pleasant lodgment at the house of William Cruikshank, in St. James's Square. Cruikshank was a genial, cultured man, for whom Burns cherished a deep regard. That is an attractive scene in which we see the Poet seated beside his landlord's lovely young daughter,—the Rosebud,—listening with keenest enjoyment to her masterly playing of the old Scotch airs he loved so well.[1]

After his return from that summer's touring, his absorbing devotion to the cause of Scottish minstrelsy becomes more and more clearly marked. During these winter months, what time remained after meeting his varied social engagements was chiefly spent in this, to him, most congenial pursuit—collecting old songs and melodies, improving and supplementing what he found rude or fragmentary, and enriching with his own finished contributions our unsurpassed heritage of national song.

Robert Ainslie, the Poet's travelling companion in his Border tour, was still his intimate friend and associate. In connection with this intimacy, Chambers recounts, on Ainslie's authority, an incident most creditable to the Poet :—

> Mr. Ainslie at this time had a lodging on the north side of the same square, so that the two friends were very ready to each other's call. . . . On Burns calling for him one afternoon, Ainslie proposed that they should spend the afternoon over a bottle ; but Burns said, "No, my friend—we'll have no wine to-day—to sit dozing in the house on such a fine afternoon as this would be insufferable. Besides, you know that you and I don't require wine to sharpen our wit, nor its adventitious aid to make us happy. No; we'll take a ramble over Arthur's Seat, to admire the beauties of nature, and come in to a late tea." The two friends adopted this plan ; and Mr. Ainslie used to declare that he had never known the Poet's conversation so amusing, so instructive, and altogether delightful, as during the cheerful stroll they had over the hill, and during the sober tea-drinking which followed.

During this period, too, Burns seems to have derived great pleasure from his acquaintance with the Harvieston family—an acquaintance which he cultivated by a series of letters to Miss Chalmers,[2] noteworthy among all his epistolary effusions for their

---

[1] The Cruikshanks : see vol. i. p. 143.
[2] Mr. Scott Douglas gives the following at page 61 of his Kilmarnock edition :—["It does not appear from Burns's letters that he ever

fine style, sense, and feeling. Though it is not clear whether he ever admired this lady as an actual *lover*, it is abundantly clear, from various letters and poems, that he held her in the very highest esteem as a friend and confidant. To her he more freely and simply unbosomed himself than to any other of his correspondents, save, perhaps, Mrs. Dunlop.

Meantime, the season wore on into mid-winter, yet the avowed object of his second sojourn in Edinburgh—settlement with Creech the publisher—was still vexatiously delayed. Chafing under this delay, and, doubtless, at the altered manner of his reception by the society of the city,—an alteration for which, however, he himself was not entirely irresponsible,—he became more and more moody in spirit and unsettled in purpose. Turning serious thoughts towards the future, he at length resolved to bid farewell to Edinburgh early in December. But the carrying out of this resolve was frustrated through his sustaining a severe injury in the leg, occasioned by his being thrown from a coach driven by a drunken coachman. At this point the famous "Clarinda episode" in his career emerges; an account of which is given in the preceding volume of this work.[1] Careful and candid study of this remarkable incident points to the conclusion that, though the position which Burns and Clarinda took up towards each other was, to say the least, an equivocal and dangerous one, it passed off free from actual moral stain. Clarinda's letters, being much pervaded by an unquestionably earnest religious tone, drew from Burns sundry statements of his ideas on religion. We reproduce one passage in particular:—

> I am delighted, charming Clarinda, with your honest enthusiasm for religion. Those of either sex, but particularly the female, who are lukewarm in

---

formally proposed marriage to Miss Margaret Chalmers, afterwards Mrs. Lewis Hay; yet the late Thomas Campbell, the poet, told me that the lady herself informed him that Burns actually made a serious proposal to her."—Note of Dr. Carruthers to the Editor.]

[1] See vol. ii. p. 46 : Agnes M'Lehose.

that most important of all things, "O my soul, come not thou into their secrets!" I feel myself deeply interested in your good opinion, and will lay before you the outlines of my belief. He who is our Author and Preserver, and will one day be our Judge, must be (not for His sake in the way of duty, but but from the native impulse of our hearts) the object of our reverential awe and grateful adoration: He is Almighty and all-bounteous, we are weak and dependent; hence prayer and every other sort of devotion.—"He is not willing that any should perish, but that all should come to everlasting life;" consequently it must be in every one's power to embrace His offer of "everlasting life;" otherwise He could not, in justice, condemn those who did not. A mind pervaded, actuated, and governed by purity, truth, and charity, though it does not *merit* heaven, yet is an absolutely necessary pre-requisite, without which heaven can neither be obtained nor enjoyed; and, by divine promise, such a mind shall never fail of attaining "everlasting life:" hence the impure, the deceiving, and the uncharitable, extrude themselves from eternal bliss, by their unfitness for enjoying it. The Supreme Being has put the immediate administration of all this, for wise and good ends known to Himself, into the hands of Jesus Christ—a great personage, whose relation to Him we cannot comprehend, but whose relation to us is a Guide and Saviour; and who, except for our own obstinacy and misconduct, will bring us all, through various ways, and by various means, to bliss at last.

These are my tenets, my lovely friend; and which, I think, cannot be well disputed. My creed is pretty nearly expressed in the last clause of Jamie Dean's grace, an honest weaver in Ayrshire: "Lord, grant that we may lead a gude life! for a gude life mak's a gude end; at least it helps weel!"

Side by side with his many rapturous outpourings to Clarinda, we find letters containing perhaps the most terrible expressions of unrest and self-upbraiding which even *he* ever penned. On the 12th December he wrote to Miss Chalmers:—

I am here under the care of a surgeon, with a bruised limb extended on a cushion; and the tints of my mind vying with the livid horror preceding a midnight thunderstorm. A drunken coachman was the cause of the first, and incomparably the lightest evil; misfortune, bodily constitution, hell, and myself, have formed a "quadruple alliance" to guarantee the other.

Again, a little later, to the same lady :—

> Now for that wayward, unfortunate thing, myself. I have broke measures with Creech, and last week I wrote him a frosty, keen letter. He replied in terms of chastisement, and promised me upon his honour that I should have the account on Monday; but this is Tuesday, and yet I have not heard a word from him. God have mercy on me! a poor damned, incautious, duped, unfortunate fool! The sport, the miserable victim of rebellious pride, hypochondriac imagination, agonising sensibility, and bedlam passions!
>
> "I wish that I were dead, but I'm no' like to die!" I had lately "a hairbreadth 'scape in th' imminent deadly breach" of love too. Thank my stars, I got off heart-whole, "waur fleyed than hurt."
>
> I have this moment got a hint. I fear I am something like—undone—but I hope for the best. Come, stubborn pride and unshrinking resolution, accompany me through this, to me, miserable world! You must not desert me. Your friendship I think I can count on, though I should date my letters from a marching regiment. Early in life, and all my life, I reckoned on a recruiting drum as my forlorn hope. Seriously, though, life presents me with but a melancholy path; but—my limb will soon be sound, and I shall struggle on.

And on the 21st January to Mrs. Dunlop :—

> After six weeks' confinement, I am beginning to walk across the room. They have been six horrible weeks; anguish and low spirits made me unfit to read, write, or think.
>
> I have a hundred times wished that one could resign life as an officer resigns a commission; for I would not take in any poor ignorant wretch by selling out. Lately I was a sixpenny private, and, God knows, a miserable soldier enough; now I march to the campaign, a starving cadet—a little more conspicuously wretched.
>
> I am ashamed of all this; for though I do want bravery for the warfare of life, I could wish, like some other soldiers, to have as much fortitude or cunning as to dissemble or conceal my cowardice.

A comparison of these passages with the contemporaneous Clarinda correspondence once more shows, in a strong light, what tumultuous and incongruous elements combined to make up the great, impassioned, erratic nature of the immortal Bard—" so miserably open," as he himself has put it, "to the incursions of a mischievous, light-armed, well-mounted banditti, under the banners of imagination, whim, caprice, and passion."

In the enforced and painful seclusion caused by his accident, turning his thoughts to the serious business of life, rightly estimating his want of steady aim and application in temporal affairs, and seeing no bright, assured, or settled prospect, he arrived at the bitter conclusion—and we ought to honour him for his honest admission of it—that, however much or little others might be to blame in their treatment of him, he, through many passionate follies, had been his own worst enemy. At the very period of which we are speaking, he must have been aware of the fresh trouble in which his previous summer's renewed intimacy with Jean Armour had involved him. At any rate, early in 1788, he received definite news from Mauchline on this score—news which could not fail to bring him feelings of keenest sorrow and shame; for he now learnt that Jean was a disgraced and hapless outcast from her home, *on his account* again. Though Burns's clamorous passions might and did lead him into many a scrape, it was not in his nature, we believe, to be *wittingly* heartless. Accordingly, we find him making haste to shield his too-confiding Jean, by securing for her a temporary refuge at the house of his friend William Muir, of Tarbolton (Willie's) Mill. This pressing claim upon his responsibility having been thus far attended to, his intimacy and correspondence with Clarinda went on as before, apparently under the belief that, after the burning of the marriage lines and his disownment by the Armours, Jean had no legal claim upon him as her *husband*.

The idea of obtaining a situation in the Excise had, as we have seen, been before Burns's mind for years. To this matter of so great importance in his after-life he now definitely addressed himself by sending an application to the Commissioners, which application he supported by privately writing to Mr. Graham of Fintry, and to Lord Glencairn. From these letters we get the most reliable idea of the Poet's motives and views at this juncture.

To Mr. Graham he wrote—

> SIR,—When I had the honour of being introduced to you at Athole House, I did not think so soon of asking a favour of you. When Lear, in Shakespeare, asked old Kent why he wished to be in his service, he answers: "Because you have that in your face which I would fain call master." For some such reason, sir, do I now solicit your patronage. You know, I daresay, of an application I lately made to your Board to be admitted an officer of Excise. I have, according to form, been examined by a supervisor, and to-day I gave in his certificate, with a request for an order for instructions. In this affair, if I succeed, I am afraid I shall but too much need a patronizing friend. Propriety of conduct as a man, and fidelity and attention as an officer, I dare engage for; but with anything like business, except manual labour, I am totally unacquainted.
>
> I had intended to have closed my late appearance on the stage of life in the character of a country farmer; but after discharging some filial and fraternal claims, I find I could only fight for existence in that miserable manner which I have lived to see throw a venerable parent into the jaws of a jail; whence death, the poor man's last and often best friend, rescued him.
>
> I know, sir, that to need your goodness is to have a claim on it; may I, therefore, beg your patronage to forward me in this affair, till I be appointed to a division—where, by the help of rigid economy, I will try to support that independence so dear to my soul, but which has been too often so distant from my situation.

And to Lord Glencairn :—

> MY LORD,—I know your lordship will disapprove of my ideas in a request I am going to make to you; but I have weighed, long and seriously weighed, my situation, my hopes, and turn of mind, and am fully fixed to my scheme, if I can possibly effectuate it. I wish to get into the Excise: I am told that your lordship's interest will easily procure me the grant from the Commissioners; and

THE EXCISE.

your lordship's patronage and goodness, which have already rescued me from obscurity, wretchedness, and exile, embolden me to ask that interest. You have likewise put it in my power to save the little tie of home that sheltered an aged mother, two brothers, and three sisters, from destruction. There, my lord, you have bound me over to the highest gratitude.

My brother's farm is but a wretched lease, but I think he will probably weather out the remaining seven years of it; and after the assistance which I have given, and will give him, to keep the family together, I think, by my guess, I shall have rather better than two hundred pounds; and instead of seeking, what is almost impossible at present to find, a farm that I can certainly live by, with so small a stock, I shall lodge this sum in a banking-house, a sacred deposit, excepting only the calls of uncommon distress or necessitous old age.

These, my lord, are my views: I have resolved from the maturest deliberation; and, now I am fixed, I shall leave no stone unturned to carry my resolve into execution. Your lordship's patronage is the strength of my hopes; nor have I yet applied to anybody else. Indeed, my heart sinks within me at the idea of applying to any other of the great who have honoured me with their countenance. I am ill qualified to dog the heels of greatness with the impertinence of solicitation, and tremble nearly as much at the thought of the cold promise as the cold denial; but to your lordship I have not only the honour, the comfort, but the pleasure of being your lordship's much obliged and deeply indebted humble servant.

The speedy granting of his application was due, in great measure, to the warm interest taken in his behalf by his medical attendant, Dr. Alexander Wood. That genial and popular citizen personally brought the Poet's case before the notice of the chairman, Mr. Graham, with the result that the name of ROBERT BURNS was entered for an appointment in due course.

A great deal has been said, in a kindly-meant but deprecating spirit, regarding this turn in the Poet's career. In remarking upon it, not a few seem to have assumed that there was something very degrading in the office of exciseman—an office honourable in itself and necessary to the trade and finance of the country. But apart from this unwarrantable assumption, it has often been asked, " Could something better than this not have been done for such an one as Burns?" To which it may be readily answered, Yes! But here again it may in all fairness and tenderness be asked, "Might not Burns have acted otherwise than he did for his own interest?" which further question must also be answered in the affirmative. Moreover, however lacking in steadiness and force of will Burns might be, he did not lack in searching perception of his own erratic conduct, or in clear estimate of his temporal circumstances and prospects. So, on this much-debated and delicate subject, it is better to refrain from strongly judging either the marvellously constituted Bard or his influential contemporaries; and to pass on, paying due heed to Burns's own statements on the point, as seen in the letters above quoted and in others, *e.g.* that to Miss Chalmers, in which he says :—

> You will condemn me for the next step I have taken : I have entered into the Excise. I stay in the west about three weeks, and then return to Edinburgh for six weeks' instructions; afterwards, for I get employ instantly, I go *où il plait à Dieu—et mon roi*. I have chosen this, my dear friend, after mature deliberation. The question is not at what door of fortune's palace shall we enter in, but what doors does she open to us? I was not likely to get anything to do. I wanted *un but*, which is a dangerous, an unhappy situation. I got this without any hanging on, or mortifying solicitation : it is immediate bread ; and though poor in comparison of the last eighteen months of my existence, 'tis luxury in comparison of all my preceding life : besides, the Commissioners are some of them my acquaintances, and all of them my firm friends.

On the 18th February, 1788, Burns left Edinburgh for Ayrshire. Travelling by Glasgow, he there met his Irvine friend, Richard Brown ; thence by Paisley to Dunlop House, where he spent a day or two ; thence home to Mossgiel. From Mossgiel, he once more went to inspect Ellisland, for which farm, if any, he now made up his mind to negotiate with Mr. Miller.

In a letter to Robert Ainslie, written about this time at Mauchline, he reveals what perplexities and complications he found himself involved in between farming and Excise, Jean Armour and Clarinda :—

> I am just returned from Mr. Miller's farm. My old friend whom I took with me was highly pleased with the bargain, and advised me to accept of it. He is the most intelligent, sensible farmer in the county, and his advice has staggered me a good deal. I have the two plans before me : I shall endeavour to balance them to the best of my judgment, and fix on the most eligible. On the whole, if I find Mr. Miller in the same favourable disposition as when I saw him last, I shall in all probability turn farmer.
>
> I have been through sore tribulation, and under much buffeting of the Wicked One, since I came to this country. Jean I found banished like a martyr—forlorn, destitute, and friendless. I have reconciled her to her mother. I have taken her a room ; I have taken her to my arms ; I have given her a mahogany bed ; I have given her a guinea. But (as I always am on every occasion) I have been prudent and cautious to an astonishing degree. I swore her solemnly and privately never to attempt any claim on me as a husband— even though anybody should persuade her she had such a claim, which she had not—neither during my life, nor after my death. She did all this like a good girl. . . .
>
> I shall be in Edinburgh the middle of next week. My farming ideas I shall keep private till I see. I got a letter from Clarinda yesterday, and she tells me she has got no letter of mine but one. Tell her that I wrote to her from Glasgow, from Kilmarnock, from Mauchline, and yesterday from Cumnock, as I returned from Dumfries. Indeed, she is the only person in Edinburgh I have written to.

On the 10th March he returned to Edinburgh. Soon after his arrival, he concluded the bargain for Ellisland, and at last obtained a provisional settlement with Mr. William Creech, who, though he had been very dilatory, seems to have been very faithful in his management of the Edinburgh edition. So far as can be gathered from various conflicting statements, the Poet had something near £400 to the good after payment of his publishing, travelling, and lodging expenses.

Leaving Edinburgh on the 24th March, he went to Dumfries to attend to urgent matters connected with his farming project. On his return home, he at once advanced about £200 to aid his brother Gilbert in the struggle to make ends meet at Mossgiel. Regarding this transaction he afterwards wrote to Dr. Moore :—

> I give myself no airs on this, for it was mere selfishness on my part. I was conscious that the wrong scale of the balance was pretty heavily charged, and I thought that the throwing a little filial piety and fraternal affection into the scale in my favour might help to smooth matters at the *grand reckoning*.

The official order for his instructions in the practical duties of an exciseman having been issued on the 31st March, anxious to have this preliminary training over before Whitsunday, Burns set to work immediately, under Mr. James Findlay, officer at Tarbolton. Meantime, Jean Armour had been (about the middle of March) again delivered of twins—daughters—both of whom died a day or two after birth. Jean, however, was left the unfortunate object of her father's wrath and of the scandal of the country-side ; but also, we rejoice to think, the object of the Poet's love and care. For some time in April he took a humble room in Mauchline for Jean and himself, and publicly acknowledged her as his wife.

In the following August this irregular marriage was regularly confirmed in accordance with the annexed minute of Mauchline Kirk-Session—

> Compeared Robert Burns with Jean Armour, his alleged spouse. They both acknowledged their irregular marriage, and their sorrow for that irregularity, desiring that the session will take such steps as may seem to them

proper in order to the solemn confirmation of said marriage. The session, taking this affair under their consideration, agree that they both be rebuked for this acknowledged irregularity, and that they be taken solemnly engaged to adhere faithfully to one another as husband and wife all the days of their life. And in regard the session had a title in law to some fine for behoof of the poor, they agree to refer to Mr. Burns his own generosity. The above sentence was accordingly executed, and the session absolved the said parties from any scandal on this account.

(Signed)   WILLIAM AULD, *Moderator.*
(,,)   ROBERT BURNS.
(,,)   JEAN ARMOUR.[1]

Mr. Burns gave a guinea note for behoof of the poor.

Thus were the various ups and downs in the Poet's relations with Jean Armour at length consummated by regular marriage. It is a consummation devoutly rejoiced in by all who cherish a wholesome regard for the name and fame of BURNS. Calling to mind of what disposition he was, the manner of his birth and upbringing, the humble social sphere which appeared to await him, and the dilemma in which he found himself, we are compelled to think that this alliance not only lay in the path of moral duty and manly honour, but was also in the whole circumstances most expedient.

Whatever Jean Armour's frailties may have been, Burns must be regarded as a largely responsible partner in her faults. From all that had happened between them, none had so great a claim upon him as Jean, whom he passionately loved, we believe, in spite of all he had experienced. And, after all, what kind of wife would some high-bred lady have been to him? And, what kind of husband would he have made to such as Miss Chalmers, Miss Hamilton, or even Clarinda? The answer must indeed be a doubtful one. It is very far from certain that his marriage with a person of high rank, culture, and sensibility would have proved so satisfactory as that

---

[1] The signature "Jean Armour" is unmistakably in Burns's handwriting.

with his industrious, homely, long-suffering, devoted Jean turned out in the main to be. The Poet's own expressed reflections on this subject are of commanding interest. To Miss Chalmers he wrote :—

> I have married my Jean. I had a long and much-loved fellow-creature's happiness or misery in my determination, and I durst not trifle with so important a deposit; nor have I any cause to repent it. If I have not got polite tittle-tattle, modish manners, and fashionable dress, I am not sickened and disquieted with the multiform curse of boarding-school affectation; and I have got the handsomest figure, the sweetest temper, the soundest constitution, and the kindest heart in the country.

To Mrs. Dunlop he wrote :—

> Your surmise, madam, is just; I am indeed a husband. . . . To jealousy or infidelity I am an equal stranger. My preservative from the first is the most thorough consciousness of her sentiments of honour, and her attachment to me; my antidote against the last is my long and deep-rooted affection for her.
>
> In housewife matters, of aptness to learn and activity to execute, she is eminently mistress; and during my absence in Nithsdale, she is regularly and constantly apprentice to my mother and sisters in their dairy and other rural business.
>
> The Muses must not be offended when I tell them the concerns of my wife and family will, in my mind, always take the *pas;* but I assure them their ladyships will ever come next in place.
>
> You are right that a bachelor state would have insured me more friends; but, from a cause you will easily guess, conscious peace in the enjoyment of my own mind, and unmistrusting confidence in approaching my God, would seldom have been of the number.
>
> I found a once much-loved and still much-loved female literally and truly cast out to the mercy of the naked elements; but I enabled her to *purchase* a shelter—there is no sporting with a fellow-creature's happiness or misery.
>
> The most placid good-nature and sweetness of disposition; a warm heart, gratefully devoted with all its powers to love me; vigorous health and sprightly cheerfulness, set off to the best advantage by a more than commonly handsome figure; these, I think, in a woman, may make a good wife, though she should

never have read a page but the Scriptures of the Old and New Testament, nor have danced in a brighter assembly than a penny pay wedding.

Part of an entry made in his Common-place Book, on the 15th June at Ellisland, runs in the same strain on the subject of his marriage:—

> Wedlock—the circumstance that buckles me hardest to care, if virtue and religion were to be anything with me but names—was what in a few seasons I must have resolved on; in my present situation it was absolutely necessary. Humanity, generosity, honest pride of character, justice to my own happiness for after-life, so far as it could depend (which it surely will a great deal) on internal peace; all these joined their warmest suffrages, their most powerful solicitations, with a rooted attachment, to urge the step I have taken. Nor have I any reason on her part to repent it. I can fancy how, but have never seen where, I could have made a better choice. Come, then, let me act up to my favourite motto, that glorious passage in Young—
>
> "On reason build resolve,
> That column of true majesty in man!"

It is with feelings of intense gratification we dwell upon the thought of his having calmly penned such worthy, and, we believe, *heartfelt* reflections as these; even as, on the other hand, we should have been forced to regard his desertion of Jean Armour as an ineffaceable stain on his memory; as, indeed, an act of most callous inhumanity.

During the period dealt with in this chapter, though Burns produced very few new poems, he managed to perform a great work by his enthusiastic co-operation with Johnson, the editor of the *Musical Museum*. In this pursuit his genius revelled in spite of many worries and perplexities. The second volume of the *Museum*, published in the middle of February 1788, contained no fewer than thirty-five songs by Burns, not to speak of the inestimable services he rendered in the general preparation of the work.

CHAPTER VIII.

ELLISLAND—JUNE 1788-DECEMBER 1791. AGE, 29-32.

In the affair of a livelihood, I think myself tolerably secure; I have good hopes of my farm; but should they fail, I have an Excise commission, which, on my simple petition, will at any time procure me bread. There is a certain stigma affixed to the character of an Excise officer, but I do not pretend to borrow honour from my profession; and though the salary be comparatively small, it is luxury to anything that the first twenty-five years of my life taught me to expect.—*Letter to Bishop Geddes.*

> To make a happy fireside clime
> To weans and wife,
> That's the true pathos and sublime
> Of human life.
> *Epistle to Dr. Blacklock.*

HOWEVER disappointed and chagrined Burns may have felt over his second winter in Edinburgh, with his fresh farming project in view he left the city and returned to Mauchline as happy as "a mayfrog leaping across the newly harrowed ridge, enjoying the fragrance of the refreshed earth after the long-expected shower." In June 1788, he entered into residence and duty at Ellisland, by far the most picturesque and romantic for situation of all his farm homes. The lands of Ellisland lie on the western side of the Nith, which here flows through a vale of richly-varied loveliness. Up and down the river the views are scarcely surpassed in Scottish lowland scenery, while on the opposite bank the meads and forests of old Dalswinton spread themselves out in majestic beauty. The farmhouse stands close by the river-side, on the brow of a steep bank clad with trees and whins, among which there winds the secluded path where the

Poet loved to stray and muse in leisure hours. It had been open to him to become tenant of a more fertile farm on the Dalswinton side of the Nith. His fixing upon Ellisland is said to have called forth the remark of the Dalswinton land-steward: "Mr. Burns, you have made a poet's, not a farmer's choice;" and the result of his three years' tenancy fully bore out Mr. Cunningham's experienced observation. To Ellisland, however, Burns repaired, with inadequate capital indeed,—less than £300,—but with more peace of mind and better hopes than he had known for many a day. The farm was in wretched condition, and, in accordance with his bargain, the Poet had also to begin the laborious task of erecting a new dwelling-house and offices. Meantime, he took up his residence in an outlying hovel on the farm, in which miserable tumble-down abode he describes himself to Mrs. Dunlop, as

> A solitary inmate of an old smoky spence, far from every object I love or by whom I am beloved, nor any acquaintance older than yesterday, except *Jenny Geddes*—the old mare I ride on—while uncouth cares and novel plans hourly insult my awkward ignorance and bashful inexperience.

And again, in his "Epistle to Hugh Parker," Kilmarnock:—

> Here, ambush'd by the chimla cheek,
> Hid in an atmosphere of reek,
> I hear a wheel thrum i' the neuk,
> I hear it—for in vain I leuk.
> The red peat gleams, a fiery kernel,
> Enhuskèd by a fog infernal:
> Here, for my wonted rhyming raptures,
> I sit and count my sins by chapters;
> For life and spunk like ither Christians,
> I'm dwindled doon to mere existence.

In fact, he had so many cares and drudgeries to face at the very outset, that it need occasion no surprise to find such a nature as his fretting under weary feelings of loneliness and misgiving. He was, for a time, literally a solitary stranger in a strange country-side. His suffering, however, in this lonely situation, proved great gain to the realm of song. His "Bonnie Jean" could not yet find a home at Ellisland, and to her his thoughts oft turned with ardent longings, to which he gave undying voice in the well-known song, "O' a' the airts the wind can blaw," and in that other glowing lyric, "Oh, were I on Parnassus' Hill," which, we fancy, is not so widely known and admired as it deserves to be:—

> Oh, were I on Parnassus' hill!
> Or had of Helicon my fill;
> That I might catch poetic skill
>   To sing how dear I love thee!
> But Nith maun be my muse's well,
> My muse maun be thy bonnie sel';
> On Corsincon I'll glower and spell,[1]
>   And write how dear I love thee.
>
> Then come, sweet muse, inspire my lay!
> For a' the lee-lang simmer's day
> I couldna sing, I couldna say,
>   How much, how dear I love thee.
> I see thee dancing o'er the green,
> Thy waist sae jimp, thy limbs sae clean,
> Thy tempting lips, thy roguish een—
>   By heaven and earth I love thee!
>
> By night, by day, a-field, at hame,
> The thoughts o' thee my breast inflame;
> And aye I muse and sing thy name—
>   I only live to love thee.

---

[1] Corsincon Hill, standing at the head of Nithsdale, on the way to Mauchline, where dwelt the absent idol of his love.

> Though I were doomed to wander on,
> Beyond the sea, beyond the sun,
> Till my last weary sand was run;
> Till then—and then I'd love thee.

During this busy summer he frequently traversed the five-and-forty miles which separated him from his wife and from the family circle at Mossgiel, only to hasten, after a brief visit, back again to his farming and building toils and cares. Jean's absence in Ayrshire, it is true, called forth from the *wearying* husband those two grand songs; but, apart from this, it would have been better in many ways for Burns if the dwelling-house at Ellisland had been ready to at once receive him and his household into quiet, settled home life. His solitary worries caused him to fret a good deal, and separation from his much-loved and devoted wife made him more than usually restless in his movements.

> He was—says Mr. Cunningham—ever on the move, on foot or on horseback. In the course of a single day he might be seen holding the plough, angling in the river, sauntering, with his hands behind his back, on the banks, looking at the running water, of which he was very fond, walking round his buildings or over his fields; and if you lost sight of him for an hour, perhaps you might see him returning from Friar's Carse, or spurring his horse through the hills to spend an evening with such friends as chance threw in his way.

His journeyings to and from Mauchline made further serious demands on his time and energy; and, worst of all, dragged him into company and indulgences which greatly interfered with his resolutions of this time towards industry and self-control. How worthy and sincere these resolutions were may be gathered from a letter to Robert Ainslie, dated 30th June 1788 :—

> There is a great degree of folly in talking unnecessarily of one's private affairs. I have just now been interrupted by one of my new neighbours, who

has made himself absolutely contemptible in my eyes by his silly, garrulous pruriency. I know it has been a fault of my own too; but from this moment I abjure it as I would the service of hell! Your poets, spendthrifts, and other fools of that kidney, pretend, forsooth, to crack their jokes on prudence; but 'tis a squalid vagabond glorying in his rags. Still, imprudence respecting money matters is much more pardonable than imprudence respecting character. I have no objection to prefer prodigality to avarice in some few instances; but I appeal to your observation if you have not met, and often met, with the same disingenuousness, the same hollow-hearted insincerity and disintegrative depravity of principle, in the hackneyed victims of profusion as in the unfeeling children of parsimony. I have every possible reverence for the much-talked-of world beyond the grave, and I wish that which piety believes and virtue deserves may be all matter of fact. But in things belonging to and terminating in this present scene of existence, man has serious and interesting business on hand. Whether a man shall shake hands with welcome in the distinguished elevation of respect, or shrink from contempt in the abject corner of insignificance; whether he shall wanton under the tropic of plenty—at least enjoy himself in the comfortable latitudes of easy convenience—or starve in the arctic circle of dreary poverty; whether he shall rise in the manly consciousness of a self-approving mind, or sink beneath a galling load of regret and remorse—these are alternatives of the last moment.

Mention has above been made of Friar's Carse, a picturesque little estate, owned by Captain Riddel[1] of Glenriddel, a man of genial temperament and literary tastes, with whom the Poet now formed a pleasant and interesting intimacy. In the romantic grounds which closely adjoined the fields of Ellisland, Captain Riddel had formed a shady retreat known as "The Hermitage," and there Burns was privileged to wander and muse amid a scene of great natural beauty and suggestive solitude. In his "Lines written in Friar's Carse Hermitage," under the assumed character of the hermit or bedesman of the place, we again discover his mind running on in a

[1] See vol. ii. p. 175.

strain of most prudent and deeply pious reflection. Burns subsequently revised and extended this poem as follows :—

  Thou whom chance may hither lead,
  Be thou clad in russet weed,
  Be thou deckt in silken stole,
  Grave these counsels on thy soul.

  Life is but a day at most,
  Sprung from night, in darkness lost ;
  Hope not sunshine every hour,
  Fear not clouds will always lower.

  As youth and love, with sprightly dance,
  Beneath thy morning star advance,
  Pleasure with her siren air
  May delude the thoughtless pair ;
  Let Prudence bless Enjoyment's cup,
  Then raptured sip, and sip it up.

  As thy day grows warm and high,
  Life's meridian flaming nigh,
  Dost thou spurn the humble vale?
  Life's proud summits wouldst thou scale?
  Check thy climbing step, elate,
  Evils lurk in felon wait :
  Dangers, eagle-pinioned, bold,
  Soar around each cliffy hold,
  While cheerful peace, with linnet song
  Chants the lowly dells among.

  As the shades of evening close,
  Beck'ning thee to long repose ;
  As life itself becomes disease,
  Seek the chimney-nook of ease ;
  There ruminate with sober thought,
  On all thou'st seen, and heard, and wrought ;

> And teach the sportive younkers round,
> Saws of experience, sage and sound.
> Say, Man's true, genuine estimate,
> The grand criterion of his fate,
> Is not, Art thou high or low?
> Did thy fortune ebb or flow?
> Did many talents gild thy span?
> Or frugal nature grudge thee one?
> Tell them, and press it on their mind,
> As thou thyself must shortly find,
> The smile or frown of awful Heav'n
> To *virtue* or to *vice* is given.
> Say, to be just, and kind, and wise,
> There solid self-enjoyment lies;
> That foolish, selfish, faithless ways
> Lead to be wretched, vile, and base.
>
> Thus resigned and quiet, creep
> To the bed of lasting sleep;
> Sleep, whence thou shalt ne'er awake,
> Night, where dawn shall never break,
> Till future life, future no more,
> To light and joy the good restore,
> To light and joy unknown before.
>
> Stranger, go! Heav'n be thy guide!
> Quod the Bedesman of Nithside!

Building operations at Ellisland proving much more tedious than he had anticipated, Burns would wait no longer in homeless solitude. Finding temporary quarters at "The Isle"[1] about a mile down the Nith from Ellisland, he there took up house in December. The advent of his Jean afforded him feelings of lively satisfaction,

---

[1] "The Isle," so called from the fact that at one time the water of the Nith formed a kind of island of the ground on which there stood the ruins of an ancient stronghold, and the farmhouse in which the poet lived.

and he celebrated the event in the jaunty little song, "I hae a wife o' my ain." A letter of this time to Mrs. Dunlop is notable for the same happy tone, and still more so on account of its enclosing the world-renowned "Auld Lang Syne," and that other famous song, "Go, fetch to me a pint o' wine."

It is, however, in the famous letter written to the same lady on New Year's Day morning, 1789, that we now find the Bard at his best and happiest :—

> This, dear madam, is a morning of wishes, and would to God that I came under the Apostle James's description—*the prayer of a righteous man availeth much*. In that case, madam, you should welcome in a year full of blessings : everything that obstructs or disturbs tranquillity and self-enjoyment should be removed, and every pleasure that frail humanity can taste should be yours. I own myself so little a Presbyterian, that I approve set times and seasons of more than ordinary acts of devotion, for breaking in on that habituated routine of life and thought which is so apt to reduce our existence to a kind of instinct, or even sometimes, and with some minds, to a state very little superior to mere machinery.
>
> This day—the first Sunday of May ; a breezy, blue-skied noon some time about the beginning, and a hoary morning and calm sunny day about the end, of autumn—these, time out of mind, have been with me a kind of holiday.
>
> I believe I owe this to that glorious paper in the *Spectator*, "The Vision of Mirza," a piece that struck my young fancy before I was capable of fixing an idea to a word of three syllables : "On the fifth day of the moon, which, according to the custom of my forefathers, I always *keep holy*, after having washed myself and offered up my morning devotions, I ascended the high hill of Bagdad, in order to pass the rest of the day in meditation and prayer."
>
> We know nothing, or next to nothing, of the substance or structure of our souls, so cannot account for those seeming caprices in them that one should be particularly pleased with this thing, or struck with that, which, on minds of a different cast, makes no extraordinary impression. I have some favourite flowers in spring, among which are the mountain daisy, the harebell, the foxglove, the wild-brier rose, the budding birch, and the hoary hawthorn, that I view and hang over with particular delight. I never hear the loud, solitary whistle of the

curlew in a summer noon, or the wild mixing cadence of a troop of grey plovers in an autumnal morning, without feeling an elevation of soul like the enthusiasm of devotion or poetry. Tell me, my dear friend, to what can this be owing? Are we a piece of machinery, which, like the Æolian harp, passive, takes the impression of the passing accident? Or do these workings argue something within us above the trodden clod? I own myself partial to such proofs of those awful and important realities—a God that made all things—man's immaterial and immortal nature—and a world of weal or woe beyond death and the grave!

Though, during the first week or two of his sojourn at Ellisland, Burns was left to fret in almost utter loneliness, he soon found ample opportunity for indulging his imperious passion for social cheer and excitement; indeed, he was almost immediately made welcome to the festive board, not only by neighbours of his own station, but by such families as the Millers of Dalswinton, the Riddels, etc.

And so, still busy with his building operations, writing many letters and not a few poems, finding time for a good deal of social enjoyment, and also for exerting himself in the laudable work of founding and furnishing a parish library in Dunscore, the spring of 1789 was laboriously yet pleasantly spent. At length, about midsummer, the *steading* at Ellisland being ready for occupation, he removed his household thither from "The Isle." Poet-like, he followed the quaint custom observed on such occasions. With his wife on his arm, and preceded by the maidservant, Betty Smith, who carried the family Bible and a bowl of salt, he entered his new abode. As soon as things were set in order, a company of neighbours assembled to celebrate the *house-heating*, and drank, with enthusiasm, "Luck to the roof-tree of the house of Burns." The dwelling-house at Ellisland stands to-day almost as the Poet designed and constructed it :—

> A neat cottage, about fifty feet long, placed near the edge of the *scaur* or broken bank overhanging the Nith. The sitting-room, in the east end, had

THE NEW DWELLING-HOUSE.

a window looking down the valley, and commanding beautiful peeps of the stream. Another room, at the west end, was the *spence*, or room reserved for important occasions. A small kitchen and a bedroom lay between, while in the garret was accommodation for domestics. The whole structure, while marking in some degree the taste of the Poet, is yet perfectly suitable in its modesty to the frugal life of a farmer of a hundred acres. On the bank below was a spring of pure water. Assisted by his brother-in-law, Armour, who helped to build the house, Burns fashioned this into a well for the supply of his household. Running back from the house in two lines of building were a barn, terminating in a stackyard, and a cow-house and stable. Such was the simple establishment in which the great Poet of Scotland designed to spend the remainder of his life in industrious and frugal state.

The above is Chambers' brief description, the exactness of which can be seen by any one who affords himself the pleasure of a visit to this sweetly-situated classic homestead.

This summer of 1789 was the happiest stretch Burns had enjoyed for a good many years, or, indeed, was ever to know again. On June 8th he wrote in joyous key to Ainslie :—

With respect to my welfare, a subject in which you once warmly and effectively interested yourself,—I am here in my old way, holding my plough, marking the growth of my corn or the health of my dairy, and at times sauntering by the delightful windings of the Nith,—on the margin of which I have built my humble domicile,—praying for seasonable weather, or holding an intrigue with the muses, the only gipsies with whom I have now any intercourse. As I am entered into the holy state of matrimony, I trust my face is turned completely Zionward; and, as it is a rule with all honest fellows to repeat no grievances, I hope that the little poetic licences of former days will, of course, fall under the oblivious influence of some good-natured statute of celestial prescription. In my family devotion—which, like a good Presbyterian, I occasionally give to my household folks—I am extremely fond of the psalm, "Let not the errors of my youth," etc., and that other, "Lo, children are God's heritage," etc., in which last Mrs. Burns—who, by the bye, has a glorious "wood-note wild" at either old song or psalmody—joins me with the pathos of Handel's "Messiah."

It is pleasant to think of Burns as *douce gudeman*, keeping up the hallowed exercise of family prayer, and as a regular attender at worship in Dunscore Kirk, to which he had to trudge fully three miles over the hills. Mr. Kirkpatrick, then minister of Dunscore, was a strict Calvinist, and, of course, the narrow, dogmatic nature of his doctrine was very far from harmonizing with the Poet's views. To this circumstance we owe the following letter to Mrs. Dunlop, wherein, be it observed, he again solemnly avows his belief in God, and human accountability now and in a world to come; also his belief in the special divinity of Christ's mission; concluding with a beautiful statement of the practical humanity of all true religion:—

I have just heard Mr. Kirkpatrick preach a sermon. He is a man famous for his benevolence, and I revere him; but from such ideas of my Creator, good Lord, deliver me! Religion, my honoured friend, is surely a simple business, as it equally concerns the ignorant and the learned, the poor and the rich. That there is an incomprehensible Great Being, to whom I owe my existence, and that He must be intimately acquainted with the operations and progress of the internal machinery, and consequent outward deportment, of this creature which He has made,—these are, I think, self-evident propositions. That there is a real and eternal distinction between virtue and vice, and consequently that I am an accountable creature; that from the seeming nature of the human mind, as well as from the evident imperfection—nay, positive injustice—in the administration of affairs, both in the natural and moral worlds, there must be a retributive scene of existence beyond the grave, —must, I think be allowed by every one who will give himself a moment's reflection. I will go further, and affirm that from the sublimity, excellence, and purity of His doctrine and precepts, unparalleled by all the aggregated wisdom and learning of many preceding ages, though, to *appearance*, He Himself was the obscurest and most illiterate of our species—therefore Jesus Christ was from God.

Whatever mitigates the woes or increases the happiness of others, this is my criterion of goodness; and whatever injures society at large, or any individual in it, this is my measure of iniquity.

APPOINTMENT AS GAUGER.

On the 18th August 1789, his wife presented him with a son, whom he named Francis Wallace, in honour of his most deeply respected friend and correspondent, Mrs. Dunlop.

Following close upon this domestic event came his application for active employment in the Excise. He was prompted to take this step, it seems, by the present and prospective increase of his family, and on account of the comparative failure of his first year's crops and the poor promise of the coming harvest. Again, through the influence of his good friend, Mr. Graham, his application was granted, and he was there and then appointed to perform the duties of *gauger* in a wide district, comprising ten parishes around Ellisland.

That Burns's pride was somewhat wounded by this turn in his affairs is evident from numerous allusions—mostly facetious in form, it is true—both in prose and verse. We quote on this point part of his letter of the 1st November, to Robert Ainslie :—

> I know not how the word exciseman, or the still more opprobrious gauger, will sound in your ears. I, too, have seen the day when my auditory nerves would have felt very delicately on this subject; but a wife and children are things which have a wonderful power in blunting these kind of sensations. Fifty pounds a year for life, and a provision for widows and orphans, is, you will allow, no bad settlement for a *poet*.

To the same effect he penned an epigram on beginning his duties as exciseman :—

> Searching auld wives' barrels,
>   Och, hon! the day!
> That clarty barm should stain my laurels;
>   But—what'll ye say!
> These movin' things ca'd wives and weans,
>   Wad move the very hearts o' stanes!

In the spirit of the above, which indicate a most creditable motive on the Poet's part, he entered manfully on his laborious task, and carried out, from the first, his not seldom disagreeable duty in a conscientious yet kindly way. Towards those who carried on an organized and extensive contraband traffic he was severe; but many incidents are recorded of his forbearance towards those who only indulged in an occasional or trifling breach of the revenue regulations. The strong good sense and kindly nature of the Poet kept him, in these cases, from officiously or tyrannically riding on the top of his commission.

Allan Cunningham tells, *e.g.*, how the Poet and a brother exciseman one day suddenly entered a widow woman's shop in Dunscore, and made a seizure of smuggled tobacco.

> "Jenny," said the Poet, "I expected this would be the upshot. Here, Lewars, take note of the number of rolls as I count them. Now, Jock, did ye ever hear an auld wife numbering her threads before check-reels were invented? Thou's ane, and thou's no ane, and thou's ane a' out—listen." As he handed out the rolls, he went on with his humorous enumeration, but dropping every other roll into Janet's lap.

And Professor Gillespie, who happened to be in Thornhill Fair in 1793, gives an account of another such incident. A certain Kate Watson was doing a little business in the shebeening way that day:—

> I saw — says the Professor — the Poet enter her door, and anticipated nothing short of an immediate seizure of a certain *greybeard* and barrel, which, to my personal knowledge, contained the contraband commodities our Bard was in quest of. A nod, accompanied by a significant movement of the forefinger, brought Kate to the doorway or trance, and I was near enough to hear the following words distinctly uttered:—"Kate, are you mad? Don't you know that the supervisor and I will be in upon you in the course of forty minutes? Good-bye t'ye at present." Burns was in the street and in the midst of the

crowd in an instant, and I had access to know that the friendly hint was not neglected.

"We see," Chambers remarks, in recording a few such anecdotes, "in these homely facts the same benevolent nature which shines in the verses to the Mouse and the Mountain Daisy."

From the time of his appointment as exciseman, however, Burns seems to have more and more neglected his duties on the farm. What work he now did on Ellisland was done with little method or interest. Increasing evidence of failure only served to increase his disgust at the necessary drudgeries of husbandry. Truth to tell, he had enough to do in thoroughly carrying out, as he did, his official duty, which compelled him to ride on an average over thirty miles a day, and also led him into many temptations most trying to one of his temperament.

On the authority of a youthful contemporary and great admirer of the Poet, Mr. David M'Culloch, Lockhart says:—

> Burns, in his perpetual perambulations over the moors of Dumfriesshire, had every temptation to encounter which bodily fatigue, the blandishments of hosts and hostesses, and the habitual manners of those who acted along with him in the Excise could present. . . . From the castle to the cottage, every door flew open at his approach; and the old system of hospitality, then flourishing, rendered it difficult for the most soberly-inclined guest to rise from any man's board in the same trim that he sat down to it. The farmer, if Burns were seen passing, left his reapers, and trotted by the side of "Jenny Geddes" until he could persuade the Bard that the day was hot enough to demand an extra libation. If he entered an inn at midnight, after all the inmates were in bed, the news of his arrival circulated from the cellar to the garret, and ere ten minutes had elapsed, the landlord and all his guests were assembled round the ingle, the largest punch-bowl was produced, and
>
> "Be ours this night; who knows what comes to-morrow?"
>
> was the language of every eye in the circle that welcomed him.

Moreover, his famous poetic and social gifts brought him a good deal of distraction and expense in the form of numerous visitors to Ellisland. "Lion-gazers," says Lockhart, "from all quarters beset him; they ate and drank at his cost, and often went away to criticise him and his fare, as if they had done Burns and his black bowl great honour in condescending to be entertained for a single evening with such company and such liquor." Of a certain afternoon's entertainment Dr. Currie gives the following graphic account, based on information furnished by one of the party:—

> In the summer of 1791, two English gentlemen, who had before met with him in Edinburgh, paid a visit to him at Ellisland. On calling at the house, they were informed that he had walked out on the banks of the river; and, dismounting from their horses, they proceeded in search of him. On a rock that projected into the stream they saw a man employed in angling, of a singular appearance. He had a cap made of a fox's skin on his head, a loose greatcoat fixed round him by a belt, from which depended an enormous Highland broadsword. It was Burns. He received them with great cordiality, and asked them to share his humble dinner—an invitation which they accepted. On the table they found boiled beef, with vegetables and barley broth, after the manner of Scotland, of which they partook heartily. After dinner, the Bard told them ingenuously that he had no wine to offer them—nothing better than Highland whisky, a bottle of which Mrs. Burns set on the board. He produced at the same time his punch-bowl, made of Inverary marble; and, mixing the spirit with water and sugar, filled their glasses, and invited them to drink. The travellers were in haste, and, besides, the flavour of the whisky to their *suthron* palates was scarcely tolerable; but the generous Poet offered them his best, and his ardent hospitality they found it impossible to resist. Burns was in his happiest mood, and the charms of his conversation were altogether fascinating. He ranged over a great variety of topics, illuminating whatever he touched. He related the tales of his infancy and of his youth; he recited some of the gayest and some of the tenderest of his poems: in the wildest of his strains of mirth he threw in some touches of melancholy, and spread around him the electric emotions of his powerful mind.

A SERVANT'S STATEMENT.

In recollection of the ungenerous and inconsiderate curiosity which actuated many of the class of visitors referred to in the above, it is with feelings of sorrow not unmixed with indignation that we think of Burns being so drawn on to 'make sport for the Philistines,' wasting his time and substance, and, worst of all, dissipating his glorious gifts of head and heart.

In making up our view of the Poet as he appeared at Ellisland, the statement, as given by Chambers, of William Clark, who was ploughman with Burns for six months of this period, must not be omitted :—

> Burns kept two men and two women servants; but he invariably, when at home, took his meals with his wife and family in the little parlour. Clark thought he was as good a manager of land as the generality of the farmers in the neighbourhood. The farm of Ellisland was said to be moderately rented, and was susceptible of much improvement, had improvement been in repute. Burns sometimes visited the neighbouring farmers, and they returned the compliment; but that way of spending time and exchanging civilities was not so common then as now, and, besides, the most of the people thereabouts had no expectation that Burns's conduct and writings would be so much noticed afterwards. Burns kept nine or ten milch cows, some young cattle, four horses, and several pet sheep: of the latter he was very fond. During the winter and spring-time, when he was not engaged with the Excise business, he occasionally held the plough for an hour or so for him (William Clark), and was a fair workman, though the mode of ploughing now-a-days-is much superior in many respects. During seed-time, Burns might be frequently seen, at an early hour, in the fields with his sowing-sheet; but, as business often required his attention from home, he did not sow the whole of the grain. He was a kind and indulgent master, and spoke familiarly to his servants, both in the house and out of it, though, if anything put him out of humour, he was *gey guldersome for a wee while:* the storm was soon over, and there was never a word of *upcast* afterwards. Clark never saw him really angry but once, and it was occasioned by the carelessness of one of the woman-servants, who had not cut potatoes small enough, which brought one of the cows into danger of being choked. His looks, gestures, and voice on that

occasion were terrible : W. C. was glad to be out of his sight, and when they met again, Burns was perfectly calm. If any extra work was to be done, the men sometimes got a dram ; but Clark had lived with masters who were more *flush* in that way to their servants. Clark, during the six months he spent at Ellisland, *never once saw his master intoxicated or incapable of managing his own business.* . . . Burns, when at home, usually wore a broad blue bonnet, a blue or drab long-tailed coat, corduroy breeches, dark blue stockings, and *cootikens*, and in cold weather a black-and-white checked plaid wrapped round his shoulders. Mrs. Burns was a good and prudent housewife, kept everything in neat and tidy order, was well liked by the servants, for whom she provided abundance of wholesome food. At parting, Burns gave Clark a certificate of character, and, besides paying his wages in full, gave him a shilling for a *fairing*.

We have seen how, almost from the first, Burns's expectations regarding success in the working of his farm were very meagre, and now, during the last summer of his tenancy, we find his farming prospect growing more and more hopeless, and his spirit more and more sad and embittered. Traces of his growing melancholy and vexation frequently appear in the letters of this season, most strikingly, perhaps, in that terrible outburst of angry, troubled discontent which he penned in his letter of 11th June to Mr. Cunningham :—

God help the children of dependence ! Hated and persecuted by their enemies, and too often, alas ! almost unexceptionably, received by their friends with disrespect and reproach, under the thin disguise of cold civility and humiliating advice. O to be a sturdy savage, stalking in the pride of his independence, amid the solitary wilds of his deserts, rather than in civilised life helplessly to tremble for a subsistence, precarious as the caprice of a fellow-creature ! Every man has his virtues, and no man is without his failings ; and curse on that privileged plain-dealing of friendship which, in the hour of my calamity, cannot reach forth the helping hand without at the same time pointing out those failings, and apportioning them their share in procuring my present distress. My friends—for such the world calls ye, and such ye think yourselves to be—pass by my virtues if you please, but do also spare my follies : the first will witness in my breast for themselves, and the last will give pain enough to the ingenuous mind without you. And since deviating more or less from the paths of propriety and rectitude must be incident to human nature, do thou, Fortune, put it in my power, always from myself and of myself, to bear the consequence of those errors! I do not want to be independent that I may sin, but I want to be independent in my sinning.

It must not be assumed, however, that want of success as a farmer was the sole cause of this gloomy and exasperated state of mind. Nor can it with fairness be set down to the self-upbraidings either of indolence or intemperance. What with his farming and Excise duties, his social engagements and correspondence, and, not least, his various poetical efforts, he must have been, in the main, a busy man; and although yielding overmuch, at times, to those festive excitements which had for him at all times so great a charm, he was by no means the victim of habitual or regardless excess. Nor could he complain of lack of recognition of his then unrivalled genius; of this he received a great deal from many of the best of his contemporaries. But whether or not these things moved him to any great extent, it is to be suspected that he was, for one thing, deeply wounded and troubled by the consequences of that passionate folly in a certain direction which had more than once before caused him keenest mental pain; and it may have been in a vain endeavour to escape from bitter reflections on his own waywardness, and to blunt the tooth of remorse, that he gave expression to such tirades of bitter, stormy feeling as the above. It should be further remarked that, about this time, he was subjected to a good deal of severe and ill-natured criticism from various quarters. That this rancorous meddling greatly annoyed him is clear from his "Third Epistle to Mr. Graham," where, *e.g.*, he writes :—

>   Critics !—appalled I venture on the name,
>   Those cut-throat bandits in the path of fame:

> Bloody dissectors, worse than ten Munroes !
> He hacks to teach, they mangle to expose.
> His heart by causeless, wanton malice wrung,
> By blockheads' daring into madness stung ;
> His well-won bays, than life itself more dear,
> By miscreants torn, who ne'er one sprig must wear :
> Foiled, bleeding, tortured, in the unequal strife,
> The hapless poet flounders on through life ;
> Till fled each hope that once his bosom fired,
> And fled each muse that glorious once inspired,
> Low sunk in squalid, unprotected age,
> Dead, even resentment, for his injured page,
> He heeds or feels no more the ruthless critic's rage !
>
> So, by some hedge, the generous steed deceased,
> For half-starved snarling curs a dainty feast,
> By toil and famine worn to skin and bone,
> Lies senseless of each tugging bitch's son.

It has also been surmised that it was while his proud and sensitive nature was wincing under the attack of some contemptible criticism, he penned the following extraordinary page :—

> Thou eunuch of language : thou Englishman, who never was south the Tweed : thou servile echo of fashionable barbarisms ; thou quack, vending the nostrums of empirical elocution : thou marriage-maker between vowels and consonants, on the Gretna Green of caprice : thou cobbler, botching the flimsy socks of bombast oratory : thou blacksmith, hammering the rivets of absurdity : thou butcher, imbruing thy hands in the bowels of orthography : thou arch-heretic in pronunciation : thou pitch-pipe of affected emphasis : thou carpenter, mortising the awkward joints of jarring sentences : thou squeaking dissonance of cadence : thou pimp of gender : thou Lion Herald to silly etymology : thou antipode of grammar : thou executioner of construction : thou brood of the speech-distracting builders of the Tower of Babel : thou lingual confusion worse confounded : thou scape-gallows from the land of syntax : thou scavenger of mood and tense : thou murderous accoucheur of infant learning : thou *ignis*

fatuus, misleading the steps of benighted ignorance : thou pickle-herring in the puppet show of nonsense ; thou faithful recorder of barbarous idiom ; thou persecutor of syllabication ; thou baleful meteor, foretelling and facilitating the rapid approach of Nox and Erebus."

The Ellisland scene of the Poet's strange, sad career—a scene which opened full of promise—was soon to close in almost complete temporal loss and disappointment. Seeing that he could no longer remain in his farm, Burns relinquished his lease, sold off his crops, and having timeously secured a transference to Excise duty in Dumfries, in December 1791 he bade farewell to lovely Ellisland, leaving there, as Cunningham with quaint force observes, "nothing but a putting-stone with which he had loved to exercise his strength, a memory of his musings which can never die, and £300 of his money sunk beyond redemption in a speculation from which all had augured happiness."

In summing up what is, after all, the most important matter in Burns's stay at Ellisland, viz. the poetical results, in addition to those already mentioned, it is our most pleasant duty now to speak of not a few songs and poems of imperishable interest, power, and beauty. On the 2nd February 1790, the third volume of Johnson's *Musical Museum* was issued, containing no fewer than forty songs by Burns. Several of these are noticed elsewhere in this chapter ; and here may be enumerated some others of the more popular songs —" John Anderson, my Jo," " Ca' the Yowes to the Knowes," " Tam Glen," " The Braes o' Ballochmyle," " A man's a man for a' that," " The day returns, my bosom burns," " I gaed a waefu' gate yestreen," and " Whistle o'er the lave o't," each one of which is a priceless poetic gift.

Of other pieces may be noted a series of four epistles addressed to Mr. Graham of Fintry, who earned immortal honour by continuing to be the poet's steadfast friend and generous patron—his "stay in worldly strife," of whom Professor Wilson has well and justly said :—

> Of all Burns's friends, the most efficient was Mr. Graham of Fintry. To him he owed exciseman's diploma, settlement as a gauger when he was gudeman at Ellisland; translation as gauger to Dumfries; support against insidious foes . . . vindication at the Excise Board ; a temporary supervisorship ; and, though he knew not of it, security from dreaded degradation on his death-bed.

In these and a few other poems, acting on the suggestion of one or two friendly critics, Burns adopted the English style, in which he does not show to advantage, but rather hampered and out of his proper element. Fortunately his own good sense and keen poetic feeling prevented him from following to any considerable extent this well-meant but mistaken advice, and called him back to his unexampled command and employment of the national Doric. Another of his English efforts is the "Address to a Wounded Hare," in sending which piece to Alexander Cunningham, he says :—

> I have just put the last hand to a little poem, which I think will be something to your taste. One morning lately, as I was out pretty early in the fields, sowing some grass seeds, I heard the burst of a shot from a neighbouring plantation, and presently a poor little wounded hare came crippling by me. You will guess my indignation at the inhuman fellow who could shoot a hare at this season, when all of them have young ones. Indeed, there is something in that business of destroying for our sport individuals in the animal creation that do not injure us materially, which I could never reconcile to my ideas of virtue.

That beautiful sympathy, amounting almost literally to fellow-feeling, which formed so great a part of Burns's nature, and to which he has so often given tenderest expression, may be once more admired in this little poem, which we give as it at first left the Poet's hands :—

> Inhuman man! curse on thy barb'rous art,
> And blasted be thy murder-aiming eye !
> May never pity soothe thee with a sigh,
> Nor ever pleasure glad thy cruel heart !
>
> Go live, poor wanderer of the wood and field,
> The bitter little that of life remains :
> No more the thickening brakes or verdant plains
> To thee a home, or food, or pastime yield.
>
> Seek, mangled innocent, some wonted form ;
> That wonted form, alas ! thy dying bed !
> The sheltering rushes whistling o'er thy head,
> The cold earth with thy blood-stain'd bosom warm.
>
> Perhaps a mother's anguish adds its woe ;
> The playful pair crowd fondly by thy side ;
> Ah ! helpless nurslings, who will now provide
> That life a mother only can bestow ?
>
> Oft as by winding Nith I, musing, wait
> The sober eve, or hail the cheerful dawn,
> I'll miss thee sporting o'er the dewy lawn,
> And curse the ruthless wretch, and mourn thy hapless fate.

Close upon the foregoing we find him writing, in quite the opposite vein and style, his inimitable descriptive " Address to the Toothache," reading which has helped many victims of this painful ailment to grimly smile in spite of its

> venom'd stang
> That shoots the tortured gums alang,
> And through the lugs gies mony a twang,
> Wi' gnawing vengeance,

and so on, as in the well-known realistic lines.

In the summer of 1789 he also wrote his famous satire, "The Kirk's Alarm." Doctor M'Gill, collegiate minister of Ayr, having ventured to publish an essay supposed to contain heretical doctrine regarding the death of Christ, was made the object of a fierce heresy-hunt. In and around the "auld toun o' Ayr" the case was exciting keen controversy, when Burns took in hand to champion the cause of Dr. M'Gill, whom he regarded as a man of worth and ability, cruelly harassed because of his enlightenment and courage of opinion. Enclosing the poem to John Logan, the author says:—

> I have, as you will shortly see, finished "The Kirk's Alarm;" but, now that it is done, and that I have laughed once or twice at the conceits in some of the stanzas, I am determined not to let it get into the public; so I send you this copy, the first that I have sent to Ayrshire, except some few of the stanzas which I wrote off in embryo for Gavin Hamilton, under the express provision and request that you will only read it to a few of us, and do not on any account give or permit to be taken any copy of the ballad. If I could be of any service to Dr. M'Gill I would do it, though it should be at a much greater expense than irritating a few bigoted priests; but I am afraid serving him in his present *embarras* is a task too hard for me. I have enemies enow, God knows, though I do not wantonly add to the number.

The keynote of the satire is struck in these lines from the second stanza, which embody, in fewest words possible, a daring "conceit" at which Burns may well have "laughed once or twice":—

> To join faith and sense
> Upon any pretence,
> Is heretic, damnable error.[1]

The autumn of this same year, 1789, was a very productive season, witnessing the composition of over half a dozen poems,

---

[1] Chambers's painstaking identification of, and notes concerning the different personages satirized should be consulted as an aid to the full enjoyment of this noted production.

several of which are of outstanding literary merit and of rich biographical interest.

As a song of jovial boon-companionship, "O Willie brewed a peck o' maut" may be said to stand without a rival. Willie (Nicol), Allan (Masterton), and the Poet formed the ever-memorable party, as may gathered from Burns's note to the song :—

> The air is Masterton's, the song mine. The occasion of it was this:— Mr. William Nicol, of the High School, Edinburgh, during the autumn vacation, being at Moffat, honest Allan (who was at that time on a visit to Dalswinton) and I went to pay Nicol a visit. We had such a joyous meeting that Mr. Masterton and I agreed, each in our own way, that we should celebrate the business.

Writing in 1799, Currie feelingly remarked, "These three honest fellows—all men of uncommon talents—are now all under the turf;" and in 1821, John Struthers, himself a man of no mean genius, gave forth a poetic wail over the "three merry boys" of the great song :—

> Nae mair in learning Willie toils, nor Allan makes the melting lay,
> Nor Rab, wi' fancy-witching wiles, beguiles the hour o' daw'ing day ;
> For tho' they werena very fou, that wicked "wee drap in the e'e"
> Has done its turn ; untimely now the green grass waves o'er a' the three.

Another of the productions of this season is "The Whistle," to which convivial ballad the author supplied the following note :—

> In the train of Ann of Denmark, when she came to Scotland with our James VI., there came over also a Danish gentleman of gigantic stature and great prowess, and a matchless champion of Bacchus. He had a little ebony whistle, which at the commencement of the orgies he laid on the table, and whoever was the last able to blow it, everybody else being disabled by the potency of the bottle, was to carry off the whistle as a trophy of victory. The Dane produced credentials of his victories, without a single defeat, at the courts of Copenhagen, Stockholm, Moscow, Warsaw, and several of the

petty courts in Germany; and challenged the Scots Bacchanalians to the alternative of trying his prowess, or else of acknowledging their inferiority. After many overthrows on the part of the Scots, the Dane was encountered by Sir Robert Lawrie of Maxwelton, ancestor of the present worthy baronet of that name; who, after three days' and three nights' hard contest, left the Scandinavian under the table,

"And blew on the whistle his requiem shrill."

Sir Walter, son to Sir Robert before mentioned, afterwards lost the whistle to Walter Riddel, of Glenriddel, who had married a sister of Sir Walter's.

Captain Riddel of Friar's Carse, who at this time held the trophy, appointed Friday, 16th October, as the day on which a drinking contest for the "whistle" championship should be held between Mr. Ferguson of Craigdarroch, Sir Robert Lawrie of Maxwelton, and himself. Burns was invited to attend, but whether or not he was actually present on the occasion, as Poet Laureate of the event he penned this highly dramatic poem, wherein is celebrated the victory (?) of Craigdarroch.

Four days after the mighty drinking contest at Friar's Carse, we find the Bard in completely altered mood and strain, on Tuesday, 20th October, the anniversary of Highland Mary's death, penning his immortal lines, "To Mary in Heaven,"—a poem which is by universal assent regarded as *peerless* in its combined tenderness and sublimity of feeling and beauty of form, "the noblest of all his ballads"—

> Thou ling'ring star, with less'ning ray,
>   That lov'st to greet the early morn,
> Again thou usher'st in the day
>   My Mary from my soul was torn.
> O Mary! dear departed shade!
>   Where is thy place of blissful rest?
> See'st thou thy lover lowly laid?
>   Hear'st thou the groans that rend his breast?

That sacred hour can I forget?
  Can I forget the hallowed grove,
Where by the winding Ayr we met,
  To live one day of parting love?
Eternity will not efface
  Those records dear of transports past;
Thy image at our last embrace—
  Ah! little thought we 'twas our last!

Ayr, gurgling, kissed his pebbled shore,
  O'erhung with wild woods, thick'ning green;
The fragrant birch, and hawthorn hoar,
  Twined am'rous round the raptured scene;
The flowers sprang wanton to be prest,
  The birds sang love on every spray—
Till too, too soon, the glowing west
  Proclaim'd the speed of wingèd day.

Still o'er these scenes my mem'ry wakes,
  And fondly broods with miser care!
Time but th' impression stronger makes,
  As streams their channels deeper wear.
My Mary! dear departed shade!
  Where is thy place of blissful rest?
See'st thou thy lover lowly laid?
  Hear'st thou the groans that rend his breast?

Keen and interesting discussion has been held regarding the exact circumstances in which Burns conceived and penned this grand, sweet ode. We find no sufficient reasons adduced, however, for losing faith in the time-honoured, affecting account as given by Lockhart in 1828:—

> This celebrated poem was, it is on all hands admitted, composed by Burns in 1789, on the anniversary day of the death of his early love, Mary Campbell. Mrs. Burns . . gave the following account to Mr. M'Diarmid

concerning the composition of this remarkable production. Burns spent that day, though labouring under a cold, in the usual work of his harvest, and apparently in excellent spirits. But as the twilight deepened, he appeared to grow "very sad about something," and at length wandered out into the barnyard, to which his wife, in her anxiety, followed him, entreating him in vain to observe that frost had set in, and to return to the fireside. On being again and again requested to do so, he promised compliance; but still remained where he was, striding up and down slowly, and contemplating the sky, which was singularly clear and starry. At last Mrs. Burns found him stretched on a mass of straw, with his eyes fixed on a beautiful planet "that shone like another moon," and prevailed on him to come in. He immediately, on entering the house, called for his desk, and wrote exactly as they now stand, with all the ease of one copying from memory, these sublime and pathetic verses.

In the almost simultaneous production of pieces so entirely different in subject-matter and style, we find one more striking illustration of the swiftly-varying moods and feelings which swayed Burns hither and thither; as also of the amazing range of his mighty genius, which could turn so easily from the extreme of joyous revelry to the opposite pole of soul-melting pathos, and touch each, as occasion offered, with the master-hand and spirit.

In the summer of this same year the poet made the acquaintance of Captain Grose, the antiquary. His intimacy with this "fine, fat, fodgel wight" is interesting, as calling forth the poem "On the late Captain Grose's Peregrinations through Scotland," and, above all, memorable in connection with the production of "Tam o' Shanter"[1]—the result, it is said, of *one day's deep musing* by the riverside at Ellisland.[2]

---

[1] See vol. i. p. 258.
[2] Speaking again on the authority of Mrs. Burns, Lockhart says:—"The Poet spent most of the day on his favourite walk by the river, where, in the afternoon, she joined him with some of her children—[there were then only two]. He was busily *crooning to himsel'*, and Mrs. Burns, perceiving that her presence was an interruption, loitered behind with her little ones among the broom. Her attention was

ELECTION BALLADS.

In 1789-90, on the occasion of a keen contest for the honour of representing the Dumfries district of burghs, in espousing the cause of Sir James Johnston of Westerhall, Burns wrote three election ballads, "The Laddies by the Banks o' Nith," "The Five Carlines," and "Fintry, my stay in worldly strife"—the first of which pieces commands special admiration for its apt personifications and splendid minstrel tone. Burns was incited to this tilt in the political arena, not so much by any feeling of strong partisanship, as by the local and temporary excitements of the campaign.[1] In the closing stanzas of the last of the above-mentioned ballads, he avows a humble yet independent position in party strife, and ends with this hearty, wild note of the deep-rooted patriotism of his nature:—

> Now for my friends' and brethren's sakes,
> And for my dear-loved Land o' Cakes,
>   I pray with holy fire:
> Lord, send a rough-shod troop o' hell
> O'er a' wad Scotland buy or sell,
>   To grind them in the mire.

During the winter of 1789-90, the Poet occasionally found his way to the theatre in Dumfries, apparently in quest of some entertainment likely to lighten the burden of melancholy and nervous depression which from time to time sat so heavily upon him. For Mr. Sutherland, the manager of the company then acting in Dumfries, he dashed off a couple of prologues, one of

presently attracted by the strange and wild gesticulations of the bard, who, now at some distance, was *agonized* with an ungovernable access of joy. He was reciting very loud, and with the tears rolling down his cheeks, those animated verses which he had just conceived—

"Now Tam, O Tam! had thae been queans,
    A' plump and strappin' in their teens;"

and so on.

[1] Perhaps Burns might be politically described in present-day phrase as a Tory Democrat.

which was spoken on the evening of 1st January, 1790, the other, shortly afterwards, on Mr. Sutherland's benefit night.

The latter half of the Ellisland period further produced several pieces of the "In Memoriam" order—"Elegy on Captain Matthew Henderson,"[1] "Elegy on Miss Burnet of Monboddo,"[2] and "Lament for James, Earl of Glencairn"—a magnificent tribute of grateful admiration and sorrowing affection, gushing warm from the Poet's great sobbing heart. In poems after this manner, we know of nothing to excel these closing stanzas :—

> Awake thy last sad voice, my harp!
>   The voice of woe and wild despair!
> Awake! resound thy latest lay—
>   Then sleep in silence evermair!
> And thou, my last, best, only friend,
>   That fillest an untimely tomb,
> Accept this tribute from the bard
>   Thou brought from fortune's mirkest gloom.
>
> In poverty's low barren vale,
>   Thick mists, obscure, involved me round;
> Though oft I turned the wistful eye,
>   Nae ray of fame was to be found:
> Thou found'st me, like the morning sun
>   That melts the fogs in limpid air,
> The friendless bard and rustic song
>   Became alike thy fostering care.
>
> O why has worth so short a date,
>   While villains ripen grey with time?
> Must thou, the noble, generous, great,
>   Fall in bold manhood's hardy prime!

---

[1] Vol. i. p. 309.
[2] The lady celebrated by Burns in his "Address to Edinburgh." See vol. ii. p. 335

> Why did I live to see that day?
>   A day to me so full of woe!
> Oh, had I met the mortal shaft
>   Which laid my benefactor low!
>
> The bridegroom may forget the bride
>   Was made his wedded wife yestreen;
> The monarch may forget the crown
>   That on his head an hour has been;
> The mother may forget the child
>   That smiles sae sweetly on her knee;
> But I'll remember thee, Glencairn,
>   And a' that thou hast done for me!

How deeply Burns mourned the loss and revered the memory of this amiable, noble friend and benefactor we further learn from his letter, enclosing the "Lament," to the Lady Cunningham, the deceased Earl's sister, wherein he says:—

> As all the world knows my obligations to the late Earl of Glencairn, I would wish to show, as openly, that my heart glows, and shall ever glow, with the most grateful sense and remembrance of his lordship's goodness. The sables I did myself the honour to wear to his lordship's memory were not the "mockery of woe." Nor shall my gratitude perish with me! If among my children I shall have a son that has a heart, he shall hand it down to his child as a family honour and a family debt, that my dearest existence I owe to the noble house of Glencairn!

When, in February 1789, the Poet paid a hurried visit to Edinburgh, to receive from Creech some £50,—the balance due for further sales of the Edinburgh edition,—he did not on that occasion see Clarinda. The estrangement, caused by his marrying Jean Armour, passed off, however, and the correspondence with Clarinda was to some extent renewed. Learning that this lady was about to set out for Jamaica to rejoin her errant husband, Burns repaired to Edinburgh about the end of November 1791, to say "Good-bye." Moved by this crisis in Clarinda's sadly romantic life, he wrote the well-known exquisite songs, "Behold the hour, the boat arrive," "Here awa', there awa'," "My Nannie's awa'," and those intensely glowing lines, which have been well described as "the alpha and omega of feeling, containing the essence of an existence of pain and pleasure distilled into one burning drop":—

> Ae fond kiss, and then we sever!
> Ae fareweel, and then for ever!
> Deep in heart-wrung tears I'll pledge thee,
> Warring sighs and groans I'll wage thee.
>
> Who shall say that Fortune grieves him,
> While the star of hope she leaves him?
> Me, nae cheerful twinkle lights me;
> Dark despair around benights me.
>
> I'll ne'er blame my partial fancy,
> Naething could resist my Nancy;
> But to see her was to love her;
> Love but her, and love for ever.
>
> Had we never loved sae kindly,
> Had we never loved sae blindly,
> Never met—or never parted,
> We had ne'er been broken-hearted.
>
> Fare-thee-weel, thou first and fairest!
> Fare-thee-weel, thou best and dearest!
> Thine be ilka joy and treasure,
> Peace, enjoyment, love, and pleasure!
>
> Ae fond kiss, and then we sever;
> Ae fareweel, alas! for ever!
> Deep in heart-wrung tears I'll pledge thee,
> Warring sighs and groans I'll wage thee.

LAST ELLISLAND SONG.

Merely observing the fact that those three years yielded various songs and minor poems which are not noticed here, we close this chapter with Burns's last poetical composition at Ellisland, his "Song of Death," a poem in some respects worthy to take rank with "Scots wha hae," by virtue of its inspiring ring of patriotic bravery. In his letter to Mrs. Dunlop, of 17th December 1791, he thus embodied this spirited ode :—

> I have just finished the following song, which, to a lady, the descendant of Wallace, and many heroes of his truly illustrious line—and herself the mother of several soldiers—needs neither preface nor apology.

SONG OF DEATH.

AIR—*Oran an Aoig*.

Scene—A Field of Battle. Time of the day—Evening. The wounded and dying of the victorious army are supposed to join in the following song :—

Farewell, thou fair day, thou green earth, and ye skies,
   Now gay with the bright setting sun ;
Farewell, loves and friendships, ye dear tender ties—
   Our race of existence is run !

Thou grim King of Terrors, thou life's gloomy foe !
   Go, frighten the coward and slave ;
Go, teach them to tremble, fell tyrant ! but know
   No terrors hast thou to the brave !

Thou strik'st the dull peasant—he sinks in the dark,
   Nor saves e'en the wreck of a name ;
Thou strik'st the young hero—a glorious mark !
   He falls in the blaze of his fame !

In the field of proud honour—our swords in our hands,
   Our king and our country to save—
While victory shines on life's last ebbing sands,
   Oh, who would not die with the brave ?

CHAPTER IX.

DUMFRIES, 1792-1795. AGE, 33-36.

But, oh! thou bitter stepmother and hard
To thy poor, fenceless, naked child—the Bard!
. . . . . .
In naked feeling and in aching pride
He bears the unbroken blast from every side.
Third Epistle to Mr. Graham.

From this time, his wit became more gloomy and sarcastic, and his conversation and writings began to assume a misanthropical tone, by which they had not been before, in any eminent degree, distinguished. But, with all his failings, *his* was still that exalted mind which had raised itself above the depression of its original condition with all the energy of the *lion pawing to free his hinder limbs from the yet encumbering earth.*
Memoir of Burns, by his contemporary, Robert Heron.

IN thus far tracing the life-story of Burns, every sympathetic student must experience, side by side with constant admiration of that amazing poetic genius, many a feeling of keen pain and sorrow at the vexing record of aberration, disappointment, and care,—a record only now and then lightened by a few evanescent gleams of joyous hope appearing amid the prevailing unrest of a swiftly alternating and almost equally saddening glare and gloom. And now, from the time of his enforced departure from Ellisland until he is laid to rest in the tomb, the story darkens as to the terrible close of a great, sad tragedy. The record of these few last years—apart, indeed, from their rich harvest of deathless song — is simply *heartrending.*

SOCIAL LIFE IN DUMFRIES.

Towards the end of December 1791, leaving Ellisland, Burns became tenant of a humble abode in the "Wee Vennel" (now known as Bank Street), Dumfries; where "the father no longer saw the sun rise over the beautiful river, the little ones[1] had no longer the gowaned sod to sport over, and the mother found that every article of household necessity had to be purchased." The dwelling consisted of three apartments—parlour and kitchen, with a small room or bed-closet between, which last served as the Poet's study. Regarding his career now, there was cause for grave apprehension in the state of things which subsisted in Dumfries one hundred years ago. There he had to encounter, of course on a smaller scale, but in no less alluring form, nearly all the temptations of city life; and also some that are peculiar to a provincial town—a small capital in its way—such as Dumfries then was:—

> The curse of country towns—says Chambers, whose earlier years reached back to the times in question—is the partial and entire idleness of large classes of the inhabitants. There is always a cluster of men living on competencies, and a greater number of tradesmen whose shop-duties do not occupy half their time. Till a very recent period, dissipation in greater or less intensity was the rule and not the exception amongst these men; and in Dumfries, sixty years ago, this rule held good. In those days, tavern enjoyments were in vogue among men who do not now enter a public place of entertainment once in a twelvemonth. The weary waste of spirits and energy at these soaking evening meetings was deplorable. Insipid toasts, petty raillery, empty gabble about trivial occurrences, endless disputes on small questions of fact, where an almanac or a dictionary would have settled all, these, relieved by a song when it was to be had, formed the staple of convivial life as I remember it in such places in

---

[1] In March 1791, his family circle was increased by the advent of an illegitimate daughter born at the Globe Tavern; and in April by the birth of a son who was named William Nicol, after the Poet's friend and quondam travelling companion. The daughter here referred to was, in common with the Poet's other two daughters, named Elizabeth. The story of Mrs. Burns taking home this child of shame, and rearing it as her own, is one of most affecting interest. This pitiful irregularity on Burns's part is said to have occurred during his faithful, patient Jean's absence on a visit to her home and kindred at Mauchline.

my own younger days. It was a life without progress, or profit, or any gleam of a tendency to moral elevation. The only redemption to be hoped for it was in such scintillations of wit and eloquence as a man like Burns could give. For him, on the other hand, to do so was to sacrifice the bread of angels before blocks and dolts.

Burns came into this society a comparatively pure man, for, though the contrary has been asserted, there is no evidence that he had as yet acquired over-convivial habits. His own inclination was to shun rather than to court the bacchanalian revel, and there was a literal truth in what he told the Countess of Glencairn as to bringing his punch-bowl from its *dusty* corner on her ladyship's birthday. Burns, however, does not seem ever to have aimed at systematically resisting the temptations of convivial society. He yielded to them when they came, and it depended on the frequency of occasion or opportunity whether he was to be much or little in merry company. Now that he was thrown into Dumfries, it was of course to be feared that he would become much more a victim to such indulgences than formerly.

The truth of the foregoing remarks finds ample illustration in country towns even now, where many a one who has withstood the allurements of city social life is seen to fall an unsuspecting victim to the half-idle, gossiping, drinking ways of some village or small town *clique* or *coterie*. While it cannot be shown that prior to this Dumfries period the Poet was *habitually* intemperate, it cannot be for a moment denied that he had indulged in many a night's hard drinking amid the revelries of hard-drinking company in a hard-drinking age. It seems to have been while suffering the consequences of one of these *carousal* nights that he self-accusingly wrote to Ainslie, in December 1791 :—

Can you minister to a mind diseased ?— can you, amid the horrors of penitence, regret, remorse, headache, nausea, and all the rest of the hounds of hell that beset a poor wretch who has been guilty of the sin of drunkenness— can you speak peace to a troubled soul?

Misérable perdu that I am! I have tried everything that used to amuse me, but in vain: here must I sit, a monument of the vengeance laid up in store for the wicked, slowly counting every click of the clock as it slowly, slowly numbers over these lazy scoundrels of hours, . . . every one with a burden of anguish on his back, to pour on my devoted head—and there is none to pity me. My wife scolds me, my business torments me, and my sins come staring me in the face, every one telling a more bitter tale than his fellow.

It was thus he bitterly upbraided himself for those occasional excesses which his sojourn in Dumfries soon multiplied and aggravated. This state of things, again, is not to be altogether accounted for by the greater temptations of his new place of residence and fresh sphere of duty and companionship. The bitterness of failure and disappointment had much to do with it. He left his farm an impoverished and embittered man; and although he had received what we may now consider a substantial increase of salary [1] on coming to the town, he was not there long, till, from one cause and another, his hopes of advancement in the Excise service were almost entirely blasted. This unhappy result was mainly brought about by his carelessly and daringly avowed sympathy with the French Revolution movement. In toast and epigram and speech, he gave open expression to sentiments which were easily construed into dangerous disaffection towards the Government and Constitution of the country, and turned upon him many watchful and suspicious eyes.

On one occasion, e.g., in a public company, when the health of the Premier, William Pitt, was about to be proposed, Burns (a Government official, be it remembered) recklessly insisted that the toast should be "the health of a greater and a better man, George

---

[1] ["I am on the list, as we call it, for a supervisor, and will be called out by and by to act as one; but at present I am a simple gauger, though t'other day I got an appointment to an Excise division of £25 per annum better than the rest. My present income, down money, is £70 per annum."—Letter to Ainslie.] Being now relieved of the expenses of keeping a horse to carry him on his duties, his income may be estimated, independent of chance additions, as equal to a present-day salary of about £120.

Washington." Language of this kind could not fail to bring the Poet into hazardous notoriety in that time of excitement and distrust.

A still more daring act of seeming disloyalty falls to be recorded,—an act which is said to have at length impelled the Excise Commissioners to institute searching inquiry into the Jacobinical speech and conduct of "Exciseman Robert Burns." This extraordinary incident in the Poet's life is thus set forth by Lockhart:—

> At that period [1792] a great deal of contraband traffic, chiefly from the Isle of Man, was going on along the coasts of Galloway and Ayrshire, and the whole of the revenue officers from Gretna to Dumfries were placed under the orders of a superintendent residing in Annan, who exerted himself zealously in intercepting the descent of the smuggling vessels. On the 27th of February, a suspicious-looking brig was discovered in the Solway Firth, and Burns was one of the party whom the superintendent conducted to watch her motions. She got into shallow water the day afterwards, and the officers were enabled to discover that her crew were numerous, armed, and not likely to yield without a struggle. Lewars, a brother exciseman, an intimate friend of our Poet, was accordingly sent to Dumfries for a guard of dragoons; the superintendent himself, Mr. Crawford, proceeded on a similar errand to Ecclefechan, and Burns was left with some men under his orders, to watch the brig, and to prevent landing or escape. From the private journal of one of the excisemen—now in my hands—it appears that Burns manifested considerable impatience while thus occupied, being left for many hours in a wet salt-marsh, with a force which he knew to be inadequate to the purpose it was meant to fulfil. One of his comrades hearing him abuse his friend Lewars in particular, for being slow about his journey, the man answered that he also wished the devil had him for his pains, and that Burns in the meantime would do well to indite a song upon the sluggard: Burns said nothing; but, after taking a few strides by himself among the reeds and shingle, rejoined his party, and chanted to them the well-known ditty—'The Deil's awa' wi' the Exciseman.'
>
> Lewars arrived shortly after with his dragoons; and Burns, putting himself at their head, waded sword in hand to the brig, and was the first to board her. The crew lost heart and submitted, though their numbers were greater than

those of the assailing force. The vessel was condemned, and, with all her arms and stores, sold next day at Dumfries; upon which occasion Burns, whose conduct had been highly commended, thought fit to purchase four carronades by way of trophy.

But his glee went a step further;—he sent the guns, with a letter, to the French Convention, requesting that body to accept of them as a mark of his admiration and respect. The present and its accompaniment were intercepted at the Custom-house at Dover; and here, there appears little room to doubt, was the principal circumstance that drew on Burns the notice of his jealous superiors.

Notwithstanding the fact that a good deal has been written, not altogether unsuccessfully, in extenuation of the Poet's conduct, it still remains, taken in conjunction with his other sayings and doings of the same tendency, an act of, to say the least, impulsive, reckless folly on the part of any one situated as he then was. "We were not, it is true," as Lockhart remarks, "at war with France; but every one knew and felt that we were to be so ere long; and nobody can pretend that Burns was not guilty, on this occasion, of a most absurd and presumptuous breach of decorum." Every one rejoices in that glowing passion which the Bard ever cherished towards whatever made for the cause of liberty and humanity. At the same time, it may justly be regretted that his enthusiasm led him in this instance to continue to so emphatically sympathize with a movement which nominally avowed the principles expressed by the formula, "LIBERTY, FRATERNITY, EQUALITY," but which, almost from the first, manifested itself as a combination of mob-force, terror, and blood-guiltiness—a terrible menace to the peace and real progress of Europe and mankind.

From the Poet's own writings,—and all we know for certain must there be looked for,—it is evident that, like his Jacobitism, his sympathy with the Revolution movement sprang from no *rooted* feelings of disaffection or disloyalty towards the British Constitution, but rather he was, by his bounding love of all forms and names of liberty, and by the stirring excitements of those days, drawn into unguarded situations and expressions, which, in calmer moments, he heartily and loyally repudiated. But before passing from this unfortunate crisis, it is well, in defence of Burns, to let Burns speak for himself, as he does so nobly in one or two letters on the matter in hand.

On learning, in December 1792, that the Commissioners of Excise were bestirring themselves against him, he wrote to his friend, Mr. Graham, as follows :—

> SIR,—I have been surprised, confounded, and distracted by Mr. Mitchell, the collector, telling me that he has received an order from your Board to inquire into my political conduct, and blaming me as a person disaffected to Government.
>
> Sir, you are a husband and a father. You know what you would feel to see the much-loved wife of your bosom, and your helpless, prattling little ones, turned adrift into the world, degraded and disgraced from a situation in which they had been respectable and respected, and left almost without the necessary support of a miserable existence. Alas! sir, must I think that such soon will be my lot! and from the d—— dark insinuations of hellish, groundless envy, too! I believe, sir, I may aver it, and in the sight of Omniscience, that I would not tell a deliberate falsehood, no, not though even worse horrors, if worse can be, than those I have mentioned, hung over my head; and I say that the allegation, whatever villain has made it, is a lie! To the British Constitution, on revolution principles, next after my God, I am most devoutly attached. You, sir, have been much and generously my friend—Heaven knows how warmly I have felt the obligation, and how gratefully I have thanked you. Fortune, sir, has made you powerful, and me impotent—has given you patronage, and me dependence. I would not, for my single self, call on your humanity; were such my insular, unconnected situation, I would despise the tear that now swells in my eye—I could brave misfortune, I could face ruin, for at the worst "Death's thousand doors stand open;" but, good God! the tender concerns that I have mentioned, the claims and ties that I see at this moment, and feel around me, how they unnerve courage and wither resolution!

To your patronage, as a man of some genius, you have allowed me a claim; and your esteem, as an honest man, I know is my due. To these, sir, permit me to appeal; by these may I adjure you to save me from that misery which threatens to overwhelm me, and which—with my latest breath I will say it—I have not deserved.

The danger which at this juncture menaced the unlucky Bard was so grave that it was even currently reported that he had been dismissed. Erskine of Mar, on hearing this report, wrote to Riddel of Friar's Carse, sympathizing with Burns, and generously offering to head a subscription on his behalf. Hence the Poet's magnificent letter to Mr. Erskine, which, notwithstanding its length, we reproduce in all its passionate, truth-laden, pathetic power.

SIR,—Degenerate as human nature is said to be,—and in many instances worthless and unprincipled it is,—still there are bright examples to the contrary; examples that, even in the eyes of superior beings, must shed a lustre on the name of man.

Such an example have I now before me, when you, sir, came forward to patronize and befriend a distant obscure stranger, merely because poverty had made him helpless, and his British hardihood of mind had provoked the arbitrary wantonness of power. My much-esteemed friend, Mr. Riddel of Glenriddel, has just read me a paragraph of a letter he had from you. Accept, sir, of the silent throb of gratitude; for words would but mock the emotions of my soul.

You have been misinformed as to my final dismission from the Excise; I am still in the service. Indeed, but for the exertions of a gentleman who must be known to you, Mr. Graham of Fintry,—a gentleman who has ever been my warm and generous friend,—I had, without so much as a hearing, or the slightest previous intimation, been turned adrift with my helpless family to all the horrors of want. Had I had any other resource, probably I might have saved them the trouble of a dismission; but the little money I gained by my publication is, almost every guinea, embarked to save from ruin an only brother, who, though one of the worthiest, is by no means one of the most fortunate of men.

In my defence to their accusations I said, that, whatever might be my sentiments of republics, ancient or modern, as to Britain I abjured the idea—that a CONSTITUTION which, in its original principles, experience had proved to be every way fitted for our happiness in society, it would be insanity to sacrifice to an untried visionary theory—that, in consideration of my being situated in a department, however humble, immediately in the hands of people in power, I had forborne taking any active part, either personally or as an author, in the present business of REFORM ; but that, where I must declare my sentiments, I would say there existed a system of corruption between the executive power and the representative part of the legislature, which boded no good to our glorious CONSTITUTION, and which every patriotic Briton must wish to see amended. Some such sentiments as these I stated in a letter to my generous patron, Mr. Graham, which he laid before the Board at large, where, it seems, my last remark gave great offence ; and one of our supervisors-general, a Mr. Corbet, was instructed to inquire on the spot, and to document me—that my business was to act, *not to think;* and that, whatever might be men or measures, it was for me to be *silent* and *obedient.*

Mr. Corbet was likewise my steady friend ; so between Mr. Graham and him I have been partly forgiven : only I understand that all hopes of my getting officially forward are blasted.

Now, sir, to the business in which I would more immediately interest you. The partiality of my COUNTRYMEN has brought me forward as a man of genius, and has given me a character to support. In the POET I have avowed manly and independent sentiments, which I trust will be found in the MAN. Reasons of no less weight than the support of a wife and family, have pointed out as the eligible, and, situated as I was, the only eligible line of life for me, my present occupation. Still my honest fame is my dearest concern ; and a thousand times have I trembled at the idea of those *degrading* epithets that malice or misrepresentation may affix to my name. I have often, in blasting anticipation, listened to some future hackney scribbler, with the heavy malice of savage stupidity, exulting in his hireling paragraphs — " Burns, notwithstanding the *fanfaronade* of independence to be found in his works, and after having been held forth to public view and to public estimation as a man of some genius, yet quite destitute of resources within himself to support his borrowed dignity, he dwindled into a paltry exciseman, and slunk out the rest of his insignificant existence in the meanest of pursuits, and among the vilest of mankind."

In your illustrious hands, sir, permit me to lodge my disavowal and defiance

ON HIS DEFENCE.

of these slanderous falsehoods. Burns was a poor man from birth, and an exciseman by necessity; but—*I will* say it—the sterling of his honest worth no poverty could debase, and his independent British mind oppression might bend, but could not subdue. Have not I, to me, a more precious stake in my country's welfare than the richest dukedom in it? I have a large family of children, and the prospect of many more. I have three sons, who, I see already, have brought into the world souls ill qualified to inhabit the bodies of SLAVES. Can I look tamely on, and see any machination to wrest from them the birthright of my boys—the little independent BRITONS, in whose veins runs my own blood? No! I will not, should my heart's blood stream around my attempt to defend it!

Does any man tell me, that my full efforts can be of no service, and that it does not belong to my humble station to meddle with the concern of a nation!

I can tell him that it is on such individuals as I that a nation has to rest, both for the hand of support and the eye of intelligence. The uninformed MOB may swell a nation's bulk; and the titled, tinsel, courtly throng may be its feathered ornament; but the number of those who are elevated enough in life to reason and to reflect, yet low enough to keep clear of the venal contagion of a court—these are a nation's strength!

I know not how to apologize for the impertinent length of this epistle; but one small request I must ask of you further—When you have honoured this letter with a perusal, please to commit it to the flames. Burns, in whose behalf you have so generously interested yourself, I have here, in his native colours, drawn *as he is;* but should any of the people in whose hands is the very bread he eats, get the least knowledge of the picture, *it would ruin the poor Bard for ever.*

Any comment of ours must appear stiff and feeble beside this glowing eloquence. For our own part, pondering such utterances as these, we can put away all doubt regarding Burns's thorough deep-rooted loyalty, and anew learn to admire and venerate his native nobility of mind and spirit.

Very soon after coming to Dumfries, the Poet made the acquaintance of Mr. and Mrs. Walter Riddel, of Woodley Park. Walter Riddel, younger brother of the laird of Friar's Carse, was a genial, sociable man; and his wife, Maria Woodley,[1] then under twenty years of age, was a person of bright, glowing temperament, and already an authoress of no mean note. Having a marked poetic turn of mind, she warmly cultivated the friendship of the Exciseman Bard, who in turn greatly esteemed her company, and often enjoyed the hospitalities of Woodley Park; but to this acquaintanceship we shall again refer. Another of Burns's heroines of this first year in Dumfries was Miss Lesley Baillie, the theme of his lays in "Saw ye Bonnie Lesley" and "Blithe hae I been on yon hill," which latter song he describes as "one of the finest songs ever I made in my life."

> Blithe hae I been on yon hill,
>   As the lambs before me;
> Careless ilka thought and free,
>   As the breeze flew o'er me:
> Now nae longer sport and play,
>   Mirth or sang can please me;
> Lesley is sae fair and coy,
>   Care and anguish seize me.
>
> Heavy, heavy is the task,
>   Hopeless love declaring;
> Trembling, I dow nocht but glower,
>   Sighing, dumb, despairing!
> If she winna ease the thraws
>   In my bosom swelling,
> Underneath the grass-green sod,
>   Soon maun be my dwelling.

Of this new "vision of beauty" he also wrote (rapturously as was his wont on such a theme) to Mrs. Dunlop:—

> Do you know that I am almost in love with an acquaintance of yours? Almost! said I—I am in love, souse over head and ears, deep as the most

---

[1] See vol. ii. p. 175.

unfathomable abyss of the boundless ocean!—but the word love, owing to the *intermingledoms* of the good and the bad, the pure and the impure, in this world, being rather an equivocal term for expressing one's sentiments and sensations, I must do justice to the sacred purity of my attachment. Know then, that the heart-struck awe; the distant, humble approach; the delight we should have in gazing upon and listening to a messenger of heaven, appearing in all the unspotted purity of his celestial home, among the coarse, polluted, far inferior sons of men, to deliver to them tidings that make their hearts swim in joy, and their imaginations soar in transport—such, so delighting and so pure, were the emotions of my soul on meeting the other day with Miss Lesley Baillie, your neighbour at M. Mr. B., with his two daughters, accompanied by Mr. H. of G., passing through Dumfries a few days ago, on their way to England, did me the honour of calling on me; on which I took my horse—though, God knows, I could ill spare the time—and accompanied them fourteen or fifteen miles, and dined and spent the day with them. 'Twas about nine, I think, when I left them, and riding home, I composed the following ballad, of which you will probably think you have a dear bargain, as it will cost you another groat of postage. You must know that there is an old ballad beginning with—

"My bonnie Lizzie Baillie,
I'll rowe thee in my plaidie," etc.

So I parodied it as follows, which is literally the first copy, "unanointed, unannealed," as Hamlet says:—

BONNIE LESLEY.

O saw ye bonnie Lesley,
   As she gaed ower the Border?
She's gane, like Alexander,
   To spread her conquests farther.

To see her is to love her,
   And love but her for ever;
For nature made her what she is,
   And never made anither!

Thou art a queen, fair Lesley,
   Thy subjects we, before thee;
Thou art divine, fair Lesley,
   The hearts o' men adore thee.

> The deil he couldna scaith thee,
>   Or aught that wad belang thee;
> He'd look into thy bonnie face,
>   And say, "I canna wrang thee!"
>
> The powers aboon will tent thee;
>   Misfortune sha' na steer thee;
> Thou'rt like themselves sae lovely,
>   That ill they'll ne'er let near thee.
>
> Return again, fair Lesley,
>   Return to Caledonie!
> That we may brag, we hae a lass
>   There's nane again sae bonnie.

In August 1792, the fourth volume of Johnson's *Musical Museum* was issued, containing some fifty songs by Burns; and in the following month the Bard began his correspondence with Mr. George Thomson,[1] the gifted and enthusiastic editor of a select collection of Scottish songs and melodies, issued with accompaniments by many of the first musicians of the day. We here give the letters with which this extensive and delightful correspondence opened:—

THOMSON TO BURNS.

EDINBURGH, *September* 1792.

SIR,—For some years past I have, with a friend or two, employed many leisure hours in selecting and collating the most favourite of our national melodies for publication. We have engaged Pleyel, the most agreeable composer living, to put accompaniments to these, and also to compose an instrumental prelude and conclusion to each air, the better to fit them for concerts, both public and private. To render this work perfect, we are desirous to have the poetry improved wherever it seems unworthy of the music; and that it is so in many instances is allowed by every one conversant with our musical collections. The editors of these seem in general to have depended on

---

[1] See vol. ii. p. 275.

the music proving an excuse for the verses; and hence some charming melodies are united to mere nonsense and doggerel, while others are accommodated with rhymes so loose and indelicate as cannot be sung in decent company. To remove this reproach would be an easy task to the author of the "Cotter's Saturday Night;" and, for the honour of Caledonia, I would fain hope he may be induced to take up the pen. If so, we shall be enabled to present the public with a collection infinitely more interesting than any that has yet appeared, and acceptable to all persons of taste, whether they wish for correct melodies, delicate accompaniments, or characteristic verses. We will esteem your poetical assistance a particular favour, besides paying any reasonable price you shall please to demand for it. Profit is quite a secondary consideration with us, and we are resolved to spare neither pains nor expense on the publication. Tell me frankly, then, whether you will devote your leisure to writing twenty or twenty-five songs suited to the particular melodies which I am prepared to send you. A few songs, exceptionable only in some of their verses, I will likewise submit to your consideration, leaving it to you either to mend these or make new songs in their stead. It is superfluous to assure you that I have no intention to displace any of the sterling old songs; those only will be removed which appear quite silly or absolutely indecent. Even these shall be all examined by Mr. Burns, and if he is of opinion that any of them are deserving of the music, in such cases no divorce shall take place.

G. Thomson.

BURNS TO THOMSON.

Dumfries, 16th Sept. 1792.

Sir,—I have just this moment got your letter. As the request you make to me will positively add to my enjoyments in complying with it, I shall enter into your undertaking with all the small portion of abilities I have, strained to their utmost exertion by the impulse of enthusiasm. Only, don't hurry me— "Deil tak' the hindmost" is by no means the *cri de guerre* of my muse. Will you, as I am inferior to none of you in enthusiastic attachment to the poetry and music of old Caledonia, and, since you request it, have cheerfully promised my mite of assistance—will you let me have a list of your airs, with the first line of the printed verses you intend for them, that I may have an opportunity of suggesting any alteration that may occur to me? You know 'tis in the way of my trade; still leaving you, gentlemen, the undoubted right of publishers to approve or reject, at your pleasure, for your own publication. Apropos, if you are for English verses, there is, on my part, an end of the matter. Whether in the simplicity of the ballad, or the pathos of the song, I can only hope to please myself in being allowed at least a sprinkling of our native tongue. English verses, particularly the works of Scotsmen that have merit, are certainly very eligible. "Tweedside;" "Ah! the poor shepherd's mournful fate!" "Ah! Chloris, could I now but sit," etc., you cannot mend; but such insipid stuff as "To Fanny fair could I impart," etc., usually set to "The Mill, Mill, O!" is a disgrace to the collections in which it has already appeared, and would doubly disgrace a collection that will have the very superior merit of yours. But more of this in the further prosecution of the business, if I am called on for my strictures and amendments—I say amendments, for I will not alter except where I myself, at least, think that I amend.

As to any remuneration, you may think my songs either above or below price; for they shall absolutely be the one or the other. In the honest enthusiasm with which I embark in your undertaking, to talk of money, wages, fee, hire, etc. would be downright prostitution of soul! A proof of each of the songs that I compose or amend I shall receive as a favour. In the rustic phrase of the season, "Gude speed the wark!" I am, sir, your very humble servant,

R. BURNS.

Into this new scheme the Poet entered with loving and unselfish enthusiasm; and, till very near the close of his life, he continued to pen to Thomson letter after letter, pregnant with his own matchless songs, accompanied by scarcely less delightsome notes and criticisms ranging over the entire field of national song, ballad, and tradition.[1]

---

[1] Of the Poet's unwearying critical and pioneer labours in this field, part of one of a multitude of such letters to Mr. Thomson may here suffice as an example:—

I have yours, my dear sir, this moment. I shall answer it and your former letter, in my desultory way of saying whatever comes uppermost.

The business of many of our tunes, wanting at the beginning what fiddlers call a starting-note, is often a rub to us poor rhymers.

"There's braw, braw lads on Yarrow braes,
That wander through the blooming heather,"

you may alter to

"Braw, braw lads on Yarrow braes,
Ye wander," etc.

My song, "Here awa', there awa'," as amended

In November 1792, Mrs. Burns brought forth a daughter, who was named Elizabeth Riddel, out of respect to Mrs. Riddel of Friar's Carse. Of this infant daughter Burns is said to have been very fond, not scorning to be seen nursing her at his own door in the Wee Vennel, or carrying her about on the green by the riverside. The protracted illness and early death of this child proved a painful wrench to his great kind heart. About this same time we find him patronizing the little theatre in Dumfries, and writing an "Address on the Rights of Woman," to be recited by a Miss Fontenelle on her benefit-night, November 26th. Of other forms of enjoyment, too,—social entertainments whereof boon-companionship and free use of stimulating liquors were the leading features,— he had enough, nay, more than enough, it is painful to relate. The winter seemed to be passing, though laboriously, yet withal pleasantly and contentedly ; but anon, we meet with startling

by Mr. Erskine, I entirely approve of, and return you.

Give me leave to criticise your taste in the only thing in which it is, in my opinion, reprehensible. You know I ought to know something of my own trade. Of pathos, sentiment, and point you are a complete judge ; but there is a quality more necessary than either in a song, and which is the very essence of a ballad —I mean simplicity ; now, if I mistake not, this last feature you are a little apt to sacrifice to the foregoing.

Ramsay, as every other poet, has not been always equally happy in his pieces ; still, I cannot approve of taking such liberties with an author as Mr. W. proposes doing with " The last time I came o'er the moor." Let a poet, if he chooses, take up the idea of another, and work it into a piece of his own ; but to mangle the works of the poor bard whose tuneful tongue is now mute for ever in the dark and narrow house—by Heaven, 'twould be sacrilege ! I grant that Mr. W.'s version is an improvement ; but I know Mr. W. well, and esteem him much ; let him mend the song, as the Highlander mended his gun—he gave it a new stock, a new lock, and a new barrel.

I do not by this object to leaving out improper stanzas, where that can be done without spoiling the whole. One stanza in " The Lass o' Patie's Mill " must be left out : the song will be nothing worse for it. I am not sure if we can take the same liberty with "Corn-rigs are Bonnie." Perhaps it might waut the last stanza, and be the better for it. "Cauld Kail in Aberdeen" you must leave with me yet awhile. I have vowed to have a song to that air on the lady whom I attempted to celebrate in the verses, "Puirtith cauld and restless love." At any rate, my other song, "Green grow the Rashes," will never suit. That song is current in Scotland under the old title, and to the merry old tune of that name, which of course would mar the progress of your song to celebrity. Your book will be the standard of Scots songs for the future ; let this idea *ever keep your judgment on the alarm.*

expressions of the now seldom-absent feverish unrest and bitter self-upbraiding. One great cause of this renewed outburst of gloomy repining was the blighting of his prospect of advancement in the Excise; in fact, at the time of which we speak, his trouble in that connexion was at its worst. But another obvious cause was his increasing indulgence in the dissipations of Dumfries social and tavern life. What these dissipations were, and with what terrible temptations they assailed the ever social Bard, may be best gathered from a notable passage by Chambers, from which we venture to give a somewhat lengthy but most appropriate quotation.

> Dumfries was then a great stage on the road from England to the north of Ireland; the Caledonian Hunt occasionally honoured it with their meetings; and the county gentlemen were necessarily often within its walls. Its hotels were consequently well frequented; and when a party of strangers found themselves assembled there, with no other means of passing an evening, they were very apt to make an effort to obtain the company of Burns, the brilliant intellectual prodigy of whom fame spoke so loudly. Now it certainly was a most unreasonable thing for such persons to expect that they were to draw Burns away from his humble home, and his wife and little ones, to bestow his time, strength, and spirits, merely for the amusement of a set of people whom he probably never saw before and was never to see again. Equally absurd was it for Burns to yield to such invitations, and render himself up a voluntarily-enslaved Samson to make sport for such a set of Philistines. Yet so it is, that gentlemen, or what were called such in those days, would send messages for Burns, bidding him come to the "King's Arms," the "George," or the "Globe," as it might be, and there drink with them. And equally true it is, though most lamentable, that Burns did not feel called upon by any principle, either of respect to himself or regard for his gentle wife and innocent children, to reject these unworthy invitations. Sure was he to answer on the spur of the moment in some such good-humoured terms as these—
>
>> The king's most humble servant, I
>> Can scarcely spare a minute;
>> But I'll be with you by and by,
>> Or else the devil's in it.

And sure was he in time to make his appearance before the strangers, meditating at first, of course, only a social hour, but certain to be detained for hour after hour, till perhaps the cock had given his first, if not his second accusing crow.

According to all accounts, it was not a love of debauchery for its own sake that rendered Burns the victim of this system. Nor can we doubt that he felt himself in error in giving way to such temptations. Why, then, could he not resist them? Need we answer that the first grand cause was his social, fervent temperament, his delight in that ideal abnegation of the common selfish policy of the world which arises amongst boon-companions over the bowl? He could not but know the hollowness of convivial friendship; yet he could not resist the pleasing deceit. Burns, moreover, though a pattern of modesty amongst poets, was not by any means so insensible to flattery as his more ardent admirers would in general represent him. He would have been more than mortal if he had been beyond all sensibility to distinction on account of his extraordinary intellect. Notwithstanding, then, his great pride, and the powerful self-assertion which he had sometimes shown, he certainly felt no small pleasure in being so signalised by these gentlemen strangers, and in seeing himself set up amongst them as a luminary. It was the ready compensation for that equality with common functionaries, and that condemnation to a constant contact with the vulgar, in which his professional fate condemned him to spend the most of his time. A vigorous will might have saved him from falling under this influence; but here again our Poet was sadly deficient. And yet he was occasionally sensible that his course was a wrong one. Of this there is proof in a very interesting anecdote preserved by the family of his neighbour, George Haugh. One summer morning, this worthy citizen had risen somewhat earlier than usual to work: Burns soon after came up to his shop-door, on his way home from a debauch in the "King's Arms." The Poet, though excited by the liquor he had drunk, addressed his neighbour in a sufficiently collected manner. "Oh, George," said he, "you are a happy man; you have risen from a refreshing sleep, and left a kind wife and children, while I am returning a self-condemned wretch to mine."

On 2nd January 1793, he had written to Mrs. Dunlop: "Occasional hard drinking is the devil to me; against this I have again and again set my resolution, and have greatly succeeded." Yet only three days after this—so greatly a prey to passionate impulse was Burns—we find him addressing the same lady in the entirely opposite vein of bacchanalian bravado :—

> Your cup,[1] my dear madam, arrived safe. I had two worthy fellows dining with me the other day, when I with great formality produced my whigmaleerie cup, and told them that it had been a family-piece among the descendants of William Wallace. This roused such an enthusiasm that they insisted on bumpering the punch round in it; and by and by never did your great ancestor lay a *suthron* more completely to rest than for a time did your cup.

Regarding this drinking scene, further information was forthcoming from the Rev. Mr. M'Morine, minister of Caerlaverock. The Poet, being then *out of touch* with ecclesiastical authority in Dumfries, had secured the services of the friendly Mr. M'Morine for the baptism of the infant Elizabeth Riddel. Proceeding to Burns's abode early in the forenoon, the minister discovered the aforementioned *bout* still in progress, the party having to all appearance been at it all night. Doubtless this debauch took place a day or two after the new year had come, and there is some extenuation for the Poet on the ground of the custom of excessive drinking at this season—a custom which has long been a curse and shame to Scotland, but which is now being rapidly superseded by more rational and innocent forms of social enjoyment. It is, nevertheless, most sad to think of Burns as at this time giving way more and more to the allurements of hard-drinking company and its attendant debasements. The marvel is how he managed to attend so efficiently as he did to his duties as exciseman, and to proceed so enthusiastically and effectively with his song-making task. As for the latter, it would seem that he lost no opportunity of official leisure, or of freedom from social duties and dissipations,

---

[1] A family heirloom gifted by Mrs. Dunlop to Burns.

but, taking his matchless lyre in hand, he would bring forth an immortal lay; or, finding some fragment of an old song, he would expand and round it off in his own great way. It was then and thus he contrived to bestow to his country and the world such fruits of his wondrous genius as "Duncan Gray," "The Lea Rig," "Ye banks and braes and streams around," "O Puirtith Cauld," "The Soldier's Return," and so on.

He had also been attending to the preparation of the new edition of his poems which was issued in April 1793. From this edition, which was in two volumes, the Bard reaped little, if any, pecuniary advantage. In presenting copies to various friends, he made some characteristic remarks. To the youthful Lord Glencairn he says :—

> I know, my lord, such is the vile, venal contagion which pervades the world of letters, that professions of respect from an author, particularly from a poet to a lord, are more than suspicious. I claim my by-past conduct, and my feelings at this moment, as exceptions to the too just conclusion. Exalted as are the honours of your lordship's name, and unnoted as is the obscurity of mine, with the uprightness of an honest man, I come before your lordship, with an offering, however humble, 'tis all I have to give, of my grateful respect; and to beg of you, my lord, 'tis all I have to ask of you, that you will do me the honour to accept of it.

And to Mr. M'Murdo, of Drumlanrig House :—

> Will Mr. M'Murdo do me the favour to accept of these volumes? a trifling but sincere mark of the very high respect I bear for his worth as a man, his manners as a gentleman, and his kindness as a friend. However inferior now, or afterwards, I may rank as a poet, one honest virtue to which few poets can pretend, I trust I shall ever claim as mine—to no man, whatever his station in life, or his power to serve me, have I ever paid a compliment at the expense of TRUTH.
>
> THE AUTHOR.

Very characteristic, too, is the letter he at this time penned to Clarinda on hearing of her return from Jamaica :—

> I suppose, my dear madam, that by your neglecting to inform me of your arrival in Europe—a circumstance that could not be indifferent to me, as indeed no occurrence relating to you can—you meant to leave me to guess and gather that a correspondence I once had the honour and felicity to enjoy is to be no more. Alas! what heavy-laden sounds are these—"No more!" The wretch who has never tasted pleasure has never known woe; what drives the soul to madness is the recollection of joys that are "no more!" But this is not language to the world: they do not understand it. But come, ye few—the children of Feeling and Sentiment!—ye whose trembling bosom-chords ache to unutterable anguish as recollection gushes on the heart!—ye who are capable of an attachment keen as the arrow of Death, and strong as the vigour of immortal being—come! and your ears shall drink a tale——But, hush! I must not, cannot tell it; agony is in the recollection, and frenzy in the recital!
>
> But, madam, to leave the paths that leads to madness, I congratulate your friends on your return; and I hope that the precious health, which Miss P. tells me is so much injured, is restored or restoring. There is a fatality attends Miss Peacock's correspondence and mine. Two of my letters, it seems, she never received; and her last came while I was in Ayrshire, was unfortunately mislaid, and only found about ten days or a fortnight ago, on removing a desk of drawers.
>
> I present you a book: may I hope you will accept of it. I daresay you will have brought your books with you. The fourth volume of the *Scots Songs* is published; I will presume to send it you. Shall I hear from you? But first hear me. No cold language—no prudential documents. I despise advice and scorn control. If you are not to write such language, such sentiments as you know I shall wish, shall delight to receive, I conjure you, by wounded pride, by ruined peace, by frantic, disappointed passion, by all the many ills that constitute that sum of human woes, a broken heart!!!—to me be silent for ever.

At Whitsunday of 1793 the Poet removed from the Wee Vennel to a more commodious dwelling in Mill Vennel, now known as Burns Street. This new house is of two storeys, containing kitchen, parlour, and several bedrooms. On the front of the adjoining house, which is now used as a ragged school, a small bust of Burns was placed by the late Mr. Ewart, Member for the Dumfries district of Burghs; also a tablet bearing this inscription :—

IN THE ADJOINING HOUSE,
TO THE NORTH,
LIVED AND DIED THE POET OF HIS COUNTRY AND OF MANKIND,
ROBERT BURNS.

The occupation of a larger, higher-rented house meant increased expense; and, without exaggerating our idea of the Bard's poverty, we may justly infer that at this juncture money was not plentiful with him. It is indeed probable that, during these war times, his income was greatly curtailed by a decrease of chance fees and perquisites owing to the prevailing stagnation of trade. Be this as it may, however, we now meet with one of the most striking of all the many manifestations of his sturdy, almost stubborn, independence and unselfishness of spirit.

On July 1st 1793, Mr. Thomson wrote the Poet as follows :—

> I cannot express how much I am obliged to you for the exquisite new songs you are sending me; but thanks, my friend, are a poor return for what you have done—as I shall be benefited by the publication, you must suffer me to enclose a small mark of my gratitude, and to repeat it afterwards when I find it convenient. Do not return it, for, by Heaven! if you do, our correspondence is at an end; and though this would be no loss to you, it would mar the publication, which, under your auspices, cannot fail to be respectable and interesting.[1]

To which Burns sent this reply, truly great and prophetic :—

> I assure you, my dear sir, that you truly hurt me with your pecuniary parcel. It degrades me in my own eyes. However, to return it would savour

---

[1] Five pounds was the sum enclosed.

of affectation; but, as to any more traffic of that debtor and creditor kind, I swear, by that Honour which crowns the upright statue of Robert Burns's Integrity — on the least motion of it, I will indignantly spurn the bypast transaction, and from that moment commence entire stranger to you! Burns's character for generosity of sentiment and independence of mind will, I trust, long outlive any of his wants which the cold, unfeeling ore can supply; at least I will take care that such a character he shall deserve.

In the usual way of publishing his poems, the Bard was willing, though never in a narrow, *screwing* way, to reap some much-needed pecuniary reward for his poetic labours. But he could not brook the idea of being an *hireling*, writing with a direct view to making money thereby. In fact, we have here only one of many evidences [1] that he nobly counted his genius as, first of all, a gift to be employed in singing the loves and joys and sorrows of humanity— that he felt it in his spirit to do what in him lay towards bringing gladness and courage and harmony into the hearts and homes of his countrymen and his kind. And thus it is that, spite of all his grievous faults and follies, "Burns's character for generosity of sentiment and independence of mind" still essentially stands and brightens as generations come and pass away.

Having now reached a middle point of time in Burns's four and a half years in Dumfries, we again pause to view him in his solitary musings, and in his daily routine of Excise duty and social

---

[1] On this point the following note is given by Chambers:—

In a brief anonymous memoir of Burns, published in the *Scots Magazine* for January 1797, and which appears to have been the composition of one who knew him and had visited him at Ellisland, it is stated that he considered it below him to be an author by profession. 'A friend,' adds the writer, 'knowing his family to be in great want [an exaggeration, certainly], urged the propriety, and even necessity, of publishing a few poems, assuring him of their success, and showing the advantage that would accrue to his family from it. His answer was: "No; if a friend desires me, and if I'm in the mood for it, I'll write a poem, but I'll be d—— if ever I write for money."'

Here, too, it will be remembered how, with the utmost self-disinterestedness, the Poet, though not seldom remonstrated with for doing so, continued to *give away*, right and left, his most valued compositions to those whom in the warmth of his generous nature he sacrificed to as his FRIENDS.

engagements. Allan Cunningham says that during the Dumfries period—

> Burns had three favourite walks: on the Dock Green by the river-side, among the ruins of Lincluden College, and towards the Martingdon Ford, on the north side of the Nith. This latter place was secluded, commanded a view of the distant hills, and the romantic towers of Lincluden, and afforded soft greensward banks to rest upon, and the sight and sound of the stream. Here he composed many of his finest songs. As soon as he was heard to hum to himself, his wife saw that he had something in his mind, and was prepared to see him snatch up his hat, and set silently off for his musing-ground. When by himself, and in the open air, his ideas arranged themselves in their natural order—words came at will, and he seldom returned without having finished a song. In case of interruption, he set about completing it at the fireside; he balanced himself on the hind-legs of his arm-chair, and, rocking to and fro, continued to hum the tune, and seldom failed of success. When the verses were finished, he passed them through the ordeal of Mrs. Burns's voice; listened attentively when she sang; asked her if any of the words were difficult; and when one happened to be too rough, he readily found a smoother—but he never, save at the resolute entreaty of a scientific musician, sacrificed sense to sound. The autumn was his favourite season, and the twilight his favourite hour of study.

While the foregoing statement regarding the Poet's musing-haunts and manner of composition commends itself by its distinct air of probability, it further closely agrees with Burns's own account in one of his letters to Thomson:—

> Until I am complete master of a tune, in my own singing (such as it is), I can never compose for it. My way is: I consider the poetic sentiment correspondent to my idea of the musical expression; then choose my theme; begin one stanza. When that is composed, which is generally the most difficult part of the business, I walk out, sit down now and then, look out for objects in nature around me that are in unison and harmony with the cogitations of my fancy, and workings of my bosom, humming every now and then the air with the verses I have framed. When I feel my muse beginning to jade, I retire to the solitary fireside of my study, and there commit my effusions to paper,

swinging at intervals on the hind-legs of my elbow-chair, by way of calling forth my own critical strictures as my pen goes on. Seriously, this, at home, is almost invariably my way.

It is easy to conjecture, apart from any definite information on the point, that the fine old ruins of Lincluden Abbey, set on a knoll at the junction of the Cluden with the Nith,—a lovely, romantic spot,—would often attract the Poet, and inspire his musings. One grand ballad, at least, clearly fixes this as the scene of its conception. We give the opening lines :—

> As I stood by yon roofless tower,
>   Where the wa'-flower scents the dewy air,
> Where th' howlet mourns in her ivy bower,
>   And tells the midnight moon her care.
>
> The winds were laid, the air was still,
>   The stars they shot alang the sky;
> The fox was howling on the hill,
>   And the distant echoing glens reply.
>
> The stream, adown its hazelly path,
>   Was rushing by the ruined wa's,
> Hasting to join the sweeping Nith,
>   Whose distant roaring swells and fa's.

And so on, in the glowing stanzas of his piece, entitled "A Vision."

But of the Exciseman Bard, in his home-circle, on his business rounds, and in his social hours, Chambers has drawn a sketch so graphically interesting and life-like as to call for its almost full insertion here :—

> So existence flows on with Burns in this pleasant southern town. He has daily duties in stamping leather, gauging malt-vats, noting the manufacture of candles, and granting licences for the transport of spirits. These duties he performs with fidelity to the king, and not too much rigour to the subject. As he goes about them in the forenoon, in his respectable suit of dark clothes, and

with his little boy Robert perhaps holding by his hand and conversing with him on his school exercises, he is beheld by the general public with respect, as a person in some authority, the head of a family, and also as a man of literary note; and people are heard addressing him deferentially as *Mr*. Burns—a form of his name which is still prevalent in Dumfries. At a leisure hour before dinner, he will call at some house where there is a piano,—such as Mr. Newall, the writer's,—and there have some young miss to touch over for him one or two of his favourite Scotch airs, such as the "Sutor's Daughter," in order that he may accommodate to it some stanzas that have been humming through his brain for the last few days. For another half hour, he will be seen standing at the head of some cross street with two or three young fellows, bankers' clerks, or "writer chiels" commencing business, whom he is regaling with sallies of his bright but not always innocent wit—indulging there, indeed, in a strain of conversation so different from what had passed in the respectable elderly writer's mansion, that, though he were not the same man, it could not have been more different. Later in the day, he takes a solitary walk along the Dock Green by the riverside, or to Lincluden, and composes the most part of a new song; or he spends a couple of hours at his folding-down desk, between the fire and window in his parlour, transcribing in his bold round hand the remarks which occur to him on Mr. Thomson's last letter, together with some of his own recently composed songs. As a possible variation upon this routine, he has been seen passing along the old bridge of Devorgilla Balliol, about three o'clock, with his sword-cane in his hand, and his black beard unusually well shaven, being on his way to dine with John Syme at Ryedale, where young Mr. Oswald of Auchincruive is to be of the party—or maybe in the opposite direction, to partake of the luxuries of John Bushby, at Tinwald Downs. But we presume a day when no such attraction invades. The evening is passing quietly at home, and pleasant-natured Jean has made herself neat, and come in at six o'clock to give him his tea—a meal he always takes. At this period, however, there is something remarkably exciting in the proceedings of the French army under Pichegru; or Fox, Adam, or Sheridan is expected to make an onslaught upon the ministry in the House of Commons. The post comes into Dumfries at eight o'clock at night. There is always a group of gentlemen on the street, eager to hear the news. Burns saunters out to the High Street, and waits among the rest. The intelligence of the evening is very interesting. The Convention has decreed the annexation of the Netherlands—or the new treason bill has passed the House of Lords, with only the feeble protest of Bedford, Derby, and Lauderdale. These things merit some discussion. The trades-lads go off to strong ale in the closes; the gentlemen slide in little groups into the King's Arms Hotel or the George. As for Burns, he will just have a single glass and a half-hour's chat beside John Hyslop's fire, and then go quietly home. So he is quickly absorbed in the little narrow close where that vintner maintains his state. There, however, one or two friends have already established themselves, all with precisely the same virtuous intent. They heartily greet the Bard. Meg or John bustles about to give him his accustomed place, which no one ever disputes. And, somehow, the debate on the news of the evening leads on to other chat of an interesting kind. Then Burns becomes brilliant, and his friends give him the applause of their laughter. One jug succeeds another, mirth abounds, and it is not till Mrs. Hyslop has declared that they are going beyond all bounds, and she positively will not give them another drop of hot water, that our bard at length bethinks him of returning home, where Bonnie Jean has been lost in peaceful slumber for three hours, after vainly wondering "what can be keeping Robert out so late the nicht." Burns gets to bed a little excited and worn out, but not in a state to provoke much remark from his amiable partner, in whom nothing can abate the veneration with which she has all along regarded him. And though he beds at a latish hour, most likely he is up next morning between seven and eight, to hear little Robert his day's lesson in *Cæsar*, or, if the season invites, to take a half-hour's stroll before breakfast along the favourite Dock Green.

Thus existence moves on, not unenjoyed, and not without its labours both for the present and future; and yet it is an unsatisfactory life, as compared with what might have been expected by those who saw Burns in his first flush of fame at Monboddo's suppers or the reunions of Dr. Ferguson.

During the closing days of July, the Poet enjoyed an excursion through part of Galloway and Wigton, his travelling companion being Mr. John Syme[1] of Ryedale, one of his most intimate associates in Dumfries. Mr. Syme afterwards communicated to Dr. Currie the following account of this brief but lively tour:—

> I got Burns a grey Highland shelty to ride on. We dined the first day, 27th July 1793, at Glendonwyne's of Parton—a beautiful situation on the

---

[1] See vol. ii. p. 257.

banks of the Dee. In the evening, we walked out, and ascended a gentle eminence, from which we had as fine a view of Alpine scenery as can well be imagined. A delightful soft evening showed all its wilder as well as its grander graces. Immediately opposite, and within a mile of us, we saw Airds, a charming, romantic place, where dwelt Lowe, the author of "Mary, weep no more for me." This was classical ground for Burns. He viewed "the highest hill which rises o'er the source of Dee;" and would have stayed till "the passing spirit" had appeared, had we not resolved to reach Kenmure that night. We arrived as Mr. and Mrs. Gordon were sitting down to supper.

Here is a genuine baron's seat. The castle, an old building, stands on a large natural moat. In front the river Ken winds for several miles through the most fertile and beautiful *holm*, till it expands into a lake twelve miles long, the banks of which, on the south, present a fine and soft landscape of green knolls, natural wood, and here and there a grey rock. On the north, the aspect is great, wild, and, I may say, tremendous. In short, I can scarcely conceive a scene more terribly romantic than the Castle of Kenmure. Burns thinks so highly of it, that he meditates a description of it in poetry. Indeed, I believe he has begun the work. We spent three days with Mr. Gordon, whose polished hospitality is of an original and endearing kind. Mrs. Gordon's lap-dog, Echo, was dead. She would have an epitaph for him. Several had been made. Burns was asked for one. This was setting Hercules to his distaff. He disliked the subject, but, to please the lady, he would try. Here is what he produced—

> In wood and wild, ye warbling throng,
>   Your heavy loss deplore!
> Now half extinct your powers of song,
>   Sweet Echo is no more.
>
> Ye jarring, screeching things around,
>   Scream your discordant joys!
> Now half your din of tuneless song
>   With Echo silent lies.

We left Kenmure and went to Gatehouse. I took him the moor road, where savage and desolate regions extended wide around. The sky was sympathetic with the wretchedness of the soil; it became lowering and dark. The hollow winds sighed, the lightnings gleamed, the thunder rolled. The Poet enjoyed the awful scene. He spoke not a word, but seemed rapt in meditation. In a little while rain began to fall; it poured in floods upon us. For three hours did the wild elements "rumble their belly full" upon our defenceless heads. "Oh! oh! 'twas foul." We got utterly wet; and, to revenge ourselves, Burns insisted at Gatehouse on our getting utterly drunk.

From Gatehouse, we went next day to Kirkcudbright, through a fine country. But here I must tell you that Burns had got a pair of *jemmy* boots for the journey, which had been thoroughly wet, and which had been dried in such manner that it was not possible to get them on again. The brawny Poet tried force, and tore them to shreds. A whiffling vexation of this sort is more trying to the temper than a serious calamity. We were going to St. Mary's Isle, the seat of the Earl of Selkirk, and the forlorn Burns was discomfited at the thought of his ruined boots. A sick stomach and a headache lent their aid, and the man of verse was quite *accablé*. I attempted to reason with him. Mercy on us, how he did fume and rage! Nothing could reinstate him in temper. I tried various expedients, and at last hit on one that succeeded. I showed him the house of Garlieston, across the bay of Wigton. Against the Earl of Galloway, with whom he was offended, he expectorated his spleen, and regained a most agreeable temper. He was in a most epigrammatic humour indeed! He afterwards fell on humbler game. There is one whom he does not love. He had a passing blow at him—

> When ———, deceased, to the devil went down,
> 'Twas nothing would serve him but Satan's own crown;
> Thy fool's head, quoth Satan, that crown shall wear never,
> I grant thou'rt as wicked, but not quite so clever.

Well, I am to bring you to Kirkcudbright along with our Poet without boots. I carried the torn ruins across my saddle in spite of his fulminations, and in contempt of appearances; and, what is more, Lord Selkirk carried them in his coach to Dumfries. He insisted they were worth mending.

We reached Kirkcudbright about one o'clock. I had promised that we should dine with one of the first men in our country, J. Dalzell. But Burns was in a wild and obstreperous humour, and swore he would not dine where he should be under the smallest restraint. We prevailed, therefore, on Mr. Dalzell to dine with us in the inn, and had a very agreeable party. In the evening we set out for St. Mary's Isle. Robert had not absolutely regained the milkiness of good temper, and it occurred once or twice to him, as he rode along, that

St. Mary's Isle was the seat of a lord; yet that lord was not an aristocrat, at least in his sense of the word. We arrived about eight o'clock, as the family were at tea and coffee. St. Mary's Isle is one of the most delightful places that can, in my opinion, be formed by the assemblage of every soft but not tame object which constitutes natural and cultivated beauty. But not to dwell on its external graces, let me tell you that we found all the ladies of the family (all beautiful) at home, and some strangers; and, among others, who but Urbani. The Italian sang us many Scottish songs, accompanied with instrumental music. The two young ladies of Selkirk sang also. We had the song of "Lord Gregory," which I asked for, to have an opportunity of calling on Burns to recite *his* ballad to that tune. He did recite it; and such was the effect, that a dead silence ensued. It was such a silence as a mind of feeling naturally preserves when it is touched with that enthusiasm which banishes every other thought but the contemplation and indulgence of the sympathy produced. Burns's "Lord Gregory" is, in my opinion, a most beautiful and affecting ballad. The fastidious critic may perhaps say some of the sentiments and imagery are of too elevated a kind for such a style of composition; for instance, "Thou bolt of heaven that passest by," and " Ye mustering thunders," etc.; but this is a cold-blooded objection, which will be *said* rather than *felt*.

We enjoyed a most happy evening at Lord Selkirk's. We had, in every sense of the word, a feast, in which our minds and our senses were equally gratified. The Poet was delighted with his company, and acquitted himself to admiration. The lion that had raged so violently in the morning was now as mild and gentle as a lamb. Next day we returned to Dumfries; and so ends our peregrination. I told you that, in the midst of the storm, on the wilds of Kenmure, Burns was rapt in meditation. What do you think he was about? He was charging the English army, along with Bruce, at Bannockburn. He was engaged in the same manner on our ride home from St. Mary's Isle, and I did not disturb him. Next day, he produced me the following address of Bruce to his troops:—

  Scots wha hae wi' Wallace bled, etc.

The reader will here observe with regret the Poet's growing bitterness of spirit and arrogant irritability of temper, as also the ominous statement, "Burns insisted at Gatehouse on our getting utterly drunk." It is, however, in connexion with the conception of "Scots wha hae" that this excursion is most memorable. In September the Poet wrote to Thomson :—

> You know that my pretensions to musical taste are merely a few of nature's instincts, untaught and untutored by art. For this reason many musical compositions, particularly where much of the merit lies in counterpoint, however they may transport and ravish the ears of your connoisseurs, affect my simple lug no otherwise than merely as melodious din. On the other hand, by way of amends, I am delighted with many little melodies, which the learned musician despises as silly and insipid. I do not know whether the old air, "Hey, tuttie tattie," may rank among this number; but well I know that it has often filled my eyes with tears. There is a tradition, which I have met with in many places in Scotland, that it was Robert Bruce's march at the battle of Bannockburn. This thought, in my yesternight's evening walk, warmed me to a pitch of enthusiasm on the theme of liberty and independence, which I threw into a kind of Scottish ode, fitted to the air, that one might suppose to be the gallant royal Scot's address to his heroic followers on that eventful morning.

Then follows the song in its finished and well-known form, to which the author appended the prayer, "So may God ever defend the cause of truth and liberty as He did that day! Amen."

The divergence between this and Mr. Syme's account may be reasonably enough got over by believing, as is most probable, that, in midst of the storm on the wilds of Kenmure, the first idea or outline of this sublimest lay of Scottish patriotism and prowess shaped itself in the Poet's glowing imagination, responsive to the raging tempest, the gleaming lightning, and rattling thunder. But whatever the exact circumstances, we shall remember with grateful pride that it was BURNS who wrote "Scots wha hae," than which the world possesses no grander, more inspiring war-song.

When the threatening cloud of his trouble with the Excise authorities had passed away, Burns expressed his resolution to put "a seal upon his lips" so far as political questions were concerned. As time went by, however, he again began to involve himself by the daring and stinging utterance of democratic sentiments which, in that suspicion-laden, unsettled war-time, could not be lightly passed over. A single instance must here suffice. One evening, in a company which had been drinking freely, Burns proposed as a toast, "May our success in the present war be equal to the justice of our cause." A military officer present angrily resented this as a quibble veiling a sentiment of marked disloyalty, and a quarrel ensued, the nature of which can be gathered from the humiliating letter which the Poet, reflecting on his conduct of the previous evening, and on his humble, dependent position under the Government, next morning forced himself to pen, with a view to having the unfortunate occurrence hushed up.

TO MR. STEPHEN CLARKE, JUN., DUMFRIES.

Sunday Morning.

DEAR SIR,—I was, I know, drunk last night, but I am sober this morning. From the expressions Capt. —— made use of to me, had I had nobody's welfare to care for but my own, we should certainly have come, according to the manners of the world, to the necessity of murdering one another about the business. The words were such as generally, I believe, end in a brace of pistols; but I am still pleased to think that I did not ruin the peace and welfare of a wife and family of children in a drunken squabble. Further, you know that the report of certain political opinions being mine, has already once before brought me to the brink of destruction. I dread lest last night's business may be misrepresented in the same way. You, I beg, will take care to prevent it. I tax your wish for Mrs. Burns's welfare with the task of waiting, as soon as possible, on every gentleman who was present, and state this to him, and, as you please, show him this letter.

Such unguarded ebullitions of democratic sentiment seem to have been at this juncture by no means infrequent on Burns's part, with the result that, in the terror and *espionage* which overspread the country, he became more than ever a marked man. That this was so, and that he himself knew his suspected situation, is evident from various measures of precaution which, on calmer after-thoughts, he adopted to disarm suspicion; *e.g.*, having in his possession Paine's *Common Sense* and *Rights of Man*, he, in alarm, was constrained to ask his former neighbour in the Wee Vennel—George Haugh, the blacksmith—to take charge of these writings, lest their being found in his possession should bring him into serious trouble with the watchful emissaries of Government. How, in such circumstances, he continued to indulge from time to time in thus implicating himself, we learn from his own pen, the fact being that his unguarded speech and conduct emanated from intoxication, in which state, alas! the nights of 1793 frequently found him.

To this same lamentable cause must also be attributed his unfortunate estrangements from some of his warmest admirers and kindest friends. As before mentioned, he was often entertained by the Riddels at Woodley Park, and one evening there, the bottle having, as usual, been going round rather freely, Burns indulged to excess, and in drunken frolic committed towards Mrs. Riddel a gross breach of decorum. In sober recollection of his rudeness to this lady, for whom he entertained a high admiration, he hastened to send her the following apology of agonized wretchedness and remorse :—

> MADAM,—I dare say that this is the first epistle you ever received from this nether world. I write you from the regions of hell, amid the horrors of the ———. The time and manner of my leaving your earth I do not exactly know, as I took my departure in the heat of a fever of intoxication, contracted at your too-hospitable mansion; but, on my arrival here, I was fairly tried, and sentenced to endure the purgatorial tortures of this infernal confine for the space of ninety-nine years, eleven months, and twenty-nine days, and all on account of the impropriety of my conduct yesternight under your roof. Here am I, laid on a bed of pitiless furze, with my aching head reclined on a pillow of ever-piercing thorn, while an infernal tormentor, wrinkled, and old, and cruel,—

his name, I think, is *Recollection*—with a whip of scorpions, forbids peace or rest to approach me, and keeps anguish eternally awake. Still, madam, if I could in any measure be reinstated in the good opinion of the fair circle whom my conduct last night so much injured, I think it would be an alleviation to my torments. For this reason, I trouble you with this letter. To the men of the company I will make no apology. Your husband, who insisted on my drinking more than I chose, has no right to blame me; and the other gentlemen were partakers of my guilt. But to you, madam, I have much to apologize. Your good opinion I valued as one of the greatest acquisitions I had made on earth, and I was truly a beast to forfeit it. There was a Miss I——, too, a woman of fine sense, gentle and unassuming manners—do make, on my part, a miserable —— wretch's best apology to her. A Mrs. G——, a charming woman, did me the honour to be prejudiced in my favour; this makes me hope that I have not outraged her beyond all forgiveness. To all the other ladies, please present my humblest contrition for my conduct, and my petition for their gracious pardon. O all ye powers of decency and decorum! whisper to them that my errors, though great, were involuntary—that an intoxicated man is the vilest of beasts—that it was not in my nature to be brutal to any one—that to be rude to a woman, when in my senses, was impossible with me—but—

. . . .

Regret! Remorse! Shame! ye three hell-hounds that ever dog my steps and bay at my heels, spare me! spare me!

Forgive the offences, and pity the perdition of, madam, your humble slave.

Also, to Mr. Riddel he sent these entreating lines :—

> The friend whom wild from wisdom's way,
>   The fumes of wine infuriate send
> (Not moony madness more astray)—
>   Who but deplores that hapless friend?
>
> Mine was th' insensate, frenzied part,
>   Ah! why should I such scenes outlive?—
> Scenes so abhorrent to my heart!
>   'Tis thine to pity and forgive.

And though he again and yet again wrote Mrs. Riddel in apologetic strain, it was in vain he pled for forgiveness—the Riddels

remained silent and unrelenting. This, however, cannot justify the
Poet in turning round, as he did, and lashing Mrs. Riddel in
sundry cruel satires. Alas! how unlike the real Burns! His
treatment of this lady, whom he had deeply offended, and who had
so greatly admired and kindly treated him, was shameful in the
extreme, and can only be accounted for by thinking that he wrote
these abusive pieces in the frenzy of drink, which, at times, seems
to have utterly perverted his great, kind, passionate nature, kindling
his mind into baleful fire, and setting him at fearful war even with
himself.

In this quarrel, the Riddels of Friar's Carse, as was to be
expected, took the side of their relatives, and turned against Burns;
and about this same time occurred the estrangement between the
unhappy Bard and his noted good friend, John Bushby [1] of Tinwald
Downs, lawyer and banker in Dumfries.

It was in the midst of this, the gloomiest and most miserable
time of all his fitful, deeply-vexed career, that he turned to Alexander Cunningham, his Edinburgh friend of brighter days, and
poured into his sympathetic ear that piercing wail of a great
disappointed life, and, it would seem, of an almost broken heart,
crying "out of the depths" for the consolations of religion, and the
vision and peace of God.

25th February 1794.

Canst thou minister to a mind diseased? Canst thou speak peace and rest
to a soul tost on a sea of troubles, without one friendly star to guide her course,
and dreading that the next surge may overwhelm her? Canst thou give to a
frame, trembling under the tortures of suspense, the stability and hardihood
of the rock that braves the blast? If thou canst not do the least of these, why
wouldst thou disturb me in my miseries with thy inquiries after me?

For these two months I have not been able to lift a pen. My constitution
and frame were, *ab origine*, blasted with a deep, incurable taint of hypochondria,

---

[1] See vol. i. p. 78.

which poisons my existence. Of late, a number of domestic vexations, and some pecuniary share in the ruin of these d———d times,—losses which, though trifling, were yet what I could ill bear,—have so irritated me that my feelings at times could only be envied by a reprobate spirit listening to the sentence that dooms it to perdition.

Are you deep in the language of consolation? I have exhausted in reflection every topic of comfort. *A heart at ease* would have been charmed with my sentiments and reasonings; but, as to myself, I was like Judas Iscariot preaching the gospel: he might melt and mould the hearts of those around him, but his own kept its native incorrigibility.

Still, there are two great pillars that bear us up amid the wreck of misfortune and misery. The ONE is composed of the different modifications of a certain noble, stubborn something in man, known by the names of courage, fortitude, magnanimity. The OTHER is made up of those feelings and sentiments which, however the sceptic may deny them, or the enthusiast disfigure them, are yet, I am convinced, original and component parts of the human soul; those *senses of the mind*—if I may be allowed the expression—which connect us with, and link us to, those awful obscure realities—an all-powerful and equally beneficent God, and a world to come, beyond death and the grave. The first gives the nerve of combat while a ray of hope beams on the field; the last pours the balm of comfort into the wounds which time can never cure.

I do not remember, my dear Cunningham, that you and I ever talked on the subject of religion at all. I know some who laugh at it, as the trick of the crafty FEW to lead the undiscerning MANY; or, at most, as an uncertain obscurity, which mankind can never know anything of, and with which they are fools if they give themselves much to do. Nor would I quarrel with a man for his irreligion, any more than I would for his want of a musical ear. I would regret that he was shut out from what, to me and to others, were such superlative sources of enjoyment. It is in this point of view, and for this reason, that I will deeply imbue the mind of every child of mine with religion. If my son should happen to be a man of feeling, sentiment, and taste, I shall thus add largely to his enjoyments. Let me flatter myself that this sweet little fellow, who is just now running about my desk, will be a man of a melting, ardent, glowing heart, and an imagination delighted with the painter, and rapt with the poet. Let me figure him wandering out in a sweet evening to inhale the balmy gales, and enjoy the growing luxuriance of the spring; himself the while in the blooming youth of life. He looks abroad on all nature, and through nature up to nature's God. His soul, by swift, delighting degrees, is rapt above this sublunary sphere, until he can be silent no longer, and bursts out into the glorious enthusiasm of Thomson,—

> These, as they change, Almighty Father, these
> Are but the varied God. The rolling year
> Is full of Thee;—

and so on, in all the spirit and ardour of that charming hymn. These are no ideal pleasures—they are real delights; and, I ask, what of the delights among the sons of men are superior, not to say equal, to them? And they have this precious, vast addition, that conscious virtue stamps them for her own, and lays hold on them to bring herself into the presence of a witnessing, judging, and approving God.

In quoting the above, Lockhart remarks: "They who have been told that Burns was ever a degraded being,—who have permitted themselves to believe that his only consolations were those 'the opiate guilt applies to grief,'—will do well to pause over this noble letter, and judge for themselves." Most heartily would we seek to commend the fine, true feeling of this remark, but we must, most reluctantly indeed, point out that this period of excessive indulgence and maddening misery had, *for the time being*, a very pernicious influence on the Poet's essentially noble nature, else he could not have permitted himself, during the first half of 1794, to make that collection of obscene and ribald doggerel known as the "Merry Muses." It is pitiful beyond expression to recall that dark time in Burns's career when drink and revelry held such strong sway over so great a life, and brought that other demon of impurity to madden and debase.

The touching incident, communicated to Lockhart by Mr. M'Culloch of Ardwell,[1] falls to be recorded at this stage:—

> Mr. M'Culloch told Lockhart that he was seldom more grieved than when, riding into Dumfries one fine summer evening, to attend a county ball, he saw

---

[1] See vol. ii. p. 344.

Burns walking alone on the shady side of the principal street of the town, while the opposite side was gay with successive groups of ladies and gentlemen, all drawn together for the festivities of the night, not one of whom appeared willing to recognise him. The horseman dismounted, and joined Burns, who, on his proposing to him to cross the street, said, "Nay, nay, my young friend—that's all over now;" and quoted, after a pause, some verses of Lady Grizel Baillie's pathetic ballad :—

> His bonnet stood ance fu' fair on his brow;
> His auld ane looked better than mony ane's new;
> But now he lets 't wear ony gate it will hing,
> And casts himsel' dowie upon the corn-bing.
>
> Oh, were we young, as we ance hae been,
> We sud hae been galloping down on yon green,
> And linking it ower the lily-white lea—
> And werena my heart light I wad die.

It was little in Burns's character to let his feelings on certain subjects escape in this fashion. He, immediately after reciting these verses, assumed the sprightliness of his most pleasing manner, and, taking his young friend home with him, entertained him very agreeably until the hour of the ball arrived, with a bowl of his usual potation, and Bonnie Jean's singing of some verses which he had recently composed.

Out of this abysmal condition Burns gradually emerged, however, during the latter half of 1794. In June he paid a visit to Ardwell and other places in its neighbourhood. From Castle-Douglas he wrote to Mrs. Dunlop, expressing fears that his constitution was beginning to suffer seriously "from the follies of his youth." At this same place and time he penned his last communication, so far as we know, to Clarinda. As such, the letter is uniquely interesting, and we give one or two of its passages :—

> Before you ask me why I have not written you, first let me be informed by you *how* I shall write you. "In friendship," you say; and I have many a

time taken up my pen to try an epistle of "friendship" to you, but it will not do; 'tis like Jove grasping a pop-gun after having wielded his thunder. When I take up the pen, recollection ruins me. Ah, my ever dearest Clarinda! Clarinda! What a host of memory's tenderest offspring crowd on my fancy at that sound! But I must not indulge that subject; you have forbid it.

I am extremely happy to learn that your precious health is re-established, and that you are once more fit to enjoy that satisfaction in existence which health alone can give us. My old friend Ainslie has indeed been kind to you. Tell him that I envy him the power of serving you. I had a letter from him awhile ago, but it was so dry, so distant, so like a card to one of his clients, that I could scarce bear to read it, and have not yet answered it. He is a good, honest fellow, and *can* write a friendly letter which would do equal honour to his head and his heart, as a whole sheaf of his letters which I have by me will witness; and though Fame does not blow her trumpet at my approach *now* as she did *then*, when he first honoured me with his friendship, yet I am as proud as ever; and, when I am laid in my grave, I wish to be stretched at my full length, that I may occupy every inch of ground I have a right to.

You would laugh were you to see me where I am just now. Would to Heaven you were here to laugh with me, though I am afraid that crying would be our first employment! Here am I set, a solitary hermit, in the solitary room of a solitary inn, with a solitary bottle of wine by me, as grave and as stupid as an owl, but, like that owl, still faithful to my old song, in confirmation of which, my dear Mrs. Mac, here is your good health! May the hand-waled benisons o' Heaven bless your bonnie face; and the wratch wha skellies at your welfare, may the auld tinkler deil get him to clout his rotten heart! Amen.

You must know, my dearest madam, that these now many years, wherever I am, in whatever company, when a married lady is called as a toast, I constantly give you, but, as your name has never passed my lips, even to my most intimate friend, I give you by the name of Mrs. Mac. This is so well known among my acquaintances, that, when any married lady is called for, the toast-master will say, "Oh, we need not ask him who it is; here's Mrs. Mac!" I have also, among my convivial friends, set on foot a round of toasts, which I call a round of Arcadian Shepherdesses—that is, a round of favourite ladies, under female names celebrated in ancient song; and then you are my Clarinda. So, my lovely Clarinda, I devote this glass of wine to a most ardent wish for your happiness.

EMERGING.

This short trip seems to have cheered and reinvigorated the Poet. For some months previous his lyric muse had cowered her wing, and almost hushed her voice. This autumn, however, she again soared aloft, and sang as sweetly as ever. Burns had met Jean Lorimer,[1] the "lassie wi' the lint-white locks," who, under the poetic name of "Chloris," was the theme of many of this productive season's songs. For Mr. Thomson's collection, too, he wrought industriously, his correspondence with that gentleman being at this period full of charming interest. Also, ere the year was out, he began to be somewhat reconciled to those friends from whom he had been so regrettably estranged. So, on the 29th December, we find him writing to Mrs. Dunlop in a more cheerful and happy strain :—

> Since I began this letter I have been appointed to act in the capacity of supervisor here; and, I assure you, what with the load of business, and what with that business being new to me, I could scarcely have commanded ten minutes to have spoken to you had you been in town, much less to have written you an epistle. This appointment is only temporary, and during the illness of the present incumbent; but I look forward to an early period when I shall be appointed in full form—a consummation devoutly to be wished! My political sins seem to be forgiven me.
>
> This is the season (New Year's Day is now my date) of wishing; and mine are most fervently offered up for you! May life to you be a positive blessing while it lasts, for your own sake; and that it may yet be greatly prolonged is my wish, for my own sake and for the sake of the rest of your friends! What a transient business is life! Very lately I was a boy; but t'other day I was a young man; and I already begin to feel the rigid fibre and stiffening joints of old age coming fast o'er my frame. With all my follies of youth, and, I fear, a few vices of manhood, still I congratulate myself on having had, in early days, religion strongly impressed on my mind. I have nothing to say to any one as to which sect he belongs to or what creed he believes; but I look on the man who is firmly persuaded of infinite wisdom and goodness

---

[1] For Jean's tragic history, see vol. ii. p. 20.

> superintending and directing every circumstance that can happen in his lot—I felicitate such a man as having a solid foundation for his mental enjoyment—a firm prop and sure stay in the hour of difficulty, trouble, and distress—and a never-failing anchor of hope when he looks beyond the grave.

And then he heralds the opening days of 1795 with world-resounding trumpet-tones, in "A Man's a Man for a' that." Now, too, when the Revolution alarms began to subside, the political atmosphere at home was greatly cleared of suspicious unrest, and Burns was rapidly regaining popular confidence and social favour. Passing on, we note that during this springtime, on the occasion of a contest for the representation of the Stewartry of Kirkcudbright, he once more rushed into the political arena, and dashed off several keen, satirical ballads in favour of the Whig candidate, Mr. Heron[1] of Kerroughtree. Learning that this gentleman had expressed a warm desire to employ his influence in obtaining for the Poet some promotion in the Excise, Burns wrote him a letter, to which we have seen the epithets "cringing" and "grovelling" applied; to which, however, in the whole circumstances, we deem the terms "frank," "sensible," and "prudent" much more appropriate. But here is the letter:—

> SIR,—I enclose you some copies of a couple of political ballads, one of which, I believe, you have never seen. Would to Heaven I could make you master of as many votes in the Stewartry—but—
>
> > Who does the utmost that he can,
> > Does well, acts nobly—angels could no more.
>
> In order to bring my humble efforts to bear with more effect on the foe, I have privately printed a good many copies of both ballads, and have sent them among friends all about the country.
>
> To pillory on Parnassus the rank reprobation of character, the utter dereliction of all principle, in a profligate junto, which has not only outraged virtue,

---

[1] See vol. ii. p. 342.

but violated common decency, spurning even hypocrisy as paltry iniquity below
their daring—to unmask their flagitiousness to the broadest day—to deliver
such over to their merited fate—is surely not merely innocent but laudable ; is
not only propriety, but virtue. You have already, as your auxiliary, the sober
detestation of mankind on the heads of your opponents; and I swear by the
lyre of Thalia to muster on your side all the votaries of honest laughter and
fair, candid ridicule.

I am extremely obliged to you for your kind mention of my interests in a
letter which Mr. Syme showed me. At present my situation in life must be
in a great measure stationary, at least for two or three years. The statement
is this : I am on the supervisors' list, and, as we come on there by precedency,
in two or three years I shall be at the head of that list, and be appointed *of
course*. Then a FRIEND might be of service to me in getting me into a place
of the kingdom which I would like. A supervisor's income varies from about
a hundred and twenty to two hundred a year, but the business is an incessant
drudgery, and would be nearly a complete bar to every species of literary
pursuit. The moment I am appointed supervisor, in the common routine,
I may be nominated on the collectors' list; and this is always a business
purely of political patronage. A collectorship varies much, from better than
two hundred a year to near a thousand. They also come forward by precedency
on the list, and have, besides a handsome income, a life of complete leisure. A
life of literary leisure, with a decent competency, is the summit of my wishes.
It would be the prudish affectation of silly pride in me to say that I do not
need, or would not be indebted to, a political friend; at the same time, sir,
I by no means lay my affairs before you thus, to hook my dependent situation
on your benevolence. If, in my progress of life, an opening should occur where
the good offices of a gentleman of your public character and political consequence might bring me forward, I shall petition your goodness with the same
frankness as I now do myself the honour to subscribe myself, etc.

Mr. Heron was successful in the contest, and he might have
found a way, as he had kindly intentions, of advancing the Poet's
interests. But the bright prospect on which Burns dwells in his
letter was, as every one knows, doomed to disappointment. His
time on earth was not to be long enough for the realization of his

natural and reasonable expectation. This fresh hope, however, served to cheer, in some measure, a few months of the one remaining year of ups and downs which was eventually to close his life in tragic sorrow.

Now from this electioneering episode we turn with unmixed pleasure to survey the Bard as a member of the Dumfries Volunteers —a force which was constituted in the spring of 1795. It was at length more and more evident that, as we have already held, Burns's imputed disloyalty was not the outcome of real deep-rooted feeling, but rather an impulsive, romantic product of his ardent love of everything that seemed to make for freedom and the dignity of man. At any rate, along with his friends, Syme and Dr. Maxwell,[1] the Poet had himself enrolled among the volunteers—none so *intelligently* loyal or so *instinctively* and intensely patriotic as he.

Allan Cunningham tells us he remembered distinctly the Poet's appearance in the ranks, "his very swarthy face, his ploughman stoop, his large dark eyes, and his indifferent dexterity in handling his arms."

But though Burns may not have been an adept at handling his sword and musket, he could, wielding his mighty pen, become the unrivalled poet-laureate of the loyal band, and kindle the heart of the nation into new patriotic flame. Apropos, we quote his well-known song of loyalty, written at this exciting time :—

THE DUMFRIES VOLUNTEERS.

> Does haughty Gaul invasion threat?
> Then let the loons beware, sir;
> There's wooden walls upon our seas,
> And volunteers on shore, sir.

---

[1] See vol. ii. p. 43.

> The Nith shall run to Corsincon,
>   And Criffel sink in Solway,
> Ere we permit a foreign foe
>   On British ground to rally!
>
> Oh, let us not like snarling tykes
>   In wrangling be divided;
> Till, slap, come in an unco loon,
>   And wi' a rung decide it.
> Be Britain still to Britain true,
>   Among oursel's united;
> For never but by British hands
>   Maun British wrangs be righted.
>
> The kettle o' the Kirk and State,
>   Perhaps a clout may fail in't;
> But deil a foreign tinkler loon
>   Shall ever ca' a nail in't.
> Our fathers' blude the kettle bought,
>   And wha wad dare to spoil it;
> By Heaven, the sacrilegious dog
>   Shall fuel be to boil it.
>
> The wretch that wad a tyrant own,
>   And the wretch, his true-born brother,
> Wh' 'ould set the mob aboon the throne,
>   May they be damned together!
> Who will not sing "God save the King,"
>   Shall hang as high's the steeple;
> But while we sing "God save the King,"
>   We'll ne'er forget the People.

Of this composition, so stirring in itself and so applicable to that time of threatened French invasion, Cunningham says, "It hit the taste and suited the feelings of the humbler classes, who added to it 'The Poor but Honest Sodger,' the 'Song of Death,' and 'Scots wha hae.' Hills echoed with it; it was heard in every street; it did more to right the mind of the rustic part of the population than did all the speeches of Pitt and Dundas or the chosen Five-and-Forty.

And yet for services such as no other Poet ever rendered to our country and constitution in such time of need, Burns received no pension or reward such as those in authority might easily have bestowed—might, indeed, have counted it an honour to bestow. But, letting "the dead past bury its dead," may we the more fondly enshrine the name of BURNS in ever-grateful and admiring memory.

In course of this year, his trusty friend, Graham of Fintry, had been renewing his efforts on the Poet's behalf. A scheme was on foot to promote him to higher office in Leith, at a salary of £200; but, from whatever cause, he was left to drudge on in Dumfries, —earning only a bare competency, yet standing well again in popular estimation, reconciled to his friends, spending perhaps too many of his evenings in the Globe Tavern, yet constantly sending to Thomson his priceless lyric effusions, accompanied by an abounding fund of uniquely valuable notes and criticisms on Scottish songs and song-makers.

Before entering upon our narrative of the last sad year, we here pause to notice a few more of the noted productions of these four years in Dumfries. In November 1792, the sixth anniversary of Mary Campbell's death, he wrote his "Highland Mary," a piece hardly inferior to his "Address to Mary in Heaven," written exactly three years before. In connexion with the career and temperament of the Bard, these two noble strains must ever exert the most strangely romantic and fascinating interest :—

> Ye banks, and braes, and streams around
> The castle o' Montgomery,
> Green be your woods, and fair your flowers,
> Your waters never drumlie!

There simmer first unfauld her robes,
    And there the langest tarry ;
For there I took the last fareweel
    O' my sweet Highland Mary.

How sweetly bloomed the gay green birk,
    How rich the hawthorn's blossom,
As underneath their fragrant shade
    I clasped her to my bosom!
The golden hours, on angel wings,
    Flew o'er me and my dearie ;
For dear to me as light and life
    Was my sweet Highland Mary.

Wi' mony a vow and locked embrace
    Our parting was fu' tender ;
And, pledging aft to meet again,
    We tore oursel's asunder :
But, oh! fell death's untimely frost,
    That nipt my flower sae early!
Now green's the sod, and cauld's the clay,
    That wraps my Highland Mary!

O pale, pale now those rosy lips
    I aft hae kissed sae fondly!
And closed for aye the sparkling glance
    That dwelt on me sae kindly :
And mouldering now in silent dust
    That heart that lo'ed me dearly!
But still within my bosom's core
    Shall live my Highland Mary.

On sending this grand, sweet song to Thomson, the Poet says :—

The foregoing song pleases myself; I think it is in my happiest manner; you will see at first glance that it suits the air. The subject of the song is one of the most interesting passages of my youthful days, and I own that I should be much flattered to see the verses set to an air which would ensure celebrity. Perhaps, after all, 'tis the still glowing prejudice of my heart that throws a borrowed lustre over the merits of the composition.

Commencing his enthusiastic and entirely disinterested labours for Thomson's collection in the autumn of 1792, ere the close of the year he produced several new songs, among which may be noted, "Duncan Gray," "My ain kind Dearie," and "Here's a health to them that's awa." Then, in 1793, he wrote, amongst others "Braw, braw lads," "Had I a cave," "O Puirtith Cauld," "Whistle, and I'll come to ye, my lad," "Logan Braes," "Scots wha hae," and "When wild war's deadly blast was blawn," a ballad of consummately dramatic power, and full of the sweetest natural pathos :—

> When wild war's deadly blast was blawn,
>   And gentle peace returning,
> Wi' mony a sweet babe fatherless
>   And mony a widow mourning;
> I left the lines and tented field,
>   Where lang I'd been a lodger,
> My humble knapsack a' my wealth,
>   A poor but honest sodger.
>
> A leal, light heart was in my breast,
>   My hand unstained wi' plunder;
> And for fair Scotia, hame again,
>   I cheery on did wander.
> I thought upon the banks o' Coil,
>   I thought upon my Nancy,
> I thought upon the witching smile
>   That caught my youthful fancy.
>
> At length I reached the bonnie glen
>   Where early life I sported;
> I passed the mill, and trysting thorn,
>   Where Nancy aft I courted:

SONGS OF BRIGHTER TIME.

    Wha spied I but my ain dear maid
      Down by her mother's dwelling!
    And turned me round to hide the flood
      That in my een was swelling.

    Wi' altered voice, quoth I, "Sweet lass,
      Sweet as yon hawthorn's blossom,
    O happy, happy may he be,
      That's dearest to thy bosom!
    My purse is light, I've far to gang,
      And fain would be thy lodger;
    I've served my king and country lang—
      Take pity on a sodger!"

And so on in other four as exquisite stanzas as these.[1]

We saw how, during the first dark half of 1794, his muse was almost silent, giving forth only one or two pieces of bitter personality against his offended friends; and how, in the brightening time, he touched anew his sweetly-sounding lyre with unabated skill, producing in quick succession many songs, of which we further note, "My Chloris, mark how sweet the groves," "Contented wi' little, an' cantie wi' mair," "She says she loes me best o' a'," "My Nannie's awa," and "A Man's a Man for a' that."

---

[1] Cunningham remarks: "Burns was a zealous lover of his country, and has stamped his patriotic feelings in many a lasting verse. His 'Poor but honest Sodger,' laid hold at once on the public feeling, and it was everywhere sung with an enthusiasm which only began to abate when Campbell's 'Exile of Erin,' and 'Wounded Hussar,' were published. Dumfries, which sent so many of her sons to the wars, rang with it from port to port; and the Poet, wherever he went, heard it echoing from house and hall. I wish this exquisite song, with 'Scots wha hae,' the 'Song of Death,' and 'Does haughty Gaul invasion threat,'—all lyrics which enforce a love of country and a martial enthusiasm into men's breasts, had obtained some reward for the Poet. His perishable conversation was remembered by the rich to his prejudice—his imperishable lyrics were rewarded only by the admiration and tears of his fellow-peasants."

CHAPTER X.

THE CLOSING YEAR, JULY 1795–JULY 1796. AGE 36–37.

Three gates of deliverance, it seems to us, were open for Burns : clear poetical activity ; madness ; or death. The first, with longer life, was still possible, though not probable. . . . . . The second was still less probable, for his mind was ever among the clearest and firmest. So the milder third gate was opened for him : and he passed not softly, yet speedily, into that still country, where the hail-storms and fire-showers do not reach, and the heaviest laden wayfarer at length lays down his load.
Carlyle on Burns.

Oh, Robert Burns ! by tempest tossed,
Storm-swept, by cruel whirlwinds crossed ;
Thy prayers, like David's psalms of old,
Make all our plaints and wailings cold.
. . . .
We know but this : his living song
Protects the weak and tramples wrong ;
Refracting radiance of delight,
His prismed genius, clear and bright,

Illumes all Scotland far and wide,
And Caledonia throbs with pride
To hear her grand old Doric swell
From Highland crag to Lowland dell ;

To find, where'er her children stray,
Her "Auld Lang Syne," her "Scots wha hae,"
And words of hope which proudly span
The centuries vast—"A man's a man."

Then welcome, Burns, from shore to shore !
All hail, our Robin, evermore !¹

A STRANGER visiting Dumfries in the summer of 1795, and inquiring about the Poet's way of life at that time, would gather

---
¹ From poem recited by the author, Mr. Wallace Bruce, U.S. Consul, Edinburgh, at the unveiling of the Ayr Burns Statue, on 8th July 1891.

from the more intelligent and liberal-minded townspeople that
"Mister"[1] Burns was regarded as altogether an extraordinary man,
who, while paying zealous heed to his duties as exciseman, spent
much of his time in company of one degree and another, and,
notwithstanding his official labours and social distractions, managed
every now and then to produce some lovely song or clever poem.
It might also be remarked that he would have passed his leisure
hours more at his own fireside, but for folks coming about and
enticing him away to the Globe Tavern, to hear his glowing
utterances as the toast and song went round; and that, as he was
then looking far from well, it was doubtful whether he would long
withstand his wearing worries and jovial excitements. Indeed, we
fancy that, among those who knew Burns well, there prevailed a
distinct opinion that his great, restless, fiery life would ere long
burn itself out. In what manner and to what extent the Bard
indulged in tavern excitements during this summer, there is now
no exact means of knowing. Moreover, the question is not one
upon which there need be minute or set discussion. We therefore
turn to survey the brighter side. Regarding Burns's industry and
efficiency as *gauger*, from a statement by Mr. Alexander Findlater,[2]
supervisor in the Dumfries district, we learn that he was most
vigilant and exemplary in attention to duty; that, in this respect,
no falling off was discernible till near the end, when he was assailed
by pain and sickness; that, in business hours, he was always able
for his work; and that he never indulged in drinking in the
forenoon, nor, at any time, in drinking apart from company. The
testimony of another highly respectable and competent witness here
deserves to be quoted at length, and will be read with grateful

---

[1] For long after the Poet's death, the inhabitants of Dumfries and its neighbourhood always spoke of him as *Mister* Burns.
[2] See vol. i. p. 194.

pleasure. Mr. James Gray,[1] then Rector of Dumfries Grammar School, and afterwards a clergyman of the Episcopal Church, knowing the Poet intimately (and *speaking from his own observation*, as he emphatically reminds us), says:—

> It is not my intention to extenuate Burns's errors, because they were combined with genius; on that account they were only the more dangerous, because the more seductive, and deserve the more severe reprehension; but I shall likewise claim that nothing may be said in malice against him. It came under my own view, professionally, that he superintended the education of his children with a degree of care that I have never seen surpassed by any parent in any rank of life whatever. In the bosom of his family, he spent many a delightful hour in directing the studies of his eldest son, a boy of uncommon talents. I have frequently found him explaining to this youth, then not more than nine years of age, the English poets, from Shakespeare to Gray, or storing his mind with examples of heroic virtue, as they live in the pages of our most celebrated English historians. I would ask any person of common candour, if employments like these are consistent with *habitual drunkenness*. It is not denied that he sometimes mingled with society unworthy of him. He was of a social and convivial nature. He was courted by all classes of men for the fascinating powers of his conversation, but over his social scene uncontrolled passion never presided. Over the social bowl, his wit flashed for hours together, penetrating whatever it struck, like the fire from heaven; but, even in the hour of thoughtless gaiety and merriment, I never knew it tainted by indecency. It was playful or caustic by turns, following an allusion through all its windings; astonishing by its rapidity, or amusing by its wild originality and grotesque, yet natural combinations, but never, within my observation, disgusting by its grossness. In his morning hours, I never saw him like one suffering from the effects of last night's intemperance. He appeared then clear and unclouded. He was the eloquent advocate of humanity, justice, and political freedom. From his paintings, virtue appeared more lovely, and piety assumed a more celestial mien. While his keen eye was pregnant with fancy and feeling, and his voice attuned to the very passion which he wished to communicate, it would hardly have been possible to conceive any being more interesting and delightful.

---

[1] See vol. i. p. 251.

I may likewise add, that, to the very end of his life, reading was his favourite amusement. I have never known any man so intimately acquainted with the elegant English authors. He seemed to have the poets by heart. The prose authors he could quote either in their own words, or clothe their ideas in language more beautiful than their own. Nor was there ever any decay in any of the powers of his mind. To the last day of his life, his judgment, his memory, his imagination, were fresh and vigorous, as when he composed the "Cotter's Saturday Night." The truth is, that Burns was seldom *intoxicated*. The drunkard soon becomes besotted, and is shunned even by the convivial. Had he been so, he could not long have continued the idol of every party. It will be freely confessed, that the hour of enjoyment was often prolonged beyond the limit marked by prudence; but what man will venture to affirm that, in situations where he was conscious of giving so much pleasure, he could at all times have listened to her voice?

The men with whom he generally associated were not of the lowest order. He numbered among his intimate friends many of the most respectable inhabitants of Dumfries and the vicinity. Several of those were attached to him by ties that the hand of calumny, busy as it was, could never snap asunder. They admired the Poet for his genius, and loved the man for the candour, generosity, and kindness of his nature. His early friends clung to him through good and bad report, with a zeal and fidelity that prove their disbelief of the malicious stories circulated to his disadvantage. Among them were some of the most distinguished characters in this country, and not a few females, eminent for delicacy, taste, and genius. They were proud of his friendship, and cherished him to the last moment of his existence. He was endeared to them even by his misfortunes, and they still retain for his memory that affection and veneration which virtue alone inspires.

Of the Poet's care and anxiety in the cultivation of the minds of his family, Mr. Gray's further testimony, addressed to Gilbert Burns, is reproduced at p. 253 of vol. i.

Such accounts as those given by Mr. Findlater and the Rev. James Gray command all respect and credence as proceeding from *men who wrote on no hearsay evidence*, and who, it is justly remarked, were altogether incapable of wilfully stating what they knew to be untrue. Setting this fairer presentment alongside the darker one by Dr. Currie, Professor Walker, Robert Heron, etc., while we marvel not a little at the wide divergence of statement, we find some explanation thereof by calling to mind what great and strangely discordant elements combined to make up the character and career of *Burns*, and we do not wrong the Poet's memory by thinking with Lockhart that probably " truth lies between."

Resuming our narrative, we find that, up till the beginning of August 1795, the Bard's notable song-correspondence with George Thomson continued with no marked intermission, except that of the troubled songless half of 1794. But now there is another ominous blank, wherein his lyre is silent, no friendly correspondence is found, and almost nothing is known of his experiences for several months. We discover, however, one pleasant incident which occurred in September, and of which an attractive account remains by Mr. John Pattison, son of Burns's friend, Mr. Pattison of Kelvin Grove. This gentleman, accompanied by his son, happening to be in Dumfries, accidentally encountered the Poet, and cordially invited him to come to dinner at the inn, and bring their mutual friend, Dr. Maxwell, with him.

> At the hour named my father sat down at the head of the table, Dr. Maxwell at the foot, and the grammar-school boy (John Pattison) opposite Burns. Upwards of half a century has passed away; but the recollection of that day is as fresh and green in my memory as if the events recorded had occurred yesterday. It was, in fact, a new era in my existence. I had never before sat after dinner; but now I was chained to my chair till late at night, or rather early in the morning. Both Dr. Maxwell and my father were highly-gifted, eloquent men. The Poet was in his best vein. I can never forget the animation and glorious intelligence of his countenance, the rich, deep tones of his musical voice, and those matchless eyes, which absolutely appeared to flash fire, and stream forth rays of living light. It was not conversation I heard;

SERIOUS ILLNESS.

it was an outburst of noble sentiment, brilliant wit, and a flood of sympathy and good-will to fellow-men. Burns repeated many verses that had never seen the light, chiefly political; no impure or obscene idea was uttered, or I believe thought of: it was altogether an intellectual feast. A lofty, pure, and transcendent genius alone could have made so deep and lasting an impression on a mere boy, who had read nothing, and who does not remember to have heard Burns named till that day.

It has already been observed that, though in youth and earlier manhood Burns was possessed of great physical strength, his was a highly-strung constitution and temperament—quickly excited and easily disordered. Further, it is well known that, all along, he suffered more or less from a certain nervous depression, and at times from alarming palpitation of the heart, brought on and aggravated, it is believed, by the straining toil and weary care of his boyhood days.

Of later years, too, he had otherwise suffered from several sharp though short attacks of illness. Nor will it be denied that many a time he was far from careful of his health. Allusion has been made to his letter of 25th June, 1794, to Mrs. Dunlop, in which he states that he had been for some time in poor health, and threatened with "flying gout." We now learn that the late autumn of 1795 brought a more serious and prolonged illness than any he had yet experienced. "For over a year before his death there was," according to Dr. Currie's account, "an evident decline in our Poet's personal appearance; and though his appetite continued unimpaired, he was himself sensible that his constitution was sinking." From October 1795 to the January following, an accidental complaint "confined him to the house." During this illness, however, he was able to employ his pen a little. About the beginning of December he wrote another "Address," to be spoken by Miss Fontenelle of the Dumfries Theatre on her benefit night, 4th December; and on 15th December he thus wrote to Mrs. Dunlop :—

> MY DEAR FRIEND,—As I am in a complete Decemberish humour, gloomy, sullen, stupid, as even the Deity of Dulness herself could wish, I shall not drawl out a heavy letter with a number of heavier apologies for my late silence. Only one I shall mention, because I know you will sympathize in it: these four months, a sweet little girl, my youngest child, has been so ill, that every day, a week or less threatened to terminate her existence. There had much need be many pleasures annexed to the states of husband and father, for, God knows, they have many peculiar cares. I cannot describe to you the anxious, sleepless hours these ties frequently give me. I see a train of helpless little folks; me and my exertions all their stay; and on what a brittle thread does the life of man hang! If I am nipt off at the command of fate, even in all the vigour of manhood, as I am—such things happen every day—Gracious God! what would become of my little flock? 'Tis here that I envy your people of fortune. A father on his death-bed, taking an everlasting leave of his children, has indeed woe enough; but the man of competent fortune leaves his sons and daughters independency and friends; while I— But I shall run distracted if I think any longer on the subject!
>
> To leave talking of the matter so gravely, I shall sing with the old Scots ballad—
>
>   O that I had ne'er been married,
>   I would never had nae care ;
>   Now I've gotten wife and bairns,
>   They cry crowdie evermair.
>
>   Crowdie ance, crowdie twice,
>   Crowdie three times in a day ;
>   An ye crowdie ony mair,
>   Ye'll crowdie a' my meal away.

This letter he continues on the 24th, and again on Christmas morning; and at the close of the year he penned the following smart little epistle to his kind-hearted friend, Excise-Collector Mitchell, showing the author in a *pinch* for want of a single guinea of ready cash, and also in resolute mood towards better care of his health, which had been so seriously impaired, but was now in the way of improvement :—

> Friend of the Poet, tried and leal,
> Wha, wanting thee, might beg or steal;
> Alake, alake, the meikle deil
>   Wi' a' his witches
> Are at it, skelpin' jig and reel,
>   In my poor pouches!
>
> I modestly fu' fain wad hint it,
> That one-pound-one, I sairly want it;
> If wi' the hizzie down ye sent it,
>   It would be kind;
> And while my heart wi' life-blood dunted,
>   I'd bear't in mind.
>
> So may the auld year gang out moaning
> To see the new come laden, groaning,
> Wi' double plenty o'er the loanin
>   To thee and thine:
> Domestic peace and comforts crowning
>   The hale design.
>
>   POSTSCRIPT.
>
> Ye've heard this while how I've been licket,
> And by fell death was nearly nicket;
> Grim loon! he got me by the fecket,
>   And sair me sheuk;
> But by gude luck I lap a wicket,
>   And turned a neuk.
>
> But by that health, I've got a share o't,
> And by that life, I'm promised mair o't,
> My hale and weel I'll tak' a care o't,
>   A tentier way;
> Then farewell folly, hide and hair o't,
>   For ance and aye!

At the beginning of the New Year, he was again able to go about a little; but, pitiful to relate, one evening in the middle of January he was allured to join a jovial party at the Globe Tavern, and to tarry long over the wine-cup. Returning home at an early hour of the morning, which was bitterly cold, with snow on the ground, becoming overpowered by the effects of the liquor, he fell asleep upon the icy street.

> In these circumstances — says Chambers — and in the peculiar condition to which a severe medicine had reduced his constitution, a fatal chill penetrated to his bones; he reached home with the seeds of rheumatic fever in possession of his already weakened frame. In this little accident—adds Chambers—and not in the pressure of poverty or disrepute, or wounded feelings or a broken heart, truly lay the *determining* cause of the sadly shortened days of our great national Poet.

Burns seems now to have lain prostrate for about a week. On 20th January he managed to pen a short note to Mrs. Riddel, whom he could again address as a sympathetic friend. "The health you wished me in your morning's card is, I think, flown from me for ever. I have not been able to leave my bed to-day till about an hour ago." On 28th January he was so far recovered as to be present at a meeting of the masonic lodge; and on the 31st he sent the following letter to Mrs. Dunlop, his ever deeply-respected friend and long-trusted correspondent, who had, however, for over a year maintained, to him, a painful silence, leaving his letters totally unanswered :—

> These many months you have been two packets in my debt—what sin of ignorance I have committed against so highly valued a friend, I am utterly at a loss to guess. Alas! madam, ill can I afford, at this time, to be deprived of any of the small remnant of my pleasures. I have lately drunk deep of the cup of affliction. The autumn robbed me of my only daughter and darling child,[1]

---

[1] Elizabeth Riddel, who died at Mauchline in September 1795.

and that at a distance, too, and so rapidly, as to put it out of my power to pay the last duties to her. I had scarcely begun to recover from that shock, when I became myself the victim of a most severe rheumatic fever, and long the die spun doubtful; until, after many weeks of a sick-bed, it seems to have turned up life, and I am beginning to crawl across my room, and once indeed have been before my own door in the street.

> When pleasure fascinates the mental sight,
> Affliction purifies the visual ray,
> Religion hails the drear, the untried night,
> And shuts, for ever shuts! life's doubtful day.

This letter tells its own sad tale of woe. Poor afflicted Burns, crying out in the restless misery of remorse and pain and care, his desolation darkened by the reflection that even Mrs. Dunlop, whose steadfast friendship he had so fondly valued and counted upon, had *turned against him!*

And now—observes Currie—his appetite began to fail; his hand shook, and his voice faltered on any exertion or emotion. His pulse became weaker and more rapid, and pain in the larger joints, and in the hands and feet, deprived him of the enjoyment of refreshing sleep. Too much dejected in his spirits, and too well aware of his real situation to entertain hopes of recovery, he was ever musing on the approaching desolation of his family, and his spirits sank into a uniform gloom.

Nevertheless, a gleam of the old grim humour darts through the serious view of his situation in the answer which he at this time returned to Colonel de Peyster,[1] his commanding officer in the Dumfries Volunteers, who had sent a kind inquiry regarding the Poet's health:—

> My honored Colonel, deep I feel
> Your interest in the Poet's weal:

---

[1] See vol. ii. p. 155.

Ah! now sma' heart hae I to speel
        The steep Parnassus,
Surrounded thus by bolus pill
        And potion glasses.

O what a canty warld were it,
Would pain and care and sickness spare it;
And fortune favor worth and merit,
        As they deserve!
And aye a rowth roast beef and claret;
        Syne, wha wad starve?

Dame Life, though fiction out may trick her,
And in paste gems and frippery deck her;
Oh! flickering, feeble, and unsicker
        I've found her still,
Aye wavering, like the willow-wicker,
        'Tween good and ill.

Then that curst carmagnole, auld Satan,
Watches like baudrons by a rattan,
Our sinfu' soul to get a claut on
        Wi' felon ire;
Syne, whip! his tail ye'll ne'er cast saut on—
        He's aff like fire.

Ah, Nick! ah, Nick; it isna fair,
First showing us the temptin' ware,
Bright wines an' bonnie lassies rare,
        To put us daft,
Syne weave, unseen, thy spider snare,
        O' hell's damned waft.

Poor man, the flee, aft bizzes by,
And aft, as chance he comes thee nigh,
Thy auld damned elbow yeuks wi' joy
        And hellish pleasure;
Already in thy fancy's eye,
        Thy sicker treasure!

> Soon, heels-o'er-gowdie! in he gangs,
> And like a sheep-head on a tangs,
> Thy girning laugh enjoys his pangs
>   And murdering wrestle,
> As, dangling in the wind, he hangs,
>   A gibbet's tassel.
>
> But lest you think I am uncivil,
> To plague you with this draunting drivel,
> Abjuring a' intentions evil,
>   I quat my pen:
> The Lord preserve us frae the devil!
>   Amen! Amen!

About this time, the wife of his old neighbour, Haugh the blacksmith, in the Wee Vennel, meeting Burns in the street, kindly and seriously talked with him about his health. She distinctly remembered one remark he made to her:—"I find that a man may live like a fool, but he will scarcely die like one!"

On February 5th, Thomson wrote:—

> The pause you have made, my dear sir, is awful! Am I never to hear from you again? I know, and I lament how much you have been afflicted of late; but I trust that returning health and spirits will now enable you to resume the pen, and delight us with your musings. I have still about a dozen Scotch and Irish airs which I wish "wedded to immortal verse."

In answer, the Bard nerved himself to produce "Hey for a lass wi' a tocher," a song remarkable, in the circumstances, for its liveliness and vigour:—"A most excellent song," Thomson rightly acknowledged it to be, adding, "and with you the subject is something new indeed":—

> Awa wi' your witchcraft o' beauty's alarms,
> The slender bit beauty you grasp in your arms:
> O gie me the lass that has acres o' charms,
> O gie me the lass wi' the weel-stockit farms.

CHORUS.

Then hey for a lass wi' a tocher, then hey for a lass wi' a tocher;
Then hey for a lass wi' a tocher—the nice yellow guineas for me.

Your beauty's a flower, in the morning that blows,
And withers the faster, the faster it grows:
But the rapturous charm o' the bonnie green knowes,
Ilk spring they're new deckit wi' bonnie white yowes.

And e'en when this beauty your bosom has blest,
The brightest o' beauty may cloy, when possest;
But the sweet yellow darlings wi' Geordie imprest,
The langer ye hae them, the mair they're carest.

This same month of February, we find the Poet writing to Mr. James Clarke, teacher in Forfar, requesting repayment of money (a considerable sum, it seems) which he had lent Clarke at the time of his troubles with the educational authorities in Moffat.[1]

During the spring of 1796, owing to the failure of the preceding harvest, food was scarce and costly; and, besides having to meet those additional expenses which illness usually occasions, Burns was apprehensive that he would only receive reduced (off-duty) salary. It was in these circumstances he at length applied to Mr. Clarke for something of his own. We give the letter which came in answer.

> MY DEAR FRIEND,—Your letter makes me very unhappy, the more so as I had heard very flattering accounts of your situation some months ago. A note [20s.] is enclosed; and if such partial payments will be acceptable, this shall soon be followed by more. My appointment here has more than answered my expectations; but furnishing a large house, etc., has kept me still very poor; and the persecution I suffered from that rascal Lord H——, brought me into expenses which, with all my economy, I have not yet rubbed off. Be so kind as write me. Your disinterested friendship has made an impression which time cannot efface. Believe me, my dear Burns, yours in sincerity,
>
> JAMES CLARKE.

---

[1] It will be remembered that, in 1791, Burns generously exerted himself on behalf of Clarke, whom he considered a deserving man suffering under spiteful persecution.

A GRATIFYING INCIDENT.

That the Bard's income was not reduced at this time, thanks and honour are due to a young Excise officer named Stobbie, who gratuitously performed the duties, thus enabling Burns to draw the full emolument of his office.

Pertaining to this swiftly-darkening time, a gratifying incident is noted by Chambers as follows :—

> Miss Grace Aiken, a very young lady, the daughter of Burns's early patron, Mr. Robert Aiken of Ayr, had occasion during spring to pass through Dumfries, on her way to pay a visit in Liverpool. In walking along the street towards the residence of her friend, Mrs. Copeland, she passed a tall, slovenly-looking man, of sickly aspect, who presently uttered an exclamation which caused her to turn about to see who it was. It was Burns; but so changed from his former self, that she could hardly have recognised him, except for the sound of his voice in addressing her. On her asking him playfully, if he had been going to pass her without notice, he spoke as if he had felt that it was proper for him, now-a-days, to leave his old friends to be the first to hold forth the hand of friendship. At her pressing request, he accompanied her to the house of Mrs. Copeland; he even yielded, but not till after much entreaty, to go home and put himself in order, that he might return at four to dinner. He spent the evening cheerfully in their temperate society, and retired about midnight. The circumstance is worthy of notice, because neither Mrs. Copeland nor any of her friends—all members of the best society in Dumfries—had any objection to entertaining or meeting Burns. The hostess had not seen him for a considerable time, but from no cause affecting the reputation of the Poet—only, she understood that he had of late shown a preference for what might positively as well as comparatively be called low society—a circumstance she greatly lamented. All this shows that Burns's social discredit in his latter days must have been the result of no universal feeling among his fellow-citizens. The fact seems to be, that, while many condemned and forsook him,—the provincial clergy to a man,—on the other hand, many, sensible that his faults were rather allied to imprudence and indecorum than to turpitude, regarded him with forbearance, if not with undiminished esteem and attention.

On 14th April, the Bard was well enough to attend (for the last time) a meeting of the masonic lodge; but that same month he thus gloomily addresses Thomson :—

> Alas! my dear Thomson, I fear it will be some time ere I tune my lyre again! "By Babel streams I have sat and wept" almost ever since I wrote you last: I have only known existence by the pressure of the heavy hand of sickness, and have counted time by the repercussions of pain! Rheumatism, cold, and fever have formed to me a terrible combination. I close my eyes in misery, and open them without hope. I look on the vernal day, and say with poor Fergusson—
>
> > Say wherefore has an all-indulgent Heaven
> > Light to the comfortless and wretched given?

And again on 17th May :—

> MY DEAR SIR,—I once mentioned to you an air which I have long admired—"Here's a health to them that's awa', hiney," but I forget if you took any notice of it. I have just been trying to suit it with verses, and I beg leave to recommend the air to your attention once more. I have only begun it.

JESSY.

Chorus.

> Here's a health to ane I loe dear!
> Here's a health to ane I loe dear!
> Thou art sweet as the smile when fond lovers meet,
> And soft as their parting tear—Jessy!

> Although thou maun never be mine,
>   Although even hope is denied:
> 'Tis sweeter for thee despairing,
>   Than aught in the world beside—Jessy!

> I mourn through the gay, gaudy day,
>   As, hopeless, I muse on thy charms;
> But welcome the dream o' sweet slumber,
>   For then I am lock't in thy arms—Jessy!

HIGH PURE LYRIC AIM.

> I guess by the dear angel smile,
> I guess by the love-rolling ee ;
> But why urge the tender confession,
> 'Gainst fortune's fell, cruel decree—Jessy !

> This will be delivered by a Mr. Lewars, a young fellow of uncommon merit ; indeed by far the cleverest fellow I have met with in this part of the world. His only fault is d-m-cratic heresy. As he will be a day or two in town, you will have leisure, if you choose, to write me by him ; and if you have a spare half-hour to spend with him, I shall place your kindness to my account. I have no copies of the songs I have sent you, and I have taken a fancy to review them all, and possibly may mend some of them : so, when you have complete leisure, I will thank you for either the originals or copies. I had rather be the author of five well-written songs than of ten otherwise. My verses to "Cauld Kail" I will suppress; as also those to "Laddie, lie near me." They are neither worthy of my name nor of your book. I have great hopes that the genial influence of the approaching summer will set me to rights, but as yet I cannot boast of returning health. I have now reason to believe that my complaint is a flying gout—a sad business !

Burns's remarks in this letter regarding his great song-making work are particularly noteworthy, as showing the clear sense and worthy feeling to leave to Scotland and the world naught of his save what was pure and elevating.[1] So may it be remembered that those who, in after years, with prying curiosity and prurient taste, hunted up and printed so many of the Bard's more hasty and less fastidious efforts, did so unmistakably against his anxious, though, alas ! unaccomplished desire to set his papers in order—to consign to irrevocable oblivion all that in matter or form was unworthy of his genius and name, and to leave only that which was masterly and finished, refined and ennobling.

The theme of the foregoing song—Burns's last *finished* contribution to Thomson's collection—was Jessie Lewars, sister of Lewars, the Poet's close friend and brother exciseman. Of how tenderly

[1] See vol. iii. p. 295.

Jessie ministered to Burns and his household throughout these last distressful months, and how the dying Bard—having no other reward to offer—in this song, and in his exquisite "Oh, wert thou in the cauld blast," and other grateful strains, conferred imperishable fame upon his gentle, faithful, self-sacrificing nurse, the affecting story is fully told in vol. ii. of this work.

During the dismal closing days his kind-hearted Jean was herself laid down by illness, but it is indeed most pleasing to think that, with Jessie Lewars near, he over whom the gentler sex ever held so great an influence—he who had sung the charms of woman as no other has done—did not lack, even for one hour of his heavy sorrows and sufferings, the priceless ministry of a sweet, true woman's tenderest care.

Several of the Poet's friends cherished the hope that the fresh bright spring and genial summer might in some measure restore his health; but though, during May and June, his illness did a little abate, it was a vain, brief hope. Disease now held him in strong and deadly-closing grasp. His malady did not, however, to any great extent crush his keen spirit or impair his marvellous mental power.

In May we find him writing, in the old satiric vein, yet another election ballad, "Wha will buy my troggin?" again in favour of Mr. Heron of Kerroughtree. The piece is humorously conceived, and wrought out in a clear and facetious manner. But, as might be expected, the prevailing tone of his mind at this period was sad and weary—so utterly sad that no one who has a heart can read those closing letters of wailing, imploring wretchedness without dropping on the woe-laden page some burning tears.

On receiving a note from Mrs. Riddel, inviting him to the King's Birthday Gathering on 4th June, and asking him to send her a copy of some song, he replied:—

I am in such miserable health, as to be utterly incapable of showing my loyalty in any way. Racked as I am with rheumatisms, I meet every face with a greeting like that of Balak to Balaam : "Come, curse me Jacob ; and come, defy me Israel ! " So say I : Come, curse me that east wind ; and come, defy me the north ! Would you have me in such circumstances copy you out a love-song ?

To his friend Dr. Maxwell, who attended him with unremitting care, he one day exclaimed, " What business has a physician to waste his time on me ? I am a poor pigeon, not worth plucking. Alas ! I have not feathers enough upon me to carry me to my grave." And though, until the very last, he now and then indulged in sallies of kindly wit, the few letters that remain are all burdened with the same bitter sense of harassing poverty, racking pain, and the most dismal forebodings concerning the future of his bonnie Jean and her soon-to-be fatherless bairns. To James Clarke he again wrote on 26th June :[1]—

My dear Clarke,—Still, still the victim of affliction ! Were you to see the emaciated figure who now holds the pen to you, you would not know your old friend. Whether I shall ever get about again is only known to Him, the Great Unknown, whose creature I am. Alas ! Clarke, I begin to fear the worst. As to my individual self, I am tranquil, and would despise myself if I were not ; but Burns's poor widow, and half a dozen of his dear little ones—helpless orphans ! —there I am weak as a woman's tear. Enough of this. 'Tis half of my disease.

Then to Johnson, editor of the *Musical Museum*, on 4th July :—

How are you, my dear friend, and how comes on your fifth volume ? You may probably think that for some time past I have neglected you and your work ; but, alas ! the hand of pain, and sorrow, and care has these many months lain heavy on me. Personal and domestic affliction have almost entirely banished that alacrity and life with which I used to woo the rural muse of Scotia.

You are a good, worthy, honest fellow, and have a good right to live in this world, because you deserve it. Many a merry meeting this publication has given

---

[1] It has been noted that about this time the Bard's handwriting appears suddenly cramped and small, as if it were that of an aged man.

us, and possibly it may give us more, though, alas! I fear it. This protracting, slow, consuming illness which hangs over me will, I doubt much, my ever dear friend, arrest my sun before he has well reached his middle career, and will turn over the poet to far more important concerns than studying the brilliancy of wit or the pathos of sentiment. However, *hope* is the cordial of the human heart, and I endeavour to cherish it as well as I can.

Let me hear from you as soon as convenient. Your work is a great one; and now that it is finished, I see, if we were to begin again, two or three things that might be mended; yet I will venture to prophesy that to future ages your publication will be the text-book and standard of Scottish song and music.

I am ashamed to ask another favour of you, because you have been so very good already; but my wife has a very particular friend of hers, a young lady [1] who sings well, to whom she wishes to present the *Scots Musical Museum*. If you have a spare copy, will you be so obliging as to send it by the very first *fly*, as I am anxious to have it soon.

In this humble and delicate manner, observes Cromek, did poor Burns ask for a copy of a work of which he was principally the founder, and to which he had contributed, *gratuitously*, not less than 184 original, altered, and collected songs. Cromek further states that he had himself seen 180 songs transcribed by Burns's own hand for the *Museum*.

On 4th July the Poet was conveyed to Brow, a hamlet on the Solway Firth, for sea-bathing and change of air—"his last and only chance." That evening he wrote to Thomson, giving a pitiable description of his wrecked condition, and adding, "Is this a time for me to woo the muses? However, I am still anxiously willing to serve your work, and, if possible, shall try."

On 7th July he wrote to his Edinburgh friend, Alexander Cunningham:—

MY DEAR CUNNINGHAM,—I received yours here this moment, and am indeed highly flattered with the approbation of the literary circle you mention—a

---

[1] Jessie Lewars, in all likelihood.

literary circle inferior to none in the two kingdoms. Alas! my friend, I fear *the voice of the bard will soon be heard among you no more.* For these eight or ten months I have been ailing, sometimes bedfast, and sometimes not; but these last three months I have been tortured with an excruciating rheumatism, which has reduced me to nearly the last stage. You actually would not know me if you saw me. Pale, emaciated, and so feeble as occasionally to need help from my chair—my spirits fled! fled!—but I can no more on the subject; only the medical folks tell me that my last and only chance is bathing and country quarters and riding. The deuce of the matter is this: when an exciseman is off duty, his salary is reduced to £35 instead of £50. What way, in the name of thrift, shall I maintain myself and keep a horse in country quarters, with a wife and five children at home, on £35? I mention this because I had intended to beg your utmost interest, and that of all the friends you can muster, to move our Commissioners of Excise to grant me the full salary; I dare say you know them all personally. If they do not grant it me, I must lay my account with an exit truly *en poëte*—if I die not of disease, I must perish with hunger.

I have sent you one of the songs; the other my memory does not serve me with, and I have no copy here; but I shall be at home soon, when I will send it you. Apropos to being at home: Mrs. Burns threatens in a week or two to add one more to my paternal charge, which, if of the right gender, I intend shall be introduced to the world by the respectable designation of *Alexander Cunningham Burns.* My last was *James Glencairn,* so you can have no objection to the company of nobility. Farewell.

The more cheerful allusion with which this otherwise doleful letter closes is but a lonely lurid ray amid the all-pervading gloom. On Sunday, the 10th, he thus addressed his brother, Gilbert:—

> DEAR BROTHER,—It will be no very pleasing news to you to be told that I am dangerously ill, and not likely to get better. An inveterate rheumatism has reduced me to such a state of debility, and my appetite is so totally gone, that I can scarcely stand on my legs. I have been a week at sea-bathing, and I will continue there, or in a friend's house in the country, all the summer. God keep my wife and children; if I am taken from their head, they will be poor indeed. I have contracted one or two serious debts, partly from my illness these many months, partly from too much thoughtlessness as to expense when I came to town, that will cut in too much of the little I leave them in your hands.

This affecting letter closes with the simple, kindly words, "Remember me to my mother."

Two days afterwards, he penned the last and saddest of all his magnificent letters to Mrs. Dunlop:[1]—

> MADAM,—I have written you so often, without receiving any answer, that I would not trouble you again, but for the circumstances in which I am. An illness, which has long hung about me, in all probability will speedily send me beyond that *bourn whence no traveller returns*. Your friendship, with which for many years you honoured me, was a friendship dearest to my soul. Your conversation, and especially your correspondence, were at once highly entertaining and instructive. With what pleasure did I use to break up the seal! The remembrance yet adds one pulse more to my poor palpitating heart. FAREWELL ! ! !

During his brief stay at Brow, the Poet spent a memorable day with Mrs. Maria Riddel, who was also there on account of failing health. Hearing of his arrival, she invited him to dinner, and sent her carriage to bring him, he being unable to walk. Of that meeting, Mrs. Riddel has left a most interesting and pathetic record :—

> I was struck with his appearance on entering the room. The stamp of death was imprinted on his features. He seemed already touching the brink of eternity. His first salutation was, "Well, madam, have you any commands for the other world?" I replied that it seemed a doubtful case which of us should be there soonest, and that I hoped he would yet live to write my epitaph. He looked in my face with an air of great kindness, and expressed his concern at seeing me look so ill, with his accustomed sensibility. At table, he ate little or nothing, and complained of having entirely lost the tone of his stomach. We had a long and serious conversation about his present situation, and the approaching termination of all his earthly prospects. He spoke of his death, without any of the ostentation of philosophy, but with firmness as well as

---

[1] We would fain believe, as it is asserted, that ere he died Burns received some explanation of this lady's silence, and an assurance of her friendship and esteem. Anyway, Mrs. Dunlop proved a warm friend to the Poet's widow and family.

AN ONLY CHANCE.

feeling, as an event likely to happen very soon, and which gave him concern chiefly from leaving his four children so young and unprotected, and his wife in so interesting a situation—in hourly expectation of lying-in of a fifth. He mentioned, with seeming pride and satisfaction, the promising genius of his eldest son, and the flattering marks of approbation he had received from his teachers, and dwelt particularly on his hopes of that boy's future conduct and merit. His anxiety for his family seemed to hang heavy upon him, and the more perhaps from the reflection that he had not done them all the justice he was so well qualified to do. Passing from this subject, he showed great concern about the care of his literary fame, and particularly the publication of his posthumous works. He said he was well aware that his death would occasion some noise, and that every scrap of his writing would be revived against him, to the injury of his future reputation; that letters and verses written with unguarded and improper freedom, and which he earnestly wished to have buried in oblivion, would be handed about by idle vanity or malevolence, when no dread of his resentment would restrain them, or prevent the censures of shrill-tongued malice, or the insidious sarcasms of envy, from pouring forth all their venom to blast his fame. He lamented that he had written many epigrams on persons against whom he entertained no enmity, and whose characters he should be sorry to wound; and many indifferent poetical pieces, which he feared would now, with all their imperfections on their head, be thrust upon the world. On this account he deeply regretted having deferred to put his papers into a state of arrangement, as he was now quite incapable of that exertion. . . . The conversation was kept up with great evenness and animation on his side. I have seldom seen his mind greater or more collected. There was frequently a considerable degree of vivacity in his sallies, and they would probably have had a greater share had not the concern and dejection I could not disguise damped the spirit of pleasantry he seemed not unwilling to indulge. We parted about sunset on the evening of that day (the 5th of July 1796), and the next day I saw him again, and we parted to meet no more.

Another incident of this time was thus related to Lockhart by Mr. M'Diarmid, Dumfries:—

> Rousseau, we all know, when dying, wished to be carried into the open air, that he might obtain a parting look of the glorious orb of day. A night or two before Burns left Brow, he drank tea with Mrs. Craig, widow of the

minister of Ruthwell. His altered appearance excited much silent sympathy; and the evening being beautiful, and the sun shining brightly through the casement, Miss Craig—now Mrs. Henry Duncan—was afraid the light might be too much for him, and rose with the view of letting down the window-blinds. Burns immediately guessed what she meant; and, regarding the young lady with a look of great benignity, said, "Thank you, my dear, for your kind attention; but oh, let him shine; he will not shine long for me!"

The sea air and bathing effected a slight improvement in the Bard's condition; but in the few days that now remained, he was to know neither freedom from pain nor mental peace. He had incurred a debt of seven pounds in procuring his volunteer uniform, and one day at Brow a lawyer's letter was handed to him, urging payment of this account, else—as it seemed to Burns in his then emaciated, nervous state—imprisonment for debt. Fearing the worst, he hastened to appeal to George Thomson, and to his cousin, James Burness, writer, Montrose.

To Thomson he wrote:—

After all my boasted independence, curst necessity compels me to implore you for five pounds. A cruel scoundrel of a haberdasher, to whom I owe an account, taking it into his head that I am dying, has commenced a process, and will infallibly put me into jail. Do, for God's sake, send me that sum, and that by return of post. Forgive me this earnestness; but the horrors of a jail have made me half distracted. I do not ask all this gratuitously; for, upon returning health, I hereby promise and engage to furnish you with five pounds' worth of the neatest song-genius you have seen. I tried my hand on *Rothiemurchie* this morning. The measure is so difficult, that it is impossible to infuse much genius into the lines; they are on the other side. Forgive, forgive me!

And to his cousin:—

MY DEAR COUSIN,—When you offered me money assistance, little did I think I should want it so soon. A rascal of a haberdasher, to whom I owe a considerable bill, taking it into his head that I am dying, has commenced a process against me, and will infallibly put my emaciated body into jail. Will you be so good as to accommodate me, and that by return of post, with ten pounds? Oh, James! did you know the pride of my heart, you would feel doubly for me! Alas! I am not used to beg. The worst of it is, my health was coming about finely. You know, and my physician assured me, that melancholy and low spirits are half my disease—guess, then, my horrors since this business began. If I had it settled, I would be, I think, quite well in a manner. How shall I use the language to you—oh, do not disappoint me! but strong necessity's curst command.

Forgive me for once more mentioning by return of post—save me from the horrors of a jail!

My compliments to my friend James, and to all the rest. I do not know what I have written. The subject is so horrible, I dare not look it over again. Farewell!

To these appeals his cousin and Thomson promptly responded, sending the desired sums. But can it fail to fill one's heart with pity and shame to think of BURNS having to pen such letters as these. Further, it may be asked, Was it to support his small request from Thomson (upon whom he had so great a claim) that the Poet, tortured both in mind and body, set himself to pen and enclose these, *his last poetic lines*, wherein we discover memory wafting him away back to the glad sweet bygone days he had spent with Peggy Chalmers and Charlotte Hamilton, in and around their Devon Valley home—

  Fairest maid on Devon banks;
   Crystal Devon, winding Devon,
  Wilt thou lay that frown aside
   And smile as thou wert wont to do.

  Full well thou know'st I love thee dear.
  Couldst thou to malice lend an ear?
  Oh, did not love exclaim, "Forbear,
   Nor use a faithful lover so?"

> Then come, thou fairest of the fair,
> Those wonted smiles, oh, let me share!
> And by thy beauteous self I swear,
> No love but thine my heart shall know.

On 14th July, he wrote lovingly, and not without some gleam of hope, to his devoted Jean :—

> My DEAREST LOVE,—I delayed writing until I could tell you what effect sea-bathing was likely to produce. It would be injustice to deny that it has eased my pains, and I think has strengthened me; but my appetite is still extremely bad. No flesh nor fish can I swallow; porridge and milk are the only thing I can taste. I am very happy to hear, by Miss Jess Lewars, that you are all well. My very best and kindest compliments to her, and to all the children. I will see you on Sunday.—Your affectionate husband.

But almost immediately after penning the above, he was seized by a fresh attack of fever. On the 18th, he was taken home in a small spring-cart.

> The ascent to his house being steep—says Cunningham—the cart stopped at the foot of the Mill-hole Brae; when he alighted, he shook much, and stood with difficulty; he seemed unable to stand upright. He stooped as if in pain, and walked tottering towards his own door: his looks were hollow and ghastly, and those who saw him then expected never to see him in life again.

In the experiences of the world's great ones, there have been few home-comings more sad than this. The frenzied letter Burns penned that evening to Jean's father in Mauchline fills up the scene of misery :—

> MY DEAR SIR,—Do, for Heaven's sake, send Mrs. Armour here immediately. My wife is hourly expecting to be put to bed. Good God! what a situation for her to be in, poor girl, without a friend! I returned from sea-bathing quarters to-day, and my medical friends would almost persuade me that I am better; but I think and feel that my strength is so gone that the disorder will prove fatal to me.—Your son-in-law.

THE CLOSING HOURS.

Having, with trembling difficulty, traced out the above, Burns laid aside his mighty pen *for ever*. Throughout that night and the two succeeding days the fever burned higher and higher, rapidly consuming his already far-spent strength, and causing his mind to wander, save when recalled by the sympathetic voices of those who watched at his bedside.

For quiet, his little ones were taken to shelter at Jessie Lewars' home. Now and then Mrs. Burns was assisted from her sick-bed to look for a little at her dying husband. Shortly before he lost all consciousness, a beam of kindly light came to him in the form of a sympathetic letter from his staunchest, best of friends, Mr. Graham, offering means towards helping him to recruit his health. This of course came too late, but, doubtless, it cheered Burns to know of it, and to believe that in such as Mr. Graham he was leaving a few friends, at least, who would not forget him, and would stand by his poor widow and helpless children.

Early in the morning of the 21st, he sank into delirium. The children were brought to take the parting look, and they stood around until he calmly passed into the repose of death. It is said that with almost his latest breath he muttered something about that threatening letter which had so tormented his closing days, and had, as he thought, brought disgrace upon the name of ROBERT BURNS.

When it became known in Dumfries, on his return from Brow, that the poet was dying, a great excitement of sorrow and sympathy prevailed.

> Dumfries—says Cunningham—was like a besieged place. It was known he was dying, and the anxiety, not of the rich and learned only, but of the mechanics and peasants, exceeded all belief. Wherever two or three people stood together, their talk was of Burns, and of him alone. . . . His differences with them on some important points were forgotten and forgiven; they thought only of his genius—of the delight his compositions had diffused; and

they talked of him with the same awe as of some departing spirit, whose voice was to gladden them no more.

Nor was the sorrow which immediately arose on his death confined to Dumfries and its neighbourhood. Surely we need not marvel that it was widespread and profound. Burns's contemporaries in Scotland, while noting his faults and follies, had not failed to mark his mighty mental grasp, his grand poetic gifts, and his essentially true and generous nature. What he had done for our nationality and for mankind was not known then as it now is; but enough was known to send a pang of shame and regret through the hearts of his countrymen, when they reflected that, after all, so little had been done towards more duly appreciating and carefully fostering a "genius so extraordinary."

Of the Bard's funeral, Dr. Currie has left the following account :—

> The Gentlemen Volunteers of Dumfries determined to bury their illustrious associate with military honours, and every preparation was made to render this last service solemn and impressive. The Fencible Infantry of Angusshire, and the Cavalry of the Cinque Ports, at that time quartered in Dumfries, offered their assistance; the principal inhabitants of the town and neighbourhood determined to walk in funeral procession, and a vast concourse of persons assembled, some of them from a considerable distance, to witness the obsequies of the Scottish Bard. On the evening of the 25th of July,[1] the remains of Burns were removed from his house to the Town Hall, and the funeral took place on the following day. A party of volunteers, selected to perform the military duty in the churchyard, stationed themselves in the front of the procession, with their arms reversed; the main body of the corps surrounded and supported the coffin, on which were placed the hat and sword of their friend and fellow-soldier. The numerous body of attendants ranged themselves in the rear; while the fencible regiments of infantry and cavalry lined the streets from the Town Hall to the burial ground in the Southern Churchyard, a

---

[1] The burial took place on Monday, 25th July, the Poet's remains being conveyed to the Town Hall on the evening of Sunday, the 24th.

distance of more than half a mile. The whole procession moved forward to that sublime and affecting strain of music, the Dead March in Saul; and three volleys fired over his grave marked the return of Burns to his parent earth. The spectacle was in a high degree grand and solemn, and accorded with the general sentiments of sympathy and sorrow which the occasion had called forth.

Burns left some £30 of debt, it is said; but at least a considerable part of the £200 he generously handed to his brother Gilbert still remained to his credit. Besides, he had scattered his immortal productions with a lavish hand, asking nothing in return. Be this as it may, however, it is matter for surprise that, in his self-forgetful way, he managed to live on his small income of £70, these four and a half years in Dumfries, with its varied social entanglements, not to speak of his protracted illness, dragging him into extra expenditure. Moreover, that the few debts he had incurred cost him so great pain and anxiety, speaks eloquently of Burns as an *honest man*, whose earnest desire is to "owe no man anything."

This paltry debt was almost immediately cleared off, nor was it long until, in loving memory of the Bard, a number of those who had been his friends, and had enjoyed the privilege, which close acquaintance gave, of knowing the real worth and greatness of his character,—the Riddels, John Syme, George Thomson, Dr. Maxwell, and others,—bestirred themselves to succour his penniless widow and children. A public subscription was set on foot, and an edition of his life and works was projected. To be his first editor and biographer, the choice happily fell on Dr. James Currie, of Liverpool—a man well qualified for the task, both on account of literary ability and sympathetic admiration of the Poet and his writings. This new edition, published in May 1800, yielded £1400; which sum being handed, along with the result of the subscription, to Mrs. Burns, placed her in a position of comfort and comparative plenty wherewith to bring up her "little flock." His painstaking and altogether disinterested labours in this connexion have justly endeared the name of Dr. Currie to the Poet's admirers everywhere.

In volume ii. of this work there already appears, by the late Dr. Rogers, a glowing estimate of Burns and his writings; and in as much as it does not fall within the scope of this narrative to further enter into general disquisition upon the Poet and his marvellous achievements, duly noting, as we ever ought to do, that his errors were those of a uniquely self-forgetful, soaring, impassioned nature, cast in and tempted by a calculating, materialistic, *hard-drinking* age, and proudly rejoicing to think that the spreading fame of the Ayrshire Peasant Bard, Scotland's great national Poet, the world's peerless lyric genius, is safely kept in the heart of humanity, we close our humble endeavour to state the facts of this great tragic life by placing before the reader the graphic description of the Poet which was penned by his first biographer "under advantages which no subsequent writer can enjoy":—

> Burns—says Dr. Currie—was nearly five feet ten inches in height, and of a form that indicated agility as well as strength. His well-raised forehead, shaded with black curling hair, indicated extensive capacity. His eyes were large, dark, full of ardour and intelligence. His face was well formed, and his countenance uncommonly interesting and expressive. His mode of dressing, which was often slovenly, and a certain fulness and bend in the shoulders,—characteristic of his original profession,—disguised in some degree the natural symmetry and elegance of his form. The external appearance of Burns was most strikingly indicative of the character of his mind. On a first view, his physiognomy had a certain air of coarseness, mingled, however, with an expression of deep penetration, and of calm thoughtfulness, approaching to melancholy. There appeared in his first manner and address, perfect ease and self-possession, but a stern and almost supercilious elevation, not, indeed, incompatible with openness and affability, which, however, bespoke a mind conscious of superior talents. Strangers that supposed themselves approaching an Ayrshire peasant

who could make rhymes, and to whom their notice was an honour, found themselves speedily overawed by the presence of a man who bore himself with dignity, and who possessed a singular power of correcting forwardness and of repelling intrusion. But though jealous of the respect due to himself, Burns never enforced it where he saw it was willingly paid; and though inaccessible to the approaches of pride, he was open to every advance of kindness and of benevolence. His dark and haughty countenance easily relaxed into a look of good-will, of pity, or of tenderness; and as the various emotions succeeded each other in his mind, assumed with equal ease the expression of the broadest humour, of the most extravagant mirth, of the deepest melancholy, or of the most sublime emotion. The tones of his voice happily corresponded with the expression of his features and with the feelings of his mind. When to these endowments are added a rapid and distinct apprehension, a most powerful understanding, and a happy command of language,—of strength as well as brilliancy of expression,—we shall be able to account for the extraordinary attractions of his conversation—for the sorcery which, in his social parties, he seemed to exert on all around him. In the company of women, this sorcery was more especially apparent. Their presence charmed the fiend of melancholy in his bosom, and awoke his happiest feelings; it excited the powers of his fancy, as well as the tenderness of his heart; and by restraining the vehemence and the exuberance of his language, at times gave to his manners the impression of taste, and even of elegance, which in the company of men they seldom possessed. This influence was doubtless reciprocal. A Scottish lady, accustomed to the best society, declared with characteristic *naïveté* that no man's conversation ever *carried her so completely off her feet*, as that of Burns; and an English lady, familiarly acquainted with several of the most distinguished characters of the present times, assured the editor, that, in the happiest of his social hours, there was a charm about Burns which she had never seen equalled. This charm arose not more from the power than the versatility of his genius. No languor could be felt in the society of a man who passed at pleasure from *grave to gay*, from the ludicrous to the pathetic, from the simple to the sublime; who wielded all his faculties with equal strength and ease, and never failed to impress the offspring of his fancy with the stamp of his understanding.

This, indeed, is to represent Burns in his happiest phasis. In large and mixed parties, he was often silent and dark, sometimes fierce and overbearing; he was jealous of the proud man's scorn, jealous to an extreme of the insolence of wealth, and prone to avenge, even on its innocent possessor, the partiality of fortune. By nature kind, brave, sincere, and in a singular degree compassionate, he was on the other hand proud, irascible, and vindictive. His virtues and his failings had their origin in the extraordinary sensibility of his mind, and equally partook of the chills and glows of sentiment. His friendships were liable to interruption from jealousy or disgust, and his enmities died away under the influence of pity or self-accusation. His understanding was equal to the other powers of his mind, and his deliberate opinions were singularly candid and just; but, like other men of great and irregular genius, the opinions which he delivered in conversation were often the offspring of temporary feelings, and widely different from the calm decisions of his judgment. This was not merely true respecting the characters of others, but in regard to some of the most important points of human speculation.

APPENDICES.

APPENDIX A.

CONCERNING THE POET'S FAMILY.

The children borne by Jean Armour, and who survived mere infancy, were:—

Robert,	. . born 3rd September 1786,	died	14th May 1857.
Francis Wallace, .	,, 18th August 1789,	,,	in his 14th year.
William Nicol, .	,, 9th April 1791,	,,	21st February 1872.
Elizabeth Riddel,	,, 21st November 1792,	,,	in her 3rd year.
James Glencairn,	,, 12th August 1794,	,,	18th November 1865.
Maxwell, . .	,, 25th July 1796,	,,	in his 3rd year.

Of these, it will be observed that only three—ROBERT, WILLIAM NICOL, and JAMES GLENCAIRN—reached the years of manhood.

ROBERT was first of all trained at Dumfries Grammar School; then attended two sessions at Edinburgh, and one at Glasgow, University. He received an appointment in the Stamp Office, London, from which he retired in 1833, on a modest pension. Returning to Dumfries, he resided there until his death in 1857, aged 71 years. When 22 years of age, he married Anne Sherwood, who died in 1835. Robert and his wife were buried in the Mausoleum in Dumfries Churchyard.

That the Poet's care in the education of his eldest son was not quite thrown away, is evident from the fact that, both in London and Dumfries, Robert was able to increase his income by giving private lessons in classics and mathematics. Like his illustrious father, however, he was not strong either in finance or self-control.

His only surviving daughter, Eliza, became the wife of Dr. Everitt, of the East India Company's Service. Widowed in 1840, she died in 1878, survived by an unmarried daughter, Martha Burns Everitt.

WILLIAM NICOL, educated at Dumfries Grammar School, sailed, in his

16th year, as a midshipman, to India. Serving for 33 years in the Madras Infantry, he at length attained the rank of lieutenant-colonel. He retired from the army in 1843, returned home, and resided with his younger brother at Cheltenham. He died in 1872, aged 81, and was buried in the Mausoleum. In 1822 he married Catherine Crone, who died, childless, in India, in 1841.

JAMES GLENCAIRN, educated at Dumfries Grammar School, and at Christ's Hospital, London, joined the 15th Bengal Native Infantry, and attained the rank of captain. He came home on a visit in 1831, and on his return to India in 1833, was appointed Judge and Collector at Cahar. Retiring in 1839, he lived in London till 1843, then took up house with his brother, William Nicol, at Cheltenham. In 1855 he attained brevet rank as lieutenant-colonel. In 1865 he died, and was buried in the Mausoleum.

In 1818 he married Sarah Robinson, who died in 1821, leaving a daughter, Sarah, who was married to Dr. B. W. Hutchinson, and bore to him three daughters and a son, Robert Burns Hutchinson, the only legitimate male descendant of the Poet.

In 1828 James Glencairn married his second wife, Mary Becket, who died in 1844, leaving one daughter, Ann Becket.

THE POET'S TWO ILLEGITIMATE DAUGHTERS.

ELIZABETH,—"wee image of his bonnie Betty,"—borne by Betty Paton, at Largie-side, Tarbolton, in 1784, was brought up under the care of the Poet's mother. At 21 she received from a fund raised in London a dowry of £200. Married to John Bishop, overseer, Polkemmet, she bore him several children. She died in 1817, aged 32, and was buried in Whitburn Churchyard, where a monument stands to her memory.

ELIZABETH, borne by Ann Park, at the Globe Tavern, Dumfries, in 1791, was reared by Bonnie Jean as one of her own family. At 21 she also received £200 from the above-mentioned fund. Married to John Thomson, Pollokshaws, she bore him two sons—Robert Burns and James—and five daughters—Jean Armour, Agnes, Eliza, Sarah, and Maggie. Robert Burns Thomson inherited a certain measure of poetic gift, and wrote some excellent pieces

APPENDIX A.

In June 1879 Maggie Thomson, the youngest daughter, was married to David Wingate, the well-known Scotch poet. From 1859 until her decease in 1873 Mrs. Thomson received £30 per annum from a fund raised in Glasgow for her behoof.

In the first chapter of this volume are found full genealogical notes regarding the Poet's brothers and sisters (see pp. 64 to 74). His mother, Agnes Brown, long surviving, found a home with Gilbert Burns until her death in 1820, in her 88th year, and in the 36th year of her widowhood.

Jean Armour lived on in comfortable circumstances in the house in Burns Street, wherein the Poet breathed his last. She died on 26th March 1834, in her 69th year, and in the 38th year of her widowhood. Her remains were placed in the Mausoleum, near to the coffin of her immortal husband, to whom she had proved a wife most faithful, long-suffering, and affectionate.

APPENDIX B.

MANUAL OF RELIGIOUS BELIEF.

THE following is the text of this remarkable compendium, compiled by worthy William Burness, and used by him in the instruction of the Poet, in common with the rest of the family circle at Lochlea.

Son. Dear father, you have often told me, while you were initiating me into the Christian religion, that you stood bound for me, to give me a Christian education, and recommended a religious life to me. I would therefore, if you please, ask you a few questions that may tend to confirm my faith, and clear its evidences to me.

Father. My dear child, with gladness I will resolve to you (so far as I am able), any question you shall ask, only with this caution, that you will believe my answers, if they are founded in the Word of God.

Question. How shall I evidence to myself that there is a God?

Answer. By the works of creation : for nothing can make itself ; and this fabric of Nature demonstrates its Creator to be possessed of all possible perfection, and for that cause we owe all that we have to Him.

Q. If God be possessed of all possible perfection, ought not we then to love Him as well as fear Him?

A. Yes; we ought to serve Him out of love, for His perfections give us delightful prospects of His favour and friendship, for if we serve Him out of love, we will endeavour to be like Him, and God will love His own image, and if God love us, He will rejoice over us and do us good.

Q. Then one would think this were sufficient to determine all men to love God ; but how shall we account for so much wickedness in the world?

A. God's revealed Word teaches us that our first parents brake His Covenant, and deprived us of the influences of His grace that were to be expected in that state, and introduced sin into the world ; and the Devil, that great enemy of God and man, laying hold on this instrument, his kingdom has made great progress in the world.

Q. But has God left His own rational offspring thus, to the tyranny of His and their enemy?

A. No: for God hath addressed His rational creatures, by telling them in His Revealed Word, that the seed of the woman should bruise the head of the Serpent, or Devil, or in time destroy his kingdom; and in the meantime, every one oppressed with the tyranny of the Devil, should, through the promised seed, by faith in Him, and humble supplication, and a strenuous use of their own faculties, receive such measures of grace, in and through this method of God's conveyance, as should make them able to overcome.

Q. But by what shall I know that this is a revelation of God, and not a cunningly devised fable?

A. A revelation of God must have these four marks. 1. It must be worthy of God to reveal; 2. It must answer all the necessities of human nature; 3. It must be sufficiently attested by miracles; and 4. It is known by prophecies and their fulfilment. That it is worthy of God is plain, by its addressing itself to the reason of men, and plainly laying before them the dangers to which they are liable, with motives and arguments to persuade them to their duty, and promising such rewards as are fitted to promote the happiness of a rational soul. Secondly, it provides for the guilt of human nature, making an atonement by a Mediator; and for its weakness by promising the assistance of God's Spirit; and for its happiness, by promising a composure of mind, by the regulation of its faculties, and reducing the appetites and passions of the body unto the subjection of reason enlightened by the Word of God, and by a resurrection of the body, and a glorification of both soul and body in heaven, and that to last through all eternity. Thirdly, as a miracle is a contradiction of known laws of Nature, demonstrating that the worker has the power of Nature in his hands, and consequently must be God, or sent by His commission and authority from Him, to do such and such things. That this is the case in our Scriptures is evident both by the prophets, under the Old, and our Saviour under the New Testament. Whenever it served for the glory of God, or for the confirmation of their commissions, all Nature was obedient to them; the elements were at their command, also the sun and moon, yea, life and death. Fourthly, that prophecies were fulfilled at a distance of many hundreds of years is evident by comparing the following texts of Scripture:—Gen. xlix. 10, 11; Matt. xxi. 5; Isa. vii. 14; Matt. i. 22, 23; Luke i. 34; Isa. xl. 1; Matt. iii. 3; Mark i. 3; Luke iii. 4; John i. 23; Isa. xlii. 1, 2, 3, 4. A description of the character of Messiah in the Old Testament Scriptures is fulfilled in all the Evangelists. In Isa. l. 5, His sufferings are prophesied, and exactly fulfilled in the New Testament, Matt. xxvi. 67, and xxvii. 26; and many others, as that Abraham's seed should be strangers in a strange land four hundred years, and being brought to Canaan, and its accomplishment in the days of Joseph, Moses, and Joshua.

Q. Seeing the Scriptures are proven to be a revelation of God to His creatures, am not I indispensably bound to believe and obey them?

A. Yes.

Q. Am I equally bound to obey all the laws delivered to Moses upon Mount Sinai?

A. No; the laws delivered to Moses are of three kinds: first, the Moral Law, which is of eternal and indispensable obligation on all ages and nations; secondly, the law of Sacrifices and Ordinances were only ordinances in which were couched types and shadows of things to come, and when that dispensation was at an end, this law ended with them, for Christ is the end of the law for righteousness; thirdly, laws that respected the Jewish Commonwealth can neither be binding on us, who are not of that Commonwealth, nor on the Jews, because their Commonwealth is at an end.

Q. If the Moral Law be of indispensable obligation, I become bound to perfect and perpetual obedience, of which I am incapable, and on that account cannot hope to be justified and accepted with God.

A. The Moral Law, as a rule of life, must be of indispensable obligation, but it is the glory of the Christian religion, that, if we be upright in our endeavours to follow it, and sincere in our repentance, upon our failing or shortening, we shall be accepted according to what we have, and shall increase in our strength, by the assistance of the Spirit of God co-operating with our honest endeavours.

Q. Seeing the assistance of the Spirit of God is absolutely necessary for salvation, hath not God clearly revealed by what means we may obtain this great blessing?

A. Yes; the Scriptures tell us that the Spirit of God is the purchase of Christ's mediatorial office; and through faith in Him, and our humble prayers to God through Christ, we shall receive such measures thereof as shall answer our wants.

Q. What do you understand by Faith?

A. Faith is a firm persuasion of the Divine mission of our Lord Jesus Christ, and that He is made unto us of God, wisdom, righteousness, and complete redemption; or as He is represented to us under the notion of a root, and we the branches, deriving all from Him; or as the head, and we the members of His body: intimating to us that this is the way or channel through which God conveys His blessings to us, and we are not to expect them but in God's own way. It is therefore a matter of consequence to us, and therefore we ought with diligence to search the Scriptures, and the extent of His commission, or what they declare Him to be, and to receive Him accordingly, and to acquiesce in God's plan of our salvation.

Q. By what shall I know that Jesus Christ is really the person that was prophesied of in the Old Testament; or that He was that seed of the woman that was to destroy the kingdom of sin?

A. Besides the Scriptures fore-cited, which fully prove Him to be that blessed person, Christ did many miracles; He healed the sick, gave sight to the blind, made the lame to walk, raised the dead, and fed thousands with a few loaves, etc. He foretold His own death and resurrection, and the wonderful progress of His religion, in spite of all the power of the Roman Empire—and that by means of His disciples, a few illiterate fishermen.

Q. You speak of repentance as absolutely necessary to salvation—I would like to know what you mean by repentance?

A. I not only mean a sorrowing for sin, but a labouring to see the malignant nature of it; as setting nature at variance with herself, by placing the animal part before the rational, and thereby putting ourselves on a level with the brute beasts, the consequence of which will be an intestine war in the human frame, until the rational part be entirely weakened, which is spiritual death, and

APPENDIX B. 313

which in the nature of the thing renders us unfit for the society of God's spiritual kingdom, and to see the beauty of holiness. On the contrary, setting the rational part above the animal, though it promote a war in the human frame, every conflict and victory affords us grateful reflection, and tends to compose the mind more and more, not to the utter destruction of the animal part, but to the real and true enjoyment of both, by placing Nature in the order that its Creator designed it, which, in the natural consequences of the thing, promotes Spiritual Life, and renders us more and more fit for Christ's spiritual kingdom; and not only so, but gives to animal life pleasure and joy that we never could have had without it.

Q. I should be glad to hear you at large upon religion giving pleasure to animal life; for it is represented as taking up our cross and following Christ.

A. Our Lord honestly told His disciples of their danger, and what they were to expect by being His followers, that the world would hate them, and for this reason, because they were not of the world, even as He also was not of the world; but He gives them sufficient comfort, showing that He had overcome the world; as if He had said, "You must arm yourself with a resolution to fight, for if you be resolved to be My disciples, you expose the world, by setting their folly in its true light, and therefore every one who is not brought over by your example, will hate and oppose you as it hath Me; but as it hath had no advantage against Me, and I have overcome it, if you continue the conflict, you, by My strength, shall overcome likewise;" so that this declaration of our Lord cannot damp the pleasures of life when rightly considered, but rather enlarges them. The same revelation tells us, that a religious life hath the promise of the life that now is, and that which is to come; and not only by the well regulated mind described in my last answer, as tending to give pleasure and quiet, but by a firm trust in the providence of God, and by the help of an honest calling industriously pursued, we shall receive such a portion of the comfortable things of this life as shall be fittest for promoting our eternal interest, and that under the direction of infinite wisdom and goodness; and that we shall overcome all our difficulties by being under the protection of infinite power. These considerations cannot fail to give a relish to all the pleasures of life. Besides the very nature of the thing giving pleasure to a mind so regular as I have already described, it must exalt the mind above those irregular passions that jar and are contrary one to another, and distract the mind by contrary pursuits, which is described by the apostle with more strength in his Epistle to the Romans (chap. i., from 26 to the end) than any words I am capable of framing; especially if we take our Lord's explanation of the parable of the tares in the field as an improvement of these doctrines, as it is in Matt. xiii., from the 37th to the 44th verse; and Rev. xx., from verse 11 to the end. If these Scriptures, seriously considered, can suffer any man to be easy, judge ye, and they will remain truth, whether believed or not. Whereas, on a mind regular, and having the animal part under subjection to the rational, in the very nature of the thing gives uniformity of pursuits. The desires, rectified by the Word of God, must give clearness of judgment, soundness of mind, regular affections, whence will flow peace of conscience, good hope, through grace, that all our interests are under the care of our Heavenly Father. This gives a relish to animal life itself, this joy that no man intermeddleth with, and which is peculiar to a Christian or holy life; and its comforts and blessings the whole Scripture is a comment upon, especially our Lord's sermon upon the Mount, Matt. v. 1-13, and its progress in the parable of the Sower in the thirteenth of Matthew.[1]

---

[1] The "Manual" bears that it was *transcribed* for William Burness by John Murdoch, the Poet's teacher; but, judging from one or two extant letters penned by William Burness, it would appear that in the preparation of the "Manual" Murdoch's part was more than that of mere transcriber.

APPENDIX C.

THE POET'S COMMONPLACE BOOKS.

The opening remarks of these very interesting documents fully explain the author's purpose and plan.

First Commonplace Book.

Observations, Hints, Songs, Scraps of Poetry, etc., by Robert Burness, a man who had little art in making money, and still less in keeping it; but was, however, a man of some sense, a great deal of honesty, and unbounded goodwill to every creature, rational and irrational.—As he was but little indebted to scholastic education, and bred at a plough-tail, his performances must be strongly tinctured with his unpolished, rustic way of life; but as I believe they are really his own, it may be some entertainment to a curious observer of human nature to see how a ploughman thinks and feels, under the pressure of love, ambition, anxiety, grief, with the like cares and passions, which, however diversified by the modes and manners of life, operate pretty much alike, I believe, on all the species.

"There are numbers in the world who do not want sense to make a figure, so much as an opinion of their own abilities to put them upon recording their observations, and allowing them the same importance which they do to those which appear in print."—Shenstone.

> " Pleasing, when youth is long expired, to trace
> The forms our pencil, or our pen, designed!
> Such was our youthful air, and shape, and face,
> Such the soft image of our youthful mind."—Ibid.

April 1783.

Notwithstanding all that has been said against love, respecting the folly and weakness it leads a young experienced mind into, still I think it in a great measure deserves the highest encomiums that have been passed upon it. If anything on earth deserves the name of rapture or transport, it is the feelings of green eighteen in the company of the mistress of his heart, when she repays him with an equal return of affection.

August.

There is certainly some connection between love and poetry; and, therefore, I have always thought it a fine touch of nature, that passage in a modern love composition:—

    As towards her cot he jogg'd along,
    Her name was frequent in his song.

For my own part, I never had the least thought or inclination of turning poet till I got once heartily in love, and then rhyme and song were, in a manner, the spontaneous language of my heart. The following composition was the first of my performances, and done at an early period of life, when my heart glowed with honest, warm simplicity; unacquainted and uncorrupted with the ways of a wicked world. The performance is, indeed, very puerile and silly; but I am always pleased with it, as it recalls to my mind those happy days when my heart was yet honest, and my tongue was sincere. The subject of it was a young girl who really deserved all the praises I have bestowed on her. I not only had this opinion of her then—but I actually think so still, now that the spell is long since broken, and the enchantment at an end.

SONG.

Tune—"I am a man unmarried."

    O once I lov'd a bonnie lass,
      Ay, and I love her still,
    And whilst that honour warms my breast
      I'll love my handsome Nell.

CRITICISM ON THE FOREGOING SONG.

Lest my works should be thought below criticism, or meet with a critic who, perhaps, will not look on them with so candid and favourable an eye, I am determined to criticise them myself.

The first distic of the first stanza is quite too much in the flimsy strain of our ordinary street ballads; and, on the other hand, the second distic is too much in the other extreme. The expression is a little awkward, and the sentiment too serious. Stanza the second I am well pleased with, and I think it conveys a fine idea of that amiable part of the sex—the agreeables, or what in our Scotch dialect we call a sweet sonsy lass. The third stanza has a little of the flimsy turn in it, and the third line has rather too serious a cast. The fourth stanza is a very indifferent one; the first line is, indeed, all in the strain of the second stanza, but the rest is mostly an expletive. The thoughts in the fifth stanza come finely up to my favourite idea—a sweet sonsy lass; the last line, however, halts a little. The same sentiments are kept up with equal spirit and tenderness in the sixth stanza, but the second and fourth lines ending with short syllables hurt the whole. The seventh stanza has several minute faults, but I remember I composed it in a wild enthusiasm of passion, and to this hour I never recollect it but my heart melts, my blood sallies, at the remembrance.

September.

I entirely agree with that judicious philosopher, Mr. Smith, in his excellent Theory of Moral Sentiments, that remorse is the most painful sentiment that can embitter the human bosom. Any ordinary pitch of fortitude may bear up tolerably well under these calamities, in the procurement of which we ourselves have had no hand; but when our own follies, or crimes, have made us miserable and wretched, to bear up with manly firmness, and at the same time have a proper penitential sense of our misconduct, is a glorious effort of self-command.

Of all the numerous ills that hurt our peace.

March 1784.

A penitential thought, in the hour of Remorse : Intended for a tragedy.

All devil as I am, a damned wretch.

I have often observed, in the course of my experience of human life, that every man, even the worst, have something good about them; though very often nothing else than a happy temperament of constitution inclining him to this or that virtue; on this likewise depend a great many, no man can say how many of our vices; for this reason, no man can say in what degree any other person, besides himself, can be, with strict justice, called wicked. Let any of the strictest character for regularity of conduct among us, examine impartially how many of his virtues are owing to constitution and education; how many vices he has never been guilty of, not from any care or vigilance, but for want of opportunity, or some accidental circumstance intervening; how many of the weaknesses of mankind he has escaped, because he was out of the line of such temptation; and, what often, if not always, weighs more than all the rest, how much he is indebted to the world's good opinion, because the world does not know all; I say, any man who can thus think, will scan the failings, nay, the faults and crimes, of mankind around him, with a brother's eye.

March 1784.

I have often coveted the acquaintance of that part of mankind, commonly known by the ordinary phrase of BLACKGUARDS, sometimes farther than was consistent with the safety of my character; those who, by thoughtless prodigality or headstrong passions, have been driven to ruin :—though disgraced by follies, nay, sometimes " Stain'd with guilt, and crimson'd o'er with crimes ; " I have yet found among them, not a few instances, some of the noblest virtues, magnanimity, generosity, disinterested friendship, and even modesty, in the highest perfection.

March 1784.

There was a certain period of my life, that my spirit was broke by repeated losses and disasters, which threatened, and indeed effected, the utter ruin of my fortune. My body, too, was attacked by that most dreadful distemper, a hypochondria, or confirmed melancholy; in this wretched state, the recollection of which makes me yet shudder, I hung my harp on the willow trees, except in some lucid intervals, in one of which I composed the following :—

O Thou Great Being! what Thou art.

April.

As I am what the men of the world, if they knew of such a man, would call a whimsical mortal; I have various sources of pleasure and enjoyment, which are, in a manner, peculiar to myself, or some here and there such other out-of-the-way person. Such is the peculiar pleasure I take in the season of winter, more than the rest of the year. This, I believe, may be partly owing to my misfortunes giving my mind a melancholy cast; but there is something even in the

Mighty tempest, and the hoary waste,
Abrupt and deep, stretch'd o'er the buried earth,

which raises the mind to a serious sublimity, favourable to everything great and noble. There is scarcely any earthly object gives me more—I do not know if I should call it pleasure—but something which exalts me, something which enraptures me—than to walk in the sheltered side of a wood, or high plantation, in a cloudy winter-day, and hear the stormy wind howling among the trees, and raving over the plain. It is my best season for devotion; my mind is wrapt up in a kind of enthusiasm to Him, who, in the pompous language of Scripture, " walks on the wings of the wind." In one of these seasons, just after a train of misfortunes, I composed the following :—

SONG.

Tune—" M'Pherson's Farewell."

The wintry west extends his blast.

APPENDIX C. 319

April.

The following song is a wild rhapsody, miserably deficient in versification; but as the sentiments are the genuine feelings of my heart, for that reason I have a particular pleasure in conning it over.

SONG.

Tune—"The weaver and his shuttle O."

My father was a farmer.

April.

Shenstone observes finely, that love-verses, writ without any real passion, are the most nauseous of all conceits; and I have often thought that no man can be a proper critic of love composition, except he himself, in one or more instances, have been a warm votary of this passion. As I have been all along a miserable dupe to love, and have been led into a thousand weaknesses and follies by it, for that reason I put the more confidence in my critical skill, in distinguishing foppery and conceit from real passion and nature. Whether the following song will stand the test, I will not pretend to say, because it is my own; only I can say it was, at the time, real.

SONG.

Tune—"As I came in by London O."

Behind yon hill where Lugar flows.

April.

EPITAPH ON WM. HOOD, SENR.,

IN TARBOLTON.

ON JAS. GRIEVE, LAIRD OF BOGHEAD,

TARBOLTON.

April.

EPITAPH

ON MY OWN FRIEND, AND MY FATHER'S FRIEND,

WM. MUIR IN TARBOLTON MILN.

April.

EPITAPH ON MY EVER HONOURED FATHER.

April.

I think the whole species of young men may be naturally enough divided in grand classes, which I shall call the *grave* and the *merry;* though, by the bye, these terms do not with propriety enough express my ideas. There are, indeed, some exceptions; some part of the species who, according to my ideas of these divisions, come under neither of them; such are those individuals whom Nature turns off her hand, oftentimes, very like *Blockheads*, but generally, on a nearer inspection, have some things surprisingly clever about them. They are more properly men of conceit than men of genius; men whose heads are filled, and whose faculties are engrossed by some whimsical notions in some art or science; so that they cannot think, nor speak with pleasure, on any other subject.—Besides this pedantic species, Nature has always produced some mere, insipid blockheads, who may be said to live a vegetable life in this world.

The *grave* I shall cast into the usual division of those who are goaded on by the love of money; and those whose darling wish is to make a figure in the world. The *merry* are the men of pleasure of all denominations; the jovial lads, who have too much fire and spirit to have any settled rule of action; but, without much deliberation, follow the strong impulses of nature : the thoughtless, the careless, the indolent—in particular *he* who, with a happy sweetness of natural temper and a cheerful vacancy of thought, steals through life— generally, indeed, in poverty and obscurity—but poverty and obscurity are only evils to him who can sit gravely down and make a repining comparison between his own situation and that of others; and lastly, to grace the quorum, such are, generally, those whose heads are capable of all the towerings of genius, and whose hearts are warmed with all the delicacy of feeling.

August.

The foregoing was to have been an elaborate dissertation on the various species of men; but, as I cannot please myself in the arrangement of my ideas, I must wait till further experience and nicer observation throw more light on the subject.—In the meantime, I shall set down the following fragment, which, as it is the genuine language of my heart, will enable anybody to determine which of the classes I belong to:—

There's nought but care on ev'ry han'.

As the grand end of human life is to cultivate an intercourse with that BEING to whom we owe life, with every enjoyment that renders life delightful; and to maintain an integritive conduct towards our fellow-creatures; that so, by forming piety and virtue into habit, we may be fit members for that society of the pious and the good, which reason and revelation teach us to expect beyond the grave, I do not see that the turn of mind and pursuits of such a one as the above verses describe—one who spends the hours and thoughts which the vocations of the day can spare with Ossian, Shakespeare, Thomson, Shenstone, Sterne, etc.; or, as the maggot takes him, a gun, a fiddle, or a song to make or mend; and at all times some heart's-dear bonnie lass in view—I say I do not see that the

APPENDIX C.

turn of mind and pursuits of such an one are in the least more inimical to the sacred interests of piety and virtue, than the, even lawful, bustling and straining after the world's riches and honours: and I do not see but he may gain heaven as well—which, by the bye, is no mean consideration—who steals through the vale of life, amusing himself with every little flower that fortune throws in his way, as he who, straining straight forward, and perhaps spattering all about him, gains some of life's little eminences, where, after all, he can only see and be seen a little more conspicuously than what, in the pride of his heart, he is apt to term the poor, indolent devil he has left behind him.

August.

A Prayer, when fainting fits, and other alarming symptoms of a pleurisy or some other dangerous disorder, which indeed still threatens me, first put nature on the alarm:—

O Thou unknown, Almighty cause.

August.

Misgivings in the hour of Despondency and prospect of Death.

Why am I loth to leave this earthly scene?

September.

SONG.

Tune—" Invercald's reel—Strathspey."

Tibby, I hae seen the day.

September.

SONG.

Tune—" Black Joke."

My girl she's airy, she's buxom and gay.

JOHN BARLEYCORN—A Song to its own Tune.

I once heard the old song, that goes by this name, sung, and being very fond of it, and remembering only two or three verses of it, viz. the 1st, 2nd, and 3rd, with some scraps which I have interwoven here and there in the following piece:—

June 1785.

There were three kings into the East.

June.

The death and dyin' words o' poor Mailie—my ain pet ewe—an unco mournfu' tale.
    As Mailie and her lambs thegither
    Were ae day nibblin' on the tether.

June.

A letter sent to John Lapraik, near Muirkirk, a true, genuine, Scottish Bard.

1st April 1785.
    While breers and woodbines budding green.

On receiving an answer to the above I wrote the following:

21st April 1785.
    When new ca't ky rowt at the stake.

August.

SONG.

Tune—"Peggy Bawn."
    When chill November's surly blast.

August.

However I am pleased with the works of our Scotch poets, particularly the excellent Ramsay, and the still more excellent Fergusson, yet I am hurt to see other places of Scotland, their towns, rivers, woods, haughs, etc., immortalized in such celebrated performances, while my dear native country, the ancient bailieries of Carrick, Kyle, and Cunningham, famous both in ancient and modern times for a gallant and warlike race of inhabitants; a country where civil, and particularly religious liberty have ever found their first support, and their last asylum; a country, the birthplace of many famous philosophers, soldiers, and statesmen, and the scene of many important events recorded in Scottish history, particularly a great many of the actions of the glorious WALLACE, the SAVIOUR of his country; yet, we have never had a Scotch poet of any eminence, to make the fertile banks of Irvine, the romantic woodlands and sequestered scenes on Aire, and the heathy mountainous source and winding sweep of DOON, emulate Tay, Forth, Ettrick, Tweed, etc. This is a complaint I would gladly remedy, but, alas! I am far unequal to the task, both in native genius and education.

Obscure I am, and obscure I must be, though no young poet, nor young soldier's heart ever beat more fondly for fame than mine—

  And if there is no other scene of being
  Where my insatiate wish may have its fill,—
  This something at my heart that heaves for room,
  My best, my dearest part, was made in vain.

August.

A FRAGMENT.

Tune—"I had a horse and I had nae mair."

When first I came to Stewart Kyle.

HAR'STE.—A FRAGMENT.

Tune—Foregoing.

Now breezy win's and slaughtering guns.

September.

  There is a certain irregularity in the old Scotch songs, a redundancy of syllables with respect to the exactness of accent and measure that the English poetry requires, but which glides in, most melodiously, with the respective tunes to which they are set. For instance, the fine old song of "The Mill, Mill, O," to give it a plain, prosaic reading, it halts prodigiously out of measure; on the other hand, the song set to the same tune in Bremner's collection of Scotch songs, which begins "To Fanny fair could I impart," etc., it is most exact measure; and yet, let them both be sung before a real critic,—one above the biasses of prejudice, but a thorough judge of nature,—how flat and spiritless will the last appear, how trite and lamely methodical, compared with the wild-warbling cadence, the heart-moving melody of the first!—This particularly is the case with all those airs which end with a hypermetrical syllable. There is a degree of wild irregularity in many of the compositions and fragments which are daily sung to them by my compeers, the common people—a certain happy arrangement of old Scotch syllables, and yet, very frequently, nothing, not even like rhyme, or sameness of jingle, at the ends of the lines. This has made me sometimes imagine that, perhaps, it might be possible for a Scotch poet, with a nice judicious ear, to set compositions to many of our most favourite airs, particularly that class of them mentioned above, independent of rhyme altogether.

  There is a noble sublimity, a heart-melting tenderness, in some of these ancient fragments, which show them to be the work of a masterly hand: and it has often given me many a heartache to reflect that such glorious old bards—

bards who very probably owed all their talents to native genius, yet have described the exploits of heroes, the pangs of disappointment, and the meltings of love, with such fine strokes of nature—and, O how mortifying to a bard's vanity! their very names are "buried 'mongst the wreck of things which were."

O ye illustrious names unknown! who could feel so strongly and describe so well; the last, the meanest of the muses' train—one who, though far inferior to your flights, yet eyes your path, and with trembling wing would sometimes soar after you—a poor rustic bard unknown, pays this sympathetic pang to your memory! Some of you tell us, with all the charms of verse, that you have been unfortunate in the world—unfortunate in love; he, too, has felt all the unfitness of a poetic heart for the struggle of a busy, bad world, he has felt the loss of his little fortune, the loss of friends, and, worse than all, the loss of the woman he adored. Like you, all his consolation was his muse: she taught him in rustic measures to complain—Happy could he have done it with your strength of imagination and flow of verse! May the turf rest lightly on your bones! and may you now enjoy that solace and rest which this world rarely gives to the heart tuned to all the feelings of poesy and love!

September.

The following fragment is done something in imitation of the manner of a noble old Scotch piece called "M'Millan's Peggy," and sings to the tune of Galla Water.—My "Montgomerie's Peggie" was my deity for six or eight months. She had been bred (though, as the world says, without any just pretence for it) in a style of life rather elegant—but, as Vanburgh says in one of his comedies, "My damn'd star found me out" there too; for though I began the affair merely in a *gaieté de cœur*, or to tell the truth, which will scarcely be believed, a vanity of showing my parts in courtship, particularly my abilities at a *billet-doux*, which I always piqued myself upon, made me lay siege to her; and when, as I always do in my foolish gallantries, I had battered myself into a very warm affection for her, she told me, one day, in a flag of truce, that her fortress had been for some time before the rightful property of another; but, with the greatest friendship and politeness, she offered me every alliance except actual possession. I found out afterwards that what she told me of a preengagement was really true; but it cost some heart-aches to get rid of the affair.

I have even tried to imitate, in this extempore thing, that irregularity in the rhyme, which, when judiciously done, has such a fine effect on the ear.

Altho' my bed were in yon muir.

September.

Another fragment in imitation of an old Scotch song, well known among the country ingle sides—I cannot tell the name, neither of the song nor the tune, but they are in fine unison with one another.—By the way, these old

APPENDIX C. 325

Scottish airs are so nobly sentimental, that when one would compose to them, to "south the tune," as our Scotch phrase is, over and over, is the readiest way to catch the inspiration, and raise the bard into that glorious enthusiasm so strongly characteristic of our old Scotch poetry. I shall here set down one verse of the piece mentioned above, both to mark the song and tune I mean, and likewise as a debt I owe to the author, as the repeating of that verse has lighted up my flame a thousand times.

Alluding to the misfortunes he feelingly laments before this verse

<blockquote>
When clouds in skies do come together
To hide the brightness of the sun,
There will surely be some pleasant weather
When a' thir storms are past and gone.
</blockquote>

<blockquote>
Though fickle fortune has deceived me,
  She promis'd fair and perform'd but ill;
Of mistress, friends, and wealth bereav'd me,
  Yet I bear a heart shall support me still.

I'll act with prudence as far's I'm able,
  But if success I must never find,
Then come misfortune, I bid thee welcome,
  I'll meet thee with an undaunted mind.
</blockquote>

The above was an extempore, under the pressure of a heavy train of misfortunes, which, indeed, threatened to undo me altogether. It was just at the close of that dreadful period already mentioned, and though the weather has brightened up a little with me, yet there has always been since "a tempest brewing round me in the grim sky" of futurity, which I pretty plainly see will some time or other, perhaps ere long, overwhelm me, and drive me into some doleful dell, to pine in solitary, squalid wretchedness. However, as I hope my poor country muse, who, all rustic, awkward, and unpolished as she is, has more charms for me than any other of the pleasures of life beside—as I hope she will not then desert me, I may even then learn to be, if not happy, at least easy, and *south a sang* to soothe my misery.

'Twas at the same time I set about composing an air in the old Scotch style. —I am not musical scholar enough to prick down my tune properly, so it can never see the light, and perhaps 'tis no great matter; but the following were the verses I composed to suit it :—

<blockquote>O raging fortune's withering blast.</blockquote>

The tune consisted of three parts, so that the above verses just went through the whole air.

October 1785.

If ever any young man, in the vestibule of the world, chance to throw his eye over these pages, let him pay a warm attention to the following observations, as I assure him they are the fruit of a poor devil's dear-bought experience. —I have literally, like that great poet and great gallant, and, by consequence, that great fool, Solomon, "turned my eyes to behold madness and folly." Nay, I have, with all the ardour of lively, fanciful, and whimsical imagination, accompanied with a warm, feeling, poetic heart, shaken hands with their intoxicating friendship.

In the first place, let my pupil, as he tenders his own peace, keep up a regular, warm intercourse with the Deity—

[*Here the MS. closes.*]

SECOND COMMONPLACE BOOK.

EDINBURGH, *9th April* 1787.

As I have seen a good deal of human life in Edinburgh, a great many characters which are new to one bred up in the shades of life as I have been, I am determined to take down my remarks on the spot. Gray observes in a letter of his to Mr. Palgrave, that "half a word fixed upon, or near the spot, is worth a cart-load of recollection." I don't know how it is with the world in general, but, with me, making remarks is by no means a solitary pleasure. I want some one to laugh with me, some one to be grave with me, some one to please me and help my discrimination with his or her own remark; and at times, no doubt, to admire my acuteness and penetration.—The world are so busied with selfish pursuits, ambition, vanity, interest, or pleasure, that very few think it worth their while to make any observation on what passes around them; except where that observation is a sucker, or branch of the darling plant they are rearing in their fancy. Nor am I sure, notwithstanding all the sentimental flights of novel-writers, and the sage philosophy of moralists, if we are capable of so intimate and cordial a coalition of friendship, as that one of us may pour out his bosom, his every thought and floating fancy, his very inmost soul, with unreserved confidence to another, without hazard of losing part of that respect man demands from man; or, from the unavoidable imperfections attending human nature, of one day repenting his confidence.

For these reasons, I am determined to make these pages my confidant. I will sketch every character that any way strikes me, to the best of my observation, with unshrinking justice. I will insert anecdotes and take down remarks, in the old law phrase, without feud or favour: where I hit on anything clever, my own applause will in some measure feast my vanity; and, begging Patroclus' and Achates' pardon, I think a lock and key a security at least equal to the bosom of any friend whatever.

My own private story likewise, my amours, my rambles, the smiles and frowns of fortune on my bardship, my poems and fragments that must never see the light, shall be occasionally inserted:—in short, never did four shillings purchase so much friendship, since confidence went first to market, or honesty was set to sale.

To these seemingly invidious, but too just, ideas of human friendship, I shall cheerfully and truly make one exception—the connection between two persons of different sex, when their interests are united or absorbed by the sacred tie of love—

"When thought meets thought ere from the lips it part,
And each warm wish springs mutual from the heart."

There, confidence, confidence that exalts them the more in one another's opinion, that endears them the more to one another's hearts, unreservedly and luxuriantly "reigns and revels." But this is not my lot, and, in my situation, if I am wise (which, by the bye, I have no great chance of being), my fate should be cast with the Psalmist's sparrow, "to watch alone on the housetops." Oh, the pity!!!

A FRAGMENT.

Tune—"Daintie Davie."

There was a birkie born in Kyle.

There are few of the sore evils under the sun give me more uneasiness and chagrin than the comparison how a man of genius, nay, avowed worth, is everywhere received, with the reception which a mere ordinary character, decorated with the trappings and futile distinctions of Fortune, meets.—Imagine a man of abilities, his breast glowing with honest pride, conscious that men are born equal, still giving that "honour to whom honour is due;" he meets at a great man's table a Squire Something, or a Sir Somebody; he knows the noble landlord at heart gives the Bard or whatever he is a share of his good wishes beyond any at table perhaps, yet how will it mortify him to see a fellow whose abilities would scarcely have made an eightpenny tailor, and whose heart is not worth three farthings, meet with attention and notice that are forgot to the Son of Genius and poverty?

The noble Glencairn has wounded me to the soul here, because I dearly esteem, respect, and love him.—He showed so much attention, engrossing attention, one day to the only blockhead, as there was none but his lordship, the dunderpate, and myself, that I was within half a point of throwing down my gage of contemptuous defiance; but he shook my hand and looked so benevolently good at parting—God bless him, though I should never see him more, I shall love him until my dying day! I am pleased to think I am so capable of the throes of gratitude, as I am miserably deficient in some other virtues.

With Dr. Blair I am more at ease.—I never respect him with humble veneration; but when he kindly interests himself in my welfare, or, still more, when he descends from his pinnacle and meets me on equal ground, my heart overflows with what is called liking. When he neglects me for the mere carcase of greatness, or when his eye measures the difference of our points of elevation, I say to myself, with scarcely any emotion, what do I care for him or his pomp either?

It is not easy forming an exact judging judgment of any one, but in my opinion Dr. Blair is merely an astonishing proof what industry and application can do. Natural parts like his are frequently to be met with; his vanity is proverbially known among his acquaintances; but he is justly at the head of what may be called fine writing; and a critic of the first—the very first rank in prose; even in poesy a good Bard of Nature's making can only take the *pas* of him.—He has a heart, not of the finest water, but far from being an ordinary one.—In short, he is a truly worthy and most respectable character.

Mr. Greenfield [1] is of a superior order.—The bleedings of humanity, the generous resolve, a manly disregard of the paltry subjects of vanity, virgin modesty, the truest taste, and a very sound judgment, characterise him. His being the first speaker I ever heard is perhaps half owing to industry. He certainly possesses no small share of poetic abilities; he is a steady, most disinterested friend, without the least affectation of seeming so; and as a companion, his good sense, his joyous hilarity, his sweetness of manners and modesty, are most engagingly charming.

The most perfect character I ever saw is Mr. Stewart.[2] An exalted judge of the human heart, and of composition. One of the very first public speakers; and equally capable of generosity as humanity. His principal discriminating feature is—from a mixture of benevolence, strength of mind, and manly dignity, he not only at heart values, but in his deportment and address bears himself to all the actors, high and low, in the drama of life, simply as they merit in playing their parts. Wealth, honours, all that is extraneous of the man, have no more influence with him than they will have at the Last Day. His wit, in the hour of social hilarity, proceeds almost to good-natured waggishness; and in telling a story he particularly excels.

The next I shall mention—my worthy bookseller, Mr. Creech—is a strange, multiform character. His ruling passions of the left hand kind are, extreme vanity, and something of the more harmless modifications of selfishness. The one, mixed, as it often is, with great goodness of heart, makes him rush into all public matters, and take every instance of unprotected merit by the hand, provided it is in his power to hand it into public notice; the other quality makes him, amid all the *embarras* in which his vanity entangles him, now and then to cast half a squint at his own interest. His parts as a man, his deportment as a gentleman, and his abilities as a scholar are much above mediocrity. Of all the Edinburgh literati and wits he writes most like a gentleman. He does not awe you with the profoundness of the philosopher, or strike your eye with the soarings of genius; but he pleases you with the handsome turn of his expression, and the polite ease of his paragraph. His social demeanour and powers, particularly at his own table, are the most engaging I have ever met with. On the whole he is, as I said before, a multiform, but an exceedingly respectable, worthy character.

---

[1] The Rev. W. Greenfield, Dr. Blair's colleague in the High Church.   [2] Dugald Stewart.

APPENDIX C.

The following poem[1] is the work of some hapless, unknown son of the muses, who deserved a better fate. There is a great deal of "The Voice of Cona" in his solitary, mournful notes; and had the sentiments been clothed in Shenstone's language they would have been no discredit even to that elegant poet.

ELEGY.

Strait is the spot and green the sod,
  From whence my sorrows flow:
And soundly rests the ever dear
  Inhabitant below.

Pardon my transport, gentle Shade,
  While o'er this turf I bow!
Thy earthly house is circumscribed
  And solitary now!

Not one poor stone to tell thy name,
  Or make thy virtues known;
But what avails to me, to thee,
  The sculpture of a stone?

I'll sit me down upon this turf,
  And wipe away this tear:
The chill blast passes swiftly by,
  And flits around thy bier.

Dark is the dwelling of the dead,
  And sad their house of rest:
Low lies the head by Death's cold arm
  In awful fold embraced.

I saw the grim Avenger stand
  Incessant by thy side;
Unseen by thee, his deadly breath
  Thy lingering frame destroy'd.

Pale grew the roses on thy cheek,
  And wither'd was thy bloom,
Till the slow poison brought thy youth
  Untimely to the tomb.

Thus wasted are the ranks of men,
  Youth, Health, and Beauty fall;
The ruthless ruin spreads around,
  And overwhelms us all.

---

[1] If not Burns's own, he at least thought it worthy of a place in his journal.

Behold where round thy narrow house
　　The graves unnumber'd lie!
The multitudes that sleep below
　　Existed but to die.

Some, with the tottering steps of Age,
　　Trode down the darksome way:
And some, in youth's lamented prime,
　　Like thee, were torn away.

Yet these, however hard their fate,
　　Their native earth receives;
Amid their weeping friends they died,
　　And fill their fathers' graves.

From thy loved friends where first thy breath
　　Was taught by Heaven to flow:
Far, far removed, the ruthless stroke
　　Surprised and laid thee low.

At the last limits of our Isle,
　　Wash'd by the western wave,
Touch'd by thy fate, a thoughtful bard
　　Sits lonely on thy grave.

Pensive he eyes, before him spread,
　　The deep outstretch'd and vast;
His mourning notes are borne away
　　Along the rapid blast.

And while, amid the silent Dead,
　　Thy hapless fate he mourns;
His own long sorrows freshly bleed,
　　And all his grief returns.

Like thee cut off in early youth
　　And flower of beauty's pride,
His friend, his first and only joy,
　　His much-loved Stella died.

Him, too, the stern impulse of Fate
　　Resistless bears along;
And the same rapid tide shall whelm
　　The Poet and the Song.

The tear of pity which he shed,
　　He asks not to receive;
Let but his poor remains be laid
　　Obscurely in the grave.

APPENDIX C.

>His grief-worn heart, with truest joy,
> Shall meet the welcome shock;
>His airy harp shall lie unstrung
> And silent on the rock.
>
>O my dear maid, my Stella, when
> Shall this sick period close;
>And lead thy solitary bard,
> To his beloved repose?

ELLISLAND, 14th June 1788.
Sunday.

This is now the third day I have been in this country. Lord, what is man! what a bustling little bundle of passions, appetites, ideas, and fancies! and what a capricious kind of existence he has here! If legendary stories be true, there is indeed an Elsewhere, where, as Thomson says, "Virtue sole survives."

>"Tell us, ye Dead;
>Will none of you in pity disclose the secret
>What 'tis you are, and we must shortly be?
>   . a little time
>Will make us learn'd as you are and as close."

I am such a coward in life, so tired of the service, that I would almost at any time, with Milton's Adam,

>"gladly lay me in my mother's lap,
>And be at peace,"—

but a wife and children—in poetics, "The fair partner of my soul, and the little dear pledges of our mutual love," these bind me to struggle with the stream: till some chopping squall overset the silly vessel, or in the listless return of years, its own craziness drive it a wreck. Farewell now to those giddy follies, those varnished vices, which, though half sanctified by the bewitching levity of Wit and Humour, are at best but thriftless idling with the precious current of existence; nay, often poisoning the whole, that, like the plains of Jericho, "The water is naught, and the ground barren;" and nothing short of a supernaturally gifted Elisha can ever after heal the evils.

Wedlock, the circumstance that buckles me hardest to Care, if Virtue and Religion were to be anything with me but mere names, was what in a few seasons I must have resolved on: in the present case it was unavoidably necessary.—Humanity, Generosity, honest Vanity of character, justice to my own happiness for after life, so far as it could depend—which it surely will a great deal—on internal peace; all these joined their warmest suffrages, their most powerful solicitations, with a rooted attachment, to urge the step I have taken. Nor have I any reason on her part to rue it. I can fancy *how*, but have never seen *where* I could have made it better. Come then, let me return to my favourite motto, that glorious passage in Young:—

"On Reason build Resolve,
That column of true majesty in man."

16th June 1788.

Copy of a letter to Lord Buchan in answer to a bombast epistle he sent me when I went first to Edinburgh.

To the Earl of Eglinton on receiving ten guineas as his lordship's subscription money.

Written in Carse Hermitage.

To Robt. Graham of Fintry, Esq.: with a request for an Excise Division.—Ellisland, Sept. 8th, 1788.

When Nature her great masterpiece design'd.

Alteration of the lines wrote in Carse Hermitage. 23rd Dec. 1788.

The everlasting surliness of a lion, Saracen's head, etc., or the unchanging blandness of the Landlord's Welcoming a Traveller, on some sign-posts, would be no bad similes of the constant affected fierceness of a bully, or the eternal simper of a Frenchman or a Fiddler.

He looked
Just as your sign-posts lions do,
As fierce, and quite as harmless too.

PATIENT STUPIDITY.
So heavy, passive to the tempest's shocks,
Strong on the sign-post stands the stupid ox.

APPENDIX C.

His face with smile eternal drest,
Just like the Landlord to his guest,
High as they hang with creaking din,
To index out the country Inn.

A head, pure, sinless quite of brain or soul,
The very image of a Barber's Poll;
Just shows a human face and wears a wig,
And looks, when well-friseur'd, too amazing big.

[*Here four pages are amissing.*]

CASTLE GORDON.

INTENDED TO BE SUNG TO "MORAG."

Streams that glide in orient plains,
Never bound by Winter's chains.

SCOTS BALLAD.

Tune—"Mary, weep no more for me."

My heart is wae, and unco wae,
To think upon the raging sea.

SONG.

Tune—"Captain O'Kean."

The small birds rejoice in the green leaves returning.

EXTEMPORE.

TO MR. GAVIN HAMILTON.

To you, Sir, this summons I've sent,
Pray whip till the pownie is fraething.

TO THE NIGHTINGALE.

ON HER LEAVING EARL'S COURT, 1784. BY MRS. DR. HUNTER, LONDON.

Why from these shades, sweet bird of eve,
Art thou to other regions wildly fled?
Thy pensive song would oft my cares relieve,
Thy melancholy softness oft would shed
Peace on my weary soul, return again,
Return, and, sadly sweet, in soothing notes complain.

At the still hour I'll come alone,
And listen to thy lovelorn trembling lay,
Or by the moon's beam on some mossy stone
I'll sit, and watch thy wing from spray to spray;
Then when the swelling cadence slow shall rise,
I'll join the plaintive strain in lowly murmuring sighs.

Ah, simple bird, where art thou flown?
What distant woodland now receives thy nest?
What distant echo answers to thy moan?
What distant thorn supports thy panting breast?
Who e'er shall feel thy melting woes like me,
Or pay thee for thy song with such true sympathy?

A SONNET AFTER THE MANNER OF PETRARCH.

BY THE SAME.

Come, tender thoughts, with twilight's pensive gloom,
Soften remembrance, mitigate despair,
And cast a gleam of comfort o'er the tomb.

Methinks again the days and years return
When joy was young, and careless fancy smiled,
When hope with promises the heart beguiled,
When love illumed the world, and happiness was born.
Where are ye fled, dear moments of delight!
And thou, O best beloved! alas, no more
The future can the faded past restore,
Wrapped in the shades of Time's eternal night.
For me remains alone, through ling'ring years,
The melancholy Muse, companion of my tears.

APPENDIX C.

TO MR. GRAHAM OF FINTRY,
ON BEING APPOINTED TO MY EXCISE DIVISION.

I call no goddess to inspire my strains.

SONG.

Tune—"Ewe buchts, Marion."

Will ye go to the Indies, my Mary,
And leave old Scotia's shore?

ON SEEING A FELLOW WOUND A HARE WITH A SHOT,
APRIL 1789.

Inhuman man! curse on thy barb'rous art.

ELEGY ON CAPTAIN MATTHEW HENDERSON.
A GENTLEMAN WHO HELD THE PATENT FOR HIS HONOURS IMMEDIATELY FROM ALMIGHTY GOD!

O Death, thou tyrant fell and bloody!

TO THE HONOURABLE THE BAILIES OF THE CANONGATE, EDINBURGH.

Gentlemen, I am sorry to be told that the remains of Robert Fergusson, etc.

EPITAPH.

Here lies Robert Fergusson, Poet. He was born 5th Sept. 1751, and died 16th October 1774.

> No pageant bearings here nor pompous lay,
> No storied urn nor animated bust,
> This simple stone directs old Scotia's way
> To pour her sorrows o'er her Poet's dust.

APPENDIX D.

BURNS AND FREEMASONRY;

WITH SPECIAL REFERENCE TO THE ST. JAMES'S, TARBOLTON, LODGE.

SHORTLY before he repaired to Irvine on his flax-dressing scheme, the Poet was entered, 4th July 1781, an apprentice Mason of the St. David's, Tarbolton, Lodge. On 1st October 1781, he travelled from Irvine to Tarbolton (twelve miles) to be passed, and raised to full masonic brotherhood. Formerly, there were in Tarbolton two lodges—the St. David's, 174, and the St. James's, 178; but these had united, as the St. David's, in June 1781. A year afterwards, however, this union was departed from, through Burns and others seceding, and reconstituting the St. James's Lodge, whose original charter had been granted by the ancient mother Kilwinning Lodge. It is in connection with the reorganised St. James's that the Poet appears most prominently as a Mason. What keen and regular interest Burns manifested in the meetings and affairs of the brotherhood is abundantly manifest from the St. James's minute-book—a volume which the lodge has carefully preserved, and which it values highly, as containing a record of its history, and, most of all, for the fact that the book holds three minutes entirely in the Bard's own handwriting, and about as many as thirty minutes signed by him as Master-Depute.

The rules of the lodge are interesting reading. One is as follows:—

> "Whereas a lodge always means a company of men, worthy and circumspect, gathered together in order to promote charity, friendship, civility, and good neighbourhood; it is enacted that no member of this lodge shall speak slightingly, detractingly, or calumniously of any of his brethren behind their backs, so as to damage them in their professions or reputations, without any certain grounds;" and any member committing such an offence must humble himself by asking "on his knees the pardon of such person or persons as his folly or malice hath aggrieved." Obstinate refusal to comply with the finding of

the brethren assembled shall be met by expulsion "from the lodge, with every mark of ignominy and disgrace that is consistent with justice and Freemasonry."

Other regulations, dealing with such offences as the breaking of dram-glasses, attending the lodge in a state of intoxication, and so on, are very suggestive of the largely convivial nature of the meetings.

Besides this unique and precious minute-book, the Tarbolton St. James's Lodge possesses various interesting relics of Brother Robert Burns, amongst which we notice the chair and footstool, and the miniature Mason's mallet, so often used by the Poet when presiding over the lodge; the silver badge referred to in his "Farewell to the Brethren of St. James's Lodge, Tarbolton;"[1] the lodge Bible, dated 1775, and referred to in the minutes as "a new Bible, per Brother Burns, 13s.;" and (carefully framed) his letter from Edinburgh, 23rd August 1787, on the business of the lodge:—

> MEN AND BRETHREN,—I am truly sorry it is not in my power to be at your quarterly meeting. If I must be absent in body, believe me I shall be present in spirit. I suppose those who owe us moneys, by bill or otherwise, will appear —I mean those we summoned. If you please, I wish you would delay prosecuting defaulters till I come home. The Court is up, and I will be home before it sits down. In the meantime, to take a note of who appear and who do not, of our faulty debtors, will be right in my opinion; and those who confess debt and crave days, I think we should spare them. Farewell!
>
> > Within your dear mansions may wayward Contention,
> > And withered Envy ne'er enter;
> > May Secrecy round be the mystical bound,
> > And Brotherly Love be the centre.
> >   ROBERT BURNS.

On penning for the *Kilmarnock Standard* a series of four articles, June 1890, dealing with the Poet's connexion with the Tarbolton Freemasons, Mr. Peter Watson, Annbank, Tarbolton, was at pains to have some photographs taken of several pages of the St. James's minute-book, on which the signature and handwriting of Burns appear, as also those of Gilbert Burns, and John Wilson (the Dr. Hornbook of the famous satire).

[1] The "Farewell," penned by Burns when he was meditating emigration to Jamaica, he thus closes:—

"And YOU, farewell! whose merits claim,
  Justly, that *highest badge* to wear!
Heaven bless your honoured, noble name,
  To MASONRY and SCOTIA dear!

A last request permit me here,
  When yearly ye assemble a',
One *round*—I ask it with a tear,
  To him, the Bard that's far awa'."

William Wallace, Sheriff of Ayrshire, and at that time Grand Master, is referred to in the above, as well fitted to wear the *highest badge* of office.

Of these photographs we give the following impressions.

The following shows two signatures with the "Burness" spelling, the body of the minutes being in the handwriting of John Wilson (Dr. Hornbook) the secretary of the lodge:—

> Machline 1st Decemr 1785
>
> Sedr St James's Lodge, Dept Master Senr & Junr Wardens & Masters present
>
> The Lodge proceeded to Pass Brothers Morrison and Tannoch and also raised them to the dignity of Masters ———
>
> Bowie also granted his promissary note & caution for Twelve Shillings and Six pence Sterling as his entry money And Brother Alexr Dove paid his entry money being Twelve Shillings and Sixpence Sterling unto the Treasurer
>
> Robt Burness D. M.
>
> Turbolton 10th Novemr 1785.
>
> Sedr Lodge Mett, Brother John Manson haveing been duely recomended, The Lodge proceeded and Entered him an Apprentice,
>
> Robt Burness.

APPENDIX D.

The following contains a full minute, written and signed by Gilbert Burns; also a full minute, written and signed by Robert Burns; also Burns's signature to another minute:—

> Tarbolton 29ᵗʰ July 1786
> This Evening the Lodge met & ballanced the Books —
> Robᵗ Burns D. M.
>
> Tarbolton 4ᵗʰ Augʳ 1786
> This evening the Lodge met when Quintin Bone and James Good being before entered apprentices were paſſed and rais'd and gave promiſſory notes with caution for their entry moneys   Gilbert Burns J. W.
>
> Tarbolton August 18th —
> This night the Lodge met, and James Tennant from Ochiltree having been recommended was admitted accordingly —
> Robᵗ Burns D. M.
>
> Tarbolton 25 Augᵗ 1786

(This last line is part of a subsequent minute.)

The following contains the signature of the Poet, with his Mason's mark (nine points); also the signature of John Wilson (Dr. Hornbook):—

Pat Cla
Jo An
Hugh Dunlop
William Smith
Jas Watson
John Gray
William Dick
Robert Burns ××
John McMath
John Wilson
John Couper
John Coopper

APPENDIX D.

The following contains the caligraphy of John Wilson (Dr. Hornbook), the secretary of the lodge, and a full minute, written and signed by Burns:—

> Br James Manson Treasurer
> Br John Manson Senior Stewart
> B: John Cunninghame Junior Stewart
> B: John Dunnoch Pass Master
> Br James McWhinnie Tyler
>
> Tarbolton June 23ᵈ 1780. —
> This night the Lodge met, and Robt Andrew a Brother of St David's Tarbolton, was admitted by unanimous vote, gratis likewise James Good having been duely recommended was entered an Apprentice. —
>
> R. Burns D.m

With the courteous permission of Mr. Watson, we append the following explanatory remarks:—

Burns must have been the life and soul of the St. James's Lodge in more ways than one. The minutes show that there were more meetings when he was an office-bearer than at any other period. Though Burns is known to have been a member from the end of 1781, it is not till 27th July 1784 that we have the record of his appointment to a position of influence in the lodge. The Deputy Mastership was then conferred upon him—a position that carried with it the active duties of the Grand Master, who was not very frequently present at the meetings. All assemblies at which the Master was not present were under the presidency of the Deputy Master, and it is in this capacity that Burns has signed so many of the minutes. There are three short minutes written in full by the Poet. The first is dated "Tarbolton, 1st September 1784," but is unsigned, a circumstance not uncommon amongst the records of that time. This minute bears marks of literary conceit at any rate, the antithesis being worthy of note. It is almost ludicrous to find the world-famed Poet writing this—

"This night the lodge met, and ordered four pounds of candles and one quire of eightpence paper for the use of the lodge, which money was laid out by the treasurer, and the candles and paper laid in accordingly."

The other minutes, written fully in the Poet's hand, are as follows :—

"TARBOLTON, 23rd June 1786.—This night the lodge met, and Robert Andrew, a brother of St. David's, Tarbolton, was admitted by unanimous vote, gratis; likewise James Good, having been duly recommended, was entered an apprentice. R. BURNS, D.M."

"TARBOLTON, 18th August [no year, but, from the dates immediately before and after, sure to be 1786].—This night the lodge met, and James Tennant, from Ochiltree, having been recommended, was admitted accordingly.
ROBT. BURNS, D.M.

It is a curious coincidence that two of the three minutes written in full by Robert Burns are near to the one written in the hand of Gilbert Burns, the three being in view at the one opening of the book. Burns, who, whether living at Lochlea or Mossgiel, must have had several miles to walk in order to attend the meetings of the lodge, was most attentive to his duties. The first minute which he signed as Depute Master is dated 29th June 1785, and the last to which his name is adhibited is dated 23rd May 1788; but this does not mark his final departure from the lodge, as Dr. Robert Chambers erroneously states in his *Land of Burns*. On 21st October 1788, and again on 11th November of the same year, the minutes record that Brother Robert Burns was in the chair, though his signature is not attached. Both of these meetings took place at Mauchline, and they must have been held during a flying visit from Ellisland, as Burns settled there on 12th June 1788, a letter of his, dated 13th June, stating that "this is the second day" he had been on his farm in Dumfriesshire. Between the first and the last signature, Burns has in all signed his name twenty-nine times, and on one occasion he has his initials placed to a postscript; but one of the signatures has been cut out by some unscrupulous admirer. The theft occurs in the second last minute that was signed by the Poet, the signature being that of the main part of the minute—the minute having been divided into three. Burns has signed a "P.S." to the same minute, and also an addition to this "P.S.," connected by the words "also at same time," and to the last of these hangs a tale. The gentleman in Tarbolton who had charge of the minute-book was at one time showing it to a visitor, but, being called away for a moment to attend a sick daughter in another room, the visitor and the book were left unwatched. After the visitor departed, the gentleman was asked by his daughter to look the book, as she was afraid something would be found wrong. Whilst her father was with her, she heard either a knife or a pair of scissors at work, and she was right in the surmise that one of the minutes had been tampered with. On discovering this, the visitor was communicated with, and ordered to return the stolen property or suffer the consequences, and the cutting was returned. The stolen part is now

APPENDIX D. 343

neatly pasted in its original place, and, being on the opposite page from the blank left by the cut out signature, eloquent testimony is borne to the rapacity of collectors, and the value placed upon relics of our national bard. Strange as the omission may appear, there is no mention in the minutes of the Poet's demission of office, nor of his leaving the district, even though Burns himself looked so favourably on the position he held amongst the Tarbolton Masons as to address a poem to them as his farewell. This was in 1786, when he seriously contemplated emigrating to the West Indies. It is curious also to note the manner in which Burns signs his name; in this there is great variety. In regard to the spelling, he continues the "Burness" up till 1st March 1786— the first under the more familiar "Burns" being of date 25th May of the same year. Whilst Burns signs "Burness" so long, it is noteworthy that the references to him in the text of the minutes are always spelt "Burns," unless on one occasion, when the name had first been spelt "Burns," but afterwards altered to "Burness," probably by the Poet himself, or at least by his instructions, as his name appears at the foot of this minute as "Burness." In regard to the Christian name, it appears once before Burness as "Robert," and thirteen times it precedes the same spelling as "Robt." Before the later spelling of "Burns" we have it once only in full as "Robert," a single time as "R.," and eleven times as "Robt."—this latter having, it is thus seen, the greatest favour with the Poet. Amongst a long list of signatures of members, many of them having their Mason's marks attached, we find Burns signing himself in full, "Robert Burns," and adding his masonic mark of nine points in the same line. This signature has less resemblance to the familiar and undoubtedly genuine form than any of the others, but there is no date to it, and it is just possible that the conditions under which he signed were what the lodge might term "unfortunate."

Burns's younger brother, Gilbert, was entered, passed, and raised as a brother on 1st March 1786 (the last date on which the Poet signed Burness), and must, for a time at least, have taken an active part in the affairs of the lodge. We find Gilbert signing the minutes on five separate occasions between 11th December 1786, and 21st December 1787, one of these, as already said, being written by him in full. The last references to either of the brothers occur on 18th November and 20th November 1788, on which dates the text of the minutes states that Brother Gilbert Burns occupied the chair. These last-named meetings were held in Mauchline, and form the closing testimony to the warm interest maintained for six or seven years by Robert, and the shorter period by Gilbert, in the affairs of St. James's, Tarbolton, Lodge.

Burns signs the minute relating to the visit of Professor Dugald Stewart to the lodge, who at that time was tenant of Catrine House, and was a friend of the Poet. The record is as follows:—

"A deputation of the lodge met at Mauchline on 25th July 1787, and entered Brother Alexander Allison of Barmuir an apprentice. Likewise admitted Brothers Professor Stewart of Cathrine; and Claud Alexander, Esq., of Ballochmyle; Claud Neilson, Esq., Paisley; John Farquhar Gray, Esq., of Gilmilnscroft; and Dr. George Grierson, Glasgow, honorary members of this lodge," the minute being signed "Robt. Burns, D.M.," in very faint ink.

John Wilson, who was parish teacher of Tarbolton, and the Dr. Hornbook of Burns's well-known poem, was secretary to the lodge from 8th August 1782, till some time in 1787, and in that capacity wrote many of the minutes. Two of them are signed by him—one as "Master *pro tempore*," and the other as "M.P.T." This last minute shows his adhesion to the lodge after his successor in the secretaryship had been appointed, and it is not shown that he was at the date the holder of any office other than that of ordinary membership. Immediately succeeding Wilson's first signature as "Master *pro tempore*," he finds an imitator in James M'Donald, the succeeding chairman, who signs his name, and adds "P.T." merely, a thing that occurs also once afterwards in the writing of another temporary president.

Two of the Grand Masters sign the minutes occasionally, viz.—Mr. James Montgomerie of Coilsfield, and Mr. James Dalrymple of Orangefield, but these are the only names adhibited of the half-dozen Grand Masters who held office during the years embraced in the minutes. The others were Mr. John Hamilton of Sundrum—a name still honoured in the county in the person of the present proprietor; Mr. Mungo Smith of Drongan; Mr. Alex. Montgomerie of Coilsfield (a branch of the Eglinton family, whose estate had to be parted with after the Eglinton tournament); and Mr. Gavin Hamilton, the well-known friend and correspondent of Burns. The name of the Montgomeries suggests the immortality shed upon the family and their estate by the Poet's works. The gratitude of the lodge is expressed at one meeting to Captain Montgomerie, the Right Worshipful Master of the lodge, for his trouble in recovering their colours, "for some time illegally retained by the Lodge of St. David."

Passing from the St. James's Lodge, it is well known that, until the close of his troubled career, the Poet manifested a warm interest in Freemasonry. It is easy to imagine what a charm he lent to the many meetings he attended, though it may be in these gatherings he gave away not a few "slices of his constitution."

On two occasions, during his first winter in Edinburgh, he was highly honoured by the craft—once at an important meeting, attended by the Grand Lodge of Scotland, on 13th January 1787, when the Grand Master gave the toast of "Caledonia, and Caledonia's Bard, Brother Burns, which rang through the whole assembly with multiplied honors and repeated acclamations;"[1] and again, at a meeting of the Edinburgh Canongate (Kilwinning) Lodge, on 1st February 1787, when, in honour of his great poetic fame, Burns was enthusiastically assumed as a member of the lodge.

Then, in the Diary of his Border Tour, there occurs under date of 19th May 1787 this entry: "Spent the day at Mr. Grieve's—made a Royal Arch Mason of St. Abb's Lodge (Eyemouth)."

[1] So Burns states in his letter of 14th January 1787, to Mr. Ballantine, banker, Ayr.

APPENDIX D. 345

As already remarked, the Poet continued his connection with the Tarbolton St. James's for some considerable time after going to reside at Ellisland, and, from the following note of his attendance at Mason meetings in Dumfries, we learn how ardently he kept up his attachment to the brotherhood until the end :—

1791—27th December.	1792—30th November.
1792— 6th February.	1793—30th November.
1792—14th May.	1794—29th November.
1792—31st May.	1796—28th January.
1792— 5th June.	1796—14th April.
1792—22nd November.	

On 30th November 1792 he was elected Senior Warden, and in the minutes of the sixteen meetings held during his stay in Dumfries his name is eleven times found in the list of those who were present.

APPENDIX E.

THE AYR BURNS STATUE—1891.

WHILE many cities and towns at home and abroad have embodied in statue or monument their admiration of the Ayrshire Peasant Poet, and though within a mile or two of Ayr there stand these three most famous shrines of the Bard—the "Monument" at the auld Brig o' Doon, "Kirk Alloway," and the "Cottage" of his birth, it seemed strange that no fitting memorial of him who had reflected so great fame upon the town had arisen in

> Auld Ayr, wham ne'er a toon surpasses
> For honest men and bonnie lasses.

There is now, however, no longer ground for this reproach ; for there, on 8th July of this year, there was unveiled a statue of Burns, which is at once a worthy memorial of the Poet, and an ornament and credit to the "auld toon." The figure is in bronze, designed by Mr. Lawson, H.R.S.A., London, and represents Burns standing with folded arms, and looking towards his natal scene with an expression of face which seems to say—

> The rank is but the guinea's stamp,
> The man's the gowd for a' that.

Perhaps the most interesting part of the ceremony of unveiling consisted in the reciting, by Mr. Wallace Bruce, United States Consul in Edinburgh, of the following lines written by him for the occasion, and which, with the author's kind permission, we here reproduce as the latest noteworthy poetic tribute to the memory of BURNS.

APPENDIX E.

THE AULD BRIG'S WELCOME.

The Auld Brig hails wi' hearty cheer,—
Uncover, lads, for Burns is here!
The Bard who links us all to fame,
And blends his own with Scotia's name.

Seven hundred years the winding Ayr
Has glassed my floating image there;
I've seen long centuries glide away,
But Robin brought our blithest day.

I heard the Thirteenth's warlike peal
Wake serried ranks of glinting steel;
All wrinkled now, yet in my prime,
I wait with joy the Twentieth's chime.

I cherish weel in memory bright
The glorious deeds of Wallace wight,
And deem the very stones are blest
Which bind the arch his feet have pressed.

I mind the time King Robert's band
With sweeping oar left Arran's strand;
The flame that lit yon beacon hill
All round the world is shining still.

Old Coila's had her share of fame,
Her bead-roll treasures many a name;
She's had her heroes great and sma',
But Robin stands aboon them a'.

The auld clay-biggin of his birth
Becomes the shrine of all the earth;
The room where rose the Cottar's prayer
The proudest heritage of Ayr.

No starlit sky, no summer noon,
But kens the banks o' bonnie Doon;
No human heart but fondly turns
Responsive to the Land of Burns.

Ah, Burns! who dares to call thee poor!
Each skylark nest on yonder moor,
Each daisy-bloom on flowery mead,
The lambs that on the meadows feed,—

Each field and brae by burn or stream
Where wandering lovers come to dream,
Are all thine own. As vassals all
We gather here from princely hall,—

From lowly cot, from hills afar,
From southern clime, from western star,
To bring our love; all hearts are thine
By title time can never tyne.

The crowning meed of praise belongs
To him who writes a people's songs,
Who strikes one note—the common good,
One chord—a wider brotherhood;

Who drops a word of cheer to bless
His fellow-mortal in distress,
And lightens on life's dusty road
Some traveller weary of his load;

Who finds the Mousie's trembling heart
Of God's great universe a part;
And in the Daisy's crimson tips
Discerns a soul with human lips.

We little dreamed when Mailie died
Those tender words would speed so wide;
Men smiled and wept and went their way,—
The prince was clad in hodden grey.

Though but a brig, it garred me greet
To hear him pour his Vision sweet,
And in one crowning climax seal
His pity even for the Deil.

To see the couthie Twa Dogs there
Their joys and griefs wi' ither share;—
A cantie tale, it made me smile
That sic a lad was born in Kyle;

Who caught the witches in a dance
And bound them all in lasting trance;
The very land is bright and gay
Since Tam o' Shanter rode this way.

The Auld Brig kens the story well
These rippling wavelets love to tell:
"Ayr, gurgling, kiss'd his pebbled shore,"—
A fonder kiss his waters bore.

That raptured hour, that sacred vow,
Are love's eternal treasures now;
Montgomery's towers may fall away,
But Highland Mary lives for aye.

And sweeter still the swelling song
Of loyal love repairing wrong;
Like mavis notes that gently fa':—
"Of a' the airts the wind can blaw."

Brave, bonnie Jean! We love to tell
The story from thy lips that fell;
The lengthened life which Heaven gave
Casts radiant twilight on his grave.

A noble woman, strong to shield;
Her tender heart his trusty bield;
The critic from her doorway turns
With faith renewed and love for Burns.

She knew as no one else could know
The heavy burden of his woe;
The carking care, the wasting pain,—
Each welded link of misery's chain.

She saw his early sky o'ercast,
And gloomy shadows gathering fast;
His soul by bitter sorrow torn,
And knew that man was made to mourn.

She heard him by the sounding shore
Which speaks his name for evermore,
And felt the anguish of his prayer:
"Farewell, the bonnie banks of Ayr."

Oh, Robert Burns! by tempest tossed,
Storm-swept, by cruel whirlwinds crossed
Thy prayers, like David's psalms of old,
Make all our plaints and wailings cold.

In weakness sown, yet raised in might,
He wept that we might know the right;
His sweetest pleasures pain-imbued;
His songs a drama's interlude.

And who dare thrust his idle word
Where God's own equities are heard?
"Who made the heart, 'tis He alone"—
Let him that's guiltless cast the stone.

We know but this: his living song
Protects the weak and tramples wrong;
Refracting radiance of delight,
His prismed genius, clear and bright,

Illumes all Scotland far and wide,
And Caledonia throbs with pride
To hear her grand old Doric swell
From Highland crag to Lowland dell;

To find, where'er her children stray,
Her "Auld Lang Syne," her "Scots, wha hae,"
And words of hope which proudly span
The centuries vast—"A man's a man."

Then welcome, Burns, from shore to shore!
All hail, our Robin, evermore!
Though late, we greet the Ploughman's name
Full in the morning of his fame.

*Edinburgh: Scott & Ferguson and Burness & Company,
Printers to Her Majesty.*

INDEX.

ABBEY CRAIG, ii. 81.
Abbotshall, iii. 68.
Abdie, ii. 302.
Abercorn, Earl of, i. 20.
  ,,   lands of, i. 241.
  ,,   parish of, i. 33.
Abercrombie, Dr., i. 86.
Abercromby, Sir Ralph, i. 191 ; ii. 101, 158.
Aberdeen, ii. 210, 211, 213, 216, 218, 383, 389 ; iii. 4, 11, 16, 76, 169, 174.
  ,,   King's College, i. 194.
  ,,   university of, ii. 231 ; iii. 21, 77.
Aberdour, i. 58.
Aberfeldy, iii. 169.
Aboukir, ii. 104.
Adair, Agnes Ponsonby, i. 308.
  ,,   Anne, i. 307, 308, 309 ; ii. 9, 10.
  ,,   Charles Makitterick, i. 308.
  ,,   Charlotte Hamilton Hay, i. 308.
  ,,   Constance Mackay, i. 308.
  ,,   Eliza Hamilton, i. 308.
  ,,   Francis Keith Dunlop, i. 308.
  ,,   Hamilton, i. 308.
  ,,   Helenora Charlotte, i. 308.
  ,,   Hugh Wallace, i. 308.
  ,,   Hughina Dennistoun Mackay, i. 308.
  ,,   Isabella Mackay, i. 308.
  ,,   Dr. James, i. 305-309 ; ii. 9, 132, 262, 333 ; iii. 174-176.
  ,,   James Warren Barter, i. 308.
  ,,   Jane, i. 309.
  ,,   Jane Reid, i. 309.

Adair, John, i. 309.
  ,,   Keith Francis Vans, i. 308.
  ,,   Ponsonby, Kelly, i. 308.
  ,,   Rebecca Mary, i. 308.
  ,,   Thomas Dundonald Cochrane, i. 308.
  ,,   Major Wallace, i. 303, 308.
  ,,   Wallace Dunlop, i. 308, 309.
  ,,   William Finlay, i. 308.
Adam, Dr., Rector of the High School, i. 146 ; ii. 136-139.
  ,,   Lord Chief Commissioner, i. 123, 312.
Adamhill, ii. 163.
Addison the poet, ii. 99, 311.
Adelaide, ii. 198.
Afghanistan, iii. 40.
Agnew, Andrew, of Lochryan, i. 187.
  ,,   Eleanor, i. 187.
  ,,   Robert Vans, of Sheuchan, i. 193.
  ,,   Vans, i. 18.
Ahmedabad, iii. 32, 34, 35.
Aiken, Andrew Hunter, i. 7, 8.
  ,,   Grace, iii. 287.
  ,,   John, i. 1, 8, 170.
  ,,   Mary, i. 8.
  ,,   Peter Freeland, i. 7, 8, 9.
  ,,   Richard, i. 8.
  ,,   Robert, i. 1-8, 31-34, 75, 170-172, 227, 279, 283, 291, 295, 296, 299 ; ii. 146, 166 ; iii. 137, 145, 146, 287.
Ailsa Craig, ii. 364, 368 ; iii. 91.
  ,,   Marquis of, ii. 187, 359.
Ainslie of Darnchester, family of, i. 9.

Ainslie, Alexander Duns, i. 9.
„ Douglas, i. 10.
„ Esther, i. 19.
„ Rachel, i. 10.
„ Robert, i. 9-19, 134 ; ii. 62, 131-137, 260 ; iii. 154, 161-163, 181, 197, 203-205, 228, 261.
„ Sir Whitelaw, i. 11.
Aird, Agnes, i. 290.
„ Dr., ii. 304.
„ Hugh, i. 202, 278, 282.
„ Janet, iii. 71.
„ John, farmer, Sorn, iii. 71.
Airds, iii. 253.
Airlie, Earls of, i. 243.
Aitken, Amelia Kate Cope, ii. 142.
„ Helen, ii. 142.
„ Isabella Howat, ii. 142.
„ James Johnstone, ii. 142.
„ J. Carlyle, i. 337.
„ Jean, of Greenock, ii. 198.
„ Margaret, ii. 142.
„ Mrs. Robert, Cupar Fife, i. 115.
„ Robert Nicol, ii. 142.
„ Rev. William, ii. 141, 299.
„ William Burns, ii. 142.
„ William Nicol, ii. 142.
Albemarle, Earl of, ii. 86, 87.
Alexander I. King of Scots, iii. 44.
„ II. „ „ ii. 316 ; iii. 45.
„ III. „ „ i. 167, 306.
Alexanders of Airdrie, i. 20.
Alexander, Boyd, i. 23.
„ Sir Claud, i. 20-24 ; iii. 343.
„ James, Kilmalcolm, i. 20.
„ James, ii. 168.
„ Janet, ii. 168.
„ Jean, ii. 168.
„ John, i. 19 ; ii. 168.
„ Margaret, ii. 168.
„ Robert, Blackhouse, i. 20, 23.
„ Robert, ii. 168.
„ Wilhelmina, i. 19, 20, 21, 23 ; ii. 352.
„ William Maxwell, i. 23.
„ „ „ ii. 168.
„ Mr. William, i. 44.
Alexandria, ii. 101.

Alison, Alexander, of Barmuir, iii. 343.
„ Sir Archibald, ii. 370.
„ Mr., iii. 146.
Allan, Alexander, iii. 61, 62.
„ Andrew, iii. 61, 62.
„ Anne, iii. 64.
„ Bryce, iii. 61.
„ Francis, iii. 62.
„ Hugh, iii. 61, 62.
„ Isabella, iii. 61.
„ James, iii. 60, 61, 62.
„ Janet, iii. 61, 62.
„ Jean, iii. 61.
„ John, iii. 62.
„ Margaret, iii. 61, 62.
Allardyce, Alexander, ii. 162.
Allen, Mr. John, i. 127-129.
Alloa, iii. 56.
Alloway Kirk, i. 6, 260-262 ; ii. 107-110, 266, 305, 361, 363 ; iii. 44, 55, 64-82.
„ Kirkyard, i. 309 ; iii. 66, 70, 111.
Alness, ii. 197.
Alnwick Castle, i. 11, 95 ; ii. 36 ; iii. 164.
Altona, i. 224.
Alva, Lord, i. 220, 221.
Ambleside, iii. 21.
America, i. 203, 359 ; ii. 101, 144, 155, 168, 231, 235, 236, 318.
„ South, iii. 74.
Amory, Mr., i. 223.
Amoy, China, iii. 73.
Anacreon, ii. 313.
Anchor Close, ii. 242.
Anderson, Dr. Alexander, R.N., iii. 41.
„ Elizabeth S., iii. 68.
„ Harriet A., iii. 41.
„ James, Calcutta, iii. 68.
„ James, i. 93.
„ Dr. James, i. 54, 55.
„ Janet, i. 353, 359.
„ Jean, ii. 48.
„ John, of Dovehill, i. 187 ; ii. 84.
„ Lilias, ii. 122.
„ Marion H., ii. 84, 85.
„ Mrs., i. 93.
„ Dr. Robert, ii. 100.
„ Thomas, i. 214.
„ William, i. 91, 93.

INDEX.

Andover, i. 306.
Andrew, Margaret, iii. 58.
  „ Robert, iii. 342.
Andrewes, Lieut.-Colonel Charles, ii. 236.
  „ Frances Mary, ii. 236.
Angus, Archibald, Earl of, ii. 383.
  „ George, Earl of, i. 242.
  „ John, Earl of, i. 242.
Annan, i. 41 ; ii. 128, 129, 375 ; iii. 164, 230.
Annandale, George, Marquis of, i. 112.
  „ i. 256, 257.
Annbank, iii. 337.
Antigua, i. 306, 307 ; ii. 167, 175, 304.
Antonio, Port, ii. 248.
Arabia, i. 323.
Arbiglands, estate of, ii. 40.
Arbroath, iii. 32, 169.
  „ Abbey of, i. 242.
Arbuckle, Rev. William, ii. 360, 375.
Arbuthnot, parish of, ii. 381, 385, 386 ; iii. 2-6, 15, 16, 32.
  „ Sir Robert, ii. 386 ; iii. 5.
Archers' Hall, i. 38.
Ardlochan, ii. 143, 144, 332, 364, 365 ; iii. 52.
Ardmillan House, ii. 186, 187.
Ardrossan, ii. 352.
Ardwell, iii. 263.
Argaum, battle of, i. 150.
Argyle, Archibald, Duke of, i. 46, 148 ; ii. 87.
  „ Earl of, iii. 6.
  „ family of, i. 148.
Argyleshire, i. 91.
Armagh, ii. 84.
Armour, Adam, iii. 43, 203.
  „ Fanny, iii. 43.
  „ James, iii. 43.
  „ Jean, the Poet's wife, i. 3, 13, 91, 154, 304, 341 ; ii. 58, 201, 206, 248, 250 ; iii. 43, 130-137, 164-166, 180-200, 223, 251, 252, 263, 290-309.
  „ John, iii. 43.
  „ Mary Smith, iii. 43.
  „ Robert, iii. 43.
  „ Thomas, iii. 43.
  „ William, iii. 43.
Armstrong, Mr. Adam, ii. 17, 18.
  „ John, i. 330.
  „ Robert, ii. 18.

Armstrong, Samuel, ii. 18.
Arnold, Dr., ii. 264.
Arran, island of, ii. 308 ; iii. 91.
  „ Regent, i. 168.
Arrochar, i. 12.
Arrol, Mr., iii. 27.
Arthur's Seat, i. 13 ; ii. 123.
Artois, Compte d', ii. 263.
Asia, i. 101.
Asia, the, iii. 41.
Assaye, battle of, i. 150.
Atheling, Edgar, ii. 36.
Athelstaneford, i. 58.
Athole, Duchess of, i. 244, 306, 307 ; iii. 170.
  „ Duke of, ii. 140, 305-311 ; iii. 170-173.
  „ House, i. 244 ; iii. 186.
Atlantic, ii. 142 ; iii. 133, 158.
Auchanmore, i. 91.
Auchenbay, ii. 271, 272.
Auchenbrain, i. 203.
Auchendrane, ii. 121 ; iii. 45.
Auchinabrig, ii. 340.
Auchinblae, ii. 383, 391 ; iii. 19, 27.
Auchinleck, Lord, i. 310.
  „ parish of, i. 303 ; ii. 1, 18, 30, 200.
Auchlin, ii. 270.
Auchtertool, i. 160.
Auchtochter, farm of, iii. 17.
Auchtywick, lands of, i. 303.
Auld, Robert, ii. 240.
  „ Rev. William, i. 24-30, 200-202, 266-300 ; ii. 240 ; iii. 129, 191.
Australia, i. 302, 328 ; ii. 168, 198, 237, 283, 284 ; iii. 38.
Avondale, i. 194, 263.
Avon, the, ii. 249, 250.
Ayr, town of, i. 2, 3, 6, 9, etc.
  „ church of, iii. 45.
  „ water of, iii. 118, 124, 322, 337.
Ayrshire, iii. 42, 44, etc.

BABYLON, ii. 361.
Bacchus, iii. 217.
Bach, ii. 72.
Bad, lands of, ii. 33.
Badenoch, iii. 173.
Baillie, Lady Grizel, ii. 344 ; iii. 263.

Baillie, Dr. Hugh, i. 217.
„ Lesley, ii. 331 ; iii. 236, 237.
„ Robert, of Mayfield, ii. 331.
Bainsford Institution, ii. 105.
Baird, Adam, iii. 60.
„ Elizabeth, ii. 121.
„ Fullarton, iii. 56.
„ Sir Gilbert, ii. 121.
„ Marion, i. 238.
„ Rev. Mr., ii. 98.
„ Samuel, iii. 56.
„ Thomas, i. 238.
„ William, of Dalrymple, iii. 56.
„ William, of Rosemount, i. 218.
Balchryston, ii. 147.
Balfour, Mr., ii. 241.
„ Margaret, ii. 302.
„ Sir Michael, of Denmyln, ii. 302.
Balgarvie, Agnes, i. 34.
Balkenran, iii. 52.
Ballantine, Hugh, i. 30.
„ James, i. 34.
„ John, i. 3, 30-34, 172 ; ii. 73, 74, 322 ; iii. 145, 344.
„ Patrick, i. 30, 31, 71.
„ William, i. 30, 31.
Ballantrae, parish of, i. 241 ; ii. 186 ; iii. 73.
Ballikinrain, ii. 274.
Balloch, ii. 316.
Ballochmyle, i. 21-24 ; ii. 318-324.
Ballochneil, ii. 144-147, 152, 187, 363-366 ; iii. 53, 59, 93.
Balmaladie, iii. 19.
Balmerino, Lord, i. 344.
Baltimore, i. 238.
Banaktin, Janet, iii. 63.
Banchory, iii. 19.
„ Ternan, ii. 238.
Banff, i. 11 ; ii. 233, 275, 276, 340 ; iii. 169, 172.
Bangor, i. 58.
Bankhead, farm of, ii. 76.
Bannatine, Mr. James, i. 71, 73.
„ Katherine, i. 71.
Bannatyne, Mr. George, ii. 90.
„ Lord, i. 162.
Bannerman, Rev. William, iii. 73.
Bannockburn, ii. 118, 231, 335, 368 ; iii. 169, 170, 255, 256.

Barbadoes, i. 58.
Barbour, John, iii. 57.
Barclay, Mr., i. 130 ; ii. 158.
„ John, ii. 297.
Bargeny, i. 210.
Barjarg, Lord, i. 220.
Barnard, Anne, ii. 369.
Barncailzie, ii. 257.
Barnhill, ii. 23.
Barossa, ii. 307.
Barr, Mr. Matthias, ii. 373.
Barr, parish of, iii. 60.
Barras, East Mains of, iii. 21-23.
Barrhead, ii. 273.
Barry, Rev. Edward M., i. 185.
Barskimming, ii. 30, 351.
Barter, Anne, i. 309.
„ Mary, i. 307.
Bath, i. 306 ; ii. 34, 70.
Beaton, Cardinal, i. 210, 242.
„ Catherine, i. 242.
„ Elizabeth, i. 242.
„ John, of Balfour, i. 242.
Beattie, Catherine, iii. 17, 28.
„ James, the poet, i. 55, 56, 132, 340 ; ii. 89, 215, 222 ; iii. 18, 78.
Bedford, iii. 251.
Becket, Mary, iii. 308.
„ Thomas à, iii. 1.
Beethoven, ii. 277.
Begbie, Ellison, ii. 331 ; iii. 97, 98, 99.
Begg, family of, iii. 66-71.
„ Margaret, ii. 18.
Belgaum, India, iii. 34.
Bell, Mr. Andrew, ii. 241.
„ Benjamin, i. 86.
„ Sir Charles, i. 170.
„ Francis, 154, 156.
„ Mr. John, i. 131.
„ Prof. Joseph, i. 170.
„ Margaret, ii. 313.
„ Peter, i. 274, 346.
„ R. C., i. 39.
„ Richard, of Cruvie, ii. 313.
Beloochistan, iii. 40.
Benares, i. 251.
Bengal, i. 21.
Benholm, parish of, ii. 386 ; iii. 3.

Bennals, ii. 340.
Bennet, David, 154.
  „   Rev. E. K., ii. 315.
Benson, Richard, i. 257.
Bent, iii. 67.
Berne, ii. 238.
Berrywell, i. 9, 12 ; ii. 131 ; iii. 162, 163.
Bertram, Andrew N., of Clober, iii. 34.
Bervie, river, ii. 381, 387.
Berwick, i. 11, 147 ; iii. 45, 163.
Betson, Elizabeth, ii. 142.
Beugo family, the, i. 34-39 ; ii. 122-124.
Beveridge, Grace, iii. 67, 69.
  „   James, of Balado, iii. 67.
Bhooj, i. 255 ; iii. 32-39.
Bield Inn, i. 161.
Biggar, family of, i. 39, 40.
Billington, ii. 314.
Birley, Mary (Mrs. Creech), i. 129, 130.
Birmingham, i. 126 ; ii. 141.
Birnes, James, iii. 22.
Birness, Robert, iii. 22.
Birniehill, iii. 52.
Birsemore, ii. 211.
Bishop, John, iii. 308.
Bisset, Christian, iii. 15.
Black, Anne, ii. 238.
  „   Dr., ii. 86.
Blackburn, lands of, i. 34.
Blackheath, i. 215.
Blackhouse, estate of, i. 20.
Blackie, Professor, iii. 104.
Blacklock, family of, i. 40-58.
  „   Dr. Thomas, i. 41-58, 97, 305, 316-319, 339, 340 ; ii. 2-7, 159, 222, 306 ; iii. 139, 143-149, 178, 194.
Blackwood, estate of, Lanarkshire, iii. 66, 67.
  „   Mr. William, i. 347.
Bladensburg, i. 238.
Blain, Margaret, iii. 60, 63.
Blair, Alexander, i. 8, 59.
  „   Castle, ii. 306 ; iii. 169.
  „   Captain, i. 8.
  „   David, i. 126 ; ii. 155.
  „   family of, i. 71-77.
  „   Dr. Hugh, i. 48, 60-71 ; ii. 2, 5, 30, 90, 306 ; iii. 145, 157, 327.
  „   John, i. 59, 60, 292.

Blair, Margaret, iii. 48.
  „   of that Ilk, i. 58 ; ii. 316.
  „   provost, of Dumfries, ii. 67.
  „   Mr. Robert, i. 58, 59, 70.
Blair Athole, ii. 140, 306, 308 ; iii. 170, 173.
Blairduff, ii. 213.
Blane, Sir Gilbert, ii. 186 ; iii. 60.
Blantyre, Lord, iii. 71, 72.
Bletchingley, i. 235.
Blore, Mr. Edward, ii. 339.
Boath, estate of, i. 185.
Bodan, Mary, ii. 185.
Bogend, ii. 261.
Boghall, estate of, i. 20 ; iii. 32.
Bogjargan, ii. 381, 386 ; iii. 6-10, 76.
Bogside, farm of, i. 241.
Bogtoun, farm of, iii. 14, 18.
Bohemia, i. 308.
Bokhara, iii. 40.
Bolingbroke, ii. 370.
Bolton, churchyard of, iii. 65, 71.
Bombay, i. 255 ; iii. 34-42.
Bonhill, i. 88.
Borrowstounness, iii. 68.
Borthwick, parish of, i. 149-152.
Boswell, Agnes, iii. 58.
  „   Sir Alexander, i. 235 ; ii. 209.
  „   James, of Balmuto, i. 312.
  „   James, i. 24, 56 ; iii. 31.
  „   John, i. 311-314.
  „   Margaret, i. 314.
Bothwell, iii. 49.
  „   Bridge, i. 206 ; ii. 362.
Botany Bay, i. 263.
Boulogne, iii. 33.
Bourdeaux, i. 193.
Bowman, Elizabeth, i. 30, 31.
  „   John, i. 30.
Boyd, Mr. Joseph, Ayr, ii. 375.
  „   Rev. William, ii. 332.
Bradefute, Mr., i. 322.
Bradley, Caroline, ii. 102.
  „   John, of Colborne Hill, ii. 102.
Braefoot, lands of, i. 271, 272, 287.
Braid Hills, ii. 123 ; iii. 149.
Braiks, lands of, iii. 24.
Brakanwra, iii. 54.
Brampton, ii. 25.

Brand, family of, iii. 26-28.
," James, ii. 236.
," Jean, ii. 236.
," Letitia, ii. 274.
," William, iii. 174.
Brant, i. 118.
Brawlinmuir, ii. 381-390 ; iii. 14-23, 77.
Breadalbane, Earl of, i. 352 ; iii. 173.
Brechin, ii. 210, 228, 229, 296, 316, 386 ; iii. 5, 10.
Breckenridge, family of, iii. 71, 72.
Breconside, ii. 37.
Brewster, Dr., ii. 309.
Briche, Madame de la, i. 222.
Bridges, Francis, i. 335.
Bridgewater Foundry, ii. 127.
Bristol, i. 7, 8, 9 ; ii. 303.
Broadshean, iii. 62.
Brock, Walter, i. 90.
," Janet, i. 90.
Brodie of Brodie, iii. 174.
Brodie, William, i. 141.
Brodrick, General, i. 250.
Brougham, Lord, i. 147, 149 ; ii. 136, 361.
Brow, the, i. 105, 161, 237 ; ii. 183; iii. 294, 295.
Brown, Agnes, i. 173 ; ii. 361, 375, 387 ; iii. 44, 70, 75, 85, 309.
," Alexander, ii. 142.
," Andrew, ii. 362.
," Elizabeth, i. 310, 311, 313.
," family of, iii. 45-63.
," George, iii. 20.
," Gilbert, i. 178 ; ii. 361-363, 375.
," Hugh, ii. 332, 333, 364.
," James, ii. 362.
," Jean, i. 195.
," John, i. 107, 311 ; ii. 362, 375.
," Samuel, ii. 144, 145, 350, 365 ; iii. 93.
," Thomas, i. 309, 310.
," Dr. Thomas, ii. 152.
," William, i. 195, 311 ; ii. 332.
Browne, Mary Ann, i. 257.
," Matthew, i. 309-314.
," Richard, ii. 332, 333 ; iii. 188.
," Robert, i. 312.
Brownhill, lands of, i. 71 ; iii. 47.
Bruar, the, ii. 307, 366.

Bruce, Mr. John, i. 113, 149.
," Alexander, ii. 334.
," Catherine, ii. 333, 334 ; iii. 175.
," Henry, ii. 334.
," Michael, ii. 48.
," Robert the, King of Scots, i. 94, 167, 242, 257 ; ii. 74, 118, 160, 368, 373 ; iii. 175, 255.
," Mr. Wallace, iii. 346.
Bryan, ii. 204.
Brydone, Mr. Patrick, i. 207.
Bryen, Robert, i. 288, 290, 295.
Buchan, Earl of, i. 226, 233 ; ii. 178, 334-339 ; iii. 157, 332.
," Dr. William, ii. 241.
Buist, Andrew M., ii. 142.
Buittle, ii. 37, 39, 41.
Bunyan, John, iii. 144.
Burnet, Alexander, of Kemnay, i. 185.
," Mr. Andrew, ii. 210.
," Bishop, ii. 158.
," James, ii. 335.
," Jane, i. 185.
," Miss, i. 158, 305 ; ii. 335 ; iii. 222.
Burn, Mr. Robert, architect, i. 333.
Burnhouse, ii. 385, 387 ; iii. 2, 6.
Burns, Ann B., iii. 308.
," David, ii. 390.
," Elizabeth R., ii. 175 ; iii. 241, 244, 282, 307.
," family of, iii. 1-44, 64-74, 307-309.
," Francis W., iii. 205, 307.
," Gilbert, i. 115, 162, 188, 252, 299 ; ii. 107, 112, 115, 201, 259, 260, 280, 282, 335, 346, 349 ; iii. 26, 42, 43, 64, 65, 70, 74, 82-118, 130, 173, 190, 277, 293, 301, 309, 342, 343.
," Mrs. Gilbert, iii. 71, 114.
," Isabella, iii. 64-74, 174.
," James Glencairn, i. 232 ; iii. 293, 307, 308.
," James Henry, iii. 38, 77, 108, 296.
," Mr. James, ii. 10, 28, 381-390 ; iii. 174.
," John, ii. 382, 387.
," Margaret, ii. 382.
," Maxwell, i. 162 ; iii. 307.
," Patrick, ii. 386.

INDEX. 357

Burns, Mrs. Robert, i. 119, 127, 192; ii. 11, 25, 112, 279, 280; iii. 85, 110, 203-219, 241, 249, 257, 299, 301.
,, Robert, the poet, i. 2, etc.; ii. 2, etc.
,, his life, iii. 78-304.
,, Sarah, iii. 308.
,, Rev. Thomas, ii. 9, 382.
,, William, i. 2, 173; ii. 28, 107-114, 153, 190, 267, 381, 382, 387; iii. 174, 310-314.
,, Col. William N., ii. 123, 135, 370; iii. 307.
Burns, monument of, i. 93; iii. 79.
Bushby, John, i. 78-82; iii. 251, 260.
,, Peter, i. 82.
,, Thomas, i. 82.
,, William K., i. 80.
Bute, Marquis of, i. 235.
Byron, Lord, i. 128; ii. 373.

Cabool, iii. 40, 42.
Cadell, Wm., i. 134, 140.
Cahar, iii. 308.
Caithness, ii. 196, 283.
Caird, family of, iii. 25, 26.
,, John, of Woodhead, iii. 25, 26, 108, 174.
Cairnbank, lands of, i. 10.
Calcutta, ii. 235, 236, 237, 239; iii. 38, 41.
Caldwell, Elizabeth, i. 241.
,, Janet, i. 278.
Callanan, Jane, iii. 72.
,, Peter, iii. 72.
Callander, Rev. Robert, i. 39.
Calton burying-ground, i. 87; ii. 140, 355.
Calvi, ii. 101.
Cambridge, ii. 103.
,, St. Catherine's College, ii. 237.
,, Trinity Hall, ii. 315.
Cambuskenneth, iii. 57.
Cambusnethan, ii. 47.
Cameron, Agnes, i. 278.
,, Mr. John, ii. 196.
,, Mr. William, i. 334.
,, Mr., i. 334.
Campbell, Alexander, ii. 294.
,, Sir Archibald Ava, iii. 5.
,, Professor Archibald, ii. 8.
,, Castle, iii. 174.

Campbell, Colonel, ii. 86.
,, David, iii. 67.
,, family of, i. 91-94.
,, Flora, ii. 347.
,, Dr. George, i. 132; iii. 44.
,, Hugh, i. 202.
,, Isabella, i. 92, 238; iii. 44.
,, Sir Islay, ii. 263.
,, Col. James M., ii. 247.
,, John, of Succoth, i. 187.
,, Sir John, Bart., iii. 5.
,, Mary, i. 91-94, 304; ii. 8; iii. 131, 132, 219, 270, 271.
,, Matthew, i. 26.
,, of Kinzeancleuch, ii. 190.
,, Stranraer, i. 241.
,, Susan, ii. 263.
,, Thomas, i. 98, 149; ii. 62, 388.
,, Walter, iii. 6.
Campbeltown, i. 33, 92.
Campsie, ii. 86.
Canada, i. 89, 93, 118, 121; ii. 106; iii. 19, 51, 61, 66.
Candlish, family of, i. 82-91, 332.
,, James, i. 340; ii. 347.
Canmore, Malcolm, ii. 36.
Canterbury, i. 263.
,, Archbishop of, ii. 264.
Cantyre, Mull of, ii. 369; iii. 91.
Cape Town, ii. 270, 274.
Cardonnel, Mr., i. 259.
Cardross, i. 242.
Cargill, Captain, iii. 73.
Carlaverock, parish of, ii. 10.
Carlisle, i. 12, 45; ii. 25, 26, 129, 264; iii. 164.
Carlyle, Dr., i. 69; iii. 180, 274.
,, Elizabeth, ii. 302.
,, Thomas, ii. 192.
,, William, ii. 302.
Carmichael, family of, ii. 105, 106.
Carnegie, Elizabeth, iii. 29.
,, William, iii. 29.
Carolina, South, i. 162.
Carsphairn, ii. 18.
Carr, ——, i. 221.
,, A. Morton, i. 251.
Carrick, i. 82, 94, 239, 261, 278; ii. 144, 209, 286, 360, 380; iii. 44, 55, 116, 322.

Carrick, Robert, ii. 102.
Carrington, Lord, i. 209.
Carruthers, Christian, i. 220.
 „ Jane, i. 257.
 „ John de, i. 257.
 „ John, of Holmains, i. 220.
 „ Dr. Robert, of Inverness, i. 98.
Carse, Friars, iii. 197, 198, 218, 233, 235.
Carson, John, ii. 20.
 „ Agnes, ii. 20.
 „ Mr., Rector of High School, i. 254.
Carthage, Queen of, ii. 137.
Cassilis, David, Earl of, i. 72 ; ii. 190, 360.
 „ Downans, ii. 365.
Castlebank, i. 192.
Castle Douglas, i. 238 ; ii. 61 ; iii. 57, 263.
Castlehill, lands of, i. 31, 34.
Castleton, iii. 18.
Castleview, ii. 13, 16.
Cathcart, Lord Alan, ii. 307, 316.
 „ Sir Andrew, of Carleton, i. 301 ; ii. 186.
 „ Grizel, i. 301, 348.
 „ Margaret, ii. 316.
 „ Miss, ii. 307.
 „ of Carnock, ii. 316.
Catrine, i. 87, 164 ; ii. 30, 320, 351 ; iii. 148, 343.
Cattanach, Elizabeth, ii. 237, 238.
Catto, James, of Aberdeen, iii. 28.
Cauwin, M. Louis, i. 35 ; ii. 130.
Cawdar, iii. 174.
Cessnock, iii. 97.
 „ burn of, ii. 331, 341.
Ceylon, i. 124.
Chalmers of Fingland, family of, i. 94-137, 305 ; ii. 53, 216, 218, 226, 261 ; iii. 170-192, 298.
 „ of Gadgirth, i. 168.
 „ Dr. Thomas, i. 256.
 „ William, ii. 335.
Chanonry, Presbytery of, ii. 188, 196.
Chapel, Lieutenant, of Maybole, ii. 375, 380.
Chapelizod, Dublin, iii. 74.
Charles I., king, i. 148, 211 ; ii. 32, 84 ; iii. 5, 14.
 „ V., emperor, i. 109.
 „ IX., ii. 155.
Charteris, Alison, ii. 65.

Charteris, Henric, i. 353.
 „ William, of Bridgemoor, ii. 65.
Chatelherault, Duke of, i. 168.
Cheltenham, iii. 34, 37, 308.
Chester, ii. 185.
Chetwood, Captain, of Woodbrook, i. 8.
 „ Constance, i. 8.
China, i. 214.
Chittoor, i. 41.
Christie, ——, i. 328 ; iii. 17.
Churchill, ii. 89.
Cicero, ii. 369.
Clackmannan, county of, i. 96, 307 ; ii. 132, 261, 263, 334.
Clapham, Sarah Kate, i. 176.
Clarinda, i. 103, 104, 137, 341 ; ii. 54-57; iii. 182-191, 223, 224, 246, 263, 264.
Clark, family of, i. 106-120, 159, 333, 343.
 „ James, Forfar, iii. 285, 291.
 „ Rev. James, ii. 47.
 „ Mary, ii. 47.
 „ Stephen, ii. 71, 336 ; iii. 257.
 „ William, ii. 336 ; iii. 209.
Cleghorn, family of, i. 122-128.
 „ James, i. 252.
 „ Robert, i. 158, 314 ; ii. 24.
Cleveland, Duke of, i. 236.
Clifton, iii. 32, 33, 34.
Clinton, Canada, iii. 66.
Clochanhill, ii. 386, 387 ; iii. 23, 25, 42, 43, 77, 78.
Cloete, Henry, i. 2, 51.
 „ Johanna Catherine, i. 251.
 „ Rodolph, of Westerford, i. 251.
Closeburn, parish of, i. 106, 330 ; ii. 160, 340, 352 ; iii. 65, 67.
Clouden, ii. 40.
Clow, Jenny, iii. 168.
Cluden, water of, iii. 250.
Clyde, iii. 133, 141.
 „ Canal, ii. 78.
 „ Firth of, i. 92 ; ii. 105, 167 ; iii. 91.
 „ Mr. James, i. 337, 338.
Coates House, i. 227, 232, 233.
Cochrane, Charles, i. 217.
 „ Elizabeth, i. 95.
 „ Lady Elizabeth, ii. 343.
 „ Grizel, i. 95.

INDEX.

Cochrane, Sir John, i. 95.
   „   Messrs. Murray &, ii. 240.
   „   Thomas, Earl of Dundonald, ii. 343.
Cockburn, Lord, ii. 282.
   „   Mrs., ii. 349.
Coil, water of, iii. 272.
Coila, iii. 124, 125, 161.
Coilsfield House, i. 91.
Coke, Edward, of Longford Court, ii. 325.
   „   Eliza Grace, ii. 325.
Coldstream, i. 11 ; iii. 162.
Colebrooke, Sir T. E., i. 149.
Coleraine, i. 172.
Coleridge, Samuel Taylor, ii. 256.
Colinton, ii. 126.
Collessie, i. 60.
Collie, William, iii. 20.
Collieston, farm of, iii. 15.
Collins the poet, ii. 89.
Colman the dramatist, i. 331.
Colmonell, parish of, i. 301, 348.
Colston, Mr. James, ii. 141.
Columbia College, ii. 343.
Colvend, ii. 41.
Colville, Margaret, ii. 272.
Colvin, Alexander, iii. 31.
   „   Christian, iii. 31.
Comely Green, ii. 298.
Commonside, ii. 201.
Comyn, John, ii. 74.
Condorcet, i. 165.
Congreve, i. 331.
Connaught, coast of, ii. 332.
Connell, Mr., i. 284 ; ii. 166.
Constable, Archibald, i. 328.
   „   George, ii. 161.
   „   William Haggerston, ii. 336.
   „   Lady Winifred Maxwell, ii. 336 ; iii. 76.
Cooke, Agnes, iii. 33.
   „   C., i. 329.
Cooper, Rev. Augustus, iii. 33.
   „   Mabel, iii. 33.
Copeland, Mrs., iii. 287.
Copland, Dr., Dumfries, i. 8.
Copenhagen, iii. 217.
Corbet, Mr., i. 119 ; iii. 234.
Corehouse, Lord, i. 162.

Corfu, ii. 236.
Cork, county, ii. 315.
Corneille, i. 331.
Cornewall, Charlotte Henrietta, ii. 314.
   „   Herbert, ii. 314.
Cornwall, iii. 34, 74.
Coromandel, i. 207.
Corra, iii. 53.
Correstown, iii. 53.
Corri, Signora Domenica, ii. 277.
Corriston Burn, ii. 144.
Corsbie, barony of, i. 206.
Corsica, ii. 101.
Corsincon hill, ii. 66 ; iii. 196, 269.
Corstorphine, barony of, i. 122, 123, 127, 128, 319.
Corton, laigh, ii. 267.
Coull, Dr. James, i. 185.
   „   Helen, i. 185.
Couper, Alexander, ii. 273.
   „   Dr. John, ii. 273.
   „   Dr. William, Glasgow, ii. 273.
Coutts, Messrs., i. 71 ; ii. 61.
Coventry, i. 226.
Covington, Archdeacon of, ii. 265.
   „   Mains, iii. 140, 141.
Cowan, Charles, i. 256.
   „   Jean, i. 238.
Cowie, Rolland, ii. 275.
Coylton parish, ii. 151, 350.
Crabb, Mr. Robert, ii. 383.
Craig, family of, ii. 46, 59.
   „   Janet, ii. 116.
   „   Mrs., iii. 295.
   „   William, of Holmes, ii. 116.
Craigdow, ii. 144 ; iii. 53.
Craigencallie, i. 94.
Craigenton, i. 178 ; ii. 362, 363, 375 ; iii. 52-56, 62.
Craigie, parish of, ii. 27, 350.
Craigieburn, ii. 20, 21, 22, 24.
Craigmill, ii. 341.
Craigs, East and West, ii. 46.
Craik, William, ii. 40.
Cramond, parish of, i. 122, 123.
Cranstoun, George, i. 129, 162.
   „   Helen D'Arcy, ii. 324.
   „   Henry Kerr, ii. 324.
   „   Lord William, ii. 324.

Crauford, Janet, iii. 61.
Craufurd of Ardmillan, ii. 186.
„ Miss, ii. 187.
Crawford, Elizabeth, i. 30.
„ family of, ii. 186 ; iii. 48.
„ John, i. 30.
„ John Innes, ii. 71.
„ Lord, ii. 388.
„ Mr., of Doonside, iii. 44, 230.
Creech, William, publisher, i. 32, 63, 100, 129-143, 227, 233, 328, 333, 344 ; ii. 75, 79, 92, 96, 117, 122, 242, 267 ; iii. 145, 154, 163, 182, 184, 189, 223, 328.
Creich, parish of, i. 129.
Creoch, estate of, ii. 272.
Crichton, Thomas, ii. 294.
Crieff, iii. 169, 173.
Criffel, i. 120 ; iii. 269.
Criric, Mr. James, i. 329.
Crochallan Club, i. 153, 180 ; ii. 70, 243 ; iii. 154.
Croftingie, iii. 53.
Croix, Marianne Louisa de la, i. 44.
Croll, David, iii. 13.
Cromarty, ii. 188, 189.
Crombie, i. 236, 237.
„ Old, iii. 19.
Cromek, Mr., ii. 114, 259, 260 ; iii. 292.
Crone, Catherine, iii. 308.
Croningberg fort, ii. 207.
Crookedholm, ii. 116.
Crosbie, Andrew, ii. 175.
Crosby, Provost, ii. 169.
Crossraguel, Abbot of, ii. 316 ; iii. 60.
„ ii. 344.
Crow, Helen Margaret, iii. 5.
„ Colonel John, iii. 5.
Croydon, ii. 265.
Cruikshank, William, i. 143-157, 251, 252 ; ii. 130-137, 159, 225, 308 ; iii. 176, 180.
Cubbingtoun, ii. 64.
Cullen, Dr., i. 38, 132.
„ village, iii. 169.
Cullie, David, i. 337.
Culloden, ii. 43 ; iii. 77.
Culross, ii. 84, 348.
Culter Fells, iii. 141.
Culzean, i. 239 ; ii. 147, 285 ; iii. 52, 53.
Cumberland, i. 41, 42, 117, 302.

Cumberland, ii. 23 ; iii. 54.
„ Duke of, ii. 213.
Cumming, Alexander, ii. 230.
„ Jean, ii. 17.
„ John, ii. 230.
„ Matilda, ii. 83.
„ Robert, ii. 230, 331.
Cumnock, i. 350 ; ii. 18, 163, 208, 302 ; iii. 49, 189.
Cunningham, Alexander, i. 148-163, 183 ; ii. 45 ; iii. 214, 260, 292, 298.
„ Alexander, of Craigends, i. 20, 108, 112, 140, 146.
„ Allan, i. 3, 201-204, 229 ; ii. 46, 76, 208, 337 ; iii. 115, 142, 195, 197, 206-213, 249, 268.
„ Anne, i. 71, 192.
„ Catherine, ii. 197, 198, 199.
„ Lady Elizabeth, i. 232, 233 ; iii. 223.
„ Colonel James, Scots Brigade, i. 17.
„ James, iii. 61.
„ Jean, i. 17.
„ John, ii. 76.
„ Lady Margaret, i. 236.
„ Margaret, iii. 47.
„ Mrs., Robertland, i. 2.
„ province of, iii. 49, 116.
„ Rev. Richard, i. 126.
„ Susan, i. 172.
„ Susanna, i. 21.
„ T. M, ii. 76.
„ William, of Enterkin, ii. 352.
Cunninghame, bailiery of, ii. 143 ; iii. 322.
„ of Cunninghamhead, i. 209.
„ of Halcraigs, i. 149.
„ of Hyndhope, i. 148-163.
„ Sir Thomas Montgomerie, ii. 149.
„ William, of Annbank, ii. 337.
„ William Allason, of Logan, ii. 337.
Cunyngham, Colonel Francis, ii. 324.
Cupar Abbey, ii. 210.
Cupar-Fife, i. 113, 115, 149.
Cupples, Mr. William, ii. 150, 365.
Currie, Andrew, of Glassmount, iii. 68.
„ Dr., i. 5, 98, 164, 190, 307, 332 ; ii. 45, 82, 107, 108, 109, 253, 259, 280, 352 ;

INDEX. 361

iii. 71, 86, 148, 175, 208, 217, 252, 278-283, 300-302.
Currie, Magdalene, iii. 68.
Cushnie, Anne, iii. 3.
Cutch, i. 255; iii. 36, 39.
    „ king of, i. 255.
Cuthbertson, Annie, iii. 68.

DAER, Lord, i. 163, 164, 165, 166; ii. 30, 351.
Dailly, parish of, ii. 144, 150.
Dalgarno, Alexander, ii. 232.
Dalkeith, i. 130, 131, 150, 151, 152, 241; ii. 158, 302.
Dallas, Robert, iii. 10.
Dalmahoy, James, ii. 9.
Dalmellington, parish of, ii. 275, 351.
Dalmeny, ii. 122; iii. 67.
Dalquhram, estate of, i. 353, 354.
Dalry, parish of, i. 78, 96; iii. 31.
Dalrymple, Mr. Andrew, iii. 48, 141.
    „ Catherine, ii. 266.
    „ Charles, i. 221; ii. 338; iii. 143, 145.
    „ family of, i. 167-176.
    „ James, of Orangefield, i. 166-176, 221, 226; iii. 344.
    „ James, ii. 266.
    „ Janet, iii. 48.
    „ Sir John, ii. 242, 243.
    „ parish of, i. 87; iii. 82.
    „ Rev. Dr., i. 6, 172, 283; ii. 108.
    „ school, i. 83.
    „ Mr. W., iii. 64, 75.
Dalrymples of Langlands, i. 5.
    „ of Stair, i. 168.
Dalswinton, ii. 34, 73-80, 83, 133; iii. 164, 194, 195, 217.
Dalton, parish of, i. 329.
Dalzell, J., iii. 254.
Dalziel, Mr. Alexander, i. 226, 231; ii. 267.
Danevale, iii. 57.
Darien Scheme, i. 309.
Darnley, ii. 273.
David I. king of Scots, i. 241, 304; ii. 169.
    „ II. „ i. 167, 206; ii. 209, 334.
    „ Prince, iii. 44.
Davidson, Betty, iii. 80.
    „ David, ii. 376.
    „ Dr., physician at Edinburgh, iii. 29.

Davidson, family of, i. 177-179.
    „ James, i. 179; ii. 376.
    „ John, i. 177, 350; ii. 146, 359, 363, 364.
    „ Margaret, ii. 179; iii. 11.
    „ Matthew, i. 179; ii. 376.
    „ Thomas, i. 179.
    „ William, i. 179; ii. 380.
Davies, Miss Deborah D., ii. 337.
Dayman, Rev. Phillipps, iii. 74.
    „ Sibylla, iii. 74.
Dean, Jamie, iii. 183.
Deeside, ii. 211, 257; iii. 25, 253.
De la Croix, Marianne Louisa, i. 44.
Delany, Captain, ii. 337.
Dempster, George, ii. 337.
Denbigh, Earl of, i. 38.
Denmark, Anne of, ii. 172; iii. 217.
Denside, iii. 25.
Derbishire, Dr., ii. 34.
    „ Stewart, ii. 34.
Derby, ii. 83, 325.
Desmond, Earl of, i. 306.
Detroit, ii. 155.
Devon, ii. 262, 366.
Devonshire, i. 129, 302.
Dewar, Anne, i. 169.
    „ Mr. Forrest, i. 154, 156.
    „ Jessie, i. 156.
Dick, Captain, ii. 152.
    „ Sir Robert, ii. 152.
    „ Susanna Stewart, ii. 152.
    „ William, i. 241.
Dickens, Charles, ii. 284.
Dickie, Adam, ii. 116.
    „ Agnes, ii. 116.
    „ Margaret, i. 240.
Dickson, George, iii. 20.
    „ James, iii. 20.
    „ Mary, iii. 20.
    „ Sarah, iii. 73.
    „ Thomas, iii. 73.
Dingwall, iii. 28.
Dinnant, College of, ii. 44.
Dinning, iii. 65.
    „ farm of, iii. 71.
Dinwoodie, lands of, ii. 41, 42.
Dirleton, ii. 47.

Ditton, Wood, ii. 315.
Dock Green, iii. 249-252.
Dods, Captain, i. 118, 119.
Doig, Dr. David, ii. 159, 229, 230.
Doig & M'Kechnie, Messrs., i. 38.
Dollar, i. 115, 117.
 „ churchyard, 116, 117.
Dolphinton, i. 195.
Don, family of, i. 235, 236.
 „ George, i. 115.
 „ William, iii. 20.
Donaghadee, i. 72.
Doon, water of, ii. 146, 204, 266, 364, 366; iii. 46, 79, 116, 124, 322.
Dornel, Laird of, ii. 18.
Douglas, Sir Alexander, of Glenbervie, ii. 385; iii. 4.
 „ Sir Archibald, of Glenbervie, iii. 4.
 „ Charlotte, ii. 42.
 „ Daniel, ii. 243.
 „ ii. 347.
 „ Dr., ii. 248; iii. 29.
 „ Elizabeth, i. 242.
 „ family of, i. 163, 164.
 „ Gavin, i. 127.
 „ Sir Henry, of Lochleven, i. 242.
 „ Heron, & Co.'s bank, i. 80, 354; ii. 320; iii. 109.
 „ James, M.D., ii. 42.
 „ James, of Dornock, ii. 65.
 „ Mr. James, iii. 4.
 „ Lord, i. 9.
 „ Philadelphia, ii. 65, 66.
 „ William, of Kelhead, ii. 42.
 „ Mr. William S., i. 91, 332, 340; ii. 12, 82, 154, 325, 338.
Doune, Dr., i. 305.
Doura, ii. 339.
Dove, John, i. 294; ii. 338.
Dover, ii. 283; iii. 231.
Down and Connor, Bishop of, i. 255.
Dreghorn family, i. 149.
 „ ii. 49.
Driesen, Baron de, i. 8.
Drumbeg, iii. 52.
Drumcondra, i. 263.
Drumdow, i. 217; iii. 53.
Drumgarloch, iii. 52.

Drumlanrig Castle, ii. 66, 67, 69, 155, 172
Drumlithie, iii. 14, 18, 27.
Drummochrian, iii. 52.
Drummond, Annabella, i. 242.
 „ General, i. 204.
 „ John, Earl of Melfort, i. 20.
 „ John, Lord, i. 242.
Drummuscan, iii. 52.
Drumore, lands of, i. 306.
Drumtochty, iii. 20.
Drumvain, iii. 52.
Dryburgh, ii. 335.
Dryden, i. 189, 331.
Dublin, i. 123, 194, 263; ii. 18; iii. 72, 74.
Duddingston, ii. 240, 297.
Dudgeon, William, i. 11.
Duff House, iii. 169, 172.
 „ Innes, ii. 234.
 „ John, ii. 234.
 „ Mr., ii. 239.
Dulwich College, i. 129.
Dumbretton, ii. 128.
Dumfres, John Murthoc, Earl of, i. 95.
Dumfries, i. 6, 40, etc.; ii. 10-27, 37, etc.; iii. 10, 54, 164, etc.
 „ Earl of, i. 30, 350.
 „ Globe Inn, i. 248.
Dumourier, Mr., i. 320.
Dun, Mr., ii. 148, 149.
Dunbar, i. 11; ii. 130.
 „ Bishop, ii. 213.
 „ Colonel, i. 332, 339.
 „ Countess of, ii. 18.
 „ Earl of, i. 166.
 „ family of, i. 179-186.
 „ Mr. John, of New Cumnock, ii. 20.
 „ Mr. William, i. 146; iii. 154.
Dunbarton, i. 88, 242, 256; ii. 250, 348.
 „ Castle of, i. 212.
Dunbeath Castle, ii. 283.
Dunblane, ii. 234.
Duncan, Admiral Lord, i. 38.
 „ family of, i. 120, 121; ii. 65-68.
 „ Dr. Henry, ii. 357.
 „ Mrs. Henry, iii. 296.
 „ John, iii. 24.
 „ King, iii. 174.
 „ Dr. Robert, ii. 338.

INDEX.

Duncan, William, i. 292.
Duncombe, Francis Barbara, ii. 325.
   „   Mr., i. 224.
   „   Thomas, of Gosgrove, ii. 325.
Dundaff, i. 242.
Dundalk, iii. 65.
Dundas, Admiral George, i. 251 ; iii. 270.
   „   family of, ii. 158–162.
   „   Maria, i. 251.
   „   Major William B., i. 251.
Dundee, ii. 16, 232, 234, 340 ; iii. 169.
   „   James, Earl of, i. 243.
Dundonald, Earl of, i. 95.
   „   parish of, ii. 302, 304, 313, 338 ; iii. 60–67.
Dunedin, iii. 73, 74.
Dunfermline, i. 307, 327 ; ii. 32, 84, 265, 368 ; iii. 41, 176.
Dunkeld, ii. 151, 152, 234 ; iii. 169, 173.
Dunlappie, ii. 210.
Dunlop, Alexander, ii. 273.
   „   family of, i. 186–193.
   „   Captain Hamilton, R.N., i. 173.
   „   House, iii. 188.
   „   Mrs., i. 93, 186–193, 250 ; ii. 57, 88–99, 331 ; iii. 42, 64, 71, 136, etc.
   „   parish of, iii. 51.
   „   Wallace, C.B., ii. 99.
Dunnichen, ii. 337.
Dunnottar, parish of, ii. 381, 386, 387 ; iii. 23–25, 42.
Dunoon, parish of, i. 91.
Duns, i. 9, 10, 19, 146, 251, 252 ; iii. 162.
Dunscore, ii. 64, 172, 252 ; iii. 202–206.
Dunskey, estate of, i. 76, 306.
Duntaggart, ii. 209.
Duntrune, i. 242.
Durham, i. 206, 236 ; ii. 236.
Durris, parish of, iii. 20.
Duthie, Alexander, iii. 20.
   „   Andrew, iii. 23.
Dysart, i. 327, 328, 335.

EAGLE & HENDERSON, Messrs., i. 328.
Eales, Major Daniel, iii. 33.
   „   Lionel, iii. 33.
   „   Maud, iii. 33.

Earn, river, iii. 56.
Easton, Esther, ii. 17.
Ecclefechan, i. 238 ; ii. 143 ; iii. 230.
Eccles, estate of, i. 79.
Echt, ii. 211, 231, 237, 238.
Eden Bank, i. 11.
   „   Dora, ii. 103.
   „   river, i. 235.
   „   Thomas, ii. 103.
Edgar, Dr., Mauchline, i. 27, 28.
Edgehill, i. 7.
Edinburgh, i. 5 et passim.
Edingham, i. 17.
Edmonstone, Messrs. Millar &, iii. 61.
Ednam, ii. 335.
Edward, John, iii. 23.
Edwards, Mr. D. H., ii. 383, 384, 390.
Eglinton, Countess of, ii. 313.
   „   Earl of, i. 189 ; ii. 31, 88, 93, 103, 202, 338 ; iii. 332.
Egypt, i. 191 ; ii. 101.
Eldin, ii. 161.
Elfhill, iii. 22.
Elgin, Earl of, ii. 334.
Elibank, Lord Patrick, i. 62.
Elibanks, iii. 163.
Elibraes, iii. 103.
Elizabeth, Queen, iii. 54.
Ellanton, Laird of, i. 24.
Elles, family of, iii. 73.
Elliot, Mr. Charles, of Edinburgh, ii. 245.
   „   Sir Gilbert, ii. 367.
   „   Mr., i. 318.
Ellisland, i. 13–15, 36, 50–52, 78, 85, etc. ; ii. 19–21, 58, 66–68, 75–80, etc. ; iii. 176, 189, 193–200, etc.
Ellison, James, M.D., of Windsor, ii. 314.
Ellon, village of, ii. 215, 231, 232.
Errol, Lord, ii. 214.
Erskine, Hon. Andrew, ii. 31.
   „   Mr. Charles, of Linwald, i. 220.
   „   churchyard, iii. 72.
   „   Mr. David, i. 243.
   ,   family of, i. 220, 221.
   „   Hon. Henry, i. 136, 227 ; ii. 338, 339 ; iii. 145.
   „   Lady Isabella, i. 233.
   „   John, of Dun, i. 242.

Erskine, Lord, ii. 245.
   „   Mrs., of Mar, ii. 336.
Esk river, ii. 39.
Essex, ii. 235, 236.
Esmeade, Mrs. Mitchell, ii. 103.
Eton, i. 88 ; ii. 159, 265, 305–313.
Etruria, ii. 369.
Ettrick, iii. 116, 322.
Eugenie, the Empress, i. 238.
Everitt, Dr., iii. 307.
   „   Martha Burns, iii. 307.
   „   Mrs., ii. 115.
Every, Sir Edward, ii. 83.
Ewart, Mr., iii. 247.
Exeter, ii. 284.
Eyemouth, iii. 344.

Fail, mill of, ii. 120, 133.
Failford, ii. 343.
Fairbairn, Mr., i. 142.
Fairlie, estate of, iii. 60.
Falconer, Sir Alexander, iii. 14.
   „   family of, iii. 18–28.
   „   Francis A. K., iii. 14.
   „   Margaret, ii. 381, 386 ; iii. 12, 23, 27.
Falkirk, i. 39 ; ii. 105, 118 ; iii. 169.
Falkland, i. 336.
   „   Islands, ii. 317.
Fallside, iii. 24.
Falmouth, i. 231, 232.
Fardincalla, ii. 365.
Farquharson, Donald, of Balfour, ii. 211.
   „   Dr., i. 19 ; ii. 211.
   „   William, ii. 211.
Fearn, ii. 296.
Fenwick, ii. 332.
Ferdinmakery, ii. 64.
Ferguson, Dr. Adam, i. 38, 62, 64, 72 ; iii. 151, 252.
   „   Mr., Craigdarroch, i. 112 ; ii. 172 ; iii. 218.
Fergusson, Sir Adam, i. 72.
   „   Mrs., of Denholm, i. 2.
   „   Robert, poet, i. 333 ; ii. 166, 252–255, 355 ; iii. 124, 142, 322, 335.
Ferrier, Agnes, ii. 239.
   „   Alexander, iii. 74.
   „   Mr. James, ii. 239, 339.

Ferrier, Jane, ii. 339.
   „   Jemima G., iii. 74.
   „   Susan E., ii. 339.
Fetchen, i. 308.
Fettercairn, iii. 19.
Fetteresso, iii. 9, 22, 25, 26, 76.
Fettes, William, ii. 210.
Fielding the poet, ii. 97, 98, 250.
Fife, i. 38, 58, 129, 327 ; ii. 301, 337, 369, 385 ; iii. 2, 26, 56, 68.
Fiji, iii. 21.
Findlater, Alexander, i. 194, 195, 196, 197, 247, 250 ; iii. 275, 277.
   „   family of, i. 194–197.
Findlay, James, ii. 27 ; iii. 190.
   „   J. R., of Aberlour, i. 39.
Fingland, ii. 261, 262.
Finlay, Agnes, of Trees, i. 302.
   „   Mr. Alexander S., ii. 49.
   „   G. L., W.S., i. 176.
   „   Jane, i. 176.
   „   John, ii. 49, 360.
   „   Rev. John, ii. 372, 375, 380.
   „   Mrs., Helensburgh, i. 178, 239.
   „   Rebecca, of Trees, i. 303.
Finlayson, Professor James, i. 151.
Finlayston House, i. 211, 226, 236 ; ii. 267.
Fintona, ii. 275.
Finzean, ii. 211.
Firth, parish of, iii. 2.
Fisher, family of, i. 197–205.
   „   William, i. 197–205, 269, 278–280, 288, 296.
   „   Dr. William, ii. 283.
Fitzgerald, John, i. 306.
Flanders, ii. 86.
Fleitz, ii. 352.
Fleming, Agnes, ii. 339.
   „   Charles, ii. 304.
   „   John, ii. 339.
   „   Mary, ii. 304.
Fletcher, Phillipps L., ii. 185.
Flint, Christian, ii. 339, 340.
Flodden, ii. 121.
Florence, ii. 352.
Flushing, ii. 86.
Fochabers, ii. 131 ; iii. 172.
Folkestone, ii. 265.

INDEX. 365

Folkesworth, ii. 315.
Fontenelle, Miss, ii. 340; iii. 241, 279.
Foote, i. 331.
Forbes, Adelaide, iii. 35.
   „   Captain Charles, iii. 32, 35.
   „   Janet, ii. 238.
   „   Louisa E., iii. 32.
   „   Mr. Robert, ii. 213.
   „   Rev. William, ii. 238.
   „   Sir William, i. 71, 103.
Fordoun, parish of, ii. 386; iii. 15-19, 27.
Fordyce, Lieutenant, R.N., i. 184.
   „   parish of, i. 194.
Foregirth, farm of, ii. 76.
Forfar, i. 113-116, 242; ii. 234, 236, 296, 337.
   „   county of, iii. 6, 30, 37, 286.
Forres, iii. 174.
Forrester, Susan, i. 197.
Forster, Jean, iii. 29.
   „   Mr., iii. 9.
Forsyth, Andrew, iii. 60.
   „   Emily, ii. 235.
   „   William, ii. 189.
Fortescue, iii. 64.
Fort George, iii. 174.
Forth Bridge, iii. 27.
   „   Firth of, ii. 36, 78.
   „   river, iii. 9, 56, 116, 124, 322.
Fotheringham, Christian, ii. 381, 382; iii. 9, 10, 11.
   „   William, iii. 22.
Foulis, Barbara, ii. 126.
   „   Sir James, ii. 126.
Fox, Hon. Charles James, i. 226; ii. 253, 309; iii. 147, 251.
Foyers, Fall of, ii. 307.
France, i. 76, 131, etc.; ii. 43, 44, 96-101, 155, etc.; iii. 231.
Frank, Elizabeth, i. 310, 311, 313.
   „   George, i. 310.
   „   William, of Bughtrig, i. 310.
Franklin, Dr., ii. 318.
Fraser, Alexander, ii. 125.
   „   Mr. James, ii. 136, 197.
   „   Luke, ii. 136.
   „   Sir William, ii. 346; iii. 57.
Freeland, Mary, i. 7.
   „   Peter, i. 7.

Freswick, ii. 283.
Friars Carse, i. 126, 146, 260, 262; ii. 169, 171, 172, 183; iii. 332.
Friars Shaw, ii. 169.
Frierland, iii. 44.
Fullarton, William, of Skeldon, and his family, i. 175, 187.
Fullerton, family of, i. 205, 210.
Fyvie, ii. 237.

GAINSBOROUGH, ii. 307.
Gairdner, Dr., ii. 266.
   „   family of, i. 212-221.
   „   Captain Robert, i. 176.
   „   William, Ladykirk, i. 172.
   „   William T., ii. 267.
Galashiels, ii. 237.
Galloway, i. 82, 94, 306, 316, 320; ii. 18, 40, 64, 174, 257, 361; iii. 55, 134, 230, 252.
   „   Lord, i. 81; ii. 319, 342; iii. 254.
Galston, ii. 4, 118, 163, 331, 341, 351; iii. 97.
Galt, William, iii. 64, 65.
Galway, county, iii. 72.
Garden, Mrs., i. 257.
Garlieston, house of, iii. 234.
Garrick, i. 331.
Garvan, David, iii. 48.
Garvock, ii. 386; iii. 16.
Gatehouse, ii. 258, 344; iii. 253-255.
Gavin, family of, iii. 12-16.
Geddes, Rev. Alexander, LL.D., ii. 224, 340, 341.
Gellatly, Rev. Robert, i. 338.
Gellie, Archibald, iii. 7.
Gemmell, Margaret, ii. 204.
Geneva, i. 307.
Genoa, i. 238.
George, James, iii. 28.
   „   Margaret, iii. 28.
Gepp, Ernest Cyril, i. 302.
   „   Hamilton, i. 302.
   „   Rev. Henry, i. 302.
Germany, i. 131; iii. 218.
Gerrard, Bishop, ii. 231.
Gesner, Mr., i. 320.
Gib, Mary, iii. 3.
Gibb, Dr. Gavin, i. 88.
   „   Robert, i. 199.

Gibson, Mr. James, ii. 115.
" Mrs., ii. 165.
Gifford, Mr., i. 149.
Gilbanks, Rev. Joseph, i. 302.
" Mary Jane, i. 302.
Gilcomstone, ii. 210.
Gilfillan, Rev. George, i. 202.
Gillespie, Alexander, i. 177, 179.
" Anne, i. 178, 179 ; ii. 363.
" Mr. John, ii. 21.
" Professor, iii. 206.
Gillis, Dr., ii. 46.
Gilmour, family of, i. 173-176.
Girvan, ii. 143, 147, 150, 271, 316, 324 ; iii. 54, 55, 58.
Gladstone, family of, i. 120.
Glasgow, i. 25, 31, 44, 83, etc. ; ii. 8, 46, 64, etc. ; iii. 19, 52, 69, etc.
" Earl of, i. 69.
" Robert, of Mountgreenan, i. 193.
Glegg, family of, iii. 31-34.
Glen, estate of, ii. 274.
" Margaret, ii. 33.
Glenarth, lands of, ii. 121.
Glenbervie, ii. 381, 391 ; iii. 2-27, 43, 46.
Glencairn, Earl of, and family, i. 210-236 ; ii. 117, 190, 267, 322 ; iii. 139, 143-145, 186, 228, 327.
" parish of, ii. 133, 142.
Glenconner, i. 226 ; ii. 267-275.
Glendevon, ii. 333.
Glendonwyne of Parton, iii. 252.
Glenfoot of Ardlochan, i. 177, 178, 179 ; ii. 363.
Glen of Cowton, iii. 22.
Goderich, Clinton, iii. 66.
Goethe, ii. 389.
Gogo, iii. 35.
Goldie, John, ii. 341, 342.
" Mr., ii. 175, 193.
Goldsmith, Dr., ii. 317.
Good, James, iii. 342.
Goozerat, iii. 36.
Gorbals, ii. 318, 355.
Gordon, Caroline Maria, i. 185.
" Castle, i. 340 ; ii. 131, 217 ; iii. 169, 172, 174, 333.
" Duchess of, i. 227 ; ii. 117, 131, 322 ; iii. 145-152, 172, 174.

Gordon, Duke of, iii. 172, 174.
" Rev. George, and family, ii. 8, 87.
" Harry, iii. 38.
" Jane, iii. 27.
" Sir John, of Lochinvar, ii. 37.
" Katherine, of Afton, ii. 351.
" Marjory, i. 302.
" Marion, ii. 42.
" M. Viscount Kenmure, ii. 257 ; iii. 253.
" Mrs., ii. 258 ; iii. 253.
" Thomas, of Balmaghie, ii. 342.
" Rev. William, Glenbervie, ii. 383.
" William, of Greenlaw, ii. 42.
" William, i. 185.
Goudie, Isabella, ii. 149.
Gould, Rev. Dr., ii. 50.
Gow, Nathaniel, i. 344.
" William, i. 344.
Gracie, family of, i. 236-239.
Graham, David, of Fintry, and family, i. 241-251.
" Douglas, i. 178, 239-241 ; ii. 145, 359, 363.
" John, i. 39.
" Sir John the, ii. 118.
" Mrs., ii. 146, 307 ; iii. 94.
" Nicol, i. 236.
" of Claverhouse, i. 186, 242 ; ii. 164, 362 ; iii. 49.
" Peter, iii. 54.
" Rev. Robert Balfour, ii. 9.
" General Samuel, ii. 339.
" Thomas, of Balgowan, ii. 307.
Grahame, Robert, of Fintry, i. 241-251 ; ii. 96, 307 ; iii. 171, 186, 205-234, 270, 297, 332.
" Robert, of Gartmore, i. 236.
Grant, Alexander, of Bogton, i. 185.
" Sir Alexander, of Monymusk, iii. 73.
" Sir Archibald, ii. 212.
" Castle, iii. 173.
" Mr. Charles, ii. 189.
" Clementina, iii. 73.
" Eliza, ii. 346.
" George, ii. 237.
" Rev. James, iii. 73.
" Sir James, of Castle Grant, ii. 346 ; iii. 173.

INDEX.

Grant, Lady, ii. 212.
" Sir Ludovick, of Grant, ii. 346.
" Pennel, ii. 346.
" Sir Robert, ii. 189.
" William, advocate, iii. 24.
Grant's Braes, iii. 65, 71.
Grantham, ii. 343.
Granton, i. 122.
Gray, the poet, ii. 89 ; iii. 326.
" Rev. James, and family, i. 250-257 ; ii. 62, 360, 375, 380 ; iii. 74, 276.
" John Farquhar, iii. 343.
Greece, i. 255.
Green, Ann, ii. 273.
" General, i. 8.
Greenbank, lands of, i. 310.
Greenfield, Professor, ii. 117 ; iii. 328.
Greenford, i. 258.
Greenholm, iii. 61.
Greenhorn, Captain, iii. 61.
Greenock, i. 92, 94, 121, 352 ; ii. 19, 27, 249 ; iii. 73, 139.
Gregory, Dr., i. 132 ; ii. 245.
Greig, family of, iii. 15-43.
" J. B., ii. 381, 383, 390.
Grenada, Bishop of, ii. 99.
Grenan, estate of, iii. 55.
Gretna, ii. 11, 23 ; iii. 230.
Grierson of Lagg, i. 257.
" Mr., i. 322.
" Dr. George, iii. 343.
" Thomas, ii. 313.
" William, ii. 304.
Grieve, James, of Boghead, iii. 319.
Groat's, John o', ii. 309.
Grose, Captain Francis, i. 258, 263 ; ii. 364 ; iii. 220.
Grub, Margaret, iii. 28, 29.
Guatemala, ii. 235.
Guernsey, i. 258.
Gustavus III. of Sweden, ii. 77.
Guthrie, Alexander, iii. 29.
" Allan, ii. 120, 133.
" James, iii. 27.
" John, ii. 272.
" Rachel, iii. 27, 28.
" Thomas, i. 202, 282.

HAARLEM, ii. 155.
Haddington, Earl of, i. 164, 312.
" shire of, i. 157, 207 ; iii. 65, 71-74.
Haddo, Lord, i. 73.
Haldane, Janet, iii. 68.
" Mary, iii. 68.
Halifax, ii. 104, 284.
Halkirk, ii. 196.
Hall, Sir James, ii. 126.
Halliday, Robert, ii. 40.
Hallifax, General, ii. 283.
Hallowshean, iii. 62.
Halyburton, Andrew, of Pitcur, i. 242.
" Sir James, of Pitcur, i. 243.
" Mary, i. 243.
Hamburg, i. 224.
Hamilton, Anne, Duchess of, i. 163.
" Charlotte, i. 98-101, 304-309 ; ii. 9, 262, 333 ; iii. 170, 174, 191, 298.
" Duke of, i. 163, 167, 212 ; ii. 87, 101, 341.
" family of, i. 263-309.
" Gavin, Mauchline, i. 2-5, 27, 29, 47, 91, 96, 164, 171, 263-304, 350 ; ii. 2, 4, 19, 117, 121, 164, 249, 262, 347 ; iii. 70, 129, 133, 144, 170, 216, 333, 344.
" Lord John, i. 163.
" John, Glasgow, i. 1 ; ii. 211.
" John, of Kype, i. 96, 299, 304.
" Mr., of Sundrum, ii. 151, 211 ; iii. 344.
" Presbytery of, i. 21, 194.
" Professor, ii. 87.
" William L., i. 234.
Hampden, John, i. 157.
Hampton Court, ii. 185.
" Mr. John, ii. 383.
Hannay, Agnes, ii. 41.
" Mr. William, ii. 41.
Hannibal, ii. 107.
Hardy, George Dalton, iii. 35.
Harris, Mary Jane, iii. 38.
Harrogate, i. 73, 149, 308.
Hartlepool, i. 236.
Harvieston, i. 96-102, 299, 304-307 ; ii. 159, 261, 333 ; iii. 16, 170.
Haugh, George, iii. 243, 258, 283.
Havannah, ii. 142.

VOL. III.   3 A

Hawhill, farm of, iii. 16.
Hawkhill, farm of, iii. 17,
Hay, Ann, i. 243.
  „ Colonel, of Keillour, i. 243.
  „ Earls of Tweeddale, family of, i. 9.
  „ family of, i. 102-105.
  „ and Henderson, ii. 375, 382.
  „ Hugh, i. 123.
  „ Isabel, i. 9.
  „ James, ii. 210.
  „ of Drumelzier, i. 9.
  „ of Duns Castle, i. 9.
  „ Robert, i. 123.
Henderson, David, of Tannoch, i. 311.
  „ family of, i. 147.
  „ Harriet, ii. 102.
  „ John, ii. 102.
  „ Margaret, iii. 26.
  „ Captain Matthew, i. 309-315 ; ii. 98 ; iii. 222, 335.
Hendon, ii. 314.
Henri, James, of Bernaldean, i. 193.
Henry, Dr., i. 64 ; ii. 129.
  „ Prince, ii. 33.
Herat, iii. 40.
Hermitage Castle, i. 11 ; iii. 199.
Heron, family of, i. 315-327.
  „ Mr., ii. 39.
  „ Patrick, ii. 342, 343.
  „ Robert, i. 51, 57, 80, 139, 316-325 ; iii. 134, 154, 226, 266, 278.
Herries, Lady Agnes, ii. 37.
  „ Helen, i. 278.
  „ James Maxwell, ii. 37.
  „ Lord John, ii. 37.
  „ W. M., of Spottes, ii. 39.
Hewatson, family of, i. 204 ; ii. 208, 209.
Hewett, Captain, iii. 32.
Hewitt, Richard, i. 46.
Hexham, i. 12 ; iii. 164.
Higham, farm of, iii. 17.
Highfield, Gillanders of, ii. 211.
Hill, family of, i. 327-336.
  „ Mrs., ii. 111.
  „ Peter, i. 85, 139, 184, 327-336, 343 ; ii. 79, 244, 380.
Hilton, iii. 20.
  „ Cloch of, iii. 23.

Hilton, Hannah, ii. 238.
  „ Henry, of Fairgirth, ii. 238.
Hobart Town, i. 236.
Hobhouse, Sir Benjamin, i. 24.
  „ Sophia Elizabeth, i. 24.
Hogarth, family of, ii. 283, 284.
Hogg, Eleanor Jane, iii. 68.
  „ James, i. 253, 257 ; ii. 65.
Hogstoun, i. 240.
Holland, i. 131 ; ii. 101, 155 ; iii. 77.
  „ family of, iii. 33-35, 39.
  „ Lord, i. 128.
Holmains, i. 222, 224, 225.
Holme, William, i. 214.
Holmes, Major-General, iii. 37.
Holmhead, ii. 116.
Holyrood, i. 122 ; ii. 37, 43, 158, 297 ; iii. 77.
Home, Earl of, i. 311.
  „ John, i. 62 ; ii. 49, 276
  „ Mr., i. 263.
Hood, William, iii. 164, 319.
Hooper, Mr. Samuel, i. 258.
Hope, Archibald, i. 149, 151.
  „ Hon. Charles, i. 167.
  „ Dr., ii. 240.
Hopetoun, Earl of, i. 109-114, 159.
Horsham, i. 209.
Houghton, family of, ii. 270.
Houston, i. 217, 219, 221, 222.
  „ Annie, i. 20.
  „ Elizabeth, i. 169.
  „ Sir John, Bart., i. 20.
Howat, Mrs., ii. 13, 15.
  „ of Mabie, i. 118.
  „ William, ii. 16.
Howe, Barbara, ii. 11.
Howison, Mary, ii. 10.
Hoy, James, i. 340.
Hudson, family of, iii. 29.
Hudson's Bay, i. 166.
Hume, David, i. 44, 61, 123 ; ii. 49, 245.
  „ Joseph, iii. 30.
  „ Lord, i. 124.
Humphry, James, ii. 343.
  „ William, ii. 343.
Hunter, Dr. Andrew, i. 6, 7.
  „ David, of Burnes, iii. 2.
  „ James, i. 30.

INDEX.

Hunter, Rev. John, i. 7, 170, 173, 214 ; ii. 213, 230.
„ John, Ayr, i. 71.
„ of Hunterson, i. 71.
„ Susan, i. 35.
„ Susannah, i. 170, 174.
„ William, ii. 165.
Huntingdonshire, ii. 315.
Huntly, Marquis of, i. 163, 243 ; ii. 225.
Hurry, Colonel, i. 213.
Hutcheson, A. B., iii. 308.
„ family of, iii. 56, 68.
„ Professor Francis, i. 123.
„ Hugh, ii. 149.
„ James, ii. 376.
Hutton, John, ii. 276.
Hyland, William, ii. 39.
Hyndford, Earl of, ii. 105.
Hyndman, Mr. John, i. 225.
Hyslop, John, iii. 252.
„ Mrs., i. 345 ; ii. 24 ; iii. 252.
„ William, ii. 11.
Hythe, ii. 10.

INCHBRECK, lands of, iii. 4, 6, 11, 18, 77.
„ Stuarts of, iii. 76.
Inglis, family of, i. 336-338.
„ Rev. James, i. 40.
„ Mr., Attorney for the Crown, ii. 345.
„ Dr. Thomas, ii. 65.
Innerleithen, i. 11 ; iii. 163.
Innerwick, ii. 47.
Innes, Gilbert, of Stow, ii. 276.
Inveraray, i. 162 ; ii. 49 ; iii. 166, 208.
Inverness, i. 306 ; ii. 188, 216, 234, 284, 306 ; iii. 15, 169, 174.
Irongray, parish of, ii. 40.
Irvine, town of, i. 205 ; ii. 31, 164, 192, 201, 204, 304, 332 ; iii. 45, 71, 91, 100-108, 116, 124, 188, 322, 338.
Irving, Dr., ii. 162.
„ Edward, i. 89.
„ Francis, iii. 57.
„ Mr. John, Glenbervie, iii. 8.
Isle, The, Ellisland, iii. 200, 202.
„ St. Mary's, iii. 254, 255.
Isles, Lord of the, iii. 55.
Isleworth, i. 210.

JACK, family of, iii. 61, 62.
Jackston, farm of, iii. 19.
Jaffray, Rev. Andrew, ii. 343.
Jamaica, i. 236, 352 ; ii. 5, 59-61, 147, 167, 249, etc. ; iii. 16, 130-137, 246, 337.
Jamestoun, farm of, i. 241 ; ii. 332 ; iii. 52.
Jamie, Agnes, Garvock, iii. 3.
Jamieson, Jean, i. 290.
„ William, ii. 33.
Jarbo, Emma, iii. 41.
Jedburgh, i. 11, 129, 147 ; ii. 16-18 ; iii. 163.
Jellie, John, iii. 13.
Jenkins, Rev. A. A., ii. 237.
„ Edward, ii. 314.
Jerdan, William, i. 169.
Jersey, i. 239, 258.
Johnson, Dr. Samuel, i. 56, 63, 84, 101, 157 ; ii. 159, 313, 317 ; iii. 32.
Johnston, Commodore, i. 207.
„ family of, i. 339-348.
„ Mr. Joseph, i. 45.
„ Lucy, ii. 258.
„ Maria, ii. 314.
„ Mary, ii. 47.
„ Mr., Drumcrieff, ii. 23.
„ Captain Robert, ii. 47.
„ Sarah, i. 45, 50.
„ William, ii. 314.
„ Wynne, of Hilton, ii. 349.
Johnstone, George, M.D., i. 176.
„ James, publisher, i. 339-348 ; ii. 336, 352-354 ; iii. 176-178, 193, 291.
„ Sir James, of Westerhall, ii. 81 ; iii. 221.
„ Margaret, i. 176.
„ Richard, iii. 67.
Jolly, William, ii. 165.
Jones, William, iii. 28.
Jonson, Ben, i. 331.

KAIR, ii. 385, 386 ; iii. 15.
Kames, Lord, i. 61, 63, 132 ; ii. 159, 240, 245, 353.
Kaüilbors, Alexandrina, Baroness, i. 8.
Kay, John, i. 259.
Kean, Helen, iii. 56.

Keating, Francesca Elizabeth, i. 121.
" J. W., i. 121.
Keay, James, of Snaigow, i. 250.
Keith, Alexander, Criggie, iii. 25.
" Isabella, of Craig, ii. 387 ; iii. 25, 28, 43.
Kells, i. 316, 320.
Kelly, Thomas, Earl of, i. 312 ; ii. 31.
Kelso, i. 11 ; ii. 36, 335 ; iii. 163.
Kelton, parish of, i. 120, 316.
Kemnis-hall, ii. 21, 23.
Kemnay, parish of, ii. 212.
Ken, river, iii. 253.
Kenmore, Taymouth, iii. 161.
Kenmure Castle, ii. 257 ; iii. 253-256.
Kennedy, Agnes, i. 168, 187.
" Mr. Alexander, i. 214 ; ii. 112, 344.
" Anne, i. 72 ; ii, 344, 365.
" Captain, of Kailzie, ii. 50.
" Francis, i. 187.
" Helen, i. 301-303, 348.
" Sir James, of Dunure, i. 242.
" Jean, ii. 344, 365.
" John, i. 350-352.
" Sir John, of Culzean, i. 239.
" John, of Dunure, i. 167.
" Margaret, i. 299, 348, 349 ; ii. 5.
" Miss, i. 102, 299.
" of Ardmillan, ii. 316.
" of Kirkmichael, ii. 324.
" of Knockdaw, i. 168, 169.
" Robert, i. 301, 348.
" Sir Thomas, i. 187.
Kent, ii. 128 ; iii. 1, 34.
Keppel, William, Viscount Barrington, i. 176.
Kerr, James, iii. 10.
" John, Morriston, i. 95.
" Mr. Robert, ii. 246.
Kerroughtree, ii. 345.
Kesson, family of, iii. 20.
Kilbarchan, ii. 273.
Kilbride, i. 352.
Kildonan, ii. 188.
Kilgour, Bishop, ii. 232.
Killiecrankie, i. 186.
Kilmaine, Lord, iii. 45.
Kilmalcolm, i. 211.

Kilmarnock, i. 1, 3, 21, 24, etc. ; ii. 2, 19, 115, etc. ; iii. 51, 67, 71, 134, etc.
Kilmaurs, Lord, i. 131, 210, 226.
" parish, ii. 116, 347.
Kilmodan, ii. 49.
Kilpatrick, Nellie, iii. 89.
Kilsyth, ii. 84.
Kilwinning, ii. 143, 338, 345, 353 ; iii. 336.
Kincaid, Mr. Alexander, i. 130, 131.
King, George, i. 303.
Kingsknowe, i. 127 ; ii. 164.
Kingston, ii. 60.
Kinbilt, lands of, i. 306.
Kinloch, George, of Kair, iii. 24, 25.
Kinmouth, ii. 386 ; iii. 23, 33.
Kinneff, parish of, ii. 381, 387 ; iii. 2, 16, 20-22.
Kinneil, iii. 68.
Kinross, iii. 67, 68, 74, 169.
Kintore, iii. 18, 21.
Kintyre, ii. 144.
Kirk, Joanna, ii. 238.
Kirkaldie, Alexander, i. 194.
" Jean, i. 194.
" Mr. Thomas, i. 194.
Kirkcolm, ii. 147.
Kirkcudbright, i. 17, 45, 51, 82, 167, etc. ; ii. 11, 39, 102, 238, etc. ; iii. 54, 254, etc.
Kirkintilloch, ii. 46.
Kirkland, ii. 149, 316, 365.
Kirkmaiden, i. 306 ; ii. 369.
Kirkmichael, ii. 1.
Kirknewton, ii. 334.
Kirkoswald, i. 39, 177, 205, 239, etc.; ii. 143-153, 185, 272, etc. ; iii. 51-64, 83-96.
Kirkpatrick, ii. 40.
" Helen, ii. 344.
" Sir James, Closeburn, i. 106.
" Mr. Joseph, ii. 252.
" Mr., of Dunscore, iii. 204.
" William, of Couheath, i. 238.
" William, of Raeberry, ii. 42.
Kirkpatrick-Juxta, i. 40.
Kirkton, Jean, iii. 94, 95.
Kirktoun Inn, ii. 365.
Kirkwood, Mr., i. 321.
Knockback, iii. 19, 20.
Knockhill, ii. 381, 389.

INDEX. 371

Knockquham, iii. 21.
Knockshinnoch, ii. 18.
Knox, Elizabeth, ii. 301.
  „   Isa Craig, iii. 1.
  „   James, ii. 273 ; iii. 25.
  „   John, ii. 301 ; iii. 60.
Krow, Robert, of Parkhead, ii. 386 ; iii. 4, 5.
Krudner, Ellen, Baroness, i. 8.
Kyle, i. 353 ; ii. 305, 363 ; iii. 116, 322, 327.

LAGGAN, lands of, ii. 133, 142.
Laing, Mr. David, i. 347, 348.
Laithers, ii. 384.
Lamb, Mr. A. C., Dundee, i. 126.
Lambeth, ii. 127.
Lambie, William, iii. 61.
Lamie, James, i. 26, 202, 269-271, 278-288 ; ii. 247.
Lamont, Dr., i. 176.
  „   Katherine, i. 176.
Lanarkshire, i. 122, 149, 194, 263, 311, 352 ; ii. 101, 142.
Langham, i. 12.
Langholm, ii. 27.
Langhorne, iii. 151.
Lapland, i. 226.
Lapraik, John, i. 352-359 ; iii. 120-122, 322.
Largie-side, iii. 308.
Largs, iii. 67.
Larpent, Sir A. de, ii. 235.
  „   Caroline Anne, ii. 235.
Latham, Harriet, ii. 283.
Lauder, farm of, ii. 10.
Lauderdale, iii. 251.
  „   Earl of, ii. 99.
Laurencekirk, ii. 381-383, 389 ; iii. 4, 15, 169.
Laurie, Archibald, i. 307, 309 ; ii. 1-10.
  „   Catherine, ii. 169.
  „   family of, ii. 1-10.
  „   Rev. George, i. 46-49, 307 ; ii. 1-10 ; iii. 157.
  „   Sir Robert, ii. 1, 169, 171 ; iii. 218.
Lawrie, Sir Walter, iii. 218.
Lawson, Rev. R., ii. 360, 375, 380 ; iii. 346.
Lebrun, Antonia, i. 236.
  „   M., of Hamburg, i. 236.
Leburn, Mary, iii. 68.

Leddrie Green, ii. 270.
Ledmacdunegil, ii. 32.
Leeward Islands, ii. 175-177, 244.
Leghorn, family of, iii. 16.
Leglen, woods of, i. 188 ; ii. 308.
Leicester, Thomas, Earl of, ii. 325.
Leigh Park, farm of, i. 239.
Lekprevick, John, i. 353.
  „   Robert, i. 352.
Lennox, Matthew, Earl of, i. 168.
Leslie, parish of, i. 336 ; ii. 301, 302.
Lesmahagow, iii. 66.
Leven, banks of, ii. 159.
  „   Earl of, i. 60.
Lewars, family of, ii. 10-16.
  „   Jessie, i. 346; ii. 10-16; iii. 289, 290, 298.
Leyden, i. 24, 256.
Ley, family of, iii. 19, 20.
Liddell of Auchtertool, i. 327.
Liff, ii. 210.
Lightshaw, farm of, i. 353.
Lilliesleaf, ii. 169.
Limekilns, ii. 265.
Limerick, i. 306.
Limond, Mr., of Darblair, i. 235.
  „   Provost, Ayr, i. 93.
Lincluden, Abbey of, iii. 250, 251.
  „   College, iii. 249.
Lindsay, Sir Alexander, i. 335.
  „   Eliza, i. 334, 335.
  „   Isabella, ii. 16-18 ; iii. 163.
  „   Sir John, i. 186, 335.
  „   John, of Edzell, iii. 3.
  „   Margaret, i. 186 ; ii. 17, 18.
  „   Dr. Robert, ii. 17.
Linlithgowshire, i. 34, 35, 97 ; ii. 33, 249, 250 ; iii. 68, 169.
Linn, Caldron, ii. 262 ; iii. 174.
Linshart, ii. 216-233.
Linton, i. 194.
Littleton, iii. 52, 56.
Livingston, Alexander, iii. 74.
  „   Henry, iii. 74.
Loanfoot, ii. 115, 120.
Lochcarron, ii. 188.
Lochlea, farm of, i. 296 ; ii. 28, 75, 109, 152, 163, 222, 343 ; iii. 3, 29, 70, 92, 96, 107-110, 113, 177, 310, 342.

Lochleven Castle, iii. 68.
Loch Lomond, iii. 167.
Lochmaben, ii. 343.
Loch Ryan, iii. 57.
Lock, Mary Rice, ii. 315.
  „ Peter, ii. 315.
Lockerbie, i. 110 ; ii. 316.
Lockhart, Alexander, of Boghall, iii. 46.
     „ Anna, i. 30.
     „ John, i. 30.
     „ John G., i. 205 ; ii. 124, 137, 161, 344, 354 ; iii. 110, 150, 207, 230, 262, 278, 295.
     „ Norman, of Tarbrax, ii. 72.
     „ of Barr, ii. 190, 248.
Lockhead, William, i. 166.
Lockie, Susanna, i. 187.
Logan, Dr. Hugh, ii. 149.
   „ James, of Lagwine, ii. 18.
   „ John, of Knockshinnoch, i. 199, 301 ; ii. 18–20 ; iii. 216.
   „ John, Leith, i. 64.
   „ Margaret, i. 213.
Logiealmond, i. 91.
Lollards of Kyle, ii. 190, 191.
London, i. 11, 41–44, 63, etc.
Londonderry, ii. 84.
Longfellow, ii. 370.
Longside, ii. 213–232, 261.
Longtown, iii. 164.
Lorimer, family of, ii. 20–26.
   „ Jean, i. 127 ; ii. 20–26, 349 ; iii. 265.
   „ Mr., Cairnmill, i. 195.
   „ William, i. 127.
Lothian, Marquis of, i. 147.
   „ Robert, Earl of, i. 130.
Loudoun, i. 46–49, 307, 309 ; ii. 2, 8, 9 ; iii. 49.
   „ Castle, i. 193, 302.
   „ Countess of, ii. 32, 347.
   „ Earl of, i. 264, 296 ; iii. 70.
Loughborough, Lord Chancellor, i. 130.
Lovat, Catherine, i. 243.
   „ Lord Hugh, i. 243.
   „ Simon, Master of, i. 60.
Love, Jean, iii. 60.
Lovell, Sir Richard, i. 242.
Low, Isabel, iii. 31.

Lowder, Charles, ii. 236.
Lowe the poet, iii. 253.
Luce bay, iii. 57.
Ludquharn, ii. 214, 261.
Lugar, water of, i. 350 ; ii. 339 ; iii. 124.
Lunan, lands of, i. 242.
Lunkyn, Ranulph de, iii. 13.
   „ Walter de, iii. 13.
Lushington, General, iii. 34.
Luthers, Cornelia, ii. 155.
Lynedoch, Lord, ii. 307.
Lyons, i. 226.

MABON, Mr., ii. 239.
Macadam, Captain, of Laight, ii. 19.
   „ Martha, ii. 19.
M'Adam, Mr., of Craigangillan, ii. 324.
   „ Miss, ii. 324.
M'Alexander, Patrick, iii. 58.
M'Bean, family of, iii. 15, 29.
Macbeth, iii. 174.
M'Calmont, Elizabeth, i. 213.
M'Cay, John, iii. 39.
M'Clatchie, Jean, ii. 269.
M'Climont, Jean, i. 316.
M'Clure, James, ii. 268.
M'Comb, Dr., ii. 111.
M'Coul, Agnes, i. 179.
M'Culloch, David, ii. 344 ; iii. 207, 260.
Maccuswel, Hugh, of Carlaverock, ii. 36.
   „ Sir John de, ii. 36.
M'Dermit, Mr. John, i. 214, 282, 283 ; iii. 219, 295.
Macdonald, Rev. C. C., ii. 383, 390.
M'Donald, James, iii. 344.
M'Donal, Colonel Andrew, i. 348, 349.
Macdowal of Freugh, i. 206.
M'Dowall, Anne, i. 336.
   „ Elizabeth, i. 38.
   „ William, i. 192, 336 ; ii. 156, 376, 380.
MacEwen, ——, ii. 198.
M'Fadzeane, Margaret, iii. 58.
Macfarquhar, Messrs. Bell &, ii. 298.
MacFarquhar, Mr., i. 318, 321 ; ii. 241.
Macfie, ——, of Liverpool, iii. 61.
M'Gibbon, Mr., i. 339.
M'Gill, Mr., i. 279, 283.

INDEX.

M'Gill, Mrs. Rachael, i. 124.
,, Dr. William, ii. 194, 345 ; iii. 216.
M'Grean, family of, ii. 362, 365, 375 ; iii. 55-63.
M'Gregor, Helen, ii. 364.
Macgregors, i. 236.
M'Guire, family of, i. 170, 173, 212-236 ; ii. 267.
Machar, parish of, ii. 211.
Macintosh, Charles, ii. 86.
,, George, of Dunhatton, ii. 86.
,, John, ii. 86.
Macintyre, Duncan Ban, i. 313.
M'Ivor, Colonel, Glasgow, i. 92.
M'Jannet, ——, i. 241.
M'Jerrow, John, i. 71.
Mackay, George, Lord Reay, i. 210.
,, Hon. Marianne, i. 210.
Mackenzie, Sir Alexander, i. 96.
,, Dorothea, i. 77.
,, Dr. ii. 28-32, 321, 351.
,, Edward Hay, i. 77.
,, family of, ii. 28-32.
,, Hannah, i. 96.
,, Hector, i. 96.
,, Henry, i. 49, 56, 133, 140 ; ii. 6, 8, 131, 321 ; iii. 143-146
,, Major H., i. 207.
,, Sir Henry, i. 97, 132, 140.
,, John Whiteford, ii. 32.
,, John, of Kincraig, i. 96.
,, Lady, ii. 262.
,, Louis, ii. 346.
,, Sir Robert, Redcastle, i. 96.
,, General Roderick, i. 96.
,, Warburton, i. 96.
M'Kie, Anthony, of Netherlaw, ii. 40.
Mackinlay, Rev. James, D.D., ii. 347, 348.
M'Kinlay, Mr., ii. 166.
Mackintosh, Charles, ii. 87, 273.
,, George, ii. 86.
,, Mr. James, ii. 256.
Macklin, i. 331.
Maclagan, family of, i. 175, 176.
,, General Robert, i. 173.
Maclaine, Flora, i. 175.
,, Murdoch, of Loch Buy, i. 175.
Maclaurin, family of, ii. 48-53.

Maclean, Dr. Allan, of Mull, i. 175.
M'Lehose, family of, 50-63.
,, Mrs., i. 16, 103, 257 ; ii. 46, 50-63, 137, 340.
Macleod, Dr., ii. 159.
M'Leod, Mr. John, of Raasay, iii. 168.
M'Leods of Raasay, ii. 347.
M'Lure, John, of Alloway, ii. 269.
,, Mary, ii. 269, 270.
M'Math, Rev. John, i. 297 ; ii. 35, 36.
M'Morine, Rev. Mr., iii. 244.
M'Murdo, family of, i. 44, 58, 112 ; ii. 64-72, 336 ; iii. 245.
Macosquin, ii. 1.
Macpherson, James, i. 62, 67 ; iii. 61.
,, Peter, i. 92.
Macquechan, Robert, ii. 160.
M'Quhae, Mr., i. 283, 284.
,, Rev. William, D.D., ii. 347.
Macrae, family of, i. 170, 212-226.
M'Rae, Allan, i. 214.
M'Taggart, family of, i. 240 ; ii. 266, 359, 364.
MacWilliam, Jean, ii. 275.
M'William, Helen, ii. 186, 187.
Madeira, ii. 176, 177, 185, 244.
Maestrich, iii. 21.
Mahaar, ii. 147.
Maidens, the (rocks), i. 241 ; ii. 144.
Maine, Mr., ii. 80.
Maistre, Maria C. le, i. 222, 225.
Maitland, Charles, Eccles, i. 78.
,, Grizel, i. 78.
Major, family of, iii. 35.
Makitterick, Captain James, i. 306.
,, John, i. 306.
Malcolm IV., King of Scots, ii. 33.
,, Sir John, i. 256, 259.
Malta, i. 207.
Malvern Link, ii. 236.
Man, Isle of, ii. 236 ; iii. 93, 230.
Mancha, La, ii. 343.
Manchester, i. 110 ; ii. 86, 127 ; iii. 37.
Manitoba, ii. 166.
Mann, Anne, i. 328.
Manners, Lord Robert, iii. 29.
Manor, Lord, ii. 162.
Mansfield, Earl of, i. 63 ; ii. 65.
Mar, Earl of, iii. 9.

Mar, Erskine of, iii. 233.
Marionville, i. 222.
Marischal College, ii. 212, 236.
" Earl, iii. 9, 76, 77.
Markinch, iii. 26.
Markland, George, ii. 27.
" Jean, ii. 27.
Marlborough, ii. 370.
Marnoch, parish of, iii. 19.
Marshall, Francis, of Park, ii. 360, 376.
Martin, Alexander, iii. 16.
" Mr., i. 80.
Martingalon ford, iii. 240.
Mary, Queen of Scots, i. 168, ii. 18, 37, 98, 243, 354.
Marykirk, iii. 31, 32.
Maryland, ii. 303, 304.
Mason, John, iii. 47.
Masson, John, iii. 20.
Masterton, Mr. Allan, i. 117, 330; ii. 32-34, 133, 136; iii. 217.
" family of, ii. 32-34.
Mauchline, i. 5, 12, 24-28, 50, 87, 102, 125, 145, etc.; ii. 19, 27-32, 95, 104, 116, etc.; iii. 43, 61, 70, 113, 129, 148, etc.
" Castle of, i. 91, 304.
Maudsley, Mr. Henry, ii. 127.
Mauritius, iii. 41.
Mavis Grove, ii. 155, 156.
Maxwell, families of, i. 20-23, 120, 190, 191; ii. 37-46.
" William, M.D., i. 127, 162; ii. 24, 43-46; iii. 268, 278, 291, 301.
" W. H., of Munches, ii. 42; iii. 57.
Maxwelltown, ii. 15, 40, 133.
Maybole, i. 39, 311; ii. 147-149, 266, 316, 360, 363, 375; iii. 58-64, 78.
Mearns, the, ii. 361, 384.
Mediterranean, ii. 101; iii. 41.
Meek, Robert, ii. 301.
Melbourne, iii. 38.
Meldrum, Isabel, iii. 3.
Melrose, i. 304.
" Abbey, ii. 64.
Melville, Henry Viscount, i. 130.
Melvin, Margaret, iii. 26.
Mendelssohn, Felix, ii. 12.

Meniwa, ii. 237.
Menteith, Rev. James Stewart, ii. 352.
" Mr., of Closeburn, i. 330.
Menzies, Mr., of Pitfoddels, ii. 45.
Merkland, iii. 53.
Merry, James, i. 223.
" John, ii. 163.
Merton, iii. 20.
Mexico, i. 207.
Meyer, Colonel de, i. 8.
Michilimackinac, ii. 155.
Middleton, ii. 235, 236.
" General, i. 212; ii. 86.
Middletoun, Robert, in Broombank, iii. 9.
Miers the artist, ii. 353.
Milbank, F. A., i. 236.
Mill, Margaret, iii. 2.
" Willie's, ii. 34, 121, 133.
Millar, Jane, ii. 260.
" Mrs., ii. 250.
" Robert, i. 26.
Miller, Alexander, ii. 32.
" Rev. Alexander, ii. 347.
" family of, ii. 30-32, 73-83.
" Hugh, ii. 387.
" of Dalswinton, i. 68, 98, 100, 102, 284, 333; ii. 73-83, 268, 336; iii. 145, 164, 176, 189, 202.
" of Glenlee, ii. 73.
Millhead, ii. 143.
Milligan, Agnes, i. 106.
Milltimber, lands of, iii. 21.
Milne, Catherine, iii. 18, 19.
" Captain Duncan, i. 185.
" Janet, iii. 2.
Milton, Lord, i. 46; iii. 165.
" the poet, ii. 366.
Minnigaff, parish of, i. 94.
Minnybee, ii. 154, 285; iii. 53.
Minorca, i. 123.
Minto House, ii. 122.
" Lord, ii. 367.
Mitchell, John, of Friendlesshead, i. 271, 272; ii. 348.
" Mr., collector, i. 246; iii. 232, 280.
" Thomas, Barras, iii. 22.
Mitchelson, Mr. Samuel, i. 9, 10.
Moat, Catherine, iii. 62.

INDEX.

Moffat, i. 107-116, 159; ii. 20-23, 34, 133, 242; iii. 217, 286.
Mohammed, Dost, iii. 40.
" Shah of Persia, iii. 40.
Moir, Agnes, i. 160.
" Dr. Henry, i. 160.
" Dr. Maitland, ii. 383, 389, 390.
Moira, Earl of, i. 302.
Molendinar burn, ii. 46.
Molière, i. 331.
Mollance House, ii. 41.
Mollison, Alexander, iii. 23.
Monboddo, Lord, ii. 340, 346, 388; iii. 43, 146, 252.
Moncrieff, Rev. Alexander, i. 336.
Monday, Black, iii. 145.
Money, Robert Cotton, i. 257.
Moniaive, ii. 143.
Monk, General, i. 212.
Monkland, ii. 172.
Monkton, i. 217, 218, 221; ii. 9, 103; iii. 73.
Montague, Duke of, i. 228.
Montgarswood, i. 198, 203; ii. 164, 168.
Montgomerie, Mr. Alexander, iii. 344.
" Andrew, ii. 11.
" Castle, iii. 97.
" family of, ii. 11.
" General, ii. 338.
" Hugh, ii. 11, 202.
" Hugh, of Bushie, i. 187.
" Mr. James, of Coilsfield, iii. 344.
" John, ii. 143.
" Mary, ii. 303.
" Sir Robert, Skermorlie, ii. 47.
Montgomery, George, ii. 16.
" Jessie Lewars, ii. 16.
Montreal, iii. 61, 62.
Montrose, i. 194, 242; ii. 133, 134; iii. 2, 11, 17, 26-42, 108, 173, 296.
" Dukes of, i. 242.
" Marquis of, i. 186.
Monymusk, ii. 212, 230.
Moody, Rev. Alexander, i. 284; ii. 348.
Moore, Dr., i. 47, 50, 138, 188, 262, 314; ii. 84-113, 285, 332, 354; iii. 75, 86, 168, 190.
" family of, ii. 84-103.
" Tom, i. 336.

Moray, Anna, i. 243.
" Robert, of Abercairny, i. 243.
" Thomas, Earl of, i. 180.
Morayshire, ii. 188.
More, Hannah, i. 2.
Morham Muir, iii. 65, 74.
Morison, family of, ii. 104-106.
" Messrs., of Perth, i. 322, 323; ii. 312.
Morpeth, iii. 164.
Morrison, Colin, i. 113.
Morriston, farm of, i. 241; iii. 53.
Morton, Agnes, iii. 58.
" Christina, ii. 106.
" Hugh, Townhead, iii. 62.
" parish of, ii. 20.
Morville, Hugh de, i. 210.
Moscow, iii. 217.
Mosgiel, i. 2, 21-23, 32, 115, 188, 296, 350, 356; ii. 4, 29, 75, 95, 116-120, 148-167, 205, 248, 320, 341, 350, 370; iii. 65, 72, 113-122, 130, 134-140, 164, 188, 190, 197, 342.
Motherwell, iii. 68.
Moultan, iii. 32, 37.
Mounsey, Mr. A. C., ii. 18.
Mount Charles, estate of, i. 176.
Mount Ulston, i. 147.
Mousewald, lands of, i. 257.
Mozzello, ii. 101.
Muir, family of, ii. 116-121, 133.
" Mary, of Cassencarry, ii. 65.
" Robert, ii. 115-120, 131, 268, 322.
" William, i. 301.
" William, Tarbolton, iii. 185, 319.
Muirkirk, i. 353, 359; ii. 105; iii. 49, 120, 322.
Muirsmill, farm of, i. 353, 354, 358, 359.
Mull, Isle of, ii. 35.
Multrare, Adam, iii. 45.
Mundell, Dr., ii. 24, 25.
Murdoch of Cumloden, family of, i. 94-96.
" Thomas, i. 95, 264, 304; ii. 262.
" John, ii. 107-115, 271; iii. 70, 81, 82, 83, 84, 107, 314.
Mure, Alice, ii. 323.
" John, of Auchindrane, iii. 46.
" of Rowallan, ii. 84.
" William, of Caldwell, i. 77.
Murray, Dr. Alexander, i. 316; ii. 246.
" David, Culzean, ii. 376.

VOL. III.   3 B

Murray, Dr. David, Glasgow, ii. 272, 360, 376, 380.
  ,, Davidson, i. 121.
  ,, Euphemia, ii. 348.
  ,, Lord, i. 335.
  ,, Margaret, i. 243, 316.
  ,, Mr., of Broughton, ii. 342.
  ,, Mrs., of Henderland, i. 335.
  ,, Sir W., of Ochtertyre, i. 243 ; ii. 75, 307, 348 ; iii. 175.
Murthoc, Earl of Dumfries, i. 95.
Musgrave, Sir George, i. 120.
Musselburgh, ii. 141, 238.
Muthill, ii. 195, 197, 198.
Mutrie, Rev. John, ii. 348.
Mutter, Dr. Thomas, i. 337.
Mylnes of Mylnefield, i. 245-250.

Nagpore, ii. 152.
Nairn, county of, i. 180, 185 ; iii. 174.
Nairne, Lady, ii. 369.
Napier, Alexander, i. 197.
  ,, Hon. Minnie Schaw, i. 6.
  ,, Lord William, i. 6.
Napoleon, i. 17.
Nasmyth, Alexander, ii. 121-128 ; iii. 152.
  ,, family of, ii. 121-128.
Neilson, Claud, Paisley, iii. 343.
  ,, Rev. Edward, ii. 96.
  ,, John, ii. 286.
  ,, Mr., i. 330.
  ,, William, of Minnybee, ii. 285, 286, 366.
  ,, William, in Bogtown, iii. 7.
Neilston, parish of, i. 302.
Nelson, Lord, ii. 207.
Netherlands, iii. 251.
Netherwood, farm of, i. 354.
New Abbey, i. 238.
Newall, Margaret, i. 78.
  ,, Mr., iii. 251.
  ,, William, of Barskioch, i. 78.
Newark, lands of, iii. 47.
Newbattle, i. 129, 130.
Newcastle, i. 12 ; ii. 68. 70, 112, 141, 164, 297.
Newcombe, Dr. Henry, i, 336.
New Dykes, farm of, i. 241.
Newgate, i. 326.

Newington, ii. 26, 27.
Newlands, i. 195 ; ii. 236 ; iii. 20.
Newmills, ii. 2, 3, 6, 9, 118, 164 ; iii. 61.
New Orleans, i. 40.
Newry, i. 306.
Newton, Sir Isaac, ii. 49,
Newton on Ayr, i. 186 ; ii. 345, 349 ; iii. 48.
Newtoun, i. 20, 23.
New York, ii. 82, 142, 155, 343 ; iii. 26, 174.
New Zealand, i. 241 ; iii. 38, 73.
Nicholson Elizabeth, i. 120.
  ,, of Kendal, i. 120.
Nicol, family of, ii. 128-143.
  ,, William, i. 143, 146, 321 ; ii. 34, 128-143, 159, 250, 262, 306, 346, 370 ; iii. 154, 165-176, 217.
Nicolson, Badenach, ii. 381, 383, 385.
  ,, Margaret, iii. 34.
  ,, William, ii. 231.
  ,, Sir William, of Glenbervie, iii. 43.
Niebuhr, i. 333.
Nimmo, Mrs. Erskine, i. 98.
  ,, Miss, i. 104 ; ii. 53.
Nisbet, James, iii. 61.
  ,, of Dirleton, i. 312.
Nith, water of, iii. 176, 194-196, 200-203, 215, 249, 269.
Nithsdale, i. 50, 126 ; ii. 64, 73, 170, 308, 366, 370 ; iii. 71, 192.
  ,, Earl of, ii. 336.
Niven, David, ii. 16, 288.
  ,, family of, ii. 143-152, 187.
  ,, Isabella, ii. 16.
  ,, John, i. 178 ; iii. 59.
  ,, Margaret, iii. 59. 63.
  ,, Robert, iii. 59.
Nivernois, Duke de, ii 309.
Noble, Andrew, i. 25-27, 267, 270, 275, 278.
Nolken, Baroness, i. 222.
Normand, James, i. 335.
Norris, Eliza, i. 76.
  ,, J., i. 76.
Northwold, iii. 32.
Norway, i. 220 ; ii. 209, 231.
Novar, ii. 210.
Novice, Mr., ii. 127.
Nugent, Captain Lawrence, i. 187.
Nuthall, ii. 325.

INDEX.

O'Brien, Anna Maria, ii. 265.
  „ Sir Lucius, ii. 265.
O'Kean, Captain, i. 125.
O'Keiffe, David, ii. 315.
  „ Mary J., ii. 315.
Ochiltree, i. 212, 213, 226, 235 ; ii. 205, 209, 267-272 ; iii. 124, 342.
Ochtertyre, ii. 132, 158, 160, 229.
Ogilvy, Ann, ii. 234.
  „ James, Lord, i. 243 ; iii. 77.
  „ Sir John, ii. 234.
  „ Margaret, i. 243.
  „ Mr., ii. 296.
  „ Mrs., 369.
Ogston, Hugh, i. 59.
  „ Martha, i. 59.
Oldbuck, Jonathan, ii. 161.
Oliphant, James, ii. 190, 193, 348, 349.
  „ Mount, ii. 107, 108, 344, 365 ; iii. 80, 83, 86-91, 96.
Oliver, John W., ii. 153.
Ontario, Province of, iii. 32, 33.
Oporto, iii. 73.
Orangefield, estate of, i. 217-221.
Ord, Ann, ii. 1.
Ormiston, Haddingtonshire, iii. 66.
Orr, Jean, iii. 55.
  „ John, ii. 128.
  „ Margaret, ii. 204, 351.
  „ Thomas, ii. 110, 152-154, 285.
  „ William, ii. 152.
Osburn, John, i. 59.
Ossian, ii. 199, 360 ; iii. 320.
Oswald, Mr., of Auchincruive, iii. 251.
  „ Mr. Richard, ii. 258, 349.
  „ Mrs. Richard, ii. 96, 258, 349.
Otago, iii. 73.
Otway, i. 331.
  „ Sylvester, ii. 253.
Oughterston, John, i. 120.
  „ Mary, i. 120.
Oxford, i. 195 ; ii. 147, 237, 264, 302.
Oxus, river, iii. 41.

Paget, Caroline, ii. 325.
  „ General Sir Edward, ii. 325.
Paisley, i. 19-21 ; ii. 64, 279, 295 ; iii. 188.

Palgrave, Mr., iii. 326.
Palmer, Mr., ii. 251.
Palnure, stream of, i. 94.
Panama, ii. 235.
Panbride, i. 239.
Paraiso, ii. 235.
Paris, i. 165, 222, 224 ; ii. 44, 99, 354.
Park, Ann, iii. 308.
  „ Dr., i. 169.
  „ General S., i. 169, 173.
Park, King's, iii. 153.
  „ Woodley, iii. 236, 258.
Parker, Euphemia S., i. 176.
  „ Hugh, iii. 195.
  „ John, i. 176.
Parkmill, lands of, ii. 33.
Parsons, Colonel, i. 186.
  „ Louisa P., i. 186.
Paterson, Agnes, i. 309.
  „ Andrew, ii. 270.
  „ family of, ii. 106.
  „ Henrietta, i. 302.
  „ Hugh, ii. 231.
  „ James, ii. 206, 287 ; iii. 56.
  „ John, i. 310.
  „ Margaret, ii. 205, 302.
Patna, iii. 43.
Paton, Betty, iii. 308.
  „ James, iii. 20.
  „ Mr. John, ii. 204.
Patrick, Alexander, ii. 199
  „ William, ii. 165.
Patten, Rev. Robert, iii. 9.
Pattison, John, ii. 44 ; iii. 278.
Patton, Colonel, St. Helena, i. 8.
  „ Eliza, i. 8.
Pau in Berne, i. 105, 166, 308.
Paul, Anne, iii. 10.
  „ Emperor, ii. 207.
Paunchgunny, India, iii. 32.
Payne, John, iii. 46.
Peacock, Mary, i. 257 ; ii. 61 ; iii. 246.
  „ Mr., iii. 99.
Pearson, Charles, C.A., i. 176.
  „ Margaret Dalziel, i. 176.
Peat, Margaret, iii. 15.
Peckham Rye, ii. 314.
Peebles, i. 194 ; ii. 274.

Peebles, Mr., i. 284, 285.
„ Dr. William, ii. 345, 349.
Pegu, i. 214.
Penicuik, ii. 123.
Penkill, stream of, i. 94.
Penpont, parish of, ii. 1, 142.
Penshurst, ii. 128.
Pentland Hills, ii. 123 ; iii. 153.
Perochon, Joseph E., i. 192.
Perry, Mr., ii. 82, 83.
Persia, iii. 40.
Perth, Lord Chancellor, ii. 210.
Perthshire, i. 130, 338 ; ii. 33, 75, 141, etc. ; iii. 56.
Peterborough, ii. 314, 316.
Peterhead, ii. 217 ; iii. 11.
Petre, Lord, ii. 340.
Pettiwood, Mr., i. 224.
Peyster, Colonel de, ii. 67, 155-158 ; iii. 283.
„ Johannes de, ii. 155.
Philadelphia, ii. 231.
Philiphaugh, battle of, i. 186.
Phillips, family of, i. 256, 257 ; ii. 65.
Phœnicia, ii. 361.
Pichegru, iii. 251.
Picton, Colonel, i. 209.
Pillans, Elizabeth, i. 35.
„ Mr., i. 254.
Pimlico, ii. 236.
Pindar, Peter, ii. 15.
Pinkie, battle of, iii. 3.
Piper, Thomas, ii. 149.
Pirie, John, ii. 29.
Pitcairn, Eleanor, i. 149.
Pitgarvie, iii. 19.
Pith, William, ii. 209 ; iii. 229, 270.
Pleydell, Counsellor, ii. 175.
Pleyel, ii. 276, 277, 336 ; iii. 238.
Plymouth, ii. 158.
Plympton, i. 207.
Polcardoch, farm of, i. 241.
Polkemmet, iii. 308.
Pollen, John, LL.D., iii. 33.
Pollokshaws, iii. 69.
Pope the poet, i. 48 ; ii. 89.
Portarlington, iii. 72.
Porteous, Mr. Matthew, i. 178.

Porteous, Dr. William, ii. 86.
Porterfield, Margaret, i. 311, 313.
„ Dr. William, i. 311.
Portland, Duke of, i. 228, 302.
Portobello, i. 224 ; iii. 56, 73.
Portpatrick, i. 72, 306 ; ii. 311.
Portrack, ii. 37.
Portugal, ii. 101.
Posso, lands of, ii. 121.
Poundstock, iii. 74.
Power, Walter, ii. 314.
Premnay, ii. 296.
Prentice, Mr., ii. 270 ; iii. 140.
Preston, farm of, i. 11 ; ii. 40.
„ George, iii. 67.
Prestonpans, battle of, i. 306 ; ii. 318.
Prestwick, i. 241 ; ii. 361 ; iii. 45.
Price, Esther, iii. 37.
Priesthill, iii. 49.
Primrose, Mr. James, ii. 33.
Princeton, New Jersey, i. 89.
Pringle, Sir John, i. 123.
„ Thomas, i. 124.
Prospect Place, iii. 21.
Pugolas, Henry, i. 258.
Punjab, iii. 37.
Pusey, Dr., ii. 264.

Quarme, family of, i. 129.
Quebec, ii. 34.
Queensberry, Duke of, i. 158 ; ii. 65-68, 96, 157.
Queensferry, iii. 169.
Quothquan Law, iii. 141.

Racine, i. 331.
Radcliffe, Mrs., i. 69.
Rae, ex-Bailie, Ayr, ii. 360, 373, 375, 380.
„ John, of Little Govan, ii. 49.
„ Lilias, ii. 49.
„ Richard, i. 41.
Raeburn, Sir Henry, i. 37, 163 ; ii. 48, 126.
Rainy, family of, iii. 57-59.
„ Dr. Robert, i. 90.

INDEX. 379

Ramsay, Allan, i. 131, 319, 335 ; ii. 122, 313 ; iii. 90, 142, 322.
„ Christian, iii. 31.
„ Mr. David, i. 334.
„ Sir George, of Bamff, i. 222, 224.
„ Lady, i. 222, 223.
„ James, ii. 158.
„ Jean, iii. 58.
„ John, of Ochtertyre, ii. 158-162, 195, 211, 229, 334 ; iii. 175.
„ Margaret, i. 169.
„ of Balmain, iii. 31.
„ Dr. William, i. 170.
Randolph, Lady Agnes, i. 180.
„ Thomas, Earl of Moray, i. 180.
Rankine, Anne, ii. 163.
„ Bailie, i. 169.
„ Captain, of Drumdon, i. 169.
„ John, i. 351, 353 ; ii. 163.
„ Margaret, i. 353.
„ William, of Lochhead, i. 353.
Raphael, ii. 373.
Raploch Moss, i. 94.
Rathven, parish of, ii. 340.
Ravenscraig, Montreal, iii. 62.
Raymond, Agnes, ii. 236.
„ Rev. Oliver, ii. 235, 236.
Reeky, Andrew, ii. 275.
Reeves, Mr., i. 149.
Reid, family of, ii. 269-275.
„ George, i. 171 ; ii. 269.
„ John, of Langlands, ii. 349.
„ Mr., i. 203.
„ Patrick, i. 264, 303.
Reith, family of, iii. 18-27.
„ Rev. John, Riccarton, ii. 383, 391.
Renfrewshire, i. 20, 90, 95, 211, 217, 221 ; ii. 149, 316 ; iii. 72.
Rennie, Agnes, ii. 362, 363, 369.
„ Andrew, ii. 149, 362.
„ family of, iii. 56-63.
„ Jean, i. 278.
„ Samuel, ii. 363.
Renwick, ——, Liverpool, ii. 343.
„ James, ii. 343.
Resolis, ii. 188.
Restalrig, i. 68, 222 ; ii. 297.
Reynolds, Sir Joshua, ii. 317.

Rhin, Sutherlandshire, iii. 56.
Rhynd, farm of, iii. 56, 57.
Riach, Margaret, iii. 35.
Riccarton, i. 25 ; ii. 348, 383 ; iii. 62.
„ Viscount, i. 163.
Richardson, ii. 97, 98.
„ John, of Kirklands, i. 149.
„ Rev. Dr., i. 17.
Richmond, i. 258 ; ii. 100.
„ family of, ii. 163-168.
„ Henry, ii. 168.
„ Jean, iii. 62.
„ John, i. 2 ; ii. 134, 163-168, 248 ; iii. 141, 147, 168.
„ Mr. Legh, i. 256.
Rickarton, Banffshire, iii. 19.
Riddel, Captain, of Friars Carse, i. 259.
„ Mrs., iii. 241, 260, 282, 290, 294.
Riddell, Anna Maria, ii. 185.
„ Captain, i. 111, 112, 259, 330 ; ii. 34, 66, 169, 185 ; iii. 198, 202, 218.
„ family of, ii. 169-185.
„ Mary, ii. 43.
„ of Glenriddell, i. 112, 343 ; ii. 286 ; iii. 233.
„ Thomas, of Swinburne Castle, ii. 43.
„ Mr. Walter, ii. 175-185 ; iii. 218, 235, 258-260.
„ William, of Commieston, ii. 133.
Riga, i. 7.
Ritchie, Rev. John W., i. 28.
Roan, iii. 63.
Robert II., King of Scots, i. 206.
„ III. „ „ i. 242.
Robertland, estate of, i. 76.
Roberts, David, ii. 125.
Robertson, A. Campbell, i. 121.
„ Ann, ii. 210.
„ family of, i. 149-151.
„ Rev. James, ii. 197, 303.
„ Janet, ii. 296.
„ Jean, ii. 246, 303.
„ Rev. John, i. 19, 130 ; ii. 349.
„ John, Cromarty, ii. 246.
„ Margaret, ii. 107.
„ Mr. Peter, i. 151.
„ Principal, i. 149-159 ; ii. 367 ; iii. 147.
„ Dr. William, ii. 232, 240.

Robertsons of Struan, ii. 361.
Robespierre, ii. 354.
Robinson, Jean, ii. 152.
　,,　　Julia, ii. 152, 365.
　,,　　Sarah, iii. 308.
　,,　　Thomas, i. 117.
Robson, Rev. Henry, i. 302.
　,,　　Marjory, i. 302.
Rockhall, lands of, i. 78.
Rockvale, ii. 198.
Rodger, Janet, i. 191.
　,,　　William, i. 191.
Roger, Hugh, i. 177; ii. 145-152, 185-187, 284, 359, 363.
　,,　　Rev. James, i. 116.
　,,　　John, ii. 185.
　,,　　Matthew, ii. 187.
Rogers, Dr. Charles, ii. 313, 360, etc.; iii. 94, 302.
Rogerson, Alexander, ii. 316.
　,,　　Mrs., ii. 315.
Rome, i. 255; ii. 103, 122, 140; iii. 1.
Rome, Old, village, iii. 60.
Ronald, Anne, ii. 349.
　,,　　Jean, ii. 349.
　,,　　John, iii. 174.
　,,　　William, ii. 349; iii. 24.
Roney, Richard, ii. 284.
Rosario, iii. 33.
Rose, Mrs., ii. 131.
Rosebery, Earl of, ii. 122, 141.
Roseneath, i. 256.
Roslin, ii. 123, 124; iii. 153.
Ross, ii. 72, 188.
　,,　　Margaret, ii. 144, 145.
Rossul, ii. 36.
Rothesay, ii. 198.
Rotterdam, i. 148.
Roxburgh Castle, i. 11.
　,,　　shire, i. 147, 235, 310; ii. 36, 118, 164, 169, 287.
Rugby, ii. 264, 265.
Rumbling Brig, iii. 174.
Runciman, Alexander, ii. 122.
Russell, family of, ii. 188-199.
　,,　　Rev. John, ii. 197, 276.
　,,　　Margaret, i. 327.
Russia, i. 8; ii. 18; iii. 40.

Rutherford, George, i. 122.
Ruthwell, ii. 65, 343, 356.
Ryedale, villa of, ii. 11, 258, 259.

SAGE, Alexander, ii. 188.
　,,　　Rev. Donald, ii. 188-190, 196.
Sainton-Dolby, Madame, ii. 147.
Salem, ii. 300, 301.
Saline, parish of, iii. 56.
Saltcoats, i. 215; iii. 61.
Salt Lake City, ii. 168.
Saltwood, ii. 265.
Samarcand, iii. 41.
Samson, Thomas, ii. 199.
Sanday, Island of, iii. 2.
Sandgate, ii. 271.
Sandilands, Barbara, i. 194.
　,,　　Mr. John, i. 194.
Sangster, Annie H., ii. 239.
Sanquhar, i. 127; ii. 66.
Sarel, Thomas, ii. 315.
Saunders, Emily Eliza, i. 236.
Savary, Mr., i. 320.
Schaw, Janet, iii. 48.
Schawfield, laird of, i. 24.
Schoreswood, Janette, iii. 51.
Scone, ii. 141.
Scot, Mr., i. 328.
Scott, Alexander, of Baldovie, iii. 26.
　,,　　Barbara, i. 243.
　,,　　Mrs. E., ii. 349, 350.
　,,　　Dr. Hew, ii. 189.
　,,　　Isabella, iii. 38.
　,,　　Sir James, of Balwearie, i. 243.
　,,　　Jean, i. 123.
　,,　　Mr. John, i. 38.
　,,　　Sir Michael, i. 243.
　,,　　Sir Walter, i. 16, 149, 235, 319, 329; ii. 136, 160, 259, 319; iii. 151.
　,,　　William, iii. 38.
　,,　　—— Wauchope House, ii. 350.
Scottish National Gallery, i. 38, 39.
Scrymgeour, Sir James, of Dudhope, i. 243.
　,,　　Margaret, i. 243.
Scutari, ii. 105.
Seaforth, i. 207.
Selcraig, ii. 130.

INDEX.

Selkirk, Earl of, i. 45, 163, 166 ; ii. 258 ; iii. 254.
  „ town of, i. 11, 134, 148 ; ii. 130, 197, 274, 301 ; iii. 163.
Seringapatam, i. 150, 191.
Seton, Sir Alexander, ii. 200.
Seville, i. 90.
Shankland, Ann, i. 290.
  „ Thomas, i. 238.
Sharp, Archbishop, i. 212.
Sharpe, Charles Kirkpatrick, i. 348 ; ii. 63.
Shaw, Agnes, ii. 27.
  „ Rev. Andrew, D.D., ii. 350.
  „ Anne, ii. 303, 304.
  „ Barbara, i. 170.
  „ Dr. David, of Coylton, i. 170, 279, 283, 284 ; ii. 350.
  „ family of, i. 175.
  „ Sir James, ii, 371 ; iii. 74.
  „ John, i. 5, 214.
  „ Sir John, ii. 143.
  „ Marion, i. 170.
  „ William, ii. 303.
Sheerness, ii. 246.
Shennas farm, ii. 186.
Shenstone, ii. 80, 110, 280, 295 ; iii. 315, 320, 329.
Shepherd, Mr., i. 284.
Sheridan, iii. 251.
Sheriff, family of, ii. 198.
  „ Rev. William, ii. 198.
Sheriffmuir, iii. 76.
Sheritt, James, iii. 26.
Sherlock, Bishop, ii. 228.
Sherwood, Anne, iii. 307.
Shetland, ii. 211, 230.
Shropshire, ii. 238.
Sibbald, Mr., i. 319 ; ii. 73 ; iii. 145.
Sicily, i. 207 ; ii. 101.
Siddons, i. 222.
Sierra Leone, ii. 142.
Sievwright, Mr. Norman, ii. 228.
Sillar, David, ii. 200-205, 287, 351 ; iii. 71, 118.
  „ family of, ii. 200-205.
  „ John, i. 202, 269, 271, 278, 282.
Silloth, i. 239.
Sim, Donald, ii. 365.

Sim, Eppie, ii. 365.
Simla, iii. 40.
Simpson, Jane, i. 117.
Simson, Andrew, ii. 208.
  „ Elizabeth, i. 338.
  „ James, ii. 208.
  „ Rev. James, ii. 100.
  „ Jane, ii. 100.
  „ Patrick, ii. 205.
  „ Professor Robert, ii. 100.
  „ Thomas, Cults, i. 338.
  „ William, ii. 205-209 ; iii. 124, 161.
Sinclair, Barbara, ii. 283.
  „ Sir John, i. 324 ; ii. 172, 242, 271.
  „ Mr., of Scalloway, ii. 213.
Singleton, Auketil, i. 263.
Sitwell, Francis, of Barmoor, ii. 263.
  „ Sir George, ii. 265.
  „ Mary, ii. 263.
Skinner, family of, ii. 209-239.
  „ Rev. John, i. 340 ; ii. 261 ; iii. 177.
Sligo, Lord, iii. 45.
Sloan, Robert, ii. 350.
  „ William, ii. 270, 350, 351.
Smart, Catherine, iii. 15.
Smellie, i. 332.
  „ family of, ii. 239-246.
  „ Mr., i. 180 ; ii. 176, 179.
  „ William, ii. 298 ; iii. 153.
Smith, Dr. Adam, i. 61 ; ii. 245, 318.
  „ Agnes, iii. 21.
  „ Mr. Alexander, i. 298.
  „ Anne, iii. 31.
  „ Captain, ii. 167.
  „ Donald, iii. 47.
  „ Dr., ii. 260.
  „ George, i. 141 ; ii. 351 ; iii. 26.
  „ Rev. George Muir, ii. 116.
  „ James, i. 97, 202, 278, 288 ; ii. 165, 247-251, 337 ; iii. 165, 167.
  „ John, iii. 19, 31.
  „ Mary, iii. 21.
  „ Mr. Mungo, iii. 344.
  „ Mrs. M. E., ii. 260.
  „ Robert, i. 87, 241 ; ii. 247.
  „ William, ii. 120.
Smollet, i. 9, 158 ; ii. 97, 100, 159.

Smyth, Howell, i. 173.
„ Margaret, iii. 48.
Smythe, David, of Methven, ii. 348.
Snaid, barony of, ii. 133.
Soho, ii. 254.
Sojourner, Janet, ii. 168.
Solway Firth, i. 105 ; iii. 230, 269, 292.
„ Moss, i. 211.
Somersetshire, ii. 274.
Somerville, John, i. 332.
Sorn, parish of, i. 202 ; ii. 164.
Soult, Marshal, ii. 101, 102.
Southdean, parish of, ii. 164.
Southesk, Earl of, ii. 40.
Southsea, ii. 236.
Spain, ii. 101, 317.
Speirs, James, ii. 326, 327.
Spence, A., i. 319.
„ Rev. Joseph, i. 44.
Spens, Dr. Nathaniel, i. 38.
Spenser, ii. 366.
Spey, river, iii. 173.
Spittleside, ii. 200, 204.
Spooner, Catherine, ii. 265.
„ William, ii. 265.
St. Andrews, i. 58, 70, 106 ; ii. 64, 105, 121, 350 ; iii. 45.
„ University of, i. 60, 115, 124, 148, 174 ; ii. 151, 210, 238.
St. Bernard's Well, ii. 126.
St. Cecilia's Hall, ii. 276.
St. Cuthbert's, i. 55, 234.
„ Churchyard, ii. 339.
St. Cyrus, parish of, iii. 19.
St. David's Lodge, ii. 319.
St. David, Fort, i. 215.
St. George, Chevalier, iii. 76.
„ Fort, i. 215.
„ Mary, iii. 33.
St. George's, Granada, iii. 16.
St. Germains, ii. 43.
St. Kitts, island, ii. 175.
St. Lawrence, river, iii. 61.
St. Margaret's Hill, ii. 2, 5.
St. Mary's Isle, i. 167 ; ii. 258.
„ Loch, ii. 133.
„ Monastery, ii. 200, 239.
St. Michael's Church, i. 118, 337.

St. Michael's Churchyard, i. 41, 43, 82, 120, 192, 328; ii. 10, 15, 42, 65, 70, 72, 156, 316.
St. Nicholas, church of, iii. 65.
St. Ninian, iii. 57.
St. Pancras, i. 327.
St. Paul's Cathedral, ii. 102, 113.
„ Churchyard, iii. 70.
St. Petersburg, ii. 18.
St. Quivox, ii. 104, 268, 271, 347.
St. Rollox, ii. 273, 274.
Staffordshire, ii. 102.
Staig, Miss Jessie, ii. 44, 83.
„ Provost, ii. 83.
Stair, Earl of, i. 123.
„ Montgomery, lands of, i. 168.
„ parish of, i. 217 ; iii. 43, 107.
Stalker, Katherine, i. 122.
Stanton, ii. 9.
Stark, Katherine, ii. 283.
„ Robert, ii. 283.
Steelepark, ii. 271.
Stein, Agnes, iii. 63, 64.
„ Grace, i. 235.
„ John, i. 235.
„ Kate, ii. 359, 365.
Stenhouse, Mr. William, i. 347, 348.
Stenness, parish of, iii. 2.
Stephen, Arthur, iii. 19.
Stephenstoun, Louth, iii. 64, 65.
Sterne, ii. 99, 110 ; iii. 320.
Stetchworth, ii. 315.
Steven, Eliza, i. 117.
„ Rev. James, ii. 352.
„ Peter, i. 117.
„ Rev. Robert, i. 87.
„ William, D.D., i. 252.
Stevenson, Agnes, ii. 150.
„ Alexander, iii. 74.
„ Douglas, iii. 74.
„ James, iii. 62.
„ Dr. John, i. 43, 44, 59 ; ii. 114, 150.
Stevinson, Margaret, iii. 2.
Steuart, Hope, of Ballechin, ii. 235.
„ Mary G. E., ii. 235.
Steward, Alan, the, i. 304.
„ James, the, i. 205.
„ Walter, i. 304.

INDEX.

Stewart, Major Alexander, ii. 337.
,, Alexander, of Stair, ii. 351, 352.
,, Anne, i. 153-156.
,, Bedford, i. 176.
,, Catherine, ii. 337.
,, Prince Charles Edward, ii. 43, 169 iii. 77.
,, Prof. Dugald, i. 47, 132, 138-140, 164, 166, 248, 314 ; ii. 30, 117, 306, 309, 323, 351, 376 ; iii. 136, 143-151, 328, 343.
,, Dr., of Luss, ii. 160.
,, Elizabeth Beaton, i. 242.
,, General, ii. 342.
,, Mr. John, i. 153 ; ii. 160.
,, John, Lord Invermeath, i. 242.
,, Professor John, iii. 4, 22.
,, Sir John, iii. 57.
,, Mrs. Katherine, of Stair, ii. 204, 351, 352.
,, Mary, i. 242 ; ii. 352.
,, Dr. Matthew, ii. 351.
,, Margaret, i. 23.
,, Sir Michael Shaw, i. 23.
,, Hon. Montgomery, i. 81.
,, Robert, Provost of Aberdeen, iii. 22, 23, 24.
,, Susannah H., i. 176.
,, Thomas, i. 176.
,, William, ii. 352.
,, William, of Inchbreck, iii. 8, 9, 77.
Stewarton, iii. 42, 60.
Stewarts of Corswall, iii. 57.
,, of Garlies, iii. 57.
Stinchar, ii. 366.
Stinson, James, Belfast, iii. 15.
,, Margaret, iii. 15.
Stirling, i. 115, 147, 220, 265, 299, 303, 307 ; ii. 13, 16, 82, 116, 132, 157-160, 197, 229, 261, 339 ; iii. 32, 56, 169, 174.
,, Ann, ii. 275.
,, Hugh, i. 278.
,, James, i. 71.
Stockholm, iii. 217.
Stodart, Robert R., iii. 57.
Stonehaven, ii. 383, 389, 390 ; iii. 3, 9-19, 23-26, 169, 174.
Stoneyroo, iii. 19.

Stormont, Lord, i. 207.
Story, Mr. Robert, i. 256.
Strachan, Sir Alexander, ii. 385, 386 ; iii. 3.
,, & Cadell, Messrs., i. 63.
,, James, iii. 13.
,, Mr., i. 63.
Straitoun, i. 214 ; ii. 209 ; iii. 53.
,, Alexander, of Straiton, iii. 3.
Strand, The, ii. 112, 317.
Stranraer, i. 306.
Strathblane, ii. 270.
Strathclyde, ii. 360, 361 ; iii. 54.
Strathearn, ii. 159 ; iii. 175.
Strathmore, ii. 348.
Strathspey, iii. 321.
Struthers, John, iii. 217.
Stuart, Alexander, of Inchbreck, ii. 383, 384, 385, 390 ; iii. 18.
,, Charles, ii. 351.
,, Daniel, ii. 256.
,, David, of Johnston, iii. 4.
,, Professor George, ii. 159.
,, Dr. Gilbert, i. 64 ; ii. 241.
,, Captain James, iii. 77, 78.
,, Jane G., ii. 256.
,, Dr. John, iii. 18, 21, 77.
,, Mary, iii. 22.
,, Peter, ii. 251-256.
,, Robert, iii. 22, 77.
Sumatra, i. 214.
Sumbroughgerth, ii. 231.
Sunderland, ii. 25.
Surat, iii. 39.
Surinam, ii. 205.
Surrey, ii. 314 ; iii. 20.
Sussex, ii. 265 ; iii. 73.
Sutherland, George S., ii. 353.
,, Mr., ii. 291, 340 ; iii. 221, 222.
Swansea, ii. 273.
Sweden, i. 226 ; ii. 101.
Swift, i. 324 ; ii. 99.
Swindon Church, iii. 37.
Swinton of Swinton, i. 19.
Switzerland, i. 131, 258.
Syme, Eleanor, i. 149.
,, Rev. James, i. 149.
,, John, i. 127, 162 ; ii. 24, 45, 63, 181, 257-261, 280, 345 ; iii. 251-256, 267, 301.

VOL. III.   3 C

Symington, iii. 72.
    „   parish of, i. 24.
    „   William, ii. 78, 79.

TACITUS, ii. 246.
Tailiour, Robert, iii. 7.
Tailor, James, iii. 13.
Tailyor, Janet, iii. 51.
Tait, Archibald Campbell, ii. 264, 265.
    „   Crawfurd, i. 96, 103 ; ii. 261-265.
    „   family of, ii. 261-265.
    „   John, i. 96-98, 264, 304.
    „   ——, iii. 21.
Talavera, battle of, i. 76.
Talleyrand, ii. 114.
Tam o' Shanter, i. 16, 39, 239 ; iii. 79, 94.
Tannahill, ii. 295.
Tarbolton, i. 91 ; ii. 27, 29, 120, 133, 200, 319, 339, 343, 349, 354, 359 ; iii. 91, 97, 104-107, 113, 148, 190, 308, 319, 336, 341-345.
Tarchun, ii. 369.
Tarshaw, ii. 120, 133.
Tasmania, i. 236 ; iii. 16.
Tasso, i. 189.
Taunton, ii. 274.
Taylor, David, iii. 23.
    „   Elizabeth, i. 257.
    „   Elspeth, iii. 10.
    „   Mr. James, ii. 78, 79, 260.
    „   William, iii. 10, 13.
Tay, river, iii. 56, 116, 124, 322.
Taymouth, iii. 169, 173.
    „   Castle, i. 352.
Teith, iii. 175.
Temple, ii. 302.
Templeton, Sarah, ii. 32.
    „   William, ii. 32.
Tenducci, Signor, ii. 277.
Tennant, Charles James, ii. 274, 376.
    „   David, i. 170, 176 ; ii. 107, 266.
    „   family of, ii. 265-275.
    „   Sir James, i. 176.
    „   Mr. John, i. 173, 226, 235 ; ii. 76, 271 ; iii. 75.
    „   William, i. 115 ; ii. 266.
Terence, ii. 240.
Terraughty, ii. 37.

Terregles House, ii. 336.
Teviotdale, ii. 36, 40, 169.
Thallon, Robert, ii. 82.
Thames, river, ii. 332 ; iii. 124.
Thankerton, iii. 140.
Thicknesse, Philip, i. 307.
Thomaston Mill, ii. 186.
Thomson, Elizabeth Allen, i. 173.
    „   „   family of, ii. 15, 16.
    „   family of, ii. 275-286 ; iii. 308, 309.
    „   George, i. 155, 161 ; ii. 22-25, 44, 275-294, 336, 354 ; iii. 238-278, 285-297, 301.
    „   Helen, iii. 10.
    „   James, ii. 15, 335, 383, 390.
    „   Rev. John, ii. 125.
    „   Peggy, ii. 153, 154, 359, 365, 366 ; iii. 95.
    „   the poet, ii. 89, 110 ; iii. 320, 331.
    „   Dr. William, i. 148.
    „   William, iii. 10, 175.
Thorburn, Thomas, of Ryedale, i. 93.
Thornhill, iii. 206.
Thornley, ——, i. 173.
Thorpe Park, ii. 314.
Thurlow, John, ii. 309.
Tiber, river, iii. 124.
Tilt, river, iii. 171.
Tinto Fells, iii. 141.
Tinwald Downs, i. 78-81.
Tipperty, farm of, iii. 18, 19, 21.
Tiree, island of, ii. 49.
Titchfield, Marchioness, i. 226.
Tod, family of, i. 303.
    „   Rev. John, i. 289, 303.
    „   Mr., i. 203.
Todd, A. B., of Cumnock, ii. 208, 376, 380.
    „   Mr. William, iii. 74.
Tomlieson, Ann, ii. 106.
Tootall, Elizabeth, iii. 15.
Toronto, i. 121.
Torphichen, Lord, i. 180.
Torthorwald, ii. 65.
Touch, George, iii. 13.
Tournier, Rev. Mr., i. 156.
Townhead, farm of, iii. 16, 62.
Townsend, Henry, ii. 314.
Tradonock, iii. 53.

INDEX. 385

Trail, Dr., i. 239.
„ Ellen, i. 239.
Tranent, iii. 66.
Traquair, Earl of, ii. 340, 385; iii. 3.
Trinidad, i. 209; ii. 237.
Troqueer, ii. 11, 44, 257, 260.
Tullibardine, Marquis of, ii. 305, 308.
Tulloch, iii. 20.
Tullybreak, farm of, i. 328.
Turnberry Castle, i. 241; ii. 144; iii. 52, 53.
„ Lodge, ii. 272.
Turnbull, Alexander, iii. 2.
„ Gavin, ii. 287-295.
„ Peter, iii. 2.
„ Thomas, of Roxburghshire, ii. 287.
Tweed, river, ii. 36, 93, 335; iii. 116, 124, 162, 322.
Tweeddale, George, Marquis of, i. 77.
Tweedsmuir, i. 161.
Twysden, Frances, ii. 103.
„ Sir William, ii. 103.
Tytler, Alexander Fraser, ii. 353.
„ family of, ii. 296-300.
„ Rev. George, ii. 296.
„ Mr., i. 340.
„ Patrick, i. 220, 221.
„ William, ii. 336, 353; iii. 76.

Ulster, i. 306.
United States, i. 241; ii. 265, 295, 300.
Uphall, parish of, i. 35.
Urbani, iii. 255.
Ure, Elizabeth, ii. 234, 235.
„ John, ii. 234.
Urquhart, Margaret, iii. 28.
„ Mr., ii. 312.
„ William, iii. 20.
Urr, parish of, ii. 11, 40.

Vallance, Mary, Cumnock, i. 278.
Valparaiso, i. 251.
Vanbrugh, i. 331.
Vane, Sir Henry, i. 120.
Vannan, Andrew, iii. 68, 69.
„ Eliza, iii. 68.

Vaus of Barnbarroch, ii. 37.
Venice, State of, i. 148.
Vennel Friar, ii. 257.
„ Mill, iii. 246.
„ Wee, iii. 227, 246, 258, 283.
Vere, Mr. James Hope, iii. 66.
Vernon, family of, ii. 325.
Vicovitch, Russian agent, iii. 40.
Virginia, i. 264; iii. 68.
Voltaire, i. 331.
Virgil, ii. 136, 299.

Waddell, Dr. Hately, i. 201, 202; ii. 342.
Wade, General, ii. 378.
Wagur, iii. 39.
Wake, Sir Charles, ii. 265.
Wales, ii. 185, 237; iii. 37.
Walker, Alice, ii. 16.
„ Arthur de Noe, ii. 185.
„ family of, ii. 301-316; iii. 25.
„ John, ii. 115, 241.
„ Professor Josiah, i. 46, 65, 88, 104, 144, 166; ii. 28, 140, 151, 280, 301, 304-315; iii. 149, 170, 278.
„ Robert, i. 60.
„ Thomas, ii. 206.
„ Rev. William, ii. 230.
„ Mr. William, ii. 104, 123.
„ ——, ii. 185.
Wallace, Adam, of Riccarton, i. 186.
„ Anna, ii. 303.
„ Elizabeth, i. 169.
„ Hew, iii. 44.
„ Sir Hugh, of Craigie, i. 186.
„ Sir Hugh, of Woolmet, i. 187.
„ General Sir James, ii. 81, 82.
„ Jean, iii. 43.
„ Sir John, i. 186.
„ John, i. 106, 115, 344; ii. 303.
„ John Alexander Agnew i. 191.
„ John, of Cairnhill, i. 168; ii. 190.
„ Margaret, i. 168.
„ Rachel, i. 87.
„ Robert, ii. 81, 274.
„ Thomas, i. 187, 191.
„ Sir Thomas Dunlop, i. 190, 191.
„ Sir Thomas, of Craigie, i. 186, 187.

Wallace, Sir William, i. 186, 191, 242, 253;
 ii. 118, 335, 368; iii. 116, 124, 161,
 162, 225, 244, 322-337.
Wallacehall, Academy of, i. 106; iii. 67, 69.
Wanlockhead, ii. 78.
Ward, Captain William, iii. 32.
Wardhouse, iii. 20.
Wardour, Sir Arthur, ii. 319.
Warkworth, iii. 164.
Warren, Charlotte Enmengarde. ii. 238.
Warrender, Sir George, i. 59.
Warsaw, iii. 217.
Washington, i. 238.
 „ General, ii. 82, 304; iii. 229.
Waterloo, i. 18, 76.
Watson, David, iii. 9.
 „ family of, iii. 26, 30.
 „ Mr. George, ii. 246.
 „ Kate, iii. 206.
 „ Mr. Peter, iii. 337, 341.
Watt of Balbarton, i. 327.
 „ Mr. W., ii. 382.
Wauchope, Elizabeth, i. 77; ii. 169.
 „ Captain Francis, ii. 169.
 „ George, i. 77.
Wauchope-Don, Sir John, i. 236.
Webb, Captain W. M., i. 257.
Weber, ii. 277.
Webster, Rev. Dr., ii. 225.
Weir, Flora, Woodend, i. 278.
Wellbrae Hill, iii. 141.
Wellington, Duke of, i. 150, 191; ii. 102.
Wellwood, Nether, i. 359.
 „ Robert, ii. 275.
Welsh, Mr. John, ii. 301.
 „ Louise, ii. 301.
Wernebald, i. 210.
West, Helen, ii. 33.
West Indies, i. 92; ii. 101, 175, 179, 248, 286,
 303; iii. 343.
Western Isles, i. 56.
Westminster Abbey, ii. 385.
Westmoreland, i. 120.
Westray, parish of, iii. 2.
Weybridge, iii. 74.
Wheeler, J. T., i. 215.
Whelpdale, Mr., ii. 23.
Whinie, Jane, ii. 332.

Whins, Frigate, i. 224.
Whish, family of, iii. 32-34.
Whitburn Churchyard, iii. 308.
White, Mr. David, i. 252.
 „ Rev. James, i. 336.
 „ Mr., ii. 248.
Whitefoord, Allan, i. 219, 220.
 „ Arms, ii. 165, 247, 338.
 „ family of, ii. 316-325.
 „ House, ii. 320, 323.
 „ Sir John, i. 231; ii. 28-31, 316-
 325; iii. 145.
 „ Maria, i. 21.
Whitefoords, i. 21.
Whitehaven, ii. 41.
Whitehill, estate of, i. 2.
Whitelaw, Catherine, i. 9.
Whiteside, i. 217.
 „ family of, i. 175, 176.
Whitevale, i. 204.
Wicklow, county, i. 303.
Wight, Alexander, ii. 276.
 „ David, i. 128.
 „ Mary, i. 118, 120.
 „ Mr. Robert, i. 118, 127, 128.
Wigtownshire, i. 72, 80, 166, 348; ii. 102, 147,
 345, 347; iii. 252, 254.
Wildman, Richard, ii. 265.
Wilkes, ii. 317.
William the Lion, iii. 13.
 „ III., i. 168, 216.
 „ IV., iii. 39.
Williams, Miss, ii. 90, 91, 93, 354.
Williamson, Mr., i. 109, 110.
Willison, George, i. 39.
Wilson, Agnes, iii. 47, 67.
 „ Alexander, ii. 8, 197, 295.
 „ Bailie, ii. 376.
 „ Catherine Martha, ii. 72.
 „ Mrs. David, ii. 123; iii. 153.
 „ Elizabeth, i. 302.
 „ family of, ii. 237, 238.
 „ Mr. George, i. 334; ii. 360, 376, 380.
 „ Isabella, i. 302.
 „ John, of Kilmarnock, iii. 134, 137,
 337-344.
 „ „ of Mauchline, ii. 325-327.
 „ „ of Tarbolton, ii. 354, 355.

Wilson, Peter, Girvan, ii. 376.
　,, 　Robert, i. 17.
　,, 　William, of Thornley, ii. 273.
　,, 　Dr. William, i. 86, 90 ; iii. 180, 214.
Wimbledon, iii. 35.
Winbolt, Captain, ii. 314.
　,, 　Eliza, ii. 314.
Winchester, i. 306 ; ii. 92.
Windsor, ii. 319.
Wingate, David, iii. 309.
Winsloe, Emma, ii. 274.
　,, 　Richard, ii. 274.
Winton, Earl of, ii. 319.
Wise, family of, iii. 6, 7.
Wishart, George, ii. 190.
　,, 　Isobel, i. 122.
Witham, Robert S. J., ii. 43.
Wodrow, Dr., i. 284.
　,, 　Margaret, i. 40.
　,, 　Patrick, Tarbolton, i. 25, 285 ; ii. 35, 355.
　,, 　Rev. Robert, Eastwood, i. 40, 215 ; ii. 197.
Wolcott, Dr., ii. 15.
Wood, Mr. Alexander, i. 159.
　,, 　Dr. Alexander, iii. 187.
　,, 　Elizabeth, iii. 22.
Woods, William, ii. 355.
Woodburn, Archibald, i. 214.
Woodfall, ii. 317.

Woodhead, ii. 237.
Woodhouselee, Lord, i. 132, 220, 340 ; ii. 281.
Woodley Maria, iii. 236.
　,, 　Park, ii. 173, 185, 244, 245.
　,, 　William, ii. 175.
Woodside, iii. 20.
Woodward, Rev. John, iii. 22.
Wrae Mill, ii. **33**.
Wright, Mr., i. 279, 283.
　,, 　Robert, ii. 298.
Wycherley, i. 331.
Wylie, William II., i. 338.
Wyllie, James, i. 278 ; iii. 61.
Wynd, College, Kilmarnock, iii. 61.

YARROW, river, iii. 124.
York, ii. 37, 104, 325.
　,, 　Cathedral, i. 70.
Young, Agnes, iii. 49.
　,, 　Alexander, i. 224.
　,, 　Dr., i. 111.
　,, 　Mr. H., i. 284.
　,, 　Jacobina, i. 264, 265.
　,, 　James, i. 173 ; iii. 75.
　,, 　John, i. 264.

ZIMMERMAN, Mr., i. 320.

www.ingramcontent.com/pod-product-compliance
Lightning Source LLC
Chambersburg PA
CBHW032014220426
43664CB00006B/244